MAKING RACE

The Politics and Economics of Coloured Identity in South Africa

Ian Goldin

Longman

London and New York

Longman Group UK Limited,
Longman House, Burnt Mill, Harlow,
Essex CM20 2JE, England
and Associated Companies throughout the world.

Published in the United States of America
by Longman Inc., New York

First published 1987

ISBN 0 582 01979 6

Set in 10 on 12 point Times.
Typesetting and reproduction by Blackshaws (Pty) Ltd.
Printed by Blackshaws (Pty) Ltd.

CONTENTS

INTRODUCTION xi

The Subject xi, The Literature xiii, Theoretical Perspectives xvi, Racial Definitions xxiii, Contents xxv

PART ONE (1652-1948)

1. THE FOUNDATIONS OF FAVOURITISM 3

Introduction 3, The Roots of Segregation 3, Bullets and Ballots 5, The Reconstitution of Coloured Identity: African and White Workers 12, The Reconstitution of Coloured Identity: Artisans and Craftsmen 16, The Reconstitution of Coloured Identity: Promises and Prejudice 19, Summary 26

2. COLOURED POLITICAL ORGANISATION AND COLOURED PREFERENCE: 1900-c.1935 29

Introduction 29, The African Peoples' Organisation 31, The Politics of Coloured Preference 33, The Civilised Labour Policy and Great Depression 40, Mass Resistance and Employers' Response 48, Summary 51

3. MAINTAINING THE PATTERN OF PREFERENCE: 1935-1948 53

Introduction 53, Coloured Opposition and Politics 53, Trade Union Organisation 60, Coloured Preference 65, Summary 72

PART TWO (1948-1961)

4. THE NATIONAL PARTY AND COLOURED IDENTITY: 1948-1961 77

The National Party and the Reconstitution of Coloured Identity 77, Nationalist Dissent 82, The Coloured Labour Preference Policy 86, Strategic Concerns 91, Summary 93

CONCLUSION

ACKNOWLEDGEMENTS

Any author of a text incurs many debts in its creation. In this case, without the assistance and support of numerous individuals and institutions this book would never have been initiated, let alone completed. The book draws heavily on my doctoral thesis submitted to the University of Oxford in 1984. The primary research involved interviews with a great number of workers, trade unionists, employers, political commentators, academics and others. My thanks are due to all those individuals interviewed in the course of the research and to the South African Labour and Development Research Unit (SALDRU), which provided me with the resources necessary for the interviewing programme. In framing the research project I was greatly assisted by Dudley Horner and, in conducting the interviews, by Dumile Mawisa, Msokoli Qotole, Alan Morris and Clare Verbeek.

My deep gratitude is owed to the librarians of Rhodes House (Oxford), the Institute of Commonwealth Studies (Oxford and London), the Jagger Library (Cape Town), the Central Archives (Pretoria) and the University of South Africa Library (Pretoria). The helpfulness of these librarians and particularly of Aninca Van Gylswyk of the University of South Africa Documentation Centre for African Studies greatly facilitated my research.

The writing of the thesis depended on the financial support of the Postgraduate Studies Committee of the University of Cape Town, the Graduate Studies Committee of the University of Oxford and a grant from St Antony's College, Oxford. In times of hardship I was fortunate to be able to rely on the material support of my family. They together with numerous friends and colleagues provided the emotional support so necessary for the completion of the thesis. In this respect, my greatest debt is to my closest friends and in particular to Caroline Cullinan, who suffered most from my involvement in this project.

The friendship and help of other scholars, especially William Beinart, Peter Delius and Brian Hackland, proved an invaluable aid in writing the thesis. By far my greatest debt, however, is to my supervisor Stanley Trapido. He provided the inspiration for my studies and the guide to their development; their completion owed much to his tireless dedication to the progress of the thesis, and to the readiness with which he bore the immense burden of giving it shape. The assistance provided by him was enhanced still further by the friendship he and his wife Barbara have shown towards me.

For the final preparation of the thesis for submission I am indebted to the typing of Anne Mills and Julie Little, to the understanding of my colleagues and to Hilary Belchak.

In revising the thesis for publication, I have been able to benefit from the comments of Shula Marks and others, the assistance of my sister Jacqui and the literary skills of Jeremy Lawrence. The patience of my publishers has ensured that this study has been made available to a wider audience. I hope that by reaching this audience the text may contribute to an understanding of current events in South Africa and in so doing assist the struggle of all those who are fighting for a democratic, non-racial society. It is to all such people that this book is dedicated.

ABBREVIATIONS

AAC	All African Convention
AFCWU	African Food and Canning Workers' Union
ANC	African National Congress
ANC(WC)	African National Congress (Western Cape)
APDUSA	African Peoples' Democratic Union of Southern Africa
APO	African Peoples'/Political Organisation
CAHAC	Cape Areas Housing Action Committee
CCC	Cape Chamber of Commerce
CCI	Cape Chamber of Industries
CEA	Cape Employers' Association
COD	Congress of Democrats
CPC	Coloured Peoples' Congress
CPRC	Coloured Persons Representative Council
CPSA	Communist Party of South Africa
FCWU	Food and Canning Workers' Union
GWU	General Workers' Union
HAD	House of Assembly Debates
ICS	Institute of Commonwealth Studies
ICU	Industrial and Commercial Workers' Union
NEUM	Non-European Unity Movement
NLL	National Liberation League
PAC	Pan African Congress
SABRA	South African Bureau of Racial Affairs
SACPO	South African Coloured Peoples' Organisation
SACTU	South African Congress of Trade Unions
SAIRR	South African Institute of Race Relations
SALB	South African Labour Bulletin
SALDRU	South African Labour and Development Research Unit
UCT	University of Cape Town
UDF	United Democratic Front
WC	Western Cape

BOTSWANA

NAMIBIA

Upington •

Kenhardt •

• Springbok

Prieska •

Britstown •

Aliwal North

Victoria West •

Middelburg •

Graaff-Reinet • Cradock

Beaufort West • Adelaide

Jansenville • Somerset East Fort Beaufort

Grahamstown •

Uitenhage

Cape Town George • Knysna Port Elizabeth

0 25 50 75 100   150 Km

EISELEN LINE 1955

WESTERN CAPE AFRICAN LABOUR REPLACEMENT LINE 1963

COLOURED LABOUR PREFERENCE AREA 1967

Coloured labour preference areas

INTRODUCTION

The subject

At the heart of the revised constitution recently imposed on South Africa lies an attempt to reconstitute Coloured political identity.[1] The constitutional changes have fuelled an intense ideological and political conflict over the subject of Coloured identity. This passionate debate cannot be separated from the wider struggle being waged against the South African regime. Indeed, therein lies its particular historical significance.

Though the conflict over Coloured identity has come to the forefront of the political struggle in the 1980s, it pre-dates it by many years. For over a century attempts have been made to foster and manipulate this identity and to engineer socially a Coloured political alliance with the ruling White parties. A distinct Coloured political identity, we shall show, is the outcome of a history of "divide-and-rule" tactics in South Africa. However, the identity cannot simply be traced to attempts by the ruling class to promote a Coloured buffer group: in part it is the result of tensions within the subordinate classes and of the resistance of sections of the population to the erosion of their position. Coloured political identity represents the peculiar outcome of a complex and conflicting set of events.

The Western Cape region of South Africa has since the turn of the century been home to over 60 per cent of the Coloured population of South Africa,[2] and it is in this region that Coloured political identity was developed. Not coincidentally, successive governments have focused their attention on the Western Cape in their attempts to promote a distinct Coloured identity in South Africa. An analysis of the development of Coloured identity in this region provides important insights into the development of racial identity in the wider context of South Africa as a whole.

---

1. It should be emphasised from the outset that the terms "Coloured", "African" and "White" refer to statutory race classifications in South Africa. As we shall see, these are rejected by many of the people so defined. A discussion of the meaning of the term "Coloured" as well as other racial classifications follows below.
2. The Western Cape, according to guidelines established by the South African Department of Planning and Environment, includes the economic regions 01 to 05; the area embraces the Cape Peninsula and its hinterland including the magisterial districts Piketberg, Worcester, Swellendam and Heidelberg.

The Western Cape is currently witnessing two major programmes of social engineering; the first is that associated with the introduction of a tricameral parliamentary system in which Coloureds elect representatives responsible for the administration of "Coloured affairs". The second is connected with the continuing onslaught on Africans in the Western Cape and the particularly brutal enforcement of controls over African residence and employment in the region. Resistance to both elements of the restructuring process has been widespread. A boycott of the election for the Coloured parliament succeeded in keeping over 83 per cent of the eligible electorate away from the polls.[3] In the case of controls over African residence and employment, urban squatting and illegal employment have confounded the authorities' attempts to reduce the African population of the region and to substitute Coloured for African labour. This remarkable resistance to policies of preference for Coloureds has a proud heritage which may be traced at least to the period of the first European settlement in the Western Cape. This book will demonstrate that resistance to the regime is as much a cause of government attempts to restructure Coloured identity as a response to such interventions. With reference to the Western Cape, resistance and restructuring cannot be viewed in isolation.

The particularly strict enforcement of influx controls in the Western Cape has been associated with what came to be termed the "Coloured Labour Preference Policy".[4] This refers to the National Party plan to limit the employment and residence of Africans, and to give preference to the employment of Coloured people, in an area West of what became known as the Eiselen line. The Coloured Labour Preference Policy, however, was only one element of a wider system of preference for Coloureds. While the policy sought to secure employment preference, the National Party also tried to improve the political and social position of Coloureds relative to Africans. Our argument focuses on the whole range of Coloured preference policies and not only the Coloured Labour Preference Policy.[5]

The Coloured Labour Preference Policy embodies the interlocking regulations which seek to restrict the influx of Africans into the Western Cape. The restrictions received widespread publicity. Attacks by agents of the Government on the African squatter settlements surrounding

3. *Argus,* 24 Aug. 1984; *Cape Times* 24 Aug. 1984. The percentage of eligible voters registered was 56,7 and the percentage poll 29,5.
4. A discussion of the policy follows in Chapter Four.
5. To avoid repetition we have adopted the convention that the phrases "the Coloured Preference Policy" or "the policy" or "the Preference Policy" all refer to the Coloured Labour Preference Policy. The phrase "Coloured preference policies", by contrast, refers to the whole range of such policies.

Cape Town led to worldwide notoriety for the Coloured Preference Policy.[6] Criticisms of the policy focused on the suffering of Africans in the Western Cape and on the undue disadvantage which the policy placed on employers in this region. However, the link between the attack on Africans and the simultaneous incorporation of Coloureds in the constitution has not always been clear to outside observers. The Coloured Preference Policy was one side of a dual-pronged attempt to restructure Coloured identity which had as its other prong the political incorporation of Coloured people.

In this study, priority has been given to an investigation of the complex interrelationship between government, employers and workers in the process of restructuring the society of the Western Cape. The book therefore confines its attention to the Western Cape and primarily to the Coloured population in that region. Our aim, however, has not been to explore the "lower levels" of Coloured identity which relate to often inarticulate and hidden expressions of identity. Rather, we focus on the *political* mobilisation of Coloured identity: the articulation and representation of Coloured identity in organisations and institutions. Of course a full understanding of Coloured identity would require a larger study which, in addition to the subject matter of this book, would focus on religion, culture, language and other complex psychological manifestations of identity. Here the aim is to examine the way in which successive policies of Coloured preference have developed and to investigate the relationship of such policies to the development of Coloured political identity.

The Literature

The roots of current conflicts over the Coloured preference policies and Coloured political identity may best be understood by means of an historical overview stretching back over at least the past century. For this reason, although the focus of the study is on the period of National Party rule, the argument in the first three chapters covers the period up to 1948. Surprisingly, this attempt to link developments in the pre-Nationalist period with the situation under apartheid has no precedent in the literature on Coloured identity in South Africa. It is suggested that a wide gulf exists between those secondary sources which seek to argue that Coloured identity has been imposed from above by a racist ruling class, and those sources which see it as the assertion by Coloured

6. See I. Goldin, "The Poverty of Coloured Labour Preference: Economics and Ideology in the Western Cape", *South African Labour and Development Research Unit* [henceforth SALDRU] Working Paper No. 59 (Cape Town, SALDRU, 1984), pp. 1-17.

people of their historical roots. With two notable exceptions, commentators fail to see Coloured identity as an area of immense struggle or to explore the ambiguities which have characterised the evolution of this identity in South Africa.

Sheila Patterson's book *Colour and Culture in South Africa* drew attention to the tensions associated with Coloured identity.[7] Published in 1953, Patterson's book highlighted the tentativeness of Coloured identity in the period preceding National Party rule. The book thus corrected decisively an imbalance in the classical treatises of W. Macmillan[8] and J.S. Marais[9]. W. Macmillan's *The Cape Coloured Question* was first published in 1927 and J.S. Marais's *The Cape Coloured People* in 1939. These books greatly influenced academic thinking on the origins and development of Coloured identity. Their preoccupation with lineage, however, led both Macmillan and Marais to underestimate the significance of political conflict in the creation of Coloured identity. This issue is considered in some depth in Jack and Ray Simons' book *Class and Colour in South Africa, 1850 to 1950*.[10] Their history, written from a radical perspective, although not primarily concerned with the question of Coloured identity in the Western Cape is of great value by reason of the scholarship of the authors and their experience of political developments in that region.

Accounts of Coloureds in the period of National Party rule focus almost exclusively on politics. A.J. Venter,[11] W.B. Vosloo,[12] S.P. Cilliers,[13] P. Hugo[14] and M. Simons[15] dominate scholarly debate on the subject. These authors deal with organised Coloured political parties in the period of National Party rule. Their work provides a valuable introduction to this subject but fails to examine the relationship between Coloured political identity and economic and political developments outside Coloured political institutions.

7. S. Patterson, *Colour and Culture in South Africa* (London, Routledge and Kegan Paul, 1953).
8. W. Macmillan, *The Cape Colour Question: An historical survey* (London, Faber and Faber, 1927).
9. J.S. Marais, *The Cape Coloured People, 1652-1937* (London, Longmans, 1939).
10. H.J. Simons and R.E. Simons, *Class and Colour in South Africa, 1850-1950* (Harmondsworth, Penguin, 1969).
11. See A.J. Venter, *Coloured: A Profile of Two Million South Africans* (Cape Town, Human and Rousseau, 1974).
12. See W.B. Vosloo, "The Coloured Policy of the National Party" in N.J. Rhoodie (ed.), *South African Dialogue* (Johannesburg, McGraw Hill, 1970).
13. See S.P. Cilliers, *The Coloured of South Africa: a factual survey* (Cape Town, 1963).
14. See P. Hugo, "Die Kleurling", *Deurbraak*, May 1972, 1, (3).
15. M. Simons, "Organised Coloured Political Movements", in H.W. van der Merwe and C.J. Groenwald (eds.), *Occupational and Social Change among Coloured People in South Africa* (Cape Town, Juta, 1976).

Apart from the published work referred to above, a number of unpublished sources have complemented our primary research. Richard van der Ross's encyclopaedic "Political and Social History of the Coloured People" provides an exhaustive overview of the subject.[16] As a bibliographic reference it is invaluable. For the most part, however, description replaces analysis and Van der Ross's project leaves the reader little the wiser as to the factors underlying the development of Coloured political identity.

By touching on issues not covered elsewhere in the literature, Stanley Trapido's doctoral dissertation (together with his essays on Cape liberalism and the early development of Coloured politics) has provided an invaluable contribution to our study.[17] In contrast to Trapido's historical analysis, I.P. Mandaza in his doctoral dissertation on Coloured identity in Southern Rhodesia is concerned simply to show that Coloured identity in Southern Africa as a whole is the outcome of a relatively recent process of miscegenation.[18] His ahistorical interpretation of Coloured identity is shared by the anthropologist Rosemary Ridd, whose doctoral thesis seeks to investigate Coloured identity in the District Six area of Cape Town in the period 1976 to 1981.[19] Ridd's dissertation provides an interesting glimpse into the attitudes of her sample. However, her attempt to generalise beyond her six sample families is marred by her failure to recognise the diversity of Coloured opinion or to locate her findings within a broader analysis of Coloured society.

The glimpse which Ridd and others provide into the Coloured community is complemented by a range of literary works which concern themselves with the daily experience of Coloured men and women. Authors such as Alex La Guma,[20] Richard Rive,[21] Adam Small[22] and Peter Abrahams[23] in their novels, plays and poetry capture many of the tensions and ambiguities which are to be found in the Western Cape. A

16. R.E. van der Ross, "A Political and Social History of the Coloured People" (Doctoral manuscript, Cape Town Univ., 1973).
17. S. Trapido, "White Conflict and Non-White Participation in the Politics of the Cape of Good Hope, 1853-1910" (London University, PhD thesis, 1970).
18. I. Mandaza, "White Settler Ideology, African Nationalism and the 'Coloured' question in Southern Africa, Southern Rhodesia/Zimbabwe and Nyasaland/Malawi: 1900-1978" (York University, DPhil thesis, 1979).
19. R. Ridd, "Position and Identity in a divided Community: colour and religion in District Six, Walmer Estate, Woodstock area of Cape Town" (Oxford University, DPhil thesis, 1981).
20. See, for example, A. La Guma, *A Walk in the night and other stories* (London, Heinemann, 1967).
21. See, for example, R. Rive, *Emergency* (London, Faber and Faber, 1970).
22. See, for example, A. Small, *Kanna Hyko Hystoe* (Cape Town, Tafelberg, 1965).
23. See, for example, P. Abrahams, *Tell Freedom* (London, Faber, 1954).

further contribution is made by a number of Athol Fugard's plays.[24] By dramatising the effects of racial segregation and the enforcement of influx controls these authors have brought the everyday reality of apartheid to a wider audience and served to break down racial stereotypes. By contrast, authors such as Sarah Gertrude Millin have often perpetuated racial prejudices.[25]

From the turn of the century, pseudo-scientific explanations of racial inferiority have been widely read in South Africa. As V. February has shown, Sarah Gertrude Millin perhaps more than any other individual popularised stereotypes of Coloured identity.[26] Notions of the racial degeneration, dishonesty and ineptitude of Coloured people abound in *God's Stepchildren* and in Gertrude Millin's other novels.[27] It was no accident that, as Minister of Interior introducing his proposed law to prohibit "mixed marriages", Dr T.E. Dönges in 1949 cited the work of Gertrude Millin as a justification for National Party policies of social engineering.[28]

Theoretical Perspectives

Notions of class, race and the state must inevitably inform a book which investigates the development of racial identities. All three of these concepts are the subjects of intense debate, but it is not feasible here to engage in this wide-ranging argument. Rather, in this section a necessarily brief account of the principal theoretical positions is provided. Such an exercise will serve to define our interpretation of the theory whilst at the same time spelling out the underlying assumptions of this book.

---

24. See, for example, A. Fugard, *The Blood Knot* (Johannesburg, Simondium, 1963). The dramatised version of E. Joubert's *The Story of Poppie Nongena* (London, Hodder and Stoughton, 1980) has popularised the plight of Africans under the Coloured Preference Policy.
25. See, for example, S.G. Millin, *God's Stepchildren* (London, Constable, 1924) and S.G. Millin, *The Dark River* (London, Collins, 1919).
26. V. February, *Mind Your Colour — The "Coloured" Stereotype in South African Literature* (London, Kegan Paul, 1981).
27. See *ibid.,* pp. 52-70.
28. D. Joubert, *Met iemand van 'n ander kleur* (Cape Town, Tafelberg, 1974), p. 56.

(1) RACE

Two broad currents may be identified in the debate concerning class and race in South Africa.[29] The first, the pluralist, seeks to assert the primacy of race, culture and tradition. For the pluralists, the awareness of a shared society is the primary determinant of ethnic or racial identities.[30] By contrast, what is often referred to as the Marxist, neo-Marxist or materialist school places its emphasis on social stratifications which arise at the level of production.[31] In capitalist societies, materialists argue, class relations (which derive from the ownership of the means of production by the capitalist class and the development of a working class) determine the fundamental sources of division and should thus provide the starting-point of any analysis.

In the 1970s materialist scholars provided a radical challenge to the pluralist orthodoxy, and this considerably advanced our understanding of South Africa.[32] But in moving beyond cultural and ethnic explanations of social identity the radicals at times became trapped in a narrow dependence on economic theory derived from a deterministic reading of Marxist writings. Their simplistic analysis showed an understanding of class but was limited in its ability to unravel the process of struggle and social change. This literature, it could be said, also failed to provide an adequate explanation of racial identity and racial politics in South Africa.

The radical explanation of race was given full expression in the works of Oliver Cromwell Cox.[33] He argued that racial divisions were a necessary resolution of capitalist industrial relations.[34] Racial divisions, he said, reflected the successful outcome of a process by which the state fragmented the working class in order to undermine its power and in order that it might create an ultra-exploitable community.[35] However, general

29. For a useful analysis of the positions see the conclusion of F.A. Johnstone, *Class, Race and Gold: A Study of Class Relations and Racial Discrimination in South Africa* (London, Routledge and Kegan Paul, 1976); see also I. Goldin, "Aspects of the Dialectic of Class and Race in South Africa", in M. Fransman *et al.* (eds.), *Southern African Studies: retrospect and prospect* (Edinburgh, Centre of African Studies, 1983); and D. Posel, "Rethinking the Race-class debate in South African Historiography" in *ibid.*

30. See, for example, P.L. van der Berghe, *South Africa: A study in conflict* (Berkeley, Univ. of California Press, 1967).

31. Johnstone, *op. cit.*, pp. 1-33, 206.

32. See, for example, M. Legassick, "South Africa: Capital accumulation and violence", *Economy and Society*, 3, (3), 1974; H. Wolpe, "Capitalism and Cheap Labour in South Africa: from Segregation to Apartheid", *Economy and Society*, 1, (4), 1972.

33. O. Cromwell Cox, *Caste, Class and Race: A study in racial dynamics* (New York, Monthly Review Press [MRP], 1970).

34. *Ibid.*, pp. 322.

35. *Ibid.*, pp. 322-330.

statements such as these have little value except at the most abstract level of analysis.

To be useful, an explanation of racist practices must be soundly based historically. The specific origins of these practices need to be understood for one to recognise how it is possible to move away from them and transform society. It is therefore necessary to go beyond the conclusion, reached by A. Sivanandan, that "capital requires racism not for racism's sake but for the sake of capital."[36] Such explanations cannot account for complex patterns of social stratification, nor for the dynamic processes which constantly reconstitute and modify these relationships over time.

Sivanandan asserted that in the "exceptional" case of South Africa "race is class, and class, race — and the race struggle is the class struggle."[37] But to argue such a case is to ignore the significance of the development of a black bourgeoisie and of powerful ideologies committed to overcoming racial divisions. The conflation of race and class serves no useful purpose. Nevertheless, the distancing of race from class should not be confused with attempts to deny the critical interrelationship between the two.

Efforts to resolve the relationship between class and race theoretically have been singularly unsuccessful.[38] Of all such attempts, that of No Sizwe is closest to our focus of attention.[39] No Sizwe rejected race as a concept which is "politically empty at best and potentially reactionary at worst" but reintroduced the notion of colour-caste into the debate about Coloured identity.[40] He adopted Berreman's definition, arguing that "a caste system occurs when a society is made up of birth-ascribed groups which are hierarchically ordered and culturally distinct." He argued that whereas in India

> caste rituals and privileges, the mode of life, are legitimised by cultural-religious criteria, in South Africa they are legitimised by so-called "racial" criteria.[41]

The South African system, he insisted, may be called a "colour-caste" system.[42] "The officially classified population registration groups in South Africa," he concluded, "are colour-castes".[43]

36. A. Sivanandan, *A Different Hunger: Writings on Black Resistance* (London, Pluto, 1982), p. 124.
37. *Ibid.,* pp. 324.
38. See J. and G. Ben Tovin, "Marxism and the Concept of Racism," *Economy and Society,* 7, (2), 1978, pp. 118-154.
39. No Sizwe, *One Azania, One Nation: The National Question in South Africa* (London, Zed, 1979).
40. *Ibid.,* pp. 136.
41. *Ibid.,* pp. 148.

No Sizwe's reliance on the notion of colour-caste is out of keeping with his otherwise radical analysis of the national question in South Africa. Although he attempted to relocate it within a "Marxian and historical framework"[44] and argued that "the development of the productive forces has broken down the walls of caste consciousness"[45], his concept of colour-caste remains rooted in the pluralist paradigm.

In the 1960s the concept of colour-caste was given an explanatory role by the liberal American scholar Pierre van der Berghe, who argued that the population was divided into four rigid colour-castes.[46] These castes, he argued, were racially determined. However, as Frederick Johnstone has shown, the notion of colour-caste is inapplicable to South Africa and cannot explain the origins or development of racial identifications and categorisations.[47] The notion describes domination by a distinct group but fails to explain the origins of the distinctions between the groups. The notion of colour-caste assumes the prior existence of institutionalised boundaries between the various castes.[48] It is thus unhelpful to an investigation of the origins and evolution of these boundaries.

Cox has shown that the notion of colour-caste rests on the existence of immutable caste barriers which are never challenged but are sacred to all members of the caste.[49] The concept of colour-caste is thus unhelpful to an analysis which seeks to examine the evolution as well as the erosion of racial boundaries. In South Africa, we shall show, racial divisions are an arena of immense conflict. The fight to break down divisions and to establish a non-racial society provides a powerful counter to separatist tendencies. Assuming caste pressures as a given in any analysis prohibits the exploration of those pressures in a larger context: how such social barriers arise and continue to exist. To operate within the confines of the colour-caste framework would be to prejudge our investigation, which is concerned to investigate the origins, conservation and dissolution of racial divisions.

We intend to demonstrate that racial divisions represent the outcome of an intense battle being waged at all levels of society between com-

42. *Ibid.*
43. *Ibid.,* pp. 141.
44. *Ibid.,* pp. 152.
45. *Ibid.,* pp. 159; see also F. Molteno, "Colour-caste and ruling class strategy in South Africa", in M. Murray (ed.), *South African Capitalism and Black Political Opposition* (Cambridge [USA], Schenkman, 1982), pp. 623-629.
46. P. van der Berghe, "Race and Racism in South Africa", in A. Beteille (ed.), *Social Inequality* (Harmondsworth, Penguin, 1969), pp. 324-5.
47. F.A. Johnstone, *op.cit.,* p. 207.
48. See Cox, *op.cit.,* pp. 453-541.
49. *Ibid.,* pp. 498.

peting ideologies. These divisions are in a state of flux; the movement reflects the changing balance of forces in the struggle to mobilise racial identity as well as the ambivalence of the ideologies.

Ideologies are not "tricks" imposed by the ruling class in order to deceive workers, nor are they spontaneous processes of thought which programme individuals to assume a particular destiny.[50] Although ideologies may arise from within one particular class their development is not restricted to that class. And though they may be associated with particular objectives, the extent to which they can perform these objectives cannot be predicted. Their power is reflected in their ability to mobilise politically.[51] The efficacy of competing ideologies is therefore integrally related to the history of struggle within society.

(2) CLASS

Class is essential to our understanding of South African society. This does not imply that class explains all the divisions within society or that our analysis will be distorted in order to fit a specific mould. On the contrary, we intend to demonstrate the significance of non-class divisions and to explore the interrelation between class and other conflicts. The key to an understanding of social relations and social change in South Africa, we suggest, lies in an appreciation of the racial and other identities which are part of the everyday experience of all South Africans. At the same time, class divisions are the fundamental characteristic of all capitalist societies and South Africa is no exception. The relations between the antagonistic classes in South Africa as well as the conflicts within the classes are critical, therefore, to an understanding of South African society.

It is useful to distinguish between a "class for itself" and a "class in itself".[52] A "class in itself" is a group of people whose place in society is objectively determined by the prevailing social order; for example, South Africa is defined to be a capitalist society characterised by the an-

---

50. For an introduction to the debate see Centre for Contemporary Cultural Studies (eds.), *On Ideology* (London, Hutchinson, 1977), pp. 5-125, and J. Larrain, *The Concept of Ideology* (London, Hutchinson, 1979).
51. Q. Hoare and G. Smith (eds.), *A. Gramsci: Selections from Prison Notebooks* (London, Lawrence and Wishart, 1971), p. 376.
52. See S. Hall, "The 'Political' and the 'Economic' in Marx's Theory of Classes", in A. Hunt (ed.), *Class and Class Structure* (London, Lawrence and Wishart, 1977), pp. 36-40; E.P. Thompson, "Revolution Again! or shut your ears and run", *New Left Review*, Nov.-Dec. 1960, No. 6; G.A. Cohen, *Karl Marx's Theory of History — A Defence* (Oxford, OUP, 1979), p. 73.

tagonistic relation of the two major classes, the capitalist and working class. As used in this Marxist thesis, the term "capitalist class" refers to the owners and controllers of the means of production, who appropriate "surplus value" from wage labourers (by paying them less than their "use value"). The term "working class" or "proletariat", in contrast, refers to all those who lack ownership or control of the means of production and who are dependent on wage labour for their subsistence.

Aside from these fundamental differences it is useful to distinguish between the "bourgeoisie" and "petty bourgeoisie". The bourgeoisie embraces the middle and upper strata of the capitalist class and includes all employers of wage labour. The petty bourgeoisie, although controlling means of production, are not engaged in the appropriation of "surplus value" from wage labourers. Though often defined as a sub-class of the capitalist class they will be referred to here as a separate class. They include the traditional petty bourgeoisie (self-employed traders, master craftsmen and others) and those whom Poulantzas terms the "new petty bourgeoisie", those employed in the administration and maintenance of capitalist society but who produce no "surplus value" — for example, teachers and nurses.[53]

The concept of the petty bourgeoisie has proved to be one of the most intractable of the many issues which have occupied the attentions of Marxist scholars. In part, this is because of the failure to appreciate that Marx's central concern was with the relationship between classes rather than with class definitions. In Marx's writing the petty bourgeoisie was seen to occupy the central ground between the fundamentally opposed capitalist and working classes, sharing in common with each of them attributes which made possible an alliance with either class. The extent to which the petty bourgeoisie may join forces with either class cannot be predetermined. At the same time, the ambivalent position of the petty bourgeoisie makes that class an uncertain ally in class alliances.

A "class for itself" refers to members of a "class in itself" who are subjectively aware of the fundamental class divisions. Their recognition of this is based on their own historical experience. The mobilisation of a "class in itself" into a "class for itself" is central to the development of organised class conflict. Class conflict, however, is never a pure and undiluted process, for in practice other social divisions play a part in the struggle. This weaving together of the various strands of opposition is integral to the mobilisation of resistance; it may well involve the straddling of class divisions and the alliance of sections of the petty bour-

---

53. N. Poulantzas, *Classes in Contemporary Capitalism* (London, Verso, 1978), pp. 109-328.

geoisie with the working class. Furthermore, as Eugene Genovese has demonstrated, it is necessary to recognise the sociological uniqueness of every class "as a product of a configuration of economic interests, a semi-autonomous culture, and a particular world outlook."[54]

(3) THE STATE

The futility of constructing a general theory of the state in capitalist societies has been forcefully demonstrated by scholars concerned to challenge "structuralist" general theories such as those advanced by Poulantzas.[55] This book will highlight some of the contradictions to be found in simplistic notions of the South Africa state. Nevertheless, in criticising these interpretations we shall be careful not to deny the attempt by sections of the capitalist class to use it to their own advantage. Nor shall we ignore the obvious benefits to the ruling party that come with control over the state. The ability of the state to implement policies is after all its *raison d'être*. We intend to explore this but at the same time to guard against mechanistic or conspiratorial interpretations of state activity.

Conflicts, corruptions and inadequacies continuously undermine and distort state policy. Many of these shortcomings derive from the tensions associated with having to meet competing needs, whilst others derive from opposition to particular state policies. Such opposition may arise from intra- or inter-class conflicts.

The state under the political control of the ruling class aims to implement the designs of that class. However, tensions within the ruling class limit the coherence of its policy; furthermore, a wide variety of political struggles which are not reducible to class conflict are fought within the ambit of the state. This makes nonsense of arguments which see it as acting exclusively as the instrument of a "ruling class". Antagonistic sections of society help to undermine the state's authority. Ultimately, opposition from those who suffer most acutely from its existence pose the most serious challenges to it. This opposition ranges from individual acts of crime and deviance to mass resistance that may culminate in the actual overthrow of the state executive.

In South Africa, resistance to the state has been associated with attempts by the state to reconstitute society in order to guarantee its survival. Successive governments, we shall show, have tried to develop a

54. E. Genovese, *In Red and Black: Marxian Explanations in Southern and Afro-American History* (New York, Vintage, 1971), p. 324.
55. See B. Jessop, *The Capitalist State* (Oxford, Martin Robertson, 1982), p. 213.

client group, who although not assimilated into the dominant class owe their allegiance to that class. The development of the group who in the late nineteenth century came to be referred to as Coloured was part of such a process. But the forging of Coloured identity cannot simply be attributed to the state and to the ruling class; the Coloured population also defined itself.

From the outset, Coloured identity was an area of conflict. The term Coloured was rejected by many of the people so defined, whilst others imputed a different meaning to the term. It became the focus of a passionate debate. This has increased in intensity over time, and the term has become overloaded with connotations which almost invariably invite confusion and criticism. To avoid ambivalence over our use of the term it is necessary to devote some attention to the linguistic conventions which we have adopted.

Racial definitions

The expression of racial identities reflects the attempt by one group of people to separate itself from one or more of the characteristics of the excluded group. Such identities are in no sense fixed; they are in a constant process of evolution.

The statutory definitions Coloured, Black, Asian and White are notoriously arbitrary and are based on pseudo-scientific notions which have long since been discredited. Yet the fact remains that in South Africa these racial categories have a pervading significance, defining the boundaries of a comprehensively divided society. For all the statutory measures, however, racial categorisation has developed a momentum of its own; and racial divisions preceded and exist alongside those enforced by the state.

The terms Coloured, Black, White and Asian in this book refer simply to the statutory definition of persons in South Africa.[56] It cannot be stressed enough that many, if not most, of the individuals so defined would reject the racial categorisations and their various permutations. Many Africans, Asians and Coloureds, particularly following the rise of black consciousness ideologies in the early 1960s, when using racial categorisations define themselves simply as "black". In this book the term "black" will therefore refer to all persons not categorised as White. Such a usage may be contrasted with that currently adopted by the South Af-

---

56. For the statutory definitions and a discussion of some of the ambiguities that have arisen see M. Horrell, *Legislation and Race Relations* (Johannesburg, SAIRR, 1971).

rican state, for whom Black refers specifically to people formerly designated as Africans, Bantu, Natives or Kaffirs. In our study the term
African will be used to refer to the category of people who today are
defined by the state as Black.

There is a further complication. In the nineteenth century the term
Coloured in official documents referred to all persons not classified as
European. By 1904, however, the term Coloured had been reconstituted
to exclude Bantu-speaking people. From 1904 until the present time the
term Coloured has designated roughly the same category of individuals.
No single definition of Coloured people exists: a succession of contradictory legislative measures and legal precedents has only added to the ambiguity surrounding the term. For our purposes, however, "Coloured"
will be used to signify the category sometimes referred to as Cape
Coloured. In terms of the Population Registration Act this is defined as
consisting "of persons who are, or who are generally accepted as, members of the race or class known as Cape Coloured."[57] In practice this
subjective definition has given a free hand to the authorities, who have
been able to alter in undisclosed ways the criteria by which people are
defined to be Coloured.[58]

Administrative confusion over the definition of Coloured is related to
the ambivalence within government over this issue. We shall show that
the definition of people as Coloured has not been based on fixed criteria
but has developed over time. Nevertheless it is unhelpful to substitute
for the word Coloured other categorisations such as "Mixed race" or
"Hottentot". These terms are neither more historically accurate nor less
obnoxious.

The term "mixed race" as used in much of the British media and by
liberal commentators in South Africa reproduces in another form many
of the racial prejudices inherent in the National Party view that
Coloureds are largely the result of miscegenation between the European
settler population and the indigenous inhabitants of the colony.[59] Although such intermixing has undoubtedly contributed substantially to the
population today defined as Coloured, it is a nonsense to attempt to

57. South Africa, *Population Registration Act,* No. 30 of 1950, Section Five.
58. G. Watson in his book *Passing for White* (London, Tavistock, 1970) records numerous
    cases in which different members of the same family are classified differently. M. Hor-
    rell, *Race Classification in South Africa* (Johannesburg, SAIRR, 1958) provides similar
    examples of the arbitrary nature of race classification as does Patterson, *"Colour and
    Culture",* pp. 323-325.
59. *The Collins Dictionary of the English Language* (Collins, London, 1979, ed. P. Hanks),
    p. 300, gives credence to this myth by defining the term Coloured in the South African
    context as "a person of racially mixed parentage or descent".

distinguish the Coloured people in this manner. "Mixed race" implies the prior existence of "pure" race-groups and gives credence to apartheid notions of racial purity. No race exists which is not mixed, least of all the supposedly pure English (Anglo-Saxon) race.

The South African White population has for its ancestry an exotic pot-pourri which (not least among Afrikaners) includes the indigenous people of South Africa.[60] What is true of the so-called European population is equally true of the population defined by the state to be made up of various African "tribes". For instance the Xhosa-speaking people, it has been established by linguists, have a diverse ancestry which includes elements of the Khoi and other Khoisan groups often referred to collectively as "Hottentot".

As to the Hottentot people, they were not simply the proto-Coloureds. But the link between Hottentot and Coloured certainly provides a substantial thread woven into the history of the people who in the twentieth century came to be defined as Coloured.

Our aim is to focus our attention on the category of people defined as Coloured in order to investigate the extent to which this categorisation has determined the political identity and racial consciousness of the people so defined, and to examine the interplay of the working class, the employers and the state in the evolution of the Coloured categorisation and identity.

Our adoption of statutory racial definitions cannot be assumed to legitimise the government's definitions. On the contrary, this study aims to examine the struggle over the statutory definitions of race and to throw light on the evolution and possible dissolution of racial divisions in South Africa.

Contents

The book is divided into four parts: the first covers the period up to 1948, the second from 1948 to 1961, the third from 1961 to 1976 and the fourth from 1976 to 1984. In each part we shall discuss the development of policies of preference for Coloureds and the evolution of Coloured political identity. Each section will include an analysis of the ruling

---

60. P. van der Berghe, *Study in Conflict*, p. 42, noted that "up to one quarter of the persons classified as 'White' in the Cape Province are of mixed descent and that every 'old family' from White Cape society has genealogical connections with Coloured families". See also A. Suzman, *Race Classification and Definition in the Legislation of the Union of South Africa, 1910-1960* (Johannesburg, SAIRR, 1960).

party, the employers and the state as well as an examination of the struggle over Coloured political identity amongst people defined as Coloured.

The four parts reflect the various phases in the development of Coloured political identity and policies of Coloured preference in the Western Cape region of South Africa. It is no accident that the period of National Party rule coincides with heightened resistance to the government. In 1961 and 1976, we shall show, the challenge to the National Party coincided with renewed attempts to implement policies of preference and to reconstitute Coloured political identity. The great economic stress of these years was equally decisive in bringing about changes in preference policies and in Coloured political identity. The significance of economic factors, and particularly of the changing occupational structure of the Coloured population, merits the prominence given to this subject.

Part One, covering the period leading up to National Party rule, is divided into three chapters. The first examines the development of policies of preference for Coloureds, and of Coloured political identity, from the time of first settlement to the turn of the twentieth century. In that period the preference patterns which later became entrenched were first adopted. But although the colonial government and the colonised population thought in terms of racial identity, a distinct Coloured political identity did not develop until the 1880s. By 1904, for reasons discussed in Chapter One, this identity had been constituted in a form approximating that which exists today.

Chapter Two focuses on the development of the African Peoples' Organisation (APO) and the conflict over Coloured identity in the period 1904 to 1935. In this period the development of policies of preference for Coloured men and women was closely related to attempts by the administration and employers to deflect opposition based on an alliance of Coloured and African people. The changing occupational position of Coloured men and women, and changes in employment associated with the Civilised Labour Policy and the Great Depression, also had an impact on Coloured political identity in this period.

In Chapter Three we demonstrate that the policies of preference for Coloureds were associated with stricter controls over the employment and residence of Africans in the Western Cape. Between 1935 and 1948 the enforcement of influx controls over Africans extended the relative advantage of an assertion of Coloured identity and deepened the structural divide between African and Coloured people. The divisions between Coloured and African men and women were entrenched by the organisation of resistance by bodies which themselves failed to overcome racial boundaries.

Part Two — concerned with the period 1948 to 1961 — begins with Chapter Four. This chapter examines the place of Coloureds in the apartheid programme and demonstrates that the reconstitution of Coloured identity was a priority of the National Party. The disfranchisement of the Coloureds as well as the simultaneous implementation of the Coloured Labour Preference Policy were central to the Party's plans. Within the National Party, however, the question of Coloured identity and the legislative programme of the government remained bitterly contested.

The Coloured Labour Preference Policy, we shall show in Chapter Five, threatened to prevent African workers from engaging in employment in the Western Cape. The Policy was thus bitterly opposed by employers reliant on African unskilled workers. Included amongst these were Afrikaner farmers, many of whom were loyal National Party constituents.

In Chapter Six we show that the development of the Coloured Labour Preference Policy stimulated resistance to the National Party and attempts by the Party to undermine the alliance of African and Coloured people. The organisation of Coloured and African workers by the South African Congress of Trade Unions (SACTU) affiliates helped to overcome many of the widening structural divisions between African and Coloured workers. Outside the factories, however, radical organisations tended to reproduce distinct Coloured and African political identities.

Chapter Seven, the first in Part Three, deals with developments within the National Party and the employer class in the period 1961 to 1976. In this chapter it will be shown that the question of Coloured identity became an increasingly important source of dissent within the National Party; there was growing uncertainty regarding the future of the Coloureds. We shall show in Chapter Eight that the uncertainty was in part the result of resistance by Coloureds to a separate Coloured political identity.

From 1976 to 1984 — the period covered by Part Four — resistance to a separate Coloured political identity forced the National Party to renew its attempt to fragment the growing alliance of Coloured and African people. The ascendancy of P.W. Botha and the close involvement of the military in state planning, we shall show in Chapter Nine, placed a priority on the political incorporation of Coloureds, even at the expense of National Party unity. The priority given to the incorporation of Coloureds, Chapter Ten notes, was supported by employers. But employers were critical of the failure of the government to secure a stable skilled African workforce. The closer alliance of employers and government, together with the development of a country-wide system of labour controls which made the Coloured Preference Policy superfluous, motivated the government's decision to abandon the policy. In Chapter Eleven the decision to abandon the policy will be shown to be closely associated with the failure of the policy to undermine the growing alliance of Coloured and African people in the Western Cape or to prevent African influx into the area.

Political resistance to the National Party overcame many of the divisions which the National Party set out to create between African and Coloured people in the Western Cape. In the Conclusion we therefore return to the theme raised in this Introduction and taken up in the following chapters, namely that whilst policies of preference for Coloureds seek to establish a separate Coloured political identity, they themselves are the subject of an intense struggle at all levels of society. It is to a consideration of this struggle that we now turn.

PART ONE
1652 – 1948

CHAPTER ONE

THE FOUNDATIONS OF FAVOURITISM

Introduction

In this chapter and the next we intend to trace the lineage of practices and perceptions which all too often are misleadingly regarded as Nationalist interventions. There can be little doubt that the development of a distinct Coloured identity and of a system of preference for Coloured labour was rooted in the period of colonial rule. In the first section we shall show that attempts by the ruling class in South Africa to incorporate elements of what later became known as the Coloured people are not a recent development; they have their origin in the endeavours of the colonial state to deflect opposition based on a mass resistance by the colonised people. In the second section we focus on the reconstitution of Coloured identity in the period 1895 to 1905. A particular constellation of circumstances at the turn of the century led to the assertion of a distinct Coloured identity and the formation of Coloured political organisations. An examination of those critical years considerably enhances our understanding of Coloured indentity and Coloured politics in the period of National Party rule.

The Roots of Segregation

Orthodox accounts of social stratification assert that social status at the time of the first European colonisation was not based on colour. The orthodoxy, which until recently remained unchallenged, was popularised by G.M. Theal and I.D. MacCrone.[1] The MacCrone thesis provided the historical foundation on which the 1939 Commission on Mixed Marriages, as well as the 1937 and 1976 Commissions of Inquiry into the Coloured Population, rested their argument.[2] According to the 1939 Commission on Mixed Marriages,

---

1. G.M. Theal, *History and Ethnography of Africa South of the Zambesi, Vol. 2* (London, Sonnenschein, 1909); I.D. MacRone, *Race Attitudes in South Africa* (London, 1937).

There does not seem to have been any "colour feeling" on the part of the
Europeans at the Cape in the early days, the distinction being rather between
"Christian" and "Heathen" than between "White" and "Coloured".[3]

Religion, not colour, it was widely accepted, provided the basis for
social differentiation in early colonial society.

The 1937 and 1976 Commissions of Inquiry into the Coloured
Population followed closely Theal's assertion that

In the middle of the seventeenth century no distinction whatever appears to
have been made on account of colour. A profession of Christianity placed
black and white on the same level.[4]

Theal and MacCrone based their arguments on evidence of
miscegenation in the infant settlement and on the absence of formal
colour bars. From this they concluded that racism was not carried onto
the shores by the first European settlers. Racism, it was asserted,
developed later, as a result of practices developed by the Boers in the
interior republics. The Afrikaner republics, the liberal thesis argued,
had been established by people committed to racial principles who
trekked away from the coastal colonies; the ascendancy of the interior
republics after 1910, culminating in the victory of the National Party,
accounted for entrenchment throughout South Africa of racial practices.[5]

As Legassick has noted, the liberal thesis attempted to absolve the
imperial and colonial administrations from racist practices and pointed
an accusing finger at the Afrikaner people.[6] In so doing, the thesis failed
to comprehend the origins of racism and the limited extent of non-racial
ideologies.

The first settlers carried on to the shores of South Africa practices
and prejudices which extended beyond the simple religious distinctions
which in the orthodoxy explained social stratification in colonial society.
The liberal thesis in part rested on evidence of intermarriage in the

2. South Africa, *Report of the Commission of Inquiry Regarding the Coloured Population of the Union* UG 54/1937; South Africa, *Report of the Commission of Inquiry
   into Matters Relating to the Coloured Population Group* RP 38/1976; South Africa,
   Report of the Commission of Inquiry on Mixed Marriages in South Africa UG 30/1939;
   Prof. Erica Theron, Chairwoman of 1976 Coloured Commission, interview, Stellenbosch, 23 September 1981, transcript, p.3.
3. South Africa, *Mixed Marriages Commission*, p. 4. para. 13.
4. Theal, *op.cit.*, p. 59.
5. M. Legassick, "The frontier tradition in South African Historiography", Inst. of Commonwealth Studies, *Collected Seminar Papers on the Societies of Southern Africa in the
   19th and 20th Centuries, Vol. 2* (London, ICS, 1971), pp. 1-3.
6. *Ibid.*

settler society. But a closer examination of the patterns of intermarriage, as George Frederickson noted, demonstrated that

> even though intermarriage was extensive . . . it was not occurring in an unbiased way . . . It is obvious, therefore, that the white settlers had some sense of ethnic hierarchy.[7]

From the outset this sense of ethnic hierarchy was expressed in discrimination against Bantu-speaking people and in the reluctance of the colonists to allow Africans to become candidates for "free black" status. Furthermore, part-White people, many of whom were descendants of the concubinage of the male settlers with slave women, together with freed slaves of Eurasian or Asian descent, were accorded a higher status than purely African people. Already, within the first two decades of colonial rule, there existed in the Cape a complex racial hierarchy in which people who were later to be designated Coloured occupied an intermediate position.[8]

Bullets and Ballots

In the first decade of colonial rule, according to Theal, the strategic concerns of the governor played an important part in the promotion of an intermediate class of mixed race:

> Mr. Van Riebeeck has left on record his opinion of the advantages derived from the large mixed population of their possessions in the East, without whose assistance their fortresses could not have been held so long.[9]

But the administration soon found that miscegenation alone could not provide a bulwark against the determined resistance of the indigenous people.

The Khoisan people of the Cape were amongst the first to suffer dispossession of their lands at the hands of the colonial regime. The diverse response of the Khoisan to proletarianisation has been outlined by Marks and Gray.[10] They observed that "some Khoi found an escape route northwards or eastwards."[11] Many of the Khoi became absorbed into the Xhosa, and by the turn of the eighteenth century mixed Xhosa-

---

7. G. Frederickson, *White Supremacy: a Comparative Study of American and South African History* (Oxford, OUP, 1981), p. 116.
8. *Ibid.*, pp. 116-117 and 131-133.
9. Theal, *op. cit.*
10. S. Marks and R. Gray, "Southern Africa and Madagascar", in R. Gray (ed.), *The Cambridge History of Africa, Vol. 4, c.1600 to 1790* (Cambridge, CUP, 1975), pp. 435-451.
11. *Ibid.*, pp. 443.

Khoi groupings existed, whilst others lived alongside the Xhosa as, to use Marks's suggestive phrase, "voor-voortrekkers"[12]. Another group of Khoi remained in the Cape and lived as bandits or as increasingly impoverished independent pastoralists. But this independent existence, particularly after the smallpox epidemic of 1713, could sustain only a small number of Khoi; by the beginning of the eighteenth century the majority, as Marks and Gray have noted, "were converted into the menials of the white man, depressed socially, economically and politically."[13]

Dispossession brought about the increasing correspondence in the socio-economic position of the Khoisan and the slaves, and, Elphick suggested, led to

> the merger of the Khoikhoi and the slaves into a labouring class which South Africans in the nineteenth century would call the Cape Coloured people.[14]

Elphick, however, underestimated the diversity of the Khoisan response to proletarianisation as well as the extent to which this process preceded the emancipation of slaves and their transformation into "free labour"; a Khoisan proletariat existed for more than a century before the emancipation of slaves, and the divergence between the position of slaves and that of "free" labourers should not be underestimated.

Marks and Gray emphasise that in the seventeenth century the Dutch were heavily dependent on "loyal" Khoi levies and that in the eighteenth century "they formed the backbone of the colonial defences against both internal and external enemies"[15]; the Khoikhoi in the Cape, Pringle found, were not only cooks, herders and labourers, wagon-drivers and interpreters, they were very often fine shots and horsemen.[16] But although, as Moodie noted, these people were "found to be the most efficient troops for dealing with the Kaffirs"[17], their loyalty to the Crown could not be assumed; the Khoi were vital to the defence of the colony, but they were also a major threat to it.

The resistance of many Khoi to conscription, and their refusal to take arms against other indigenous people, undermined attempts by the embattled governor to recruit Khoi as soldiers. The response of many Khoi to conscription was to seek refuge outside the colony. Some, such as the

---

12. *Ibid.*, p. 435.
13. *Ibid.*, p. 451.
14. R. Elphick, *Kraal and Castle; Khoikhoi and the founding of White South Africa* (New Haven, Yale Univ. Press, 1977), p. 35.
15. Marks and Gray, *op.cit.*, p. 443.
16. Cited in M. Wilson, "Co-operation and Conflict: The Eastern Cape Frontier", in M. Wilson and L. Thompson (eds.), *The Oxford History of South Africa* (Oxford, OUP, 1969), p. 246-247.
17. J. Moodie, *Ten Years in South Africa* (London, 1835), p. 304.

"Bastards", fled to Namaqualand in order to avoid military service whilst others migrated north-east, later to join up in a powerful alliance with the Xhosa. Already, by the turn of the eighteenth century, the alliance of Khoi and Xhosa posed for the colonial military its most serious internal threat.

In 1799 the Khoi in the Graaff-Reinet district rose in defiance of the local administration. Seething with the indignities they had suffered, which had culminated in an attempt to disarm them and to introduce a Vagrancy Law, the Khoi joined forces with the Xhosa. The alliance of disaffected Khoi and Ndhlambe's warriors shattered the complacency of the first British administration (1795-1803). For, as J.S. Marais observed, if the rising had spread to the western Hottentots and slaves, the White man's hold on the colony would have been "shaken to its foundations"[18]. This, however, was not to be; the skilful intervention of Dundas, the acting governor, deflected the resistance and the Khoi were appeased through offers of land and employment. According to Macmillan these measures, introduced simultaneously with the vetoing by D'Urban of Wade's Vagrancy Law, saved the country from a Hottentot rebellion.[19] Eric Walker came to a similar conclusion, noting that

> under the growing rule of law, most of the Hottentots took service, and not only ceased to be a peril to the Colony, but in due course became a reinforcement to it against the Kaffirs.[20]

The strength of resistance had forced the administration on the defensive. Nevertheless, in their retreat they were able to lay a minefield of legislation which served to weaken the dangerous alliance of Khoi and Xhosa. The Xhosa bore the brunt of the new regulations; their settlement in the colony was prevented and their ability to migrate in search of work greatly restricted. The Khoi, by contrast, were allowed to remain in the colony and encouraged by law to enter fixed employment contracts. The regulations placed a yoke on the Khoi and other proletarianised inhabitants of the Cape. At the same time, the growing rule of law served to entrench the differences between the Cape proletariat and Bantu-speaking people residing beyond the colony's borders.

The Khoi pacification programme was embodied in regulations which imposed an employment contract on landless people in the Eastern Cape. For the dispossessed people, the growing rule of law raised a

18. J. Marais, *The Cape Coloured People, 1652-1937* (Johannesburg, Wits. Univ. Press, 1957) p. 114; see also S. Newton-King, *The Rebellion of the Khoi in Graaff-Reinet, 1799 to 1803* (Cape Town, University of Cape Town, 1980).
19. W.M. Macmillan, *Bantu, Boer and Britain* (London, UCT, 1929), p. 145.
20. E. Walker, *A History of South Africa* (London, Longmans, 1968), p. 135.

hope that abuses of power by employers would be prevented and that employees at last would have a recourse to law. Their optimism was ill-founded; the regulations had the opposite impact and the position of landless people deteriorated further as the power of White settler farmers to prevent desertions and bind workers to a fixed abode was enhanced. The effect was such that even Cory, an historian not known for his humanitarian perspective, was moved to note:

> Thus without the regulations violated, their intention in this particularly has been defeated and the Hottentots condemned to become a slave or a prisoner, for an indefinite time to the farmer who secured his service.[21]

The Batavian government, which ruled the Cape from 1803 to 1806, extended the regulations to all parts of the colony. In 1806 the reassertion of British rule led to the ending of the slave trade. In 1809 Governor Caledon, partly in an attempt to overcome the labour shortage which had resulted, extended further the rule of law binding workers to their employers. In 1811 the expulsion of the Xhosa from the Zuurveld increased the significance of the distinction between Xhosa and other people.

Cory has referred to Caledon's proclamations as the "Magna Carta" of the Hottentots.[22] Duncan Innes, a modern commentator, has attached a similar significance to the Caledon codes, suggesting that

> *In this way Coloured people gained for themselves legal recognition of their position as a special class of protected workers in the Cape, no longer subjected to quite the same sort of exploitation as was suffered by indigenous African workers.*[23]

At the time, however, there were virtually no "indigenous African workers" at the Cape, and when they were incorporated into the colony they came under similar laws. Furthermore, although Innes implies that the codes were associated with the development of an already existing "Coloured people", such a cohesive group did not come into existence until the turn of the twentieth century, as will become apparent later in this book.

Cory and Innes failed to note that the Caledon codes had a profoundly ambiguous impact on the class of dispossessed people in the Cape. In part, this was because the application of the codes rested on the discretion of local officials — it was not long before these "land-

---

21. G. Cory, *The Rise of South Africa, Vol. 1* (London, Longmans, 1910), p. 199.
22. *Ibid.*, p. 200.
23. D. Innes, *Forced Removals in South Africa* (London, Africa Publ., 1975), p. 4 (emphasis in original).

drosts" became a focus of Khoi grievances. Eric Walker has emphasised that

> The intention was to provide a supply of labour and to encourage farmers to look after whole families of dependants; but it only needed Somerset's permission to Landdrosts to inboek orphans and to reduce Hottentots to the level of serfs at the disposal of local officials.[24]

Clearly, the "Magna Carta", far from bringing rights and privileges to workers, in many instances placed further restrictions on the already severely constrained rights of the landless people.

By the end of the eighteenth century, as Trapido has noted, the "Khoikhoi had already become a landless proletariat."[25] They were increasingly forced into wage labour and subjected to a rule of law which could not be relied upon to defend their interests. The fact that they had been made landless earlier and forced through a different process to rely on wage labour meant that the Hottentots came to occupy a position in colonial society which fundamentally differed from that occupied by the overwhelming majority of Bantu-speaking people. By 1828, therefore, a distinguishable class of individuals of intermediate social status had come into existence in the Cape. This class included the core of individuals whom in the twentieth century came to be defined as Coloured.

In 1828, following the passage of Ordinance 50, which repealed the Caledon codes, the position of the Hottentots in the Cape was considerably improved. After this date, according to S. Newton-King, the legal category of Hottentot ceased to exist.[26] Newton-King suggests that the abolition of slavery and the emergence of a new class of proletarianised people in the 1820s and 1830s was associated with the coming into being of a new class of Coloured people who were freed from pass and other restrictions. Here Newton-King is in broad agreement with W. Macmillan.[27] According to Macmillan, at the time of the emancipation of slaves the "Hottentots and the slaves were merged together as the 'Cape Coloured' people."[28] The "Coloureds", Macmillan estimated, were about twice as numerous as the European population of the colony.[29] However, as this book shows, Macmillan overstated the extent to which the

---

24. E. Walker, *op.cit.*, p. 149. "Inboek" means "indenture".
25. S. Trapido, "White conflict and non-white participation in the politics of the Cape of Good Hope, 1853-1910" (London Univ., PhD thesis, 1970), p. 381.
26. Newton-King, *op.cit.*, p. 192.
27. W. Macmillan, *The Cape Colour Question: an historical survey* (London, Faber, 1927), p. 141.
28. *Ibid.*
29. *Ibid.*

1820s marked a rupture in the development of a distinct Coloured identity.

The assertion by Newton-King that the Coloureds emerged in the 1820s and 1830s fails to draw attention to the long process by which Coloured identity was forged. The gradual evolvement of ethnic identities cannot be reduced to the restructuring of social relations at the time of emancipation. Though Newton-King suggests that after 1828 the legal term Hottentot ceased to exist, it remained in official use in census and other government documents for at least half a century after emancipation. (Throughout the nineteenth century, we show below, the category Coloured in the Cape census included all people not classified as European, whilst Hottentots until 1904 were classified as a distinct sub-group of the Coloured category.) Following emancipation it would appear that, far from the term Hottentot disappearing, it was increasingly associated with the colonial assimilation of various landless people into the category of a homogeneous (Hottentot) labouring class. So, for example, Commissioner Brigge at the time referred to "the Hottentots . . . in which class is generally included the mixed race of Hottentots and the white and free coloured inhabitants."[30]

With the emancipation of slaves (1834-1838), the Cape proletariat more than doubled in size. For the slaves themselves, the emancipation had a contradictory impact because, as Abe Desmore discovered,

> While the emancipation resulted in technical freedom, it virtually transformed the whole community into one of wage slavery. It made dependants into helpless and hopeless vagrants.[31]

The ending of slavery brought about increased competition for jobs and the rapid growth of the dispossessed and disaffected class of people within the Cape. Although a substantial number took refuge in mission stations and some were able to engage in peasant production, the restlessness of this landless class was a cause of growing concern to the administration. In 1848 widespread agitation against a revised Vagrancy Act forced Sir Harry Smith to reappraise the new law.[32] Two years later the rising at Kat River, and the sympathy of Hottentot groups in the West to the rebellion, compounded the administration's anxieties. The rebellion at Kat River failed but, Trapido suggested, it had created a disposition among sections of the colonial ruling class to enfranchise a

30. Cited in Cory, *op.cit.*, p. 192. See also Legassick, *op.cit.*, pp. 2-4.
31. A. Desmore, "The Cape Coloured People Today", *Journal of the Royal African Society*, Vol. 36, 1937, p. 350.
32. S. Trapido, "The Friends of the Natives: Merchants, Peasants, and the political and ideological structure of Liberalism in the Cape, 1854-1910", in S. Marks and A. Atmore (eds.), *Economy and Society in Pre-Industrial South Africa* (London, Longmans, 1980), p. 273.

section of the colonised class.[33] In 1852 further agitation served to strengthen the hand of those pressing for an incorporative strategy. For, as the Cape Attorney General, William Porter, successfully reasoned,

> I would rather meet the Hottentot at the hustings voting for his representative than meet the Hottentot in the wilds with a gun on his shoulder. If these people have much physical force, — are armed, and, as you say, disaffected — is it not better to disarm them by letting them participate in the privileges of the constitution than by refusing them those long expected privileges to drive them into laagers?[34]

In 1853, with the granting of self-rule to the colony, a franchise was introduced which gave the vote to a limited number of men who were not regarded as being of European extraction. However, only a small minority of non-Europeans met the franchise's wealth and educational qualifications. For in the words of Sir Harry Smith, the governor at the time,

> except at the missionary institutions very few of the Coloured people own or occupy any property, but are principally labourers on the farms of their employers.[35]

At that time the term Coloured embraced the whole non-European population of the Cape. The majority were employed in the rural areas, with men engaged in labouring work and women mainly employed as domestic servants. Within these mission stations Coloured deacons and teachers constituted an élite. Their education set them apart from the rest of the non-European population, and within the missions they were able to command considerable influence. The pivotal role of the educated non-Europeans within their own communities, and the potential leadership role of these people in mobilising non-European resistance, were regarded by the Cape colonial administration as a threat. Those favouring the enfranchisement of this group argued convincingly that the parliamentary representation would serve to incorporate within the political arena people who, by their exclusion, may have provided a vocal leadership for extra-parliamentary opposition. The Cape colonial administration perceived a need for an incorporative strategy and, according to Macmillan, thus

> retained the devoted loyalty of its coloured citizens . . . As a partial experiment the constitution of 1853 has been abundantly justified . . . But the very success of this experiment was won at the price of economic well-being. The

33. *Ibid.,* pp. 262.
34. Trapido, "White Conflict", p. 39.
35. Cited in Trapido, "White Conflict", p. 14.

coloured people have remained a community of poor and backward dependants . . . Their contentment is testimony chiefly to the beneficent effects of a
freedom that allowed at any rate the more able and fortunate individuals
among them to rise to competence. The great mass of them were still a poor
servant class and were left to find their own level.[36]

The Reconstitution of Coloured Identity:
African and White Workers

Long before 1853, Frederickson has shown, a complex racial hierarchy
was firmly established in the Cape.[37] However, this had not yet led to
the exclusion of all Bantu-speaking people from the franchise. Nor had
racial ideologies crystallised around the distinction between Bantu-
speaking and other colonised people. Class allegiances and to a lesser
extent religious criteria remained important. A critical distinction was
between heathen, uneducated "blanket kaffirs" and the small number of
missionary-education Africans. "Blanket kaffirs" were mainly confined
to the Eastern district.[38] The 1865 Cape census recorded that 674 "Kaffirs" resided in the Greater Cape Town area and that this sub-group
constituted less than 5 per cent of the population categorised as "Coloured" in the Western Cape.[39]

Until the turn of the twentieth century the term Coloured generally
referred to all non-European people. Its use was thus not unlike that
current in North America. The official Cape census of 1875 included in
the category "Coloured" all "non-European" people, including "Fing-
oes" and "Kaffir proper".[40] The 1892 census maintained the same distinctions, declaring that the Cape population "falls naturally into two
main classes, the European or White and the Coloured."[41] Private employers tended to perceive similar distinctions. So, for example, in 1890
A.R. McKenzie, the principal labour contractor in the Cape Town
docks, referred to the fact that he employed "principally Kaffirs; all our

36. Macmillan, *op.cit.*, p. 267.
37. Frederickson, *"White Supremacy"*, pp. 116-119.
38. South Africa, *"Coloured Commission, 1937"*, para. 1058.
39. Cape of Good Hope, *Census 1865*, G20/66 (Cape Town, Govt. Printer, 1866), p. 4.
40. Cape of Good Hope, *Census 1875*, G18/76, (Cape Town, Govt. Printer, 1876), pp. 1-
    4.
41. Cape of Good Hope, *Census 1891*, G6/92 (Cape Town, Govt. Printer, 1892), p. xvii,
    para. 98.

labourers are Coloured, and are of different nationalities and tribes."[42]

Yet by 1904 this wide definition of Coloured was no longer acceptable. In marked contrast to the census of 1892, the Cape census of 1904 distinguished between three "clearly defined race groups in this colony: White, Bantu and Coloured."[43] Included in the last category were "all intermediate shades between the first two."[44]

A decisive shift in terminology therefore took place at the turn of the century. The identification of a distinct Coloured category was not only associated with changes within the colonial administration and ruling class. It simultaneously reflected a reorientation of allegiances and ideas within the subordinate society.

It was no accident that the period which saw the evolution of a distinct Coloured identity also saw a dramatic transformation of labour. A cycle of depressions, precipitated by the international banking crisis of 1866, tore the fabric of Cape society and marked a further step in the proletarianisation of rural Coloured people. Many migrated to the towns of the Cape colony, including Kimberley, and after 1886 to the Witwatersrand. The recession of 1877 to 1879 accentuated further the differential between town and country. In 1880 farmers were faced by what they regarded as a "serious want of labour"[45]. Their response was to recruit Bantu-speaking workers from the Eastern frontier and, as Patrick Harries has shown, from as far afield at Mozambique.[46] From the 1880s, despite mounting unemployment in the urban areas, the Cape proletariat increasingly successfully resisted working in the rural areas, where the most arduous and lowest-paid jobs were to be found. However, it was not only farmers who sought unskilled, low-wage labour by recruiting Bantu-speaking workers from far afield; urban employers began to display similar preferences.

In 1854 the first strike in Southern Africa had taken place, in the Cape Town docks. For the next 25 years the workforce was engaged in a series of running skirmishes with management. In 1880 this discontent culminated in a strike which threatened to cripple the Table Bay docks.

42. Cape Colony, *Select Committee Report*, A12 — 1890, p. 40, cited in V. Bickford-Smith, "Black Labour in the docks at the beginning of the twentieth century", in C. Saunders and H. Phillips (eds.), *Studies in the History of Cape Town, Vol. 2* (Cape Town, UCT, 1980), p. 87.
43. Cape Colony, *Cape Census 1904* G19/1905, p. xxi, para. 102.
44. *Ibid.*
45. S. Greenberg, *Race and State in Capitalist Development; Comparative Perspectives* (New Haven, Yale Univ., 1980), pp. 151-2.
46. See P. Harries, "Mozbiekers: The immigration of an African community to the Western Cape, 1876-1882" in C. Saunders (ed.), *Studies in the History of Cape Town, Vol. 1* (Cape Town, UCT, 1979).

However, the recruitment of over 200 workers from the Transkei led to the dismissal of the striking "Cape Boys" and the resumption of harbour activities. Employers were relieved to find that resistance had been deflected; for the next 20 years the docks experienced the most trouble-free period in the harbour's labour history. The success of the experiment inspired other employers to imitate the dock employers; it was not long before Bantu-speaking workers from the Eastern Cape and Mozambique were recruited for employment in a variety of other unskilled and arduous tasks.

By 1890 the principal employer in the Cape Town docks, A.R. Mac-Kenzie, had contracted over 1 000 "Natives", and his Bantu-speaking workforce had outnumbered his 600 "Cape Boys".[47] "Natives from up-country" were preferred by MacKenzie for unskilled and heavy manual tasks, whilst the "Cape Boys", who were regarded as "well trained and experienced", were kept on to work in more skilled jobs.[48] By 1901 the division of labour at the docks had become so entrenched that harbour employees asserted that

> the docks of Table Bay can no more be effectively worked without a good and constant supply of native labour than the mines of the Witwatersrand.[49]

Farm employers by this time endorsed the dock contractors' preference for migrant African labour, as did other employers of unskilled labour.[50] From 1893, over 200 Mfengu had been contracted to carry coal in the Cape Peninsula, and a growing number of urban and rural employers came to rely on Mfengu and Xhosa workers.[51] By 1899 it was noted by Prime Minister Schreiner that

> in the neighbourhood of Cape Town some ten thousand raw natives lived all over the place . . . We could not get rid of them: they were necessary for work. What we wanted was to get them practically in the position of being compounded.[52]

In the space of 20 years the labour process in the Western Cape had been radically restructured and Bantu-speaking men from outside the region had come to occupy the poorest-paid, most arduous and lowest-status heavy manual occupations. This restructuring of the division of

47. Bickford-Smith, "Black Labour", p. 87.
48. Cited in *ibid.*
49. C. Saunders, "The creation of Ndabeni", in C. Saunders (ed.), *Studies in the History of Cape Town Vol. 1* (Cape Town, UCT 1979), p. 135.
50. J. Whittingdale, "The development and location of industries in Greater Cape Town, 1652-1972" (Cape Town Univ. MA thesis, 1973).
51. Bickford-Smith, "Black Labour", p. 87.
52. Cited in Saunders, "Ndabeni", p. 138.

labour was associated with marked shifts in the ethnic composition of the Western Cape population; whereas previously Bantu-speaking people had comprised an insignificant proportion of the working class, by 1904 they accounted for over 45 per cent of the unskilled occupations in the region.[53] It was this rapid increase in the Bantu-speaking population of the Western Cape, we shall argue, that in part accounted for the development of a reconstituted Coloured identity at the turn of the century.

In 1865, 13 339 people were classified as Coloured in the Greater Cape Town region.[54] "Kaffirs" accounted for 674 of this Coloured category whilst 13 065 people were classified as belonging to other sub-groups within the Coloured category.[55] By 1904, we have noted, over 10 000 Bantu-speaking people were reported to be living in the Greater Cape Town area.[56] The growth in their numbers was more than matched by the explosion in the rest of the urban population not classified as "European". Whereas in 1865 over 80 per cent of this "non-European" group has been classified as agricultural labourers, by 1891 the proportion in agriculture had declined to barely 50 per cent and by 1904 to less than 18 per cent of the total workforce.[57] Agriculture's loss was urban employers' gain: whereas in 1891 less than 9 per cent of Coloureds had been engaged in industry or commerce, by 1904 over 15 per cent were in these occupations.[58] But despite the rapid growth of industrial and commercial employment, job opportunities failed to keep pace with the growing tide of urban work-seekers. By the turn of the century the migration to the towns of farm workers coupled with the recruitment of unskilled Bantu-speaking workers from the Eastern districts had resulted in chronic unemployment in the Greater Cape Town area. By 1899, according to a local paper, in Cape Town "the question of unemployment with us here" was "well-nigh chronic"[59] whilst a Cape Town clergyman observed that "this is the city of the unemployed"[60].

---

53. Cape of Good Hope, *Census 1904*, pp. lxxxv-xc.
54. Cape of Good Hope, *Census 1865*, pp. 4, 85-105.
55. *Ibid.*, p. 4.
56. Saunders, "Ndabeni", p. 135.
57. Calculated from Cape of Good Hope, *Census 1865*,, pp. 85-105; Cape of Good Hope, *Census 1891*, pp. 9-14, 18-19; Cape of Good Hope, *Census 1904*, pp. cxxxix-cxlvi. It should be emphasised that the term Coloured in both censuses included all people not identified as European.
58. *Ibid.*, and Cape of Good Hope, *Census 1904*, pp. 90-91, 380-381.
59. *South African News*, 19 Aug. 1899, cited in E. van Heyningen, "Refugees and relief in Cape Town, 1899-1902", in C. Saunders *et al.* (eds.), *Studies in the History of Cape Town, Vol. 3* (Cape Town, UCT, 1980), p. 71.
60. Rev. J. McLure, cited in *ibid.*, p. 70.

The problems faced by the Western Cape working class were compounded by the arrival in Cape Town of immigrants and refugees. The arrival between 1857 and 1863 of nearly 10 000 immigrants, and then between 1873 and 1883 of a further 20 000, served to increase competition for already scarce jobs.[61] Coming on top of the recessions of 1866 and 1877, and the move of many "non-European" people — those not classified as "European" — out of the worst-paid occupations into higher-status urban occupations, these mass immigrations probably fuelled the growing distinction between European and other skilled workers. Significantly, the competition between "European" and "non-European" people was greatest amongst the colony's skilled workers and artisans. It is no accident, we shall show, that this stratum of "non-Europeans" provided the driving force for the development of a distinct Coloured identity. Until 1900, however, the competition between "European" and other skilled workers did not lead to overtly ethnic organisations. But in 1900 the first ethnically exclusive trade unions were established in the Western Cape.

The Reconstitution of Coloured Identity: Artisans and Craftsmen

The number of "Hottentot", "Mixed race" and "Malay" people in industrial and commercial occupations rose from 9 per cent in 1891 to 20 per cent in 1904.[62] The educated and skilled strata did particularly well; the number of retail and general dealers more than tripled whilst the number of carpenters, joiners and stonemasons more than doubled.[63] The number of Coloured people occupying skilled and commercial trades increased rapidly, from 6 263 in 1891 to 11 885 in 1904.[64] This expansion strengthened the muscle of the skilled Coloured community. At the same time it served to raise further expectations regarding Coloured advancement. But the artisans and other skilled workers were soon disappointed; already by 1900 their prospects of advancement were being frustrated by the activities of White trade unionists.

61. C. Bundy, "Poor Whites before Poor Whiteism", Oxford University Seminar Paper, Feb. 1983, p. 5.
62. Cape of Good Hope, *Census 1904,* pp. cxxxix-cxlvi, Cape of Good Hope, *Census 1891,* pp. lxxxv-xc, 264-265.
63. Trapido, "White Conflict", p. 400.
64. *Ibid.*

Craftsmen and artisans were prominent amongst the immigrants who from 1857 arrived at the Cape in increasing numbers. These skilled men brought with them to South Africa their experience of organisation and craft unionism. Until the turn of the century, in the Western Cape, this legacy of trade unionism was not used to exclude Coloured workers. However, in 1900, owing largely to events associated with the South African War, and to the increasing ethnic identification within the working class, White stonemasons instituted a closed-shop excluding Coloured workers.

The South African War had brought a brief period of prosperity to certain sections of the Western Cape economy. However, much of the economy continued to stagnate, and this tended to undermine rather than foster working-class unity. The construction industry suffered particularly badly during the War years, as public expenditure was directed to the War effort. It was this sector, which had grown rapidly between 1891 and 1899, which accounted for the largest concentration of Coloured artisans.[65] The stagnation of the construction industry by 1900 had led to increased competition for jobs within the industry. It was in this climate of despair that White craftsmen combined their knowledge of craft unionism learnt in Europe with the developing ethnic identification of their White colleagues to form closed-shop unions excluding non-Europeans. In 1900 non-European stonemasons were excluded from work on public buildings. The following year, the Plasterers' Union barred non-European labour and forbade its members to work "on a scaffold with a Coloured or a Malay under pain of a fine"[66].

Whilst the construction industry stagnated, other sectors of the economy, and particularly those involved in servicing the War effort, prospered. Blacksmiths, coach- and cab-drivers and proprietors did particularly well, as did retailers and general dealers; employment in the docks also increased rapidly. In the docks, expansion provided the opportunity for job mobility, and "Cape Boys" came to occupy the more skilled occupations such as stevedoring.[67]

Between 1880 and 1900 the recruitment of African workers at the docks had served to undermine militancy, but during the short-lived period of prosperity the docks once again became a focus of non-racial militancy.[68] By 1901 skilled and unskilled dockers had been mobilised around the issue of wages, and for the next two years they engaged in a

---

65. *Ibid.*
66. *South African Spectator,* 23 March 1901, cited in S. Trapido, "White Conflict", p. 399.
67. *Ibid.,* p. 400; Bickford-Smith, "Black Labour", p. 87.
68. D. Budlender, "A history of Stevedores in Cape Town docks" (Univ. of Cape Town, BA (Hons) thesis, 1976), pp. 2-5.

running battle with management, involving strikes, lock-outs and numerous meetings and demonstrations. In 1903 the discontent culminated in a strike. However, this failed to advance the conditions of the dockers' employment, particularly as by now the short-lived boom was over and employment in the harbour was being contracted in line with the overall downturn in the economy. But the onset of the 1903-1909 depression did not in the docks lead to the development of ethnic divisions within the workforce. Trade union organisation there was dominated by socialists committed to forging non-racial unity.[69]

By contrast, in other sectors of the economy, and notably in the construction industry, the depression served to reinforce ethnic prejudices. By 1904 Coloured bricklayers were excluded from major building projects, and Coloureds had come to discover that even in those occupations which they had come to regard as their own, such as those linked to the construction industry, their position had been usurped by White craftsmen.[70] Their disadvantage in this respect was reinforced by the preference of immigrant craftsmen for young European apprentices. Immigrant craftsmen at the turn of the century had a near monopoly on many of the new skills associated with the development of mining and manufacturing in South Africa. Apprenticeship in the rapidly growing jewellery, optical, electrical, metallurgical and engineering crafts was largely restricted to White youth. The effect was to confine Coloured apprentices to the traditional occupations, some of which, such as blacksmith and coach-driver, were being affected by technological change.

Not surprisingly, therefore, Coloured artisans and craftsmen developed a growing antipathy for semi-skilled and skilled White workers and came to distrust Cape trade unions as being, in the words of John Tobin (a founder member of the first Coloured political organisation), "rotten with colour prejudice"[71].

From 1902 the demobilisation of servicemen increased the anxiety of skilled and semi-skilled Coloured people, who correctly predicted that this would lead to a further deterioration in their position in the job market. The onset of the depression of 1903 to 1909, which in 1938 the economic historian Schumann described as one of the severest South Africa had ever experienced, served to compound the situation as the protectionist policies of the White workers were entrenched further.[72]

69. *Ibid.*
70. H.J. and R.E. Simons, *Class and Colour in South Africa, 1850-1950* (Harmondsworth, Penguin, 1969), pp. 74-6.
71. *Ibid.*
72. C. Schumann, *Structural changes and business cycles in South Africa, 1806-1936* (London, King and Son, 1938), pp. 93-4.

Furthermore, it was not long before their prejudices were exploited politically; their growing political muscle and that of the demobilised servicemen, and the declining influence of the Coloured vote, led White parties to solicit their support.[73] Before long, election promises had been translated into discriminatory industrial legislation; in 1906 amendments to the Mines Act reserved many of the skilled, supervisory and managerial jobs for Whites.[74]

The increasingly discriminatory tactics of the White unionists served to foster an ethnic identity amongst the non-European skilled and artisan class at the Cape. This class comprised mainly people of Khoisan descent and descendants of freed slaves and other non-Bantu-speaking people. Their common position in society, together with their shared anxieties regarding the erosion of their place in the labour market, provided further fertile ground for the growing ethnic identity.

The Reconstitution of Coloured Identity: Promises and Prejudice

In 1899 the arrival in the Cape of over 5 000 "Cape Boys" who had been deported from the South African Republic served to stimulate awareness of an incipient Coloured identity. By October 1899 the refugees were arriving in Cape Town "by the hundreds"[75]. These exiles brought with them stories of ill-treatment and of the absence of civil rights in the interior. Many of the refugees shared familial, religious and other bonds with the Malays and people of Khoisan descent in the Cape. The concerns of the refugees were shared by many of the non-Europeans in the Cape who saw in the War a chance to extend the rule of British law to the interior republics.[76] It was also felt that the loyalty of non-European people in the Cape to the British cause would advance the Coloured case for full enfranchisement and equal treatment.

The British had in fact made Coloured rights a feature of their war propaganda. Chamberlain promised the British parliament that victory over the interior republics would bring "equal laws, equal liberty" to all[77], whilst Milner, the British High Commissioner in South Africa,

---

73. Trapido, "White Conflict", p. 152.
74. Simons and Simons, *"Class and Colour"*, pp. 77-79.
75. Van Heyningen, "Refugees and relief", p. 82.
76. B. Nassan, "These Natives think the War to be their own", Institute of Commonwealth Studies, Seminar Paper on the Societies of Southern Africa in the 19th and 20th Centuries, London Univ., 1979, p. 8.

presented discrimination against Coloureds as a justification for intervention in the interior.[78] Not surprisingly Coloureds, according to Marais, "gave the British cause their enthusiastic support"[79] and, G.H. Le
May noted, over 2900 bore arms in the Cape.[80] It must therefore have
come as a bitter disappointment to the Coloureds to discover that their
position was unlikely to have improved with the victory of the British
forces. The Vereeniging Treaty of May 1902 left the franchise question
open and failed to advance non-European rights. Increasingly, Coloured
men and women came to fear that, with the proposed Union, the practices of the interior republics would be extended to the Cape, and the
Coloured rights would be sacrificed in the process of reconciliation.

The anger of Coloureds was fuelled by the growing realisation that
Coloureds had played an important part in the British victory and had
proved to be amongst its most loyal supporters. The artisan class was
particularly indignant that the Crown had failed to reward the support
which a clandestine network of artisans had offered to the imperial
forces. The case of the blacksmith, Abraham Essau, became a rallying
point for the disaffected artisans.[81] Essau, who had been acting as a secret agent for the British forces, had been tortured to death by the
Boers without revealing details of the artisan spy network: despite being
drawn between two horses, Essau had refused to renounce his loyalty to
the Crown. But, his fellow artisans observed, the loyalty of the British
administration to Coloureds was less robust.

The end of the War left Coloured artisans and the Coloured petty
bourgeoisie cynical of the colonial administration and of White political
parties. It was increasingly felt by the educated and skilled Coloured
class that their reluctance to campaign independently of White political
parties had left them in the political wilderness. With the failure of the
White parties to honour their promises and with the growing power of
the White working class, the Coloured electorate at the turn of the century felt compelled to re-evaluate their support for White political parties. Up to this time, Trapido has noted, "Coloured people were
anxious, on the whole, not to establish for themselves a political identity
separate to the White population."[82] In part the explanation lies in the

77. Cited in G. Lewis, "'Your votes are your guns': the emergence of Coloured Political
    Organisation at the Cape", Seminar Paper, Univ. of Cape Town, Sept. 1983, p. 21.
78. Marais, *"Cape Coloured People"*, pp. 275-276.
79. *Ibid.*
80. G. Le May, *British Supremacy in South Africa, 1899-1907* (London, OUP, 1965) p. 101.
81. Nassan, "These Natives", pp. 4-5.
82. S. Trapido, "The Origins and development of the African Peoples' Organisation", Inst.
    of Comm. Studies, *Collected Seminar Papers on the Societies of Southern Africa in the
    19th and 20th Centuries, Vol. 1* (London, ICS., 1970), pp. 92-93.

fact that a distinct Coloured ethnic identity existed only in an incipient form prior to the South African War. It was feared that separate political organisations would reduce the claim of enfranchised people for assimilation into the ruling class.[83]

White political parties from 1853, Trapido has documented, had solicited the non-European vote through a combination of "patronage, corruption and intimidation"[84]. However, despite the promises and polemics of White politicians, no lasting alliance of non-European voters and White parties was sustained in the latter half of the nineteenth century. Throughout this period the non-European share of the total vote decreased. Nevertheless the more rapid erosion of the franchise of Africans increased the relative importance of the "Hottentot", "mixed race" and "Malay" vote to White politicians. From 1883, when the Afrikaner Bond was established by "Onze" Jan Hofmeyr, Cape political parties increasingly came to cultivate notions of a distinct Coloured identity. Non-Bantu-speaking people had been led to believe that by supporting White parties and by dissociating themselves from the Bantu-speaking population they would be spared the political and economic humiliation suffered by Africans.

The disfranchisement of Africans, occurring simultaneously with the dispossession of the African peasantry, had increased the significance of the distinction between Africans and other non-European people. The annexation of British Kaffraria into the Cape Colony in 1865 and the incorporation of the Transkei territories between 1872 and 1894 made it more difficult for Africans in the colony to qualify for the franchise. The 1887 and 1892 changes in the educational and property qualifications were intended to reduce further the number of Africans eligible to vote. But although these measures were primarily directed at Africans they also raised considerable disquiet amongst the Malay population of the Cape. A short-lived political organisation was established by the Malay groups in order to oppose the 1892 Franchise and Ballot Act and the 1893 Constitution Amendment Act.[85] The 1893 Act abolished the composite vote, thereby preventing a Malay candidate, A.H. Effendi, from entering parliament. The exclusion of this candidate increased the anxieties of Malay and other non-European voters. They came to question the wisdom of their support for the hollow promises of White politicians. At the same time they regarded with forboding the mounting racism of the White population and the failure of racial prejudice to dis-

---

83. *Ibid.*
84. Trapido, "Friends of the Natives", p. 267.
85. Lewis, "Your votes", pp. 14-15.

tinguish between the relatively well-educated, richer non-Europeans and the rest of the non-European population.

At the turn of the century, late-Victorian notions of social-Darwinism (see below) had a decisive impact on the Cape Colony. The pseudo-scientific writing of Benjamin Kidd[86] together with that of Karl Pearson and his associate Francis Galton, the father of "eugenics", informed the prejudices of the English ruling class and the activities of the British High Commissioner in South Africa.[87] In South Africa these notions were popularised in the writing of John Buchan[88] and in later years by Sarah Gertrude Millin.[89] Imported to South Africa, social-Darwinism and eugenics provided a source of leverage for poor Whites and a legitimation for politicians who were eager to entrench White privileges.

Theories of social-Darwinism encouraged a belief in a hierarchical racial order in which people of European blood were seen to represent an advance in the evolutionary ladder. In terms of this doctrine, miscegenation was regarded as a peril to the survival of European civilisation, and people branded as "mixed-race" were seen as the physically and mentally mutant offspring of an illegitimate mixing of European purity and African savagery.[90] Simultaneously, however, these people were regarded, because of their claim to European blood, as hierarchically above African people. Their skills and superior education, it was argued, were testimony to this superiority. The social-Darwinians warned that the strains of European blood within this group provided it with a unique potential to lead the non-European people, and they demanded that "mixed-race" people be prevented from entering into an alliance with other non-Europeans.

In South Africa the ideology of social-Darwinism added a further dimension to late-Victorian rethinking on poverty. The redefinition of poverty led to calls for greater state intervention to alleviate the "poor-white problem". In this process, according to C. Bundy, "assumptions of

86. See, for example, B. Kidd, *Social Evolution* (London, Macmillan, 1894); K. Pearson, "Socialism and Natural Selection", in *The Chances of Death and other Studies in Evolution* (London, Scott, 1897), p. 111; F. Galton, *Inquiries into the Human faculty and its Development* (London, Macmillan, 1883).
87. B. Semmel, *Imperialism and Social Reform: English social-imperial thought, 1895-1914* (London, Allen and Unwin, 1960), pp. 29-52, 177-187.
88. J. Buchan, *Prester John* (London, Nelson Sons, 1910).
89. S.G. Millin, *God's Stepchildren* (London, Constable, 1924); see also V. February, *Mind your Colour; the "Coloured" Stereotype in South African literature* (London, Routledge, 1982), pp. 52-70, and N. Etherington, "Imperialism in literature: the case of John Buchan", Collected Seminar Papers on the Societies of Southern Africa in the 19th and 20th centuries (London, ICS, 1980).
90. B. Shephard, "Peter Lobengula and 'savage South Africa'", Seminar Paper, Inst. of Comm. Studies, London, Imperialism and Popular Culture Seminar, 15 May 1983, p. 3.

[White] ethnic solidarity replaced the older forms of ideological distance and hostility along class lines."[91] In the poorer areas of Cape Town there had been, Bundy notes, "a very real blurring of ethnic identity."[92]

The metropolitan redefinition of poverty was associated with increasingly strident attacks on the "dangerous classes" of society.[93] In the Western Cape, ethnic stereotyping had by the late nineteenth century caused the non-European population to be defined as the criminal classes. Throughout the 1890s in the principal Cape papers, the *Cape Argus* and the *Cape Times,* the ethnic identification of Coloureds as the dangerous elements of society continued to feed the prejudices of Whites and fears of non-Europeans.[94] (At this time, it will be recalled, the term Coloured denoted all non-European people.) By 1895 the *Cape Argus* had embarked on a crusade against crime which as a result of crude ethnic stereotyping served as an attack on all Coloureds. The paper declared that there was "a need for stringent regulations of the Coloured classes in Cape Town" as Coloureds were "a danger to society"[95]. Cartoon caricatures of Coloureds served to further the ethnic prejudices and identification of poor-Whites and to alienate Coloured people from the White society. In this process, older class distinctions were broken by new ethnic alliances. The Coloured artisan and educated class, who previously had not borne the brunt of ethnic discrimination, began to suffer from the impact of the reconstruction of ethnic boundaries. Their anxieties were increased by events associated with what Swanson had labelled the "sanitation syndrome"[96].

In 1882 a smallpox epidemic had led to claims that "the sooner the Malays are forced to reside in a separate district the better for all concerned"[97], whilst an outbreak of enteric fever in 1887 had prompted the Dean of Cape Town to call for the establishment of a separate quarter for Coloured people.[98] However, the Coloured vote, which could influence voting in at least nine constituencies, and the indignation of the six Coloured city councillors, prevented any such action.

In 1901 a plague epidemic again brought matters to a head. But

---

91. Bundy, "Poor Whites", p. 3.
92. *Ibid.,* p. 8.
93. See G. Stedman-Jones, *Outcast London: a study in the relationship between classes in Victorian Society* (Oxford, OUP, 1971).
94. V. Bickford-Smith, "Dangerous Cape Town: middle class attitudes to poverty in Cape Town in the late nineteenth century," in C. Saunders *et al.* (eds.), *Studies in the History of Cape Town, Vol. 4* (Cape Town, UCT, 1981), pp. 50-59.
95. *Cape Argus,* 27 Jan. 1895, cited in *ibid.,* p. 55.
96. M. Swanson, "The sanitation syndrome", *Journal of African History,* 18 (3), 1977.
97. *The Lantern,* 23 Sept. 1882, cited in Bickford-Smith, "Dangerous Cape Town", p. 37.
98. *Ibid.*

whereas in the past the power of the Coloured electorate had prevented any action being taken against non-European people, the reconstitution of ethnic identities by 1901 facilitated a divisive attack on only one section of the non-European population. The African population of Greater Cape Town, it will be recalled, had grown rapidly in the period 1880 to 1900. This increase, together with the confinement of Africans to unskilled tasks, the declining significance of the African vote, the increasing ethnic identity of skilled and educated non-European people and the development of social-Darwinism, had by 1901 fundamentally reshaped Cape society to the extent that the City Council could place the blame for the plague on the Bantu-speaking section of the non-European population of Cape Town. Although the plague was by no means confined to Africans, racial stereotyping by 1901 was reflected in the local authority's ethnic diagnosis of the problem. Africans were forced to bear the full force of the health and housing ordinances which were hurriedly invoked to calm the mounting hysteria.[99]

The Cape Town medical officer of health, citing the success of the compound system instituted in the interior, called for the relocation of Africans within strictly controlled and segregated locations.[100] "Matabele" Thompson, a public servant with considerable experience of the Kimberley diamond compounds, also argued strongly for the institution in the Peninsula of the system "so easily managed" in Kimberley; this included arresting under a pass law "every native out and abroad after the [curfew] bell"[101]. Before long, over 7 000 Africans were hounded out of the premises in the inner city and forced to move to the hastily erected Uitvlugt compound. The unprecedented attack on people defined as Africans dramatically restructured the social hierarchy of the Western Cape. An African identity was now associated with subjugation to pass legislation and rehousing in a prison-like compound. The assertion of a different non-European identity provided the means to escape the onslaught. In the process of restructuring, the term Coloured increasingly came to mean a non-African non-European. The new definition of Coloured identity is reflected in the claim in the 1904 Cape census that there existed three "clearly defined race groups in this colony, White, Bantu and Coloured",[102] whereas in the previous census only two broad groups, "Coloured" and "European", were identified.[103]

99. Saunders, "The Creation of Ndabeni", p. 143; van Heyningen, "Refugees and relief", p. 102.
100. Saunders, "The Creation of Ndabeni", p. 137.
101. *Ibid.*, p. 136.
102. Cape Colony, *1904 Census,* p. xxi.
103. Cape Colony, *1891 Census,* p. xvii.

The assertion of a distinct Coloured identity for many people provided an escape from the health and housing ordinances invoked by the Cape Town City Council. The ability of the skilled and artisan class of Coloured to secure their exemption from the ordinances affecting Africans is testimony to their continued political strength and influence. Coloured councillors, it will be recalled, occupied six seats on the Cape Town City council and the Coloured electorate exercised a decisive influence in at least nine constituencies.[104] People defined as "Bantu", particularly after the franchise and other legislation referred to above, exercised a far less significant influence.

In the process of reconstitution at the turn of the century, then, the Coloured petty bourgeoisie and skilled strata attempted to defend their position, in the face of mounting prejudice against all non-European people, by the assertion of a distinct identity and the sacrifice of African interests. Adopting the language of social-Darwinism, this group sought to defend itself from the mounting racial prejudice, arguing that "respectable Coloured men" should not be classed with the "barbarous native"[105].

It was the Coloured petty bourgeoisie who took a lead in the assertion of the new Coloured identity. By no accident, this class had suffered most from the late-Victorian substitution of ethnic for class alliances. Prior to this time, Trapido noted,

> Coloured men who prospered were able to gain readmission into the White population, and some became prominent in the Afrikaner middle class.[106]

The ability to be admitted into White society depended to a large extent on the class position of the individual concerned, although skin pigmentation also was important. The effect of the permeable colour line, Frederickson observed, was to facilitate admission on a substantial scale.[107] But in his study *Passing for White,* Watson found that "those who rank below the artisan class seldom possess the characteristics necessary for successful passing."[108]

Until the turn of the century, the "passing" process facilitated the absorption into the European population of many intellectual and edu-

104. University of South Africa, Documentation Centre for African Studies (henceforth UNISA), Acc. A223, "Abdullah Abdurahman Family Papers", Box 2 Folder 4, "Report on Cape elections", p. 2.
105. See Lewis, "Your votes", pp. 38-42; Trapido, "The Development of the APO", pp. 90-94.
106. *Ibid.,* pp. 90-91.
107. Frederickson, *"White supremacy",* p. 131.
108. G. Watson, *Passing for White* (London, Tavistock, 1970), p. 120.

cated people who otherwise may have provided a vocal source of leadership for non-European opposition to the colonial regime. With the ascendancy of late-Victorian ideology and its ethnic expression in South Africa, a brake was placed on the passing process. In the construction of White identity ethnic boundaries were increasingly strictly demarcated. In this process the bridge by which petty-bourgeois, non-Bantu-speaking non-Europeans had entered into the White population was rapidly undermined.

These people had until now rejected ethnic organisations, fearing that their chances of assimilation would be reduced if they did not lend their full support to White political organisations. Disillusioned by the failure of White organisations to advance their claim to assimilation, and increasingly unable to pass for White, they began to organise along ethnic lines. Their aim was not to campaign for the rights of all non-Europeans or Coloureds. On the contrary, their objective was to impress on the administration that educated and petty-bourgeois non-Bantu-speaking people exercised a special claim for inclusion into the ruling polity and should not be classed with other non-European people. The establishment of the first Coloured organisations, we shall show in the next chapter, aimed to provide a springboard by which this group could launch its campaign for inclusion in the White society.

Summary

By 1904 a distinct Coloured identity had been established in the Western Cape which stood in marked contrast to that which had existed only 10 years previously. Whereas in 1894 the term Coloured in the census and in other published sources referred to all "non-European" people, by 1904 the term referred to an intermediate category of people. The exclusion of Bantu-speaking people from the category Coloured and the development of a separate category of "Bantu" marked the triumph of social-Darwinism in South Africa. The growing awareness of ethnic identity served to entrench within the Western Cape a racially hierarchical ordering of society in which Coloured people were seen to occupy a position intermediate between "European" and "Bantu".

From the period of first settlement the colonial administration and the settlers had fostered notions of ethnic identity and ethnic prejudices. With the growing threat to the colony posed by an alliance of dispossessed people, successive colonial governors had sought to deflect opposition by resort to ethnic divisions. The overall effect was to stratify the population of the Cape in a manner which entrenched an ethnically hierarchical ordering of social status and employment. Until the turn of the twentieth century there was no Coloured identity distinct from Africans; but at the turn of the century a profound restructuring of the racial and social division of labour took place in the Western Cape. Associated with this was the reconstitution of Coloured identity and the development of distinct Coloured organisations.

We have shown that in the eighteenth and nineteenth centuries policies of preference had served to deflect opposition and prepare the ground for the formation of what in the twentieth century was to become the Coloured group. Coloured identity reflected in part the determination of the skilled stratum of Coloureds to defend their position vis-à-vis the African population and to provide a means to assert their claim for preferential treatment. From the beginning, however, the commitment to a Coloured identity was at best ambiguous. The continued existence of an intermediate group, it was recognised, depended on the success of policies which sought to promote the interests of Coloured people relative to Africans whilst at the same time preventing the assimilation of Coloured and White people. It is the shaping of these policies and the development of Coloured identity in the period 1904 to the early 1930s which forms the focus of the next chapter.

CHAPTER TWO

COLOURED POLITICAL ORGANISATION AND COLOURED PREFERENCE: 1900 — c.1935

Introduction

The reconstitution of Coloured identity at the turn of the century provided the bedrock on which the future generations would built separate coloured organisations. By 1902 the new Coloured identity had been expressed in the establishment of an organisation devoted to the advancement of Coloured rights in isolation from Africans.

Coloured political consciousness, as Trapido has shown, had existed prior to the development of the African Peoples' Organisation in 1902.[1] But this had not led to a sustained political mobilisation of Coloured people. In part this reflected a concern to establish a political identity separate from that of the White population.

In the Western Cape, Malay people shared a common religion, language and ancestry. Their sense of community in times of economic and social stress gave birth to short-lived organisations which sought to bind the Malay in defence of the status quo. In 1869 the extension of the Masters and Servants Act was vigorously opposed by Malay voters, led by Abdol Burns, the "Mahdi of Cape Town".[2] Further infringements on the rights of the Malay community served to politicise Malay people and in 1886 culminated in rioting in the streets of Cape Town.[3] But it did not lead to the development of separate political parties. On the contrary, Malay voters in the Western Cape were encouraged to increase their support for White political parties.[4]

In Kimberley the development of a distinct Coloured identity was hastened when White workers showed their eagerness to capture for themselves a greater share of the diamond wealth: in 1883 discrimina-

---

1. Trapido, "White Politics", pp.14, 39.
2. Lewis, "Your votes", p.14-15.
3. *Ibid.*
4. *Ibid.;* Trapido, "Friends of natives", pp.262-267.

tion against the Malay alluvial diamond diggers and transport riders led to the establishment of the Afrikaner League (Coloured). Although the League failed to establish roots and soon died, it added to the growing self-awareness of Coloureds. In 1892 the Franchise and Ballot Bill prompted renewed activity, throughout the Cape, under the banner of the "Coloured Peoples' Association of South Africa". The CPA collected 10 341 signatures against the bill.[5] In so doing the CPA served to heighten the political awareness of Coloured people and to increase the resentment of Coloured voters towards White political parties. The Coloured Peoples' Association did not exclude African people, however. As we have shown in the previous chapter, in the nineteenth century the term Coloured generally referred to all non-European people and not simply to the class of people who in the twentieth century were to become defined as Coloured. In the Western Cape, in contrast to the situation in the Northern Cape, African people constituted only a small minority of the Coloured electorate; and so in this region the CPA in effect devoted its attentions to the defence of the franchise of non-Bantu-speaking non-European people.

In June 1901 the Coloured People's Vigilance Society was established by F. Z. Peregrino, a West African committed to pan-African ideologies. Peregrino through his mouth-piece, the *Spectator,* from December 1900 sought to instil "race pride" amongst the black community of Cape Town. In the Western Cape the society was open to all "who are not known as white".[7] However, in Kimberley, where the large African population outnumbered the rest of the non-European population, the society segregated its "colored Africander" and "native" members.[8] This divisive tactic, Peregrino explained, was necessary to avoid ethnic tensions undermining the organisation. It would appear that by the turn of the century Coloured and African ethnic identity had been firmly entrenched in the Northern Cape. In Kimberley the establishment of separate branches indicated the depth of identity of "Coloured Afrikaner" people as distinct from Bantu-speaking people.

In the Western Cape, at the turn of the century, Coloured organisations still embraced all non-Europeans. This was reflected in the activities of Peregrino's societies and in the content of the "Stone" meetings: the meetings, which derived their name from the boulders at the District Six meeting place in Cape Town, aimed to provide "political education

5. Lewis, "Your votes", p.17.
6. *South African Spectator,* 14 Jan. 1901 and 8 Feb. 1901, cited in Trapido, "White Politics", p.419.
7. Lewis, "Your votes", p.31.
8. *Ibid.,* pp.31-32.

for the masses"[9]. Peregrino (a supporter of the pro-British Progressive Party), together with a prominent Coloured businessman, John Tobin, was amongst the organisers of the meetings. But Peregrino's failure to condemn the British government for the "betrayal" of the Vereeniging Treaty led Tobin to switch allegiances to the anti-imperialist South African Party.[10] At the Stone meetings and elsewhere, Peregrino revealed in clandestine reports to the colonial police, Tobin called on Coloured and African people to support the South African Party.[11]

By 1900 over 10 000 Africans resided in the Western Cape. The overwhelming majority of them were unskilled labourers, and less than 1 per cent of the African population was eligible to vote.[12] The numerical insignificance of the African vote in the Western Cape meant that organisations which sought to mobilise the non-European vote focused their attention on Coloured and not African people. Furthermore, the preoccupation of political organisations with the franchise meant that in the Western Cape the incipient non-European organisations made little effort to include unskilled and disenfranchised people: their intention from the outset was to defend the embattled position of the skilled and petty-bourgeois Coloured people. By the turn of the century, as we suggested in the previous chapter, the Coloured petty bourgeoisie and skilled workers in the Western Cape had come to see themselves, and to be seen, in terms which set them apart from the rest of the non-European population. Nevertheless, ethnic divisions remained ill-defined and for at least half a century would continue to be a source of immense concern and confusion. From 1902 this uncertainty was seen in the programmes and proceedings of the first explicitly Coloured political organisation, the African Peoples' Organisation (APO).

The African Peoples' Organisation

The APO was established in September 1902, largely as a result of the commitment of a group of Cape Town professionals, led by J. Tobin and W. Collins. Tobin and Collins had served their political apprenticeship at the Stone meetings. In 1901 they had rallied Coloured people to oppose residential segregation. Their experience, it was later recalled,

9. *South African Spectator,* 4 May 1901, cited in R.E. van der Ross, "Political History", Vol. 1, p.11.
10. Lewis, "Your votes", p.34.
11. *Ibid.*
12. Saunders, "Creation of Ndabeni", p.12; L.M. Thompson, *The Unification of South Africa, 1902-1910* (Oxford, OUP, 1960), p.55, Table 2.

led them to decide to "form a permanent organisation to protect the lib-
erties of the Coloured people."[13] But whereas the Stone meetings had
been open to all and set out to address issues of concern to all sections
of the working class, the APO from the outset was an élite organisation
which sought to defend the franchise, residence and employment of
"civilised" Coloureds.[14] The first president, W. Collins, announced that
the aim of the APO was to show the administration that "an educated
class of Coloured people in Cape Town" existed.[15] "Civilised
Coloureds", he observed, wanted to take their place alongside Whites as
"civilised men".[16]

In February 1903 the president of the APO, W. Collins, told the assembled delegates at the oganisation's first conference that "this is the
first time in history that we are meeting together to discuss our affairs."[17] The conference marked a crucial point in the development of
Coloured political identity and placed the élite on a different trajectory
to that of other non-Europeans. Before long the APO leadership was
campaigning for the advancement of Coloureds at the expense of Africans. In March 1903 an APO delegation visited the mayor of Cape
Town and secured the assurance that "Coloureds would be excluded"
from the residential segregation which Africans had endured.[18]

The first aim of the APO, according to its founder members, was "to
promote unity between the coloured races."[19] And yet one of the first
achievements of the organisation's leadership was the defence of
Coloured residence rights in isolation from those of the African population of Cape Town. Clearly, the leadership of the APO from the outset was inconsistent in its defence of a wider interpretation of non-
European unity and in its claim to be a truly *African* Peoples' Organisation. The APO, despite its wider rhetoric, aimed to defend the position
of the enfranchised, skilled and petty-bourgeois peoples of the Western
Cape. It was thus almost exclusively confined to issues of concern to
non-Bantu-speaking people in the Western Cape. Increasingly the organisation came to regard itself, and to be regarded, as the representative
organisation of this category of people. But it was never representative
of Coloured people; even at its peak it embraced fewer than 5 per cent
of the population classified as Coloured and seldom penetrated below

13. *The Sun,* 18 May 1934, in Lewis, "Your votes", p.35.
14. *Ibid.*
15. *S.A. News,* 2 Oct. 1905, in Lewis, "Your votes", p.36.
16. *Ibid.,* p.35.
17. Unisa Acc. 223, Box 1, Folder 11, "Report of first APO conference", p.3.
18. *S.A. News,* 35 March 1903, in Lewis, "Your votes", p.38.
19. *Ibid.,* p.39.

the petty-bourgeois and skilled strata. Nevertheless its impact should not be underestimated; within the upper levels of Coloured society the APO exercised an important influence, keeping alive a separate Coloured political identity which stood in marked contrast to the radical ideas being articulated in the docks and elsewhere by members of the International Socialist League and other organisations.

The APO from the start was preoccupied with the franchise. This preoccupation indicated the narrow base of the APO, which failed to extend beyond the artisan and skilled classes of Coloureds. In 1904 registered voters in the Cape accounted for only 3,7 per cent of the Coloured population (14 836 people) compared with 20,7 per cent of the White population.[20] The APO aimed to extend Coloured education and wealth in order that the "civilised Coloured" population would increase its numerical significance and that the Coloured share of the franchise would accordingly be increased. But the APO failed to challenge the legitimacy of the franchise qualifications or to devote attention to the Coloured working class, who were not eligible for the franchise.

The Politics of Coloured Preference

The history of the APO was intimately linked to the politics of Abdullah Abdurahman. From 1904 until his death in 1940 Abdurahman, a medical doctor by profession, exercised a decisive influence over the APO. He was consistent only in his commitment to the advance of the Coloured franchise and the defence of the skilled and petty bourgeois; on other issues of substance he displayed a remarkable ambivalence. This ambivalence was to become a hallmark of the APO.

As we suggested in the previous chapter, the development of the APO was associated with the forging of a reconstituted Coloured identity in the Cape. Such an identity was promoted by Abdurahman; he advocated that the APO specifically exclude Africans. Abdurahman argued that

> as we [meet] as an organisation of the Coloured people of South Africa . . . it is my duty as President of the APO to deal with the rights and duties of the Coloured people of South Africa as distinguished from the native races.[21]

20. *Ibid.*, p.36.
21. Unisa Acc. 223, Box 1, Folder 12, "Speech of Dr. Abdurahman to 1910 APO Conference."

The exclusion of Africans allowed Abdurahman to advance the cause of the reconstituted Coloured population in isolation from, and often at the expense of, Africans. In his dealings with the administration he skilfully manipulated the administration's strategic goal of entrenching the divisions between Coloured and African people. By advancing the cause of an independent Coloured organisation, whilst at the same time maintaining an ambivalent commitment to non-European unity, Abdurahman was able to extend his leverage in negotiations with the administration.

It is no accident that the evolution of a distinct Coloured identity and the development of a separate Coloured political organisation took place during a period in which the colonial authorities were increasingly committed to a strategy of "divide and rule". Lord Selborne, a former British cabinet minister and the High Commissioner in South Africa from 1905 to 1910, actively encouraged the development of a distinct Coloured identity. He argued that

> Our object should be to teach the Coloured people to give their support to the white population. It seems to me sheer folly to classify them with Natives, and by treating them as Natives to force them away from their natural allegiance with the whites and into making common cause with the Natives.[22]

Abdurahman adroitly exploited the concerns voiced by Selborne and other influential administrators to press the administration to treat Coloured people differently from Africans. So, for example, he criticised Lord Milner for allowing Coloureds in the Transvaal to be treated "like the barbarous native" and argued that "although natives were excluded from the vote the Coloured should not be".[23] However, Abdurahman failed in his attempt to defend the franchise of the Coloured in the Transvaal.

From the outset he was engaged in a rearguard attempt to defend the position of educated and skilled Coloured people. In the period 1904 to 1919 this defensive manoeuvring became more and more desperate as the power of the White working class grew from strength to strength and the significance of the Coloured electorate declined. Increasingly, the only advances open to Coloured politicians were to improve the position of Coloured men and women relative to African people.

---

22. "Notes on a suggested policy towards Coloured People and Natives", 9 Jan. 1908, in W. Hancock and J. van der Poel, *Selections from the Smuts Papers* (Cambridge, CUP, 1966), Vol. 2, pp.375-376, Document 364.
23. Cited in R. van der Ross, *The Founding of the African Peoples' Organisation in Cape Town in 1903 and the role of Dr. Abdurahman* (Pasadena, Munger, 1975), pp.22-23.

In the period 1900 to 1919, growing numbers of unskilled Coloured workers were squeezed out of their jobs by lower-paid African workers. At the same time, skilled and semi-skilled Coloured men were feeling the pinch as White men monopolised skilled occupations in manufacturing and industry. The end of the First World War compounded the difficulties of the Coloured artisan class, a large part of whom had benefited from the short-lived boom which the disruption of shipping had brought to sections of the Western Cape economy. In particular, Coloured artisans during the War benefited from the expansion of the clothing industry; whilst in 1914 only one clothing factory existed in the Western Cape, by the end of the War a further seven had been established.[24] With the resumption of shipping, however, domestic producers were again unable to compete with the higher-quality and cheaper imported products, and the incipient manufacturing industry was forced into decline. As a result, the employment opportunities of many skilled and semi-skilled Coloured workers were restricted.

In this climate of uncertainty, the APO encouraged skilled and semi-skilled Coloured workers to assert their identity in the formation of Coloured trade unions. Abdurahman insisted that skilled Coloured workers could have little faith in White unionists. Pointing to the development of White trade unions at the turn of the century, he reminded artisans that

> The Coloured people have not yet forgotten that the white unions of Cape Town hounded Coloured carpenters out of their workshops and kicked Coloured bricklayers off the scaffold.[25]

Since the turn of the century, the power of White workers had been enhanced further and Coloured artisans were even less able to defend their positions than they had been earlier on. Under the changed circumstances Abdurahman was unable to moderate the support of the government for White workers. Nevertheless he was able to secure from the administration promises of preferential treatment for Coloureds relative to Africans. Whereas the position of skilled Coloureds was not enhanced, a policy of preference for Coloureds relative to Africans met with the administrations's approval.

Until 1919 the APO confined its activities to issues relating to the franchise and education, but in that year it established the APO Federation of Labour. That this departure for the APO should coincide with the emergence of the Industrial and Commercial Workers' Union (ICU)

---

24. J. Whittingdale, "The Development and Location of Industries in Cape Town, 1652-1972" (Univ. of Cape Town, MA thesis, 1973), p.34.
25. Cited in Simons and Simons, *"Class and Colour"*, p.226.

was significant. The APO Federation of Labour aimed to defend the employment of skilled and semi-skilled Coloured workers. In 1921, following Abdurahman's petitioning to the Railways and Harbours Board, 800 African dockers were dismissed and their jobs in the Cape Town docks taken over by Coloured workers.[26] The action may have served to enhance the prestige of Abdurahman within sections of the Coloured community, but it served equally to promote African antagonism towards Coloureds and to add strength to the Africanist tendencies within the ICU.[27] Policies of Coloured preference improved the position of Coloured workers relative to African men and women only at the expense of the African population.

The growing preference shown towards Coloured men and women in the Western Cape served to heighten further the ethnic identification of Coloured and African people and to increase the significance of the racial divide. Perhaps most important in this respect was the continued exemption of Coloureds from influx control and residential segregation. These regulations caused immense hardship for people defined as African. Simultaneously, the assertion of Coloured identity provided a means to escape the obnoxious laws. In 1923, with the passage of the Native Urban Areas Act, the relative advantage of Coloured men and women was extended even further. The Act clearly stated that

> any existing law or regulation, which makes compulsory the carrying or possession of a pass, shall be deemed to be repealed in so far as it effects Coloured persons.[28]

However, in the 1920s the central government was not the principal protagonist of Coloured preference policies. For in the Western Cape the Cape Town City Council from 1920 took a lead in attempts to institutionalise a system of employment preference for Coloured men and women.

At the turn of the century, it will be recalled, the Cape Town City Council had introduced residential segregation for Africans and attempted to control their influx and employment in Cape Town.[29] Coloureds were exempted from the controls. The overall effect was to place Coloureds in a position of preference relative to Africans. In 1920 the Cape Town City Council renewed its campaign to regulate the entry

26. D. Budlender, "A history of Stevedores", p.5.
27. D. Budlender, "A history of Stevedores", pp. 5-6.
28. South Africa, *Native (Urban Areas) Act*, No. 21 of 1923, Section 28.
29. See Saunders, "The creation of Ndabeni", p. 143.
30. *Ibid.*, p.171, fn.17.
31. *Ibid.*, p.171.

of Africans into Cape Town. Criticising the failure of the government to take action against African influx, it vigorously argued that Cape Town "possessed its own reservoir of labour in the Coloured community".[30] Coloured people should be protected from competition from African labour, and

> it was most unfair on the part of the Government to take no steps to prevent the indiscriminate entry of these people into urban areas.[31]

In 1923, the passage of the Urban Areas Act came to the Council's help: in terms of the Act local authorities were given the power to control the administration and influx of Africans. The Act provided for the compulsory registration of all Africans and for the deportation from the urban areas of "idle and undesirable" Africans.[32] The council sought to use the legislation to deport over 3 000 Africans from the Peninsula.[33] However, the intervention of the Native Affairs Department, who were eager not to increase the agitation of the disaffected African population, prevented the Council from enforcing its draconian plan.[34] The restraining influence of the Native Affairs Department provided a brake on the early attempts by the Council to impose a policy of preference for Coloured labour. But from 1924 the resistance of the central government to the Council began to crumble; with the introduction of the civilised labour policy and Hertzog's segregation scheme, the department was increasingly to collaborate with the Council in an attempt to prevent African influx into the Peninsula.

The election of the Hertzog government in 1924 added impetus to the policy of preference for Coloureds. Hertzog, following in the footsteps of William Porter and Selborne, insisted that

> It would be foolish to drive the Coloured people to the enemies of the Europeans — and that will happen if we expel him, to allow him eventually to come to rest in the arms of the native.[35]

He proposed, therefore, that "economically, industrially and politically the Coloured man must be incorporated with us".[36] In order to effect his strategy Hertzog developed a comprehensive segregation programme,

---

32. *Native (Urban Areas) Act,* No. 21 of 1923, Section 17.
33. Saunders, *op. cit.,* p. 1984.
34. *Ibid.,* pp. 167-199.
35. South Africa, *Parliamentary Debates,* Joint Sitting of Parliament, 12-15 Feb. 1929, Col. 169.
36. Smithfield Speech 1914, cited in S. Patterson, *Colour and Culture in South Africa; a study of the Cape Coloured people within the social structure of the Union of South Africa* (London, Routledge, 1953), p.14.

which he later incorporated into four bills.[37] The bills aimed on the one hand to enfranchise Coloured men and to extend the vote to White women, whilst at the same time totally disfranchising and segregating Africans.

Significantly, the policy of incorporation promoted by Hertzog most forcefully was devised at a time characterised by signs of increased Coloured and African unity, as shown in the growth of Garveyism, the development of the ICU, the attempt by the Cape ANC to widen its ranks and the flirtation of the APO with notions of non-European unity. In 1926 Abdurahman assured the ANC that "I do not want to sell the Native's rights or be bribed by the Government to leave the Native in the lurch."[38] The following year, together with Sol Plaatjie, the president of the African National Congress (ANC), Abdurahman convened the first Non-European Convention. Under the joint auspices of the APO and the ANC, the convention "resolved to find ways and means of uniting non-Europeans."[39] In this climate of growing non-European unity it is not surprising that the administration renewed its commitment to policies aimed to entrench the division between Coloured and African people.

Hertzog's bills, the Chairman of the Select Committee entrusted with the drafting of the legislation explained, were designed to achieve just such a purpose. For, he insisted,

> It is not safe for the Europeans themselves to force the Coloured people into the hands of the natives. I recall Lord Selborne's warning to the European people that if they did not treat the Coloured people on separate lines from the natives the Coloureds would get the natives against the white man. That will take place unless General Hertzog's wise policy is carried out to discriminate between the Coloured person and the native. It is the salvation of both the white and the Coloured that these two (viz. Coloured and native) should be treated on separate lines.[40]

Parliament, however, was unprepared to enfranchise Coloured men. Nevertheless, the renewed commitment of the administration to policies of Coloured preference led, among other things, to a more flexible attitude on the part of the Department of Native Affairs to the Cape Town

---

37. South Africa, *Government Gazette Extraordinary, No. 1570*, 23 July 1926. See also *Draft Bill* 796/1926; *Coloured Persons Rights Bill* 757/1926; *The Report of the Committee on the Coloured Persons Rights Bill* AB 37/1927; *Select Committee* 10/1927; *Select Committee* 19/1927; *Joint House of Assembly and Senate Select Committee on Representation* 1927/1929.
38. *Cape Times*, 17 June 1926.
39. T. Karis and G Carter (eds.), *From Protest to Challenge: a documentary history of African politics in South Africa, Vol. 1* (Stanford, Hoover Inst. Press, 1973), p. 257, document 44. See also Simons and Simons, *Class and Colour*, pp. 343-344.
40. South Africa, *Select Committee* 10/1927, Evidence on 10 June 1927, para. 325.

City Council's attempts to tighten influx control in the region. By June 1926 the Council was able to get away with proclamations which forced all non-property-owning Africans to live in designated locations, and which compelled all Africans not in registered employment to leave the Greater Cape Town area.[41] In 1929, with regional unemployment rising to record levels, Hertzog's administration increased further its support for the Cape Town Council's influx controls; the Transkei authorities were instructed not to issue passes to Africans wishing to travel to Cape Town to seek employment.[42]

The Hertzog government's policy of preference for Coloureds relative to Africans failed to live up to Hertzog's desire to "economically, industrially and politically" incorporate Coloured people.[43] In fact, apart from minor concessions such as those embodied in the Mines and Works Amendment Act of 1926, which allowed Coloureds to enter certain occupations barred to Africans, the position of Coloureds declined rapidly. In industry and commerce Coloured people were for a variety of reasons further disadvantaged, whilst in politics, following the passage of the Women's Enfranchisement Act and the defeat of the Coloured Persons' Enfranchisement Act, Coloured people's share of the vote was halved from 20 per cent of the Cape electorate in 1929 to 10 per cent in 1930.[44]

The declining share of the Coloured vote and the corresponding increase in the White vote drastically undercut the influence of the Coloured electorate. Until 1930 the Coloured electorate exercised a considerable influence and could turn the scale in favour of one or other of the main parties in at least 10 of the 58 Cape constituencies.[45] Prior to 1930 this electoral clout had forced White political parties into alliance with Coloured politicians.

In 1919 the APO, whose weekly newspaper had suspended publication during the First World War and which had lost both political influence and many of its members, had been lifted out of its financial and organisational crisis after receiving financial help from J.W. Jagger, a Unionist.[46] In return, the APO campaigned on the Unionists' behalf. In the same year, organising in opposition to the APO-Unionists alliance, the Cape Nationalists, who "saw the brown voter as decisive in their attempts to gain political control in the Cape", founded the United Afri-

41. Saunders, "Ndabeni", p. 184.
42. S. van der Horst, *Native Labour in South Africa* (London, Frank Cass, 1971), p.273, fn.3.
43. Cited in Patterson, *"Colour and Culture"*, p. 14.
44. L. Thompson, *The Cape Coloured Franchise* (Johannesburg, SAIRR, 1949), appendix 1.
45. Marais, *"Cape Coloured"*, p. 279.
46. M. Simons, in Van der Merwe's *Occupational Change*, p. 212.

kaner League (UAL).[47] By 1924 the UAL had given way to another specifically Coloured organisation, the Afrikaner National Bond. The ANB was subservient to the National Party and opposed the support given by Abdurahman to the South African Party (SAP). Setting the pattern for subsequent collaborationist parties, the ANB under the leadership of George Oliver vigorously promoted the idea of a distinct Coloured identity. Dr D.F. Malan, Minister of Interior, had told the first ANB conference that "If the Coloured people are to be coupled with the natives they will never get political rights."[48] By 1927 the ANB leadership had taken up the refrain, noting that

> The Coloured people resent Natives entering into our spheres of labour . . .
> Not only are we losing our bread but our vote as well . . . It is a matter of
> self-preservation with us.[49]

The close alliance of Coloured political parties and White parties after 1930 continued to underlie the development of separate Coloured parties. Abdurahman, until his death in 1940, remained a loyal supporter of the South African Party and then the United Party, whilst the ANB, under the leaderships of George Olivier, lent its support to Malan and, after 1948, to the National Party. But from 1920, with the dramatic erosion of the Coloured vote, the influence of Coloured politicians waned. By 1930 the inability of the APO to defend the Coloured franchise or to arrest the slide of Coloured workers had led to widespread disaffection from the APO, even within the Coloured artisan class which previously had proved to be the organisation's most loyal constituency. There could be little doubt that separate Coloured organisations had failed in the task they had originally set themselves to defend and advance Coloured rights.

The Civilised Labour Policy and Great Depression

In the 1920s the rearguard defence of Coloured interests by Coloured political parties, and the support of successive governments for policies of preference for Coloureds, were associated with marked changes in the racial and sexual division of labour in the Western Cape. These

47. *Ibid.*
48. T. Oberst, "The Coloured Persons Rights Bill and the Colonisation of the Coloured" (London Univ., MA thesis, 1973), p. 21.
49. South Africa, *Select Committee* SC 10/1927, Evidence, para. 329.

changes in turn were connected with the Civilised Labour Policy and the Great Depression.

In 1921 less than 1 per cent of Coloured people were employed in white-collar or professional occupations whilst fewer than 3 per cent occupied other higher-status occupations such as those in retailing, commerce and recreation. Unskilled occupations accounted for 77 per cent of the total employed in farming and fishing. Over 90 per cent of the Coloured women in the Cape were classified as unskilled, with 87 per cent of Coloured women classified as domestic servants. Less than 5 per cent of Coloured women were engaged in skilled and semi-skilled jobs. By contrast, 15 per cent of Coloured men occupied semi-skilled and skilled occupations. This sizeable stratum included apprentices and artisans. It was this upwardly mobile sector of the Coloured population which felt itself increasingly disadvantaged by the protection afforded to White unionists. In the 1920s skilled and semi-skilled Coloureds were squeezed further by the Apprenticeship Act and the Civilised Labour Policy.

Eric Walker has noted that the passage of the 1922 Apprenticeship Act set "a well-nigh unattainable educational standard for apprentices, [and] threatened to extinguish the invaluable class of skilled Coloured artisans."[50] In terms of the Act, a minimum educational level of Standard Six was specified for all apprentices. But Coloureds had suffered from a segregated system of education and were confined to the inferior mission schools. The impact of the Act, therefore, was greatly to restrict the entry of Coloured youth into apprenticeships, even in trades in which Coloured craftsmen predominated. The Superintendant-General of Education in 1899 had left no doubt that

> The first duty of the Government has been assumed to be to recognise the position of European colonists as holding the paramount influence, social and political, and to see that the sons and daughters of the colonists should have at least such education as their peers in Europe enjoy, with such local modifications as will fit them to maintain their unquestioned superiority and supremacy in this land.[51]

By 1927 the situation was essentially unchanged and, in the entire Cape Province, only 785 Coloured pupils were enrolled in the first year of high school compared with 13 128 White children.[52] The successful completion of this first year of school, in terms of the Apprenticeship

---

50. E. Walker, *A history of South Africa* (London, Longmans, 1968), p. 657.
51. Sir Langham Dale, cited in D. Innes, *Forced Removals of Coloureds in South Africa* (London, Africa Publ. Trust, 1975), pp. 4-5.
52. R. Leslie, "Coloured Labour and Trade Unionism in Cape Town", *Journal of the Economic Society of South Africa*, 1930, 3, (2), pp. 59-60.

Act, was a prerequisite for entry into the trades. The Act therefore restricted further the upward mobility of Coloureds. In the words of Abdurahman, the Act was "the most potent weapon ever forged for the
purpose of carrying on a callous and brutal one-sided war against the
Coloured youth."[53] The Apprenticeship Act established strict educational, age and service conditions for apprentices. The effect, Sheila van
der Horst has documented, was to exclude the overwhelming majority
of poorly educated Coloureds from skilled work.[54]

In 1924 the position of Coloureds was eroded further by the passage
of the Industrial Conciliation Act, dubbed by W. Hutt the "Coloured
Oppression Act".[55] Together with the Wage Act of 1925, the Industrial
Conciliation Act legitimised the closed-shop practices of White craftsmen and prevented wage-undercutting by Coloured workers. Employers
had previously preferred to employ Coloured and African workers at
lower rates of pay than their White counterparts. However, a Government Commission found the effect of wage-fixing was to "influence
many Europeans to prefer to pay these (uniform) wages to persons of
their own race."[56] Abdurahman had been assured that the legislation,
which was an integral aspect of the Civilised Labour Policy, had not
been intended to discriminate against Coloureds. But although the brunt
of the restructuring policy was directed at Africans, Coloureds also suffered from the impact of a policy which was widely interpreted to imply
that only White men and women were civilised.

From 1924, in terms of the policy, Coloured and African workers in
the public service were replaced by White workers. Whereas in 1924, in
the Western Cape, Coloured men and women accounted for 44 per cent
of all government employees, by 1932 they constituted only 30 per cent
of the region's public service employees. The fall in African numbers
was equally steep; whereas in 1924 Africans accounted for 12 per cent of
government employees, their share of public employment by 1932 had
fallen to barely 2 per cent. This loss of employment by Coloured and
African workers as a result of the Civilised Labour Policy was, for
White workers, a gain; between 1924 and 1932 White workers' share of
government employment in the Western Cape increased from 44 to 68
per cent.

53   Unisa Acc. 223, Box 3, Folder 7, "Presidential address to the 1939 APO Conference",
     p.2.
54   S. van der Horst, "Statutory and Administrative measures affecting the Employment of
     Coloured persons", in H.W. van der Merwe and C.J. Groenewald (eds.), *Occupational
     and Social Change among Coloured People in South Africa* (Cape Town, Juta, 1976), p.
     149.
55   W. Hutt, cited in Oberst, "The Coloured Persons", p.13; South Africa, *Industrial Con-
     ciliation Act*, No. 11 of 1924.
56   South Africa, *"Coloured Commission, 1937"*, p.57.

In his book *Brown South Africa* C. Ziervogel observed that as a result of the Civilised Labour Policy

> most of the avenues of employment formerly open on the railways and harbour services and in other government departments are definitely now closed to the Coloured man . . . There is absolutely no doubt that the Coloured man has been ousted from his position in the economic system because of colour prejudice.[57]

This colour prejudice was not confined to the public sector; Sheila van der Horst found that in the private sector "many employers believed that the civilised labour policy was designed to substitute White for Coloured labour."[58] In 1924, in private manufacturing in the Western Cape, Coloured people comprised 50 per cent of the workforce. By 1929 their relative share had fallen to 46 per cent and by 1932 had slipped to 43 per cent. During the same period, from 1924 to 1932, the share of African workers fell from 14 to 12 per cent. The loss of African and Coloured workers, as in the public sector, was the White workers' gain; whereas in 1924 White workers accounted for only 35 per cent of the workforce, by 1932 they had overtaken Coloureds and constituted 44 per cent of the labour force in private manufacturing.

In the 1920s Coloured and African workers suffered as a result of a renewed commitment on the part of government and private employers to a racially hierarchical division of labour. By 1929 the Civilised Labour Policy in the Western Cape had placed Coloured workers at an increasing disadvantage relative to White workers and undercut the economic base of the Coloured artisan class. The effect, as the Cape Federation of Trades noted in October 1929, was that apprentices engaged in industry "were being employed as cheap labour. For these the future held no hope or no opportunity as skilled men."[59]

In the 1920s the plight of skilled Coloured men was closely related to the development in the Western Cape of manufacturing industry and of the de-skilling, as a result of production-line techniques, of many of the occupations (for example, furniture-making) which Coloured men had come to regard as their own. Between 1929 and 1933 the position of the skilled Coloured man deteriorated even more rapidly. For in these years the Great Depression led to the restructuring of the labour process and the further loss of job opportunities for Coloured craftsmen.

By the end of the Depression, Coloured artisans had been shaken out of virtually all the traditional crafts and prevented by apprenticeship barriers and prejudice from entering the new electrical, machine and

57   C. Ziervogel, *Brown South Africa* (Cape Town, Maskew Miller, 1937), p.35.
58   Van der Horst, *Native Labour*, p.250.
59   Cited in J. Lewis, "Industrialisation and Trade Union Organisation in South Africa, 1924-1955" (Cambridge Univ., D Phil Thesis, 1982), p.99.

metallurgical crafts. Coloured craftsmen were left clinging to certain building trades and in 1933 still accounted for over 90 per cent of all bricklayers and plasterers.[60] But Coloured people, Ziervogel observed in 1937, had in the space of 15 years "lost almost every [other] occupation that was regarded as previously their own (blacksmiths, carpenters, masons, bookmakers, tailors, coachmen, painters)."[61]

The Depression provided the opportunity for a radical transformation which fundamentally reshaped the racial and sexual division of labour in the Western Cape. The process of job fragmentation and the introduction of closely supervised mass-production techniques were associated with the substitution of female for male labour and the substitution of White for Coloured and African labour. In the period 1928 to 1933 private employers increased their complement of White women by over 25 per cent, while the number of White men declined by over 13 per cent. And whilst the overall number of Whites (men and women) increased, the number of Coloureds and Africans employed declined, with men bearing the main impact of the restructuring process; the number of Coloured and African men employed declined by 35 per cent whilst the total number of Coloured women employed fell by less than 5 per cent. Coloured youth in the Western Cape were particularly adversely affected by the depression. By 1935, the Cape Coloured Commission found,

> Coloured youth had great difficulty in obtaining work; and that even when work was found, it was generally in blind alley occupations.[62]

Coloured men in the Western Cape were particularly hard hit by the restructuring process which had been initiated during the Civilised Labour Policy and given added impetus during the Great Depression. Though the policy was not intended to disadvantage Coloured workers, Coloured men found that during the 1920s and 1930s private employers increasingly substituted White men for skilled Coloured men, and White and Coloured women for semi-skilled Coloured men, whilst African men were preferred to Coloured men in unskilled occupations.

The 1937 Commission of Inquiry into Matters Affecting the Coloured Population found that in the inter-War years many employers had regarded "unskilled Coloureds to be less dependable and less efficient compared with Africans" and had substituted unskilled African men for unskilled Coloured men.[63] After 1920, Abe Desmore observed, unskilled Coloured men had been ousted from employment in unskilled work in

60. Leslie, "Coloured Labour", p.60; Van der Horst, *"Native Labour"*, p.149.
61. Ziervogel, *Brown South Africa*, p.39.
62. South Africa, *"Coloured Commission, 1937"*, p.57.
63. *Ibid.*, p.16

construction, and in the delivery of milk.[64] We have suggested that by the turn of the century employers were displaying a preference for the employment of African men in unskilled jobs in farming and in the docks. African workers, employers had found, were prepared to accept lower wages and more arduous working conditions than their Coloured counterparts. In the nineteenth century Africans may have been able in part to supplement their income through peasant production. By the 1920s, however, the peasant economy had all but collapsed.[65]

The undercutting of unskilled job opportunities by Africans served to increase racial awareness among unskilled Coloured workers and to lead to resentment against African men. For skilled Coloured men, on the other hand, White workers were the immediate competitors. White workers had established closed-shop trade unions excluding Coloured men from many occupations. In addition, the growing electoral power of the White working class had secured for that class protection in terms of the Apprenticeship Act, the Wage Act, the Industrial Conciliation Act and other industrial legislation. Skilled Coloured men were employed in many occupations covered by the Wage Act and by Industrial Conciliation legislation. In these regulated occupations the effect of wage-fixing, we have noted, was to influence many employers to prefer to pay the (uniform) wages to White workers.[66] As a result, skilled Coloured men found themselves at an increasing disadvantage to White men.

In 1921, in Greater Cape Town, over 85 per cent of Coloured women were employed as domestic servants, the proportion having remained unchanged since the 1865 census. By 1936 the proportion of Coloured women employed in domestic service had fallen to 66 per cent. Coloured women, a comparison of the census data reveals, had managed in the intervening period to capture a growing share of semi-skilled occupations. Whereas in 1921 less than 4 per cent of Coloured women had been employed in semi-skilled jobs, by 1936 over 19 per cent were categorised as semi-skilled. In the rural areas, however, Coloured women remained largely confined to domestic service, and in 1936 this sector still accounted for the employment of approximately 82 per cent of the Coloured women in South Africa.

Between 1926 and 1933 the ability of the Coloured women in the Cape Peninsula to advance their position, during a period characterised by increased preference for White workers and the rapid deterioration

---

64. A. Desmore, "The Cape Coloured People Today", *Journal of the Royal Africa Society*, 1937, Vol. 36, p.350.
65. C. Bundy, *The Rise and Fall of the South African Peasantry* (London, Macmillan, 1979).
66. South Africa, *"Coloured Commission, 1937"*, p.57.

in the position of Coloured men, may be attributed mainly to the employment of Coloured women in the rapidly expanding garment industry. From 1926, with the introduction of the Pact government's pledge to restrict by means of tariffs the import of completed garments, the domestic clothing industry was given a new lease of life. In 1926 fewer than 1 170 people were employed in the clothing manufacture in the Western Cape.[67] But between 1929 and 1934, despite the Depression, the Cape clothing industry doubled in size.[68] For the clothing manufacturers the Depression years brought increased profits as real wages declined more rapidly than the slackening demand for clothes. At the same time the Depression facilitated the restructuring of production and the substitution of semi-skilled Coloured women, and to a lesser extent White women, for skilled Coloured tailors. In 1929, a Cape employer explained, one person had made a whole garment: "A shirt-hand made the whole shirt and the pyjama-hand made the whole pair of pyjamas."[69] Five years later the work was "divided into definite operations".[70]

The preference of Cape clothing manufacturers for young Coloured women was indicative of the relatively low wages paid to this sector of the workforce. Martin Nicol in his study of the Cape Garment Workers' Union has shown that from the outset employers justified the low wages paid to their employees on the grounds that the "majority of girls live with their parents and have their parents behind them", or that the "girls" aimed simply to supplement the income of their husbands, who were considered to be the principal wage-earners.[71] From the outset, the preference of the employers in the Cape garment industry for young Coloured women reflected the ability of the employers to reduce the wages of these women to levels below those paid to African men and White women in the Transvaal, and to African men and women in Natal. After materials, wages constituted the major element of costs in the highly competitive industry, and with all manufacturers faced by similar material costs, competition in the garment industry took the form of undercutting wages. The success of the Cape in this respect was due chiefly to the ability of the Cape employers to prevent the development of a powerful trade union.

67. National Development and Management Foundation, "Stagnation or Growth", Proceedings of Conference held in Cape Town, May 1980. Paper by N. Nol, p.4.
68. *Ibid.*
69. Cited in M. Nicol, "Riches from Rags: bosses and unions in the Cape Clothing Industry, 1926-1937", Inst. of Commonwealth Studies, Seminar on the Societies of Southern Africa in the 19th and 20th centuries, Seminar Paper, 12 May 1979, p.6.
70. *Ibid.*
71. SC 4/1917 cited in M. Nicol, "The Garment Workers' Union of the Cape Peninsula and the Garment Workers Unity Movement" (Cape Town Univ., BA (Hons) thesis, 1977) p.3.

From 1926, following a Wage Board investigation, wages in the garment industry were set on a regional basis by industrial councils.[72] The Industrial Council machinery provided for the representation of workers by trade unions. In the Transvaal a well-organised and representative union, the South African Garment Union, was established by Solly Sachs and others. In the Cape, however, employers were able to pre-empt establishment of a representative union by creating a nominal union under the leadership of Bob Stuart. Until 1935 this Cape Union had fewer than 400 members and served only to legitimise employers' wage determinations. Year after year, Cape employers were able to set wages at levels which increased the differential between the Cape and the higher-paying Transvaal employers. The growing differential, Nicol observed, became a perpetual threat to the Transvaal garment workers and provided employers with a ready argument with which to rebut demands for wage rises. In order to overcome this threat and prevent undercutting by the coastal union, Solly Sachs tried on repeated occasions to get the Cape Union to join a national federation which could agree on a national pattern of wages. In 1930 when this failed he, together with John Gomas and Ben Weibren, attempted to organise in the Cape in opposition to the Cape Union. But Cape management conniving with police and the Cape Union were able to frustrate Sachs's plans. In 1935 Sachs, this time together with Weinberg, Forsyth and Andrews, again tried to organise in opposition to the Cape Union. In response, management instituted a compulsory stop-order in favour of their client union; within three months the Cape Union's membership had leapt from barely 400 to over 2 500 members. Employees, according to Nicol, were given little choice: "if they refused they were told very plainly that they either sign the stop-order or take a week's notice".[73]

By 1935, in large part because of their success in combating representative unionism, Cape employers had laid the foundation for the rapid growth of the Cape garment industry. Simultaneously, the Union, by accepting wage settlements at levels below those acceptable to White workers, was able to ensure that White workers would not compete with Coloureds for jobs in the Cape industry. The threat of competition from Africans was removed by the Union's insistence on the employment of Coloured workers. Until 1941 this prejudice was not embedded in the Union's Constitution. In that year, as a result of a closed-shop agreement secured by the Union, Africans were formally excluded from the industry.

---

72. R. Close, *New Life* (Cape Town, FCWU, 1950), pp.10-25.
73. M. Nicol, "The Garment Workers", p.34.

The exclusion of African men and women from the garment industry and from other avenues of semi-skilled and skilled employment, we have noted, cannot simply be attributed to the activities of White employers, White workers and politicians. Political organisations such as the APO and trade unions such as the Cape Garment Workers' Union catered for Coloured and not African people, and so served to reinforce racial awareness. But these racially divisive organisations were not unchallenged; from the turn of the century, attempts were made in the Western Cape to organise workers on a non-racial basis. Indeed, it is the very success of the non-racial challenge which forced the administration to strengthen its resolve to distinguish between Coloured, African and White workers.

Mass Resistance and Employers' Response

The period which saw an unprecedented racial restructuring of labour and renewed attempts to institute a policy of economic preference for Coloured people was also one of mass organisation and resistance by Coloured and African workers. In the Western Cape, non-racial organisations had taken root first in the Cape Town docks. In 1913 the organisation of dockers, which had been initiated at the turn of the century by members of the International Socialist League and Labour Party, was given expression in the formation of the Industrial Workers' Union (IWU). In 1919 the IWU gave way to the Industrial and Commercial Workers' Union (ICU). By December 1919 the ICU had welded a powerful alliance of Coloured, African and White dockers, and in order to press its wage demands had initiated industrial action. The ensuing strike involved African, Coloured and White workers and for two weeks brought the docks to a standstill. The forceful intervention of the police and the withering of the White workers' support for the action facilitated the resumption of services. But the success of the strike, which Budlender notes secured an "unprecedently high" wage increase, served to rally Cape Town's African and Coloured workers around the ICU.[74]

---

74. D. Budlender, "A history of Stevedores", p.5. For this period see also E. Roux, *Time Longer than Rope* (London, Univ. of Wisconsin, 1978); W. Harrison, *Memoirs of a socialist in South Africa, 1903-1947* (Cape Town, 1948); R.K. Cope, *Comrade Bill: the life and times of W.H. Andrews, Workers' leader* (Cape Town, Stewart, n.d.); and P. Wickins, *The Industrial and Commercial Workers' Union of South Africa* (Cape Town, OUP, 1978).

From 1919 to 1923 the ICU attracted large numbers of Coloured and African workers and provided a home and hope for Coloured radicals such as James La Guma and John Gomas. The rapid growth and initial radicalism of the ICU posed a challenge to employers and the administration as well as to Coloured organisations such as the APO. The successful example of the ICU, Abdurahman feared, would erode the support for the APO. At the same time, dock employers and the government were anxious to stem the rising tide of militancy. In 1921 the Harbours Board, which represented the Department of Transport as well as private employers, agreed to Abdurahman's request that 800 African dock workers be replaced by Coloured workers.[75] The impact of the substitution was to increase the resentment of African workers. Coloured workers by contrast were able to benefit from the relative privilege derived from their identification as a group distinct from Africans.

From 1921 racial awareness intensified and for over a generation undermined attempts to revive non-racial organisation at the docks. The position of relative preference enjoyed by Coloureds in the Western Cape strengthened the hand of those members of the ICU executive who were seeking to reorientate the ICU behind a separatist Africanist ideology. By 1925 the working-class ideology of the ICU had been replaced by an increasingly vitriolic anti-communist and Africanist ideology. The following year Gomas, who had become regional secretary, and La Guma, the national secretary, were forced to resign. These two, together with other members of the Communist Party of South Africa (CPSA) turned their attention to the African National Congress (ANC).

Between 1926 and 1930 members of the CPSA exercised a powerful influence over the Western Cape branch of the ANC. "In practice," Willie Hofmeyer noted in his history of the ANC in the Western Cape, the slogan of a black republic, adopted by the Comintern in 1927, "provided a coherent basis for a fruitful alliance between the CPSA and the ANC in the Western Cape."[76] In the late 1920s, because of the dedication of the CPSA activists and the power of the CPSA's broad alliance, Hofmeyer found that "it was only in the Western Cape that there was a revival of the ANC as a mass-based organisation"[77].

In 1927 the revitalisation of the ANC(WC) was heralded by a series of mass meetings. At these the need for organisation and unity was emphasised:

75. Budlender, "A history of Stevedores", pp.6-7.
76. W. Hofmeyer, "Rural Popular Organisation Problems: Struggles in the Western Cape, 1929-1930", *Africa Perspective*, 1983, No. 22, p.27.
77. *Ibid.*, p.28.

All non-whites are advised to organise in order to bring the government to its knees through a general strike — their only weapon . . .[78]

The executive stressed that the success of resistance depended on the participation of Coloured people. It was the executive's hope that

every Coloured man will join the ANC in the new year . . . The white man wants to prevent the co-operation — the unity between the native and the Coloured. But the ANC will do everything in its power to bring about co-operation and community.[79]

Not surprisingly, the rapid growth of this broad-based organisation rekindled the anxieties which the infant ICU had brought to the attention of the Cape Town bourgeoisie. These concerns were shared by the Hertzog administration. Hertzog, it will be recalled, had insisted that "it would be foolish to drive the Coloured people to the enemies of the Europeans"[80].

The growing ANC(WC) extended its influence into the Cape Town hinterland. In 1929, after successfully organising in Paarl, the Congress recruited more than 1 000 members in Worcester. Using Worcester as a base, the ANC then set about overcoming the extraordinary difficulties in organising farm workers. Despite victimisation, dismissals and organised thuggery, which led to the death of at least six ANC members, the ANC managed to establish branches as far afield as Carnarvon, Ladismith and George. Before long the growing strength of the organisation had led employers to call for more effective police action. The authorities obliged and, following a hasty amendment to the Riotous Assemblies Act, ANC meetings in the Cape hinterland in June 1930 were outlawed. By October 1930, following the arrest of the regional executive and other activists, it was clear that the radical movement had been dealt a serious blow.[81.]

In 1930 the appointment of James Thaele to the post of president of the ANC(WC) signalled a further defeat for the ANC radicals. Thaele suspended the Communist Party members and other militants and reoriented the ANC(WC) towards Garveyism and passive resistance. The racial reorientation of the ANC(WC) alienated Coloured rank and file members of the ANC, who felt they had no place in the increasingly Africanist organisation. The shift in the ANC served to reinforce notions of racial identity. Equally divisive, in the long run, was the alienation of

---

78. *Ibid.*, p.30.
79. *Ibid.*
80. South Africa, *House of Assembly Debates* (henceforth *HAD)* 12-15 Feb. 1929, Col. 169.
81. R. Kingwill, The African National Congress in the Western Cape: a preliminary study (Cape Town Univ., BA (Hons) thesis, 1977), p.28.

coloured intellectuals from the ANC. The African reorientation of the ANC forced Coloured intellectuals either to confine themselves to the organisation of Coloureds or else to support political movements which aimed to organise African people in competition to the ANC. By 1930 racial identities had become entrenched within radical organisations. In consequence, the divisions which up to that time had not permeated all sections of society were manifest within a wide range of political organisations.

Summary

In the period 1904 to 1935 the development of policies of preference for Coloured men and women were closely related to attempts by the administration and employers to deflect opposition based on non-racial organisation. At the same time, these preference policies were not simply the result of the conspiratorial bestowal on the Coloured population of a racial identity devised by White ideologues.

Throughout the period under consideration, confusion continued to exist within the administration as to the meaning of the term Coloured. The ambivalence of successive ruling parties was reflected in the differing treatment of the term Coloured in various items of legislation and by the failure of government departments to agree on a common definition of Coloured people. In 1921, for example, the Supreme Court ruled that "a 'Coloured person' meant a person other than White or European."[82] This interpretation was different to that of the Department of Native Affairs or, from 1904, to the racial divisions of the Population Census.

The continuing conflict within the administration over the question of Coloured identity cannot be disassociated from the struggle within the Coloured population itself over the very existence and development of a separate identity.

The entrenchment of racial boundaries within South African society as a whole was the result of a complex process; and one element of this was the development of policies of preference for people defined as Coloured. Such policies preceded the period of National Party rule and were not, as Callinicos suggested, a product of National Party rule.[83] By

82.   Central Archives, Pretoria, File CIA M250 Vol. 21 1/M/250, "Definition of Coloured Person."
83.   A. Callinicos, *Southern Africa after Soweto* (London, Pluto, 1981), p.130.

1920 the Cape Town City Council had called for the stricter control of African influx into the Western Cape. Their call had been supported by many Cape employers, the APO, and the Hertzog administration. But, contrary to Marion Lacey's assertion that the policy was initiated by the central government in the 1920s in order satisfy the demands of the mines to shore up the Eastern Cape as a reserve of African labour[84], we have shown that the policy was opposed initially by the central government and had its origins in concerns arising out of the Western Cape. It was in this region that the local authorities together with local employers and politicians began to campaign for the development of a policy of Coloured preference.

In this chapter we have examined some of the issues pertaining to the development of policies of Coloured preference and Coloured racial identity in the period 1904 to 1935. In the next chapter we continue our argument, focusing on the period 1935 to 1948.

---

84. M. Lacey, *Working for Boroko: the origins of a coercive labour system in South Africa* (Johannesburg, Ravan, 1981), p.373, fn.3.

CHAPTER THREE

MAINTAINING THE PATTERN OF PREFERENCE: 1935 — 1948

Introduction

In the period 1902 to 1935 racial prejudices that had been crystallised by the turn of the century were further entrenched. The development of political organisations, which in effect served to advance the interests of Coloured men and women in isolation from Africans, and the development of trade unions, which excluded Africans, reinforced the growing racial stratification of society. From 1922 to 1933 the Civilised Labour Policy followed by the Great Depression undermined the economic position of African and Coloured people. In this climate of insecurity some Coloured workers sought to defend their place in the labour market at the expense of African workers. At the same time the erosion of the Coloured vote and of Coloured jobs led to a growing disillusionment with White politics, leading in certain circumstances to the development of organisations embracing both Coloured and African opponents of the government. Between 1919 and 1921 the ICU, and between 1929 and 1930 the ANC (WC), provided powerful challenges to the ethnic organisations. But the non-racial commitment of these organisations was short-lived, and both the ICU and ANC capitulated to Africanist sentiment. By 1932 Coloured radicals found themselves once again isolated from the mainstream of African resistance. In the period 1935 to 1948, as we shall show, this had a marked impact on the development of Coloured political identity.

Coloured Opposition and Politics 1933 — 1948

It will be recalled that in the reorientation of the ANC (WC) in 1930 Communist Party members were expelled. Many of them were Coloured intellectuals who were resolute in their commitment to mass organisations which included Africans and Coloureds. Increasingly excluded from the ANC (WC), these individuals began to organise independently. The effect was to create in the Western Cape two axes of mass organisation. On the one hand, the ANC (WC) remained until the 1950s committed to the advance of African nationalism, and any radical tendencies within the movement were swamped. By contrast, the organisations dominated by Coloured intellectuals were non-racial in principle and more radical in rhetoric. They sought to mobilise a broad non-racial alliance against the government. But largely because of the narrowness of their base in the Coloured communities, these organisations were restricted to issues which concerned only Coloureds. The overall impact of the polarisation of African and Coloured intellectuals was to reproduce within the resistance movements racial divisions between African and Coloured people. Ironically Coloured intellectuals who were vocal in their condemnation of racial divisions found themselves operating in a political arena preoccupied with issues affecting only Coloured people and with a constituency which seldom stretched into the African communities.

By the mid-1930s Coloured radical organisations had come to exert a powerful influence within the Coloured communities. These organisations had entered into Coloured politics at a time when pre-existing Coloured organisations were near-dormant. Whereas in the previous three decades the APO had dominated Coloured politics and resisted the development of a radical Coloured challenge, by 1935 the APO was virtually defunct.

The failure of the APO and Abdurahman to advance the position of Coloured voters and the Coloured skilled and petty bourgeois strata had discredited Abdurahman's tactics of collaboration with White political parties.[1] The better-off Coloureds had previously proved to be the APO's most loyal constituency. However, the Depression had led to the decline of the Coloured artisan class and the dramatic erosion of the Coloured vote (the enfranchisement of White women had reduced the Coloured vote from 20 per cent in 1929 to 10 per cent in 1930).[2] Increasingly disillusioned, skilled and semi-skilled Coloureds turned their backs on the old-guard of Coloured notables. These notables, who since the turn of the century had promised to lead "civilised" Coloured people back into the European camp, had by 1935 been effectively replaced by a new breed of intellectuals.[3]

---

1. See Unisa Acc. 223, Box 2, Folder 12, "Political situation; memos", and Simons and Simons, *"Class and Colour"*, p.541.
2. L. Thompson, *The Cape Coloured Franchise* (Johannesburg, SAIRR, 1949), Appendix 1.
3. See, for example, G. Lewis, "Your votes", p.35.

Prominent amongst the old-guard were Abdurahman and his close allies Hoedemaker and Triegaardt. The plight of these ineffective intellectuals is vividly outlined in a letter from Triegaardt to Hoedemaker, written in 1938:

> Don't forget that most of us are working in a haphazard way for some sort of cause, but we don't really know what it is, and those of us who do know what we are striving for cannot get any support, moral or otherwise.[4]

By 1938, the face of Coloured politics had been altered. The leadership of Coloured politics had passed into the hands of radicals, such as James La Guma, Johnny Gomas and Goolam and Cissie Gool, the daughter of Abdurahman. These people exercised a decisive influence over a wide cross-section of the Coloured community of the Western Cape.[5]

The resurgence of Coloured radicalism led in 1935 to the formation of the National Liberation League (NLL), established to provide a radical and non-racial lead for opposition to the regime. But, although non-sectarian in policy, in practice the League mainly confined its organisational activities to the Coloured communities whilst Coloured intellectuals, including La Guma and Cissie and Goolam Gool, dominated its leadership.[6] These radicals, aware of the danger of the League's developing into a narrow sectarian organisation, attempted on numerous occasions to broaden the NLL to include African people.[7] To this end the League was closely associated with the All African Convention (AAC), which had been established in 1935 in order to mobilise mass opposition to the disfranchisement of Africans. But the Convention failed to remain immune from the tensions which had frustrated previous attempts to develop non-racial mass organisations. In 1937 tensions between the ANC, which refused to moderate its Africanist tendencies, and the rest of the Convention, which followed broadly the line of the NLL, culminated in the withdrawal of the ANC from the AAC.[8] The AAC from that time on, although still holding the support of prominent African intellectuals such as Tabata in the Western Cape, failed to gain a mass following within the African communities or to successfully challenge the mobilisation of Africans by the ANC.

---

4. ICS Archives, M. 858 (Hoedemaker Collection), Item 27. Hoedemaker to H.E. Triegaardt, 29 Nov. 1938.
5. See Simons and Simons, *"Class and Colour"*, pp. 486-507, and M. Simons, "Organised Coloured Political Movements", in H.W. van der Merwe and C.J. Groenewald, *"Occupational and social change"*, pp. 220-227.
6. Unisa Acc. 223, Box 4, Record Book 1, "National Liberation League (NLL) Minutes", and Folder 1, "NLL General Council Minutes, 1938-1941".
7. *Ibid.*
8. See E. Roux, *Time Longer than Rope*, pp. 286-317, and Unisa Acc. 223, Box 5, Folder 1, "NEUF Speech handbills".

The National Liberation League remained firmly committed to the establishment of a united, non-racial opposition and in March 1938 initiated the Non-European United Front. From the outset the Front
aimed to provide mass opposition; it was radical in rhetoric, seeking to
break from ballot-box politics and to embrace working-class as well as
petty bourgeois Coloureds and Africans. However, it was dominated by
members of the Coloured petty bourgeoisie, and the opposition that the
Front provided had little bearing on the African people.[9] From 1938 to
1943 it diverted much of its attention to the spread of European fascism
to South Africa as well as to the growing discrimination of the government against Coloured men and women.

In 1939 the Cape Provincial Council introduced an ordinance giving
municipal councils the power to segregate residential areas, buses and
other public places.[10] The NEUF opposed this measure and demanded
the repeal of racial laws. On 27 March 1939 the NEUF campaign culminated in a large demonstration in Cape Town; this demonstration (which
ended in a riot) pressurised the cabinet into vetoing the Provincial
Council's segregation ordinance.[11]

The success of the NEUF, Simons and Simons observed, hastened the
decline of the APO.[12] Abdurahman said he preferred peaceful change to
forceful threats and refused to join the NEUF or to admit NEUF members to the APO conference held in April 1939.[13] In the following year
Abdurahman died. His successor, Dr F.H. Gow, supported the government's segregation policy and urged the APO to support the government's "gesture of goodwill".[14] But the issue only served to undermine
the already ineffective APO and it was not long before Gow, who later
agreed to become chairman of the government-appointed Coloured Affairs Council, found himself presiding over a divided organisation.

In 1943 the Smuts government segregated the administration of
Coloured affairs from the sections of the administration dealing with the
White population. The creation of a Coloured Affairs Department
(CAD) rallied Coloureds around a common cause: the overwhelming
majority of Coloured men and women were bitterly opposed to Smuts's
plans which, it was argued, heralded the further political segregation of
Coloured people.[15] In May 1943 the anger of Coloureds was channelled

 9. *Ibid.*
10. Simons and Simons, *"Class and Colour"*, p. 502.
11. *Ibid.*
12. *Ibid.*
13. *Ibid.*, p. 503; Roux, *Time Longer than Rope*, p. 357.
14. Simons and Simons, *"Class and Colour"*, p. 541.
15. *Ibid.*, pp. 540-548.

into the formation of the Anti-Coloured Affairs Department (Anti-CAD) organisation. Amongst the 200 delegates to the first conference of Anti-CAD were representatives of a wide range of Coloured civic, cultural and political organisations, including members of dissident APO branches. By 1944, Anti-CAD had penetrated virtually every Coloured community and claimed the support of the majority of Coloured people, including most members of the APO.[16]

The Anti-CAD concentrated narrowly on issues affecting Coloureds and failed to broaden its scope to embrace Africans. The executive, under the leadership of Goolam Gool and Ben Kies, was drawn from the Coloured petty bourgeoisie and the organisation's activities were restricted to the Coloured communities of the Western Cape.[17] In these communities the Anti-CAD was able to exert a considerable influence. In part this may be attributed to the key positions which Anti-CAD activists held in schools and community organisations. Teachers, lawyers and doctors led the Anti-CAD alliance. These professionals enjoyed high status within their communities, and their commitment to the Anti-CAD enhanced the legitimacy of the alliance. The popularity of the Anti-CAD also rested on the adoption by the alliance of the tactics of passive resistance. The main thrust of the Anti-CAD campaign was to organise a political and social boycott of the Coloured Affairs Department and the Coloured Affairs Council. The Anti-CAD stopped short of calling for strikes or demonstrations — tactics which would have been illegal and placed the leadership of the Anti-CAD, many of whom were employed by the Coloured Affairs Department as teachers, in danger of losing their jobs.[18]

Despite the narrow focus of the campaign, the leaders of the Anti-CAD movement were aware of the hazards of the movement's "eventually foundering on the rock of isolation" if it restricted itself to Coloured issues.[19] They therefore set about forging a common front with other non-European organisations. The All-African Convention and the Non-European United Front had been founded in order to pursue similar goals and a number of anti-CAD activists had played a prominent part in those organisations. In December 1943 Anti-CAD activists took the lead in forging a new organisation based on non-sectarian principles, the Non-European Unity Movement (NEUM).

16. See *ibid.,* and Unisa Acc. 233, Box 5, Folder 3, "Anti-CAD Bulletin 1944".
17. See *ibid.,* and Unisa Acc. 233, Box 5, Folder 2, "Anti-CAD Organisation Speeches", and Box 6, "Campaign literature."
18. *Ibid.*
19. Simons and Simons, *"Class and Colour",* p. 544.

The NEUM programme was more radical than that of the Anti-CAD movement. Its aims were to "draw the community into struggle, prepare the masses for a direct onslaught against oppression and ally them in the fight for liberation."[20] This radical rhetoric was regarded with misgiving by less militant supporters of the Anti-CAD campaign. These moderates organised themselves into the Coloured Peoples' National Union (CPNU) and the Teachers' Educational and Professional Association (TEPA). Under the leadership of George Golding, the CPNU supported the Smuts administration, providing a home for members of the APO who wished to collaborate with the Coloured Affairs Department and who had been ousted by the successful penetration of Anti-CAD into the APO.[21]

Despite the commitment of the NEUM to a "direct onslaught against oppression", the Movement failed to extend beyond the tactics of non-collaboration which preoccupied the Anti-CAD campaign.[22] Teachers dominated the leadership of the NEUM. These people, as had been the case in the Anti-CAD movement, were vulnerable to dismissal by the Coloured Affairs Department. Non-collaboration provided the petty bourgeois and skilled strata of Coloureds with a release for their frustrations while at the same time insulating them from economic sacrifice and state repression. Non-collaboration became a synonym for inactivity.[23] This inactivity, apart from isolated exceptions, steered the leadership away from trade-union or community organisation, and the NEUM failed to organise below the level of skilled workers and failed to carry their message of unity to the African communities.[24] The Anti-CAD movement and NEUM in effect turned the attention of Coloured radicals to issues narrowly affecting Coloureds and to tactics which failed to provide a foundation for effective mass mobilisation. The organisation opposed links with other radical organisations, and refused to participate in campaigns organised by the Communist Party. According to the Communist Party activists, Simons and Simons,

> The main achievement of the Anti-CAD was to immobilise a generation of Coloured intellectuals, immunise them against Marxist theory, and isolate them from the rest of the liberation movement.[25]

20. *Ibid.*
21. M. Simons in Van der Merwe, *"Occupational Change"*, pp.220-227.
22. Simons and Simons, *"Class and Colour"*. p. 544.
23. *Ibid.*, p. 546.
24. *Ibid.*, and N. Alexander, former NEUM activist, interview, Cape Town, 25 Nov, 1981, transcript, p.4, and L. Erentzen, General-Secretary Cape Town Municipal Workers' Union, interview, Cape Town, 7 Dec. 1981, transcript, p.1.
25. Simons and Simons, *"Class and Colour"*, p. 546.

Marxist theory, however, informed the activities of the Anti-CAD and NEUM leadership as it did the leadership of the Communist Party. But whereas the Communist Party considered itself to be Marxist-Leninist the Anti-CAD rejected mainstream communism in favour of what some of their leaders regarded as a Trotskyist approach.

By the mid-1940s the ANC (WC) had begun to overcome the divisions and conservatism which had been a cause of its dormancy. The ANC Youth League, which had been formed in 1944 specifically to revive what its members saw as the "moribund" ANC, had by 1949 replaced the old-guard of that organisation. However, despite its rejection of racial oppression the youth League remained committed to a "country of four chief nationalities": Africans, Coloureds, Indians and Whites.[26] Such a policy stood in marked contrast to the NEUM's principles of non-racialism. In policy as well as in practice the revitalisation of the ANC, occurring simultaneously with the development of the NEUM, had the effect of reproducing racial divisions. On the level of policy, the ANC programme remained avowedly racial in content. In practice both the NEUM and the ANC failed to escape the racial divisions deeply ingrained in South African society; both organisations energetically agitated over issues which coincided with racial divisions. The focus of the resuscitated ANC (WC) was influx control and the pass law system. This issue was not of immediate concern to Coloureds and, in the absence of an active drive to include Coloureds, it is not surprising that demonstrations organised in 1946 failed to attract Coloured participants and that Coloureds saw the ANC (WC) as an organisation devoted to African interests.[27]

The effect of the Anti-CAD campaign and the NEUM, on the other hand, was equally divisive. These movements concentrated on issues of concern to Coloureds and failed to involve their members actively in issues of concern to Africans. By 1948 the polarisation of resistance around the opposed leaderships of the NEUM and the ANC (WC) had led liberation movements in the Western Cape to mirror the racial divisions which were promoted by the state. The only exceptions to this racial bifurcation were to be found in the emerging non-racial trade union movement.

26. *Ibid.*, p. 22
27. R. Kingwill, "The African National Congress in the W. Cape", pp. 46-47; *The Guardian*, (Cape Town), 7 August 1947.

Trade Union Organisation, 1935 — 1948

The periods 1919 to 1921 and 1928 to 1930 stand out as high points in the organisation of unskilled workers in the Western Cape. The first period was associated with the initial radicalism of the ICU and the second with the period of mass organisation by the ANC (WC) in the Western Cape hinterland. In 1930 the silencing of the radical leadership of the ANC (WC) and the ascendancy of a more conservative leadership had been a serious setback for non-racial working-class organisations in the Western Cape. Prevented from addressing public meetings, and excluded from Thaele's ANC, communist and other radical activists increasingly turned their attention to the organisation of industrial trade unions.

In the 1930s the development of industrial trade unions was facilitated by the rapid growth of manufacturing industry. This period of dramatic economic change was associated with the fragmentation of many skills and the introduction of techniques of mass production. In the Western Cape, the garment industry was most affected by the restructuring process; the industry more than doubled in size in the period 1926 to 1935 and by 1935 employed 3 500 workers.[28] In the next decade the clothing industry expanded even more rapidly and by 1947 the workforce totalled 10 350.[29]

We have noted that the dramatic restructuring of employment relations in the garment industry in the period 1926 to 1935 led to the development of a client union in the industry. In 1935 clothing manufacturers, fearing that the success of Solly Sachs in organising garment workers would be repeated in the Cape, instituted compulsory stop-orders in favour of the docile Cape Garment Workers' Union under the leadership of Bob Stuart.[30] By 1937 employers, in collaboration with the police and the Cape Union, had thwarted attempts by radicals to organise in the Cape garment industry. In 1941 a closed shop agreement institutionalised the Cape Union's monopoly over the Cape clothing employees. At the same time the agreement served to exclude African workers from the industry.[31]

In terms of the Industrial Conciliation Act of 1924 pass-bearing African workers had been excluded from the definition of "employee" and

---

28. N. No 1, "The Cape Garment Industry", paper presented to National Development and Management Foundation conference on "Stagnation or Growth'" Cape Town, May 1980, p.3.
29. *Ibid.*
30. M. Nicol, "The Garment Workers' Union of the Cape Peninsula", pp. 32-34.
31. *Ibid.*, pp. 47-76.

hence were not permitted to join registered trade unions. Until 1937, however, Africans in the Western Cape were excluded from the pass provisions operating elsewhere in the country and in terms of the Industrial Conciliation Act were thus eligible for trade union membership. From 1937, Africans in the Western Cape were no longer classed as "employees".[32] The institution of a closed shop agreement by the Cape Garment Workers' Union therefore served to exclude Africans from the garment industry. Furthermore, in terms of the agreement, dissident workers, who during the War Years had established a Vigilance Committee with the aim of democratising the Cape Union, were expelled from the Union and the industry.[33]

The failure of progressive trade unionists in the Western Cape to organise garment workers was offset by their success in penetrating the food and canning industry and the docks. In these and other industries, the period 1935 to 1948 heralded a new awareness of radical trade unionism in the Western Cape which stood in contrast to the docile Cape Garment Workers' Union and to the conservatism of the ANC (WC). In 1935, despite the dampening influence of the ANC (WC) under Thaele, labour organisation again peaked. According to R. Cope, this organisation

> . . . bore magnificent fruit. Mass demonstrations were held in Cape Town in 1935 and 1936 . . . In 1937 labour leaders initiated the *Guardian* weekly . . .[34]

Prominent amongst the labour leaders referred to were Ray Alexander, John Gomas, James La Guma and Bill Andrews.[35]

From the mid-1930s Alexander and others devoted much of their attention to the organisation of workers employed in the food and canning industries.[36] In 1925 food-processing accounted for over 40 per cent of the value of the region's output and 20 per cent of the region's industrial employment, and during peak seasons it employed up to 7 000 people.[37] The industry stagnated during the Great Depression but by 1948 employed over 18 000 people.[38] Together with the garment industry, the food-processing industry from the 1920s provided the foundation of the Western Cape economy. Both industries in 1935 employed mainly Coloured people. But whereas the Cape Garment Workers' Union sought to perpetuate this preference for Coloureds, the development of

32. South Africa, *The Industrial Conciliation Amendment Act, 1937.*
33. M. Nicol, "The Garment Workers' Union of the Cape Peninsula", p. 76.
34. R. Cope, *"Comrade Bill"*, pp. 329-331.
35. *Ibid.*
36. R. Close, *"New Life"* (Cape Town, FCWU, 1950), pp. 26-33.
37. Whittingdale, "The Location of Industry", p. 135, Table 7.
38. South Africa, *Industrial Census No. 33,* UG 30/1954, pp. 75-86.

a more radical union in the food and canning industry served to undermine attempts to entrench further racial divisions.

The Food and Canning Workers' Union (FCWU) was formally established on 30 August 1941 after having first built up a strong following
through the organisation of a number of factory branches.[39] Within a
month of its formation, the dismissal of union activists at the Jones
Brothers factory was opposed by a strike by the predominantly
Coloured workforce.[40] The reinstatement of the activists was a direct and
important victory for the Union. However, as Rex Close observed,

> the great achievement of the Jones' strike was ...less tangible but of deeper
> significance and more enduring. For the first time Coloured workers of Paarl
> felt their strength ... They had learnt the power of organisation ... There was
> new hope for the Coloured workers of the Platteland.[41]

Within a month of its formation the Union had instilled a new radicalism amongst Coloured workers and had through their joint organisation
with African workers chiselled at the racial division of labour. By 1942
the FCWU had enlisted over 2 000 members and the Union was well
and widely organised, with branches in Cape Town, Paarl, Wellington,
Groot Drakenstein, Daljosaphat and Worcester.[42] This success is even
more remarkable given the well-known difficulties associated with organising in rural areas. Farmers, rural employers and rural officials in the
Western Cape were more conservative than their urban counterparts
and exercised a particularly coercive system of labour relations which
sought to secure an abundant and obedient supply of labour at low
wages; a web of tied-cottages, the "tot" system (by which wine was provided as payment in kind, and workers were consequently at times
bound to work through alcoholic addiction), the employment of juve-
niles and the indebtedness of workers to the farmers in the Western
Cape served to bind rural workers to their employers. At the same time
the problems of the union activists were compounded by the geograph-
ical isolation of many of the food-processing plants and by the collaboration of rural employers and the police in repeated attempts to intimidate
and harass the union.[43]

In contrast to the Cape Garment Worker's Union, which used the industrial conciliation legislation to exclude the African workers from the

39. R. Close, *"New Life"*, pp. 10-25.
40. *Ibid.* p. 26.
41. *Ibid.*
42. *Ibid.*, p.34.
43. L. Abraham, FCWU Organiser , interview, Paarl, 22 Dec. 1981, transcript p.3; Central
     Archives Pretoria, Evidence to the Cape Coloured Liquor Commission of Inquiry (UG
     33/1945), Pretoria, Dr S. du Plessis, 14 December 1944; B. Bunting, "Liquor and the
     Colour Bar", *Africa South*, Vol.2, No.4, 1958.

industry, the FCWU in 1947 decided to continue operating inside the law by means of establishing a separate union, the African Food and Canning Workers' Union (AFCWU), to function as an unregistered union alongside the registered FCWU. The division of the Union from the outset was a tactic devised to strengthen the commitment of the Union to the organisation of African as well as Coloured workers; the division between the AFCWU and the FCWU was a nominal one which aimed to give the union some protection in law. Despite its legal division, the FCWU remained at the forefront of attempts to forge non-racial organisation in the Western Cape. In the garment industry, unionists had hidden behind the legislation in order to promote a policy of Coloured preference at the expense of Africans. In the food-processing industry and in the docks, by contrast, radical unionists manipulated the legislation to their own advantage.

The dockers of Table Bay, it will be recalled, had since the 1850s organised collectively in defence of their interests. At the turn of the century and again in the period 1919 to 1922, dock-workers of all races joined forces to press their claim for higher wages and improved working conditions. However, by 1924 the replacement, on Abdurahman's insistence, of African workers by Coloured men, together with the increasingly Africanist content of the ICU and the growing political power of White workers, had brought about the strengthening ethnic identification of dock-workers. A radically hierarchical division of labour was entrenched; in it, White workers monopolised supervisory tasks, Coloured workers claimed a growing share of stevedoring, and African workers increasingly were confined to unskilled, heavy manual and cold-storage jobs. But from 1926 a trade union began to overcome some of the racial divisions within the workforce.

In 1926 the stevedores established a registered union, the Cape Town Stevedores and Dockers Workers' Union (CTSDWU).[44] Until 1937 the 700 African stevedores working in the Cape docks were legally members of the Union,[45] but in that year an amendment to the Industrial Conciliation Act forced the Union to exclude Africans. Both in terms of participation in union affairs and in terms of the wage agreement negotiated by the Union, however, African stevedores continued *de facto* to be part of the Union. At the same time, partly in order to prevent wage-undercutting by the African stevedores, the Union secured agreements with management which extended to African stevedores and secured for these dockers minimum wages which were well in excess of

---

44. D. Budlender, "A history of Stevedores", pp. 6-9.
45. *Ibid.,* p.9.

the rates paid to Africans outside the industry. The agreements, which were unique at the time, ensured that Cape Town dockers remained, in the words of R. Cope, "among the best-organised and -paid groups of African workers in the country."[46] Despite being legally excluded from the Union, the CTSDWU continued to operate in a manner designed to minimise the racial division between Coloured and African stevedores. Africans continued to play an active part in union affairs to the extent that, according to the 1951 industrial legislation commission, the CTSDWU was a "body largely organised by Africans".[47]

The CTSDWU was remarkable for its success in overcoming the division between African and Coloured workers which had been an intended outcome of prohibition of African membership of the Union. Whilst the FCWU had maintained its commitment to organising African workers by establishing a separate African unregistered union, the CTSDWU had achieved the same ends by *de jure* excluding Africans whilst they in practice continued their involvement with the Union. The Stevedores' Union, however, was criticised by Communist Party activists, including Alexander, La Guma and Driver, for its failure to advance further the position of unskilled African workers.[48] In 1943 these activists formed the Non-European Railways and Harbour Workers' Union (NERHWU), which by the following year claimed to have an affiliation of 1 300 in the Cape Town docks.[49] This union, together with the unregistered AFCWU, was virtually alone in its endeavour to organise unskilled African workers in the Western Cape. Elsewhere in the country, however, the period of fast economic growth which followed the Great Depression saw the rapid development of unregistered unions; by 1945 over 150 000 unskilled African workers had been organised into 119 unregistered trade unions.[50] The organisation of unskilled Africans was least advanced in the Western Cape. In part, the relatively small size of the African population of the Western Cape, when compared with the other regions of South Africa, accounts for the dearth of unregistered unions in the region. But other factors, and in particular the insecurity of African workers and their subjection to policies of preference for Coloureds, also hampered union organisation.

---

46. R. Cope, *"Comrade Bill"* p. 214.
47. D. Budlender, "A history of Stevedores," p. 15.
48. *Ibid.*
49. K. Luckhardt and B. Wall, *Organise ... or starve. The story of the South African Congress of Trade Unions* (London, Lawrence and Wishart, 1980), p.172.
50. N. Coetzee, "Nie-blanke vakbonde in Suid-Afrika", *Inst. vir bevordering van Calvinisme, Studie Nr. 84*, Sept. 1974, p.12.

Coloured Preference in the Period 1935 — 1948

Since the eighteenth century, African influx into the Western Cape had been strictly regulated. However, at the turn of the twentieth century the African population grew rapidly and by 1904, according to the census, 13 416 Africans resided in the Western Cape.[51] From that time the tightening of the controls further restricted African influx; by 1921 the registered African population had grown by less than 1 000. During the next decade controls associated with the passage of the Native (Urban Areas) Act, and with the introduction of the Civilised Labour Policy and the advent of the Depression, put a further brake on African influx; by 1932 the African population had contracted to 1920 levels. After the Depression, however, the rapid development of manufacturing placed a new premium on the employment of African labour. Between 1932 and 1936 the African population of the Cape Peninsula grew by over 50 per cent, whilst in the following decade the African population more than doubled, from 16 450 in 1936 to 42 580 in 1946. For the Western Cape as a whole, the growth in the African population, after 30 years of near-stagnation, was equally spectacular; in 1921 according to the census only 14 400 Africans resided in the region. By 1936 their numbers had grown to 21 559 and by 1946 to 57 947.

In the period 1935 to 1948 the rapid growth in the African population of the Western Cape was partly due to the development of manufacturing and the accompanying restructuring of the racial division of labour. By 1933 South Africa had begun to recover from the Depression. The manufacturing sector recovered particularly rapidly and between 1932 and 1940 the total industrial labour force in the Western Cape increased by 43 per cent, and between 1940 and 1945 the industrial workforce grew by a further 30 per cent; by 1949 the number of people employed in industry had virtually doubled.[52] In the Western Cape, as was the case elsewhere in South Africa, manufacturing by 1948 had overtaken the primary and tertiary sectors. In 1928 manufacturing had accounted for 13 per cent of national output, compared with 18 per cent for mining and 19 per cent for agriculture.[53] By 1948, whilst the relative share of the primary sectors had declined, manufacturing had increased to the extent that it accounted for 25 per cent of national production.[54]

51. Cape Colony, *Census 1904*, p. cxxxix.
52. Whittingdale, "The Location of Industry", Tables 63, 66, 67.
53. S. van der Horst, "The changing face of the economy", in E. Hellman and H. Lever (eds.), *Race Relations in South Africa, 1929-1979* (London, Macmillan, 1980), p. 98.
54. *Ibid.*

The remarkable growth of manufacturing was mirrored in the growth in industrial employment. In the Western Cape this surge in industrial employment saw an increase in the share of African workers from 14 per cent of the industrial labour force in 1935 to 24 per cent in 1949.[55] The share of Coloured workers increased by a mere 2 per cent, from 44 per cent to 46 per cent, whilst the share of White workers fell from 42 per cent in 1935 to 27 per cent in 1949.[56] Africans, clearly, benefited from the manufacturing revolution although a closer examination of the underlying sexual division of labour reveals that in the Western Cape African women were excluded from employment; in 1949 less than 150 African women were registered in manufacturing employment.[57] On the other hand the number of Coloured women employed in Western Cape industry over the period 1933 to 1949 leapt by 132 per cent, whilst the number of White women employed over the same period grew by 68 per cent.[58] The number of White men employed over the period 1933 to 1949 grew by 62 per cent whilst the number of African men employed increased from 3 500 in 1933 to 23 439 in 1949, a growth of 570 per cent.[59]

African men gained more than Coloured men from the boom in construction which accompanied the economic recovery of the 1930s and which was given added impetus by the construction of defences and stores during the Second World War. Whereas previously Coloured men had dominated the construction industry, African men in 1949 constituted the majority of building employees.[60] But in construction and in other manufacturing sectors African men were confined to unskilled tasks. The employment of African men led to the substitution of unskilled African for unskilled Coloured men, but never threatened the livelihood of skilled Coloured men or White workers. In fact the greatest threat to skilled Coloured men came not from Africans but from the deskilling of their crafts and the employment of semi-skilled Coloured men and women in manufacturing, whilst the biggest threat to White workers came from skilled Coloured workers employed at lower rates of pay.[61]

In 1935 Western Cape employers had not yet begun to feel the pinch on their African labour supplies. The Cape Town City Council, with the

55. S. van der Horst, *Native Labour in South Africa*, p.264; South Africa, *Industrial Census No. 33*, pp.75-86.
56. *Ibid.*
57. *Ibid.*, p.85.
58. South Africa, *Industrial Census No. 16, 1932-1933*, UG 31/1935, Table 2b; South Africa, *Industrial Census No. 33*, Table 2.
59. *Ibid.*
60. *Ibid.*
61. South Africa, *"Coloured Commission, 1937"*, p.61.

approval of local employers, therefore continued to collaborate with the government in the stricter enforcement of influx controls. In May 1935 the Minister of Labour announced that

> The Minister of Native Affairs in conjuction with the City Council of Cape Town is now taking steps to regulate the influx of Natives in the Cape Peninsula.[62]

By 1939, however, the development of manufacturing and the rapid economic recovery had led to a tightening of the labour market and the drying up of what employers termed the "native labour pool".[63] Before long, employers demanded that the controls over recruitment of Africans be eased. The Cape Town City Council, which from the turn of the century had pressed central government to tighten the controls over African influx, by 1939 had been convinced by local employers to reverse its stand. Declaring that it "refused to have any part or lot in the proclamation of Cape Town as a closed area to the native people", the City Council attempted to convince the Government that "so far as native labour is concerned there was ... actually a shortage of labour and not a surplus"[64]. The Government had previously proved a moderating influence on the Council's attempts to regulate African labour; by 1939 it had taken the lead in the enforcement of influx controls. In Parliament the Minister of Native Affairs, Henry Fagan, defended the influx controls on the grounds that "it is considered that unrestricted entry must tend to aggravate the unemployment position particularly as regards the Coloured people"[65]. In response to this assertion Donald Molteno, the opposition Western Cape spokesman, reiterated the findings of the Government's own Commission of Inquiry into Matters Affecting the Coloured Population of the Union. The Commission had concluded that with regard to measures

> . . . controlling the influx of native labour to the urban areas, we are of the opinion that the adoption of such a policy in the case of only one section of the population is economically and ethically unsound.[66]

According to Molteno, "not one single Coloured organisation came before them and asked for discrimination" of the kind which was being proposed by the Minister of Native Affairs.[67]

By 1939 a growing number of Cape employers had begun to call for a relaxation of the influx controls. Nevertheless certain employers' group-

---

62. South Africa, *Senate Debates,* 25 May 1935, Col. 590.
63. South Africa, *HAD,* 1939, Col. 2456.
64. *Ibid.;* S. van der Horst, *Native Labour in South Africa,* p.74, fn.4.
65. South Africa, *HAD,* 1939, 33, Col. 2456.
66. *Ibid.,* Col. 2458.
67. *Ibid.,* Col. 2457-8.

ings, and notably the Cape Engineers, Founders and Shipwrights Association, continued to support stricter controls. In March 1939 its executive
noted that

> this association is of the opinion that the unrestricted influx of Native labour
> into the Cape is, both from a social and public point of view, undesirable, as
> in the Association's view the natural unskilled labour supply is found among
> the Cape Coloured community who are rate-paying citizens.[68]

The "social and public" considerations used by the Shipwrights Association were mobilised to the opposite effect by organisations calling
for the relaxation of the controls. The Commission of Inquiry into Matters Affecting the Coloured Population of the Union in 1937 had called
for the abolition of the controls on the grounds that they were "economically and ethically unsound".[69] In 1943 the *Report of the Commission
of Inquiry into Conditions on the Cape Flats* used similar language to call
for the relaxation of the influx controls. It concluded that

> *employers of Non-European labour should not be subjected to any restraint in
> their choice of employing either Coloured or Native labour and, for this reason, it
> cannot support the plea that special protection be afforded the Coloured worker in
> his competition with the Native in the Cape Division.*[70]

The government, however, refused to budge from its commitment to a
policy of employment preference for Coloureds in the Western Cape.
From June 1939 the City Council was compelled to house all Africans in
the metropolitan area in registered locations.[71] By 1941 over 2 300 African men had been refused entry into the Cape Town municipal area on
the grounds that accommodation was not available for them.[72]

From 1902, it will be recalled, the Department of Native Affairs had
attempted to control African influx into the Cape Peninsula by this
method. From that time African resistance to influx controls increasingly
took the form of squatting; Africans seeking to remain in the urban
areas who were not able to acquire registered accommodation found in
the squatter settlements homes from which they could attempt to live
and work outside the law.

68. Cape Town Chamber of Commerce, Unsorted Archives, Cape Engineers, Founders and
     Shipwrights Association, Minutes of meeting held in Cape Town, March 1939.
69. South Africa, *HAD*, 1939, 33, Col. 2458.
70. South Africa, *Report of the Commission of Inquiry into the Cape Flats and Other Areas,*
     UG 18/1943, para. 89. (Emphasis in original.)
71. M. Budow, Urban Squatting in Greater Cape Town, 1939-1948 (Cape Town Univ.,BA
     (Hons) thesis, 1976), p.39 (in terms of Proclamation 105 of 30 May 1939).
72. South Africa, *Cape Flats Commission,* para. 75-76.

By June 1939 the accomodation-employment nexus had become the focus of the government's attempts to control the influx of Africans into the urban areas. In 1939, the Commission of Inquiry into the Conditions on the Cape Flats found, over 50 000 squatters were living in the Cape Peninsula in "deplorable conditions".[73] These squatters provided a direct challenge to the authorities' renewed attempts to regulate the influx of Africans into the Western Cape. In fact the success of the squatters in evading the authorities in large part facilitated the doubling of the African population of the Greater Cape Town area during the period 1939 to 1948.[74] During this period the number of Africans in registered accomodation increased by less than 10 per cent; the overwhelming majority of Africans who streamed into the Peninsula during the decade preceding National Party rule settled in unregistered accommodation in the Western Cape.[75] By 1948, Oscar Wolheim estimated, over 150 000 squatters were resident in the Greater Cape Town area.[76]

The failure of the government to enforce more strictly its policy of influx control in the Western Cape partly reflected the wartime needs of the economy; the recruitment of Coloureds into the allied force occurred at the same time as the construction of several defence establishments. This caused a temporary shortage of unskilled labour which compelled the government to permit greater recruitment of African labour despite the non-availability of registered accomodation.[77] But this registered employment accounted for only a fraction of African influx; the ineffectiveness of attempts to control urban squatting, rather than any easing in the government's commitment to the influx controls, accounted for the rapid increase in the African urban population in the period 1939 to 1948.

Alf Stadler in his essay on squatter movements in the Johannesburg area has suggested that the remarkable growth in squatter settlements in the 1940s was due primarily to the collapse of the rural reserves and the rapid development of urban employment opportunities at a time when the need for wage income was increased by rises in the prices of staple foodstuffs and shortages of maize.[78] In the Cape Peninsula, we have noted, the government was committed to the particularly strict enforcement of controls to regulate squatting. Nevertheless, the rate of growth

---

73. *Ibid.,* pp.7,17.
74. M. Wilson and A. Mafeje, *Langa* (Cape Town, OUP, 1963),p.2.
75. Budow, *op.cit.,* pp. 35,58.70
76. *Ibid.,* Appendix 1, p.2.
77. City of Cape Town, Mayor's Minutes, *Annual Report of 1943,* p.9.
78. A.W. Stadler, "Birds in the Cornfields: squatter movements in Johannesburg, 1944-1949", in B. Bozzoli (ed.), *Labour, Township and Protest* (Johannesburg, Ravan, 1979), pp. 20-22.

in the African population in that area during the 1940s exceeded that of the Johannesburg area.[79] In the Western Cape the authorities were singularly unsuccessful in their attempts to control African squatting.

The ineffectiveness of the policy of influx control in the Western Cape was due in large part to the refusal of the local authorities or the judiciary to implement either the spirit or the letter of the Native (Urban Areas) Act. The Department of Justice time and time again refused to prosecute Africans who were found to be illegally resident in the Greater Cape Town area.[80] Africans who had been refused registered accomodation in the Peninsula, according to the Cape Flats Commissioners, took up residence "in the peri-urban belt".[81] This area was beyond the jurisdiction of the Cape Town City Council and under the direct control of the Department of Native Affairs.[82] The effective implementation of influx control, however, rested on the powers of search, arrest and deportation which in terms of the amended Urban Areas Act had been given to the police.[83] But the police came under the authority of the Department of Justice, which refused to make stricter controls a priority.[84] In 1942, the Attorney-General of the Cape confirmed that "there had been no prosecutions locally" in terms of the legislation dealing with the illegal residence of Africans in the peri-urban belt.[85] In the Western Cape the Deputy-Commissioner of Police the following year was moved to

> state emphatically that he was not prepared to take action against Natives who are living illegally in the area unless some provision is made for them after they have been evicted from their premises.[86]

There can be little doubt that during the War years the police frustrated the Department of Native Affairs' plans to enforce a policy of stricter influx control in the Western Cape.

The end of the War saw the return to the Western Cape of Coloured and White servicemen. Coloured men, who had prided themselves on their contribution to the allied victory, found in their return to civilian life little reward for their efforts. Their growing disillusionment was aggravated by their belief that the War years had facilitated the employ-

79.   *Ibid.*, p. 19, and Budow , *op.cit.*, Appendix 1.
80.   South Africa, *Cape Flats Commission,* paras. 79-80.
81.   *Ibid.*, para. 79
82.   *Ibid.*, para. 79.
83.   *Ibid.*
84.   *Ibid.*
85.   *Ibid.*
86.   *Ibid.*, para. 80.

ment of unskilled African men at the expense of Coloured men. In Cape Town the six Coloured Councillors in the City Council voiced the resentment of Coloured ex-servicemen and made the Council fully aware of the growth in the African population during the War years. In 1945 it was widely accepted that a surplus of unskilled African and Coloured labour existed in the Western Cape. With employers' demand for unskilled labour temporarily satisfied, the City Council reversed its commitment to an open labour market and reverted to its earlier support for stricter controls over African labour.[87]

The Consolidated Urban Areas Act of 1945 had effect first in the Western Cape. Within months of the passage of the Act, Africans in the region felt the full force of the draconian legislation. By October 1946, over 9 000 Africans had been endorsed out of the region and further influx into the region severely constrained.[88] Employers, in terms of the Act, were from this time on compelled to guarantee the "repatriation" of all African employees not previously resident in the region, whilst the residence of the African population was strictly circumscribed by the notorious Section Ten clauses of the Act.[89] By Section Ten, Africans not legally resident in the urban "prescribed" areas were prevented from entering these areas except under special circumstances.[90] Africans in the reserves were thus effectively trapped in those increasingly desolate areas. The distance of the Western Cape from the closest reserves compounded the difficulties of migrants seeking to travel to the Western Cape and increased the power of the authorities in their bid to control African influx into the Peninsula; the prohibition of rail tickets to unregistered Africans effectively cut off the main routes to the Western Cape.[91] The effect of this measure, which was strongly supported by the Cape Town City Council, according to a 1946 report of the City Council could be "gauged from the fact that the number of Natives which [sic] had arrived at Maitland by the M'bombela train is about 30" whereas previously the number had ranged from 300 to 800.[92]

By 1946 the Cape Town City Council, in collaboration with the central government and local employers, had instituted a strict policy of African influx control in the Western Cape. Influx controls throughout

87. Budow, *op.cit.*, pp. 41-42.
88. *Ibid.*, p.42, citing Major Piet van der Byl.
89. South Africa, *Urban Areas Act,* No. 25 of 1945, Section 10. For an outline of the Act see M. Horrell, *Legislation and Race Relations* (Johannesburg, SAIRR, 1970), pp. 35-45.
90. *Ibid.*
91. Budow, *op.cit.*, p.41.
92. *Ibid.*, and City of Cape Town, Native Affairs Department, *Annual Report, 1946,* (Cape Town, CTCC, 1947), p.8.

South Africa in terms of the Consolidated Urban Areas Act were implemented more strictly than had previously been the case, but, in the
Western Cape, the legislation had had a particularly harsh impact. In
that region the City Council colluded with local employers in order to
implement a policy of labour preference for Coloured men and women.

Summary

In the period 1935 to 1948 the distance between Coloured and African
people increased further. The strict enforcement of influx controls over
Africans served to extend the relative advantages of an assertion of
Coloured identity and to deepen the structural division between African
and Coloured men and women. At the same time, resistance to the government was increasingly divided along racial lines; the ANC pursued a
path to liberation which excluded Coloureds. The Non-European Liberation League and NEUM, although in theory non-racial, were in practice preoccupied with issues of immediate concern to Coloured but not
African people. Only in the trade union movement was there a practical
attempt to challenge and break down the growing barrier between
Coloured and African workers. The Food and Canning Workers' Union
and the CTSDWU combated racial divisions within the workers with
some success. The Cape Garment Workers' Union had the opposite effect, serving to entrench further the racial divisions within the workforce
of the Western Cape.

By 1948 there existed within the Western Cape an ideological and political war of great intensity over the issue of Coloured identity. The
Smuts government had by this time imposed punitive influx controls
over African people and segregated virtually every aspect of their lives
from the remainder of the population. The government had not advanced as far with regard to the Coloured population of the Western
Cape. On the political level the power of Coloured men and women had
been drastically eroded, but the Coloured electorate continued to be
counted on the common voters' roll and to be represented on the Cape
Town City Council. On the economic level Coloured men had been
ousted from virtually all skilled crafts, and the Coloured population,
with some exceptions, had been reduced to an unskilled proletariat.

Coloured workers, however, were able to join registered trade unions
and were not yet subject to statutory job reservations in favour of White
workers. The remaining links between Coloureds and Whites were testi-

mony, we suggest, to the fact that the Smuts government had not fundamentally reviewed pre-existing policies affecting the Coloureds.

In the period 1935 to 1948 existing patterns of preference for Coloureds were entrenched further and a renewed commitment made to the strict control of African influx and residence. The overall effect of these policies, together with the schisms between the ANC and NEUM and other factors discussed above, was that Coloured identity developed rapidly from 1935 to the period of National Party rule.

In establishing the Coloured Affairs Department and the Coloured Affairs Council the Smuts Government provided a focus for resistance in an issue which only affected Coloureds. The fact that resistance was restricted to Coloureds served to stimulate Coloured identity — but this was the unintended outcome of the government's actions rather than the result of a fully developed and coherent attempt on the part of the Smuts administration to develop Coloured identity.

The period 1935 to 1948, we shall show in the following chapters, stands in marked contrast to the era of National Party rule. From the outset the National Party was engaged in a reasonable coherent but increasingly desperate attempt to build a Coloured identity. This active drive was the cause of massive dissent from the regime and a growing challenge to Coloured identity. Ironically, the challenge to Coloured identity was in large part the result of attempts by means of political, economic and social segregation to stimulate the development of separate ethnic identities. It is to an analysis of Coloured identity and Coloured preference in the period of National Party rule that we now turn.

PART TWO
1948 – 1961

CHAPTER FOUR

THE NATIONAL PARTY AND COLOURED IDENTITY: 1948 — 1961

The National Party and the Reconstitution of Coloured Identity

The mobilisation of racial identity in 1948 propelled the National Party into office: ethnic fibres bound together the Party's disparate elements and classes. The Party made racial identification a central plank in its election campaign, and when it came to power this preoccupation was translated into the Party's legislative programme.

The central design of the National Party's scheme, apartheid, had been evolved in the run-up to the election. Apartheid did not entail a complete rejection of the existing system of segregation; rather, it aimed to remould it in terms of an ideology rooted in Afrikaner Christian-nationalism, of which ethnic identification provided a pillar. National Party policy soon became associated with unprecedented attempts to cement ethnic divisions in South Africa.

The victory of the National Party owed much to the successful consolidation of disparate economic classes around a common cause. Under a petty-bourgeois political leadership the resources of Afrikaner agricultural capital were combined with the pooled contributions of Afrikaner workers to provide the financial reserves and the numerical muscle necessary to win the election. In this process, class differences were subsumed in the new-found unity of the Afrikaner "volk". The unity of the "volk", as O' Meara has elaborated, was the vehicle for the success and prosperity for all categories within it.[1]

The notion of "volk" wove together various strands of Afrikaner history and language, rearticulating popular culture in order to mobilise the Afrikaners politically and economically.[2] At the same time the re-arrangement of the webbing binding Afrikaners served to exclude from the "volk" many who might previously have considered themselves Afri-

---

1. D. O'Meara, *Volkskapitalisme — class, capital and ideology in the development of Afrikaner Nationalism, 1934-1948* (Cambridge, CUP, 1983), p. 164.
2. See I. Hofmeyer, "Building a nation from words: Afrikaans language, literature and 'ethnic identity', 1902-1904" (Univ. of London, MA thesis, 1983).

kaners. Afrikaans has been the mother tongue of most people categorised as Coloureds. Yet the ideology of the new "volk" proclaimed that
its purpose was to preserve the purity of the all-White nation. Admission to the "volk" was restricted to White, Afrikaans-speaking Christians. The notion of "volk" crystallised Afrikaner identity and provided
the foundation for the political supremacy of the National Party. Simultaneously, for many Afrikaner Nationalists the unity of the "volk" was
associated with the gospel of Christian-nationalism. In terms of this
philosophical justification for apartheid, the establishment of separate
nations in South Africa was the divine mission of the National Party.[3]

The most urgent task facing the National Party was to resolve the
"native problem". The South African Bureau of Racial Affairs (SA-
BRA) and the Broederbond provided the ideological and organisational
foundations of the party and were entrusted with the reformulation of
state policy. SABRA was an academic institution close to the leadership
of the National Party. The Broederbond was a secret organisation of the
National Party élite. The solution to the "native problem", SABRA and
Broederbond intellects insisted, lay in the segregation of Africans into a
multitude of "nations", each forcibly relocated in fragmented "homelands".[4] The same policy, it was suggested, should be applied to the resolution of the "Coloured" problem.[5] But whereas the support of the
National Party for the African "homeland" policy was unequivocal, the
Party was divided on issues affecting Coloured people. Already by 1950
differences concerning the Coloured "problem" provided a major source
of friction; while within SABRA, the subject of the Coloureds led to
conflicts between the Stellenbosch academics led by Erica Theron and
the Pretoria group led by W.W. Eiselen.[6]

The ambiguity of the Nationalist administration's conception of
Coloured identity was reflected in the imprecision of the definition of
Coloureds in the Population Registration Act of 1950. The Act was re-
garded as a "foundation-stone to the whole apartheid structure."[7] Yet
this pivotal measure could provide no more than a residual definition of
Coloureds, declaring them to be all those who were not defined as
"White" or "Native".[8] The Cape Coloured group was defined to com-

3. O' Meara, *op. cit.,* pp. 68, 175.
4. See, for example, W. Eiselen, "The meaning of apartheid", *Race Relations*, XV, 3,
   1948, pp. 69-86.
5. *Ibid.*
6. E. Theron, interview, transcript, pp. 7-8; see also conflicting views in Central Archives,
   Evidence to the 1954 Commission of Inquiry into the Separate Representation of Voters' Act, "SABRA submission", para. 29
7. *HAD,* 1950, 71, Col. 2651, D.J. van der Heever.
8. South Africa, *Population Registration Act,* No. 30 of 1950, Section 5.

prise one sub-group of the broader Coloured category; it consisted of "persons who are, or who are generally accepted as, members of a race or class known as Cape Coloured."[9]

The Cape Coloureds (henceforth Coloureds) posed a dilemma for the Nationalist. They shared a common language (Afrikaans) and historical homeland (the rural areas of the Western Cape), and many — although this was never publicly admitted — shared a common ancestry. In addition, due to the close involvement of Coloureds in Cape politics and to the language bond, many Cape Nationalists were well disposed to Coloured intellectuals and considered Coloureds to be "brown Afrikaners", "a part of Western civilisation" and deserving of a closer association with the Whites.[10]

The symmetry of apartheid, many prominent Nationalists claimed, demanded the forging of a Coloured "nation", even though it was widely recognised that a national identity did not yet exist amongst the Coloured.[11] The task, as H.S. Erasmus, a Nationalist ideologue, argued in parliament, was for the government to nurture "new ideas and ideologies in the minds of the Coloureds."[12] Paul Sauer, the Minister of Transport and self-appointed nation-builder, expounded at length that

> There has been a tendency among the Coloured people of late for one section to do its best to become White, while another section has been engaged in taking up by the Natives. A sense of national awareness ... has not been developed among them ... and if one wants to stop him from splitting up one can only hope to succeed if one develops that sense of national awareness and that sense of pride in himself and his people [sic].[13]

National Party ideologues talked at length about their ambitions to develop a sense of pride and achievement amongst Coloureds which would herald the birth of a Coloured nation. But in the end their strategy rested on a cruder, but nevertheless effective, two-pronged attack. Recognising that identification is firmly rooted in material experience, the National Party set about restructuring the social, political and economic world inhabited by the people they defined as Coloureds. Before long, interlocking legislation had been introduced which served to segre-

---

9. *Ibid.*
10. See, for example, *Die Burger,* 2 Dec. 1970 and 24 April 1971 (translations from Afrikaans are by author and David Muggleston, for whose assistance I am grateful); *Woord en Daard,* May 1974, p. 4.
11. E. Theron, interview, p. 4.
12. *HAD,* 1951, 71, Col. 2703.
13. *HAD,* 1951, 75, Col. 5426. Sauer, it should be noted, was from the Cape. His commitment to the development of a separate Coloured nation provided a focus for the Cape National Party. Sauer was not, however, in favour of a fully fledged Coloured "homeland".

gate Coloureds and break their links with people defined as White, Native or Asian.

Allied to the realisation that the establishment of a "Whites only" "volk" demanded the forceful extraction of the Coloured components was a clear desire to restrict the absorption into the White population of the Coloured middle class. Until the turn of the century, as Trapido and Watson have shown, it was relatively easy for wealthy and skilled Coloureds to "pass for White".[14] Findlay estimated that by 1936 38 per cent of the people classified as White in the Cape Province were of "mixed descent".[15] Although obviously limited by the lightness or otherwise of the skin pigmentation of the people concerned, the passing process had provided a mechanism for the siphoning of the Coloured petty bourgeoisie into the White political arena, thereby incorporating many of the potential Coloured leaders. Until 1950 "passing for White" remained an escape route for many Coloureds. In that year, however, the passage of the Population Registration Act, the Immorality Amendment Act and the Group Areas Act set out to block many of the remaining avenues of escape.[16]

Legislation governing the interaction of Whites and Coloureds was designed both to prevent Whites from becoming part of the Coloured society and to prevent the movement of people in the opposite direction. By cutting off all escape for the Coloured middle class, the Nationalists hoped to promote the development of that class. It was envisaged that the middle class would provide the intellectual and economic core for the new Coloured nation. Without the inspiration of a successful Coloured élite, it was stated, the Coloured working class would have no ambition to work for an improvement within the apartheid system. The logic of the government's position was outlined by H.J. Erasmus:

> What it will do will be to arouse a sense of national pride in the Coloureds. In the past ... their chief aim has been to filter into the ranks of the Europeans ... By means of the different laws we have enacted, for example, the Prohibition of Mixed Marriages Act, the door is being closed to them and they are given the opportunity in their own ranks to aspire to a higher status for themselves ... They will now attain a separate status.[17]

---

14. S. Trapido, "The Origins and development of the African Peoples' Organisation", Institute of Commonwealth Studies, *Collected Seminar Papers on the Societies of Southern Africa, Vol. 1* (London ICS, 1970), pp. 90-91; G. Watson, "Passing for White" (London, 1970), p. 120.
15. G. Findlay, *Miscegenation* (Pretoria, *Pretoria News*, 1936), p. 44.
16. For a discussion of the legislation see M. Horrell, *Legislation and Race Relations* (Johannesburg, SAIRR, 1971), pp. 9-84; A. Suzman, *Race Classification and Definition* (Johannesburg, SAIRR, 1960).
17. *HAD*, 1950, 71, Col. 2703.

It was not long before Coloureds felt the brunt of apartheid. The first apartheid measure to be introduced in the Western Cape introduced segregation on trains in the Cape Peninsula. This measure affected passengers travelling first class and its impact was thus mainly restricted to petty-bourgeois Coloureds.

A few months later, by the Prohibition of Mixed Marriages Act, marriage across the statutory racial divides was declared illegal. In 1950 the Population Registration Act and Group Areas Act continued the process of segregation.[18] The aim, the Minister of the Interior, T.E. Dönges, roundly declared, was "to remove the points of contact" between people defined to be members of different racial groups.[19]

Miscegenation was an anathema to apartheid. Nationalists insisted that the survival of the White race was threatened by the merest trace of non-White blood. Coloureds were singled out for particular attention. Poor-Whites, it was widely recognised, had for years resided alongside Coloureds in District Six and other areas of Cape Town. The assertion of distinct ethnic identities demanded that these communities be destroyed and that legislation be enforced which would prevent miscegenation and residential mixing of races. According to Nationalist parliamentarians, the mixed residential areas of Cape Town were the "death-beds of the European race" in which poor Whites stood "in danger of being absorbed by the Coloured community" and where there is "the inevitable miscegenation".[20] Urban segregation, Nationalists explained, would prevent the "colour feelings of the Europeans becoming dulled" and thereby guarantee the "White man's protection".[21]

The National Party's victory at the 1948 polls was secured with a slim majority of five seats.[22] The role of the 50 000 Coloureds eligible to vote was regarded by the Party as a serious threat to the survival of the government, as the Coloured vote was considered to be decisive in seven constituencies.[23] The removal of the remaining Coloured common roll representation, it was argued within the Party, would bring several seats within the grasp of the Party.[24] The Separate Representation of Voters Act of 1951 may be understood at least in part as a means to further this objective. But this measure also had a deeper significance; the disfranchisement of the Coloureds, together with their complete segrega-

18. See Horrell, *Race Relations*, pp. 9-21, 35-45.
19. *HAD*, 1951, 68, Col. 5387.
20. Cited in M. November, "The Origins of the Group Areas Act" (University of London, MA thesis, 1981), p. 16.
21. *Ibid.*, p. 17.
22. L. Marquard, *The Peoples and Politics of South Africa* (Oxford, OUP, 1962), p. 80.
23. *Ibid.*
24. E. Theron, interview, p. 4.

tion in terms of the Population Registration Act, Group Areas Act and other legislation, was a focal point of National Party ideology.

In 1951 the Separate Representation of Voters Bill was tabled for discussion. Five years later, after steam-rollering through constitutional and extra-parliamentary resistance, the Act was implemented.[25] The Act removed the remaining direct representation of Coloureds in parliament and provided for the representation of Coloureds on a separate voters' roll. The legislation, the Minister of the Interior argued, was designed to "place the Coloured vote beyond the zone of fear"[26]. In so doing the Nationalists were able to disfranchise a source of vocal opposition which, Paul Sauer explained, many Whites saw "as a threat to the survival of the white race"[27]. The disfranchisement of Coloureds led to the further alienation of many Coloureds from the regime. Many Nationalists feared that this would inevitably lead Coloureds to add momentum to the campaign of resistance being waged against the Nationalist government.

Nationalist Dissent

In 1948 the election victory of the National Party was secured by an alliance of highly differentiated, shifting and at times contradictory class interests. The divergent sectional interests within the party at certain times aligned themselves along provincial lines. The federal structure of the National Party facilitated this regionalism and the relatively autonomous provincial parties over time developed their own ideological and political priorities. These commitments reflected the particular social basis of each province's membership and leadership. Each provincial party, Dan O'Meara has shown, represented a distinct class alliance.[28] The Transvaal Party in the 1950s was built on an alliance of White workers with the Afrikaner petty bourgeoisie and farmers. The Broederbond and SABRA exercised great influence on the ideological development of this alliance. These organisations were less influential in the Cape National

25. For a discussion of the process by which the constitution was manipulated see W. Beinart, "The Political and Constitutional Crisis over the Separate Representation of Voters Act" (Univ. of Cape Town, BA (Hons) thesis, 1971).
26. *HAD*, 1957, 68, Col. 5388.
27. *HAD*, 1957, 68, Col. 5429.
28. D. O'Meara, "'Muldergate', the politics of Afrikaner nationalism and the crisis of the capitalist state in South Africa", Seminar Paper, Dar es Salaam, 1980, p. 13, and D. O'Meara, *Volkskapitalisme*, p. 251.

Party, which rested on an alliance of relatively wealthy Afrikaner farmers with a small number of capitalists based in Sanlam and other financial institutions. The Cape party was thus closely associated with large business concerns whilst the Transvaal party was more representative of White workers and the Afrikaner petty bourgeoisie.

The influence which the diverse constituencies of the National Party were able to exercise depended to a large extent on the warring factions' abilities to secure the appointment of their candidates to key posts in the state legislature and executive. The ability of the Transvaal party to secure control over the Department of Native Affairs provided the party with the means to implement its apartheid strategy. The ascendancy of the Transvaal party in 1958 was confirmed with the appointment of Verwoerd as Prime Minister. The Transvaal Party was unequivocal in its commitment to a separate Coloured identity. Coloureds were regarded as a distinct race and, in terms of the Christian-nationalist apartheid scheme, were destined to develop their own national consciousness. Verwoerd referred to the Coloureds as a "nation in the making"[29]. For Verwoerd the implication was that

> We definitely do not accept that there will be integration or intermingling of the political structure for the Coloured and for the White man.[30]

Verwoerd proposed instead the establishment of a segregated parliament, executive and administration for Coloureds.[31]

The sense of purpose which informed the National Party's political programme for Coloureds was less evident in matters concerning the establishment of a Coloured nation state. For although the Transvaal National Party was unequivocal in its commitment to such an independent identity for Coloureds, there was little agreement on the precise formula for its implementation. Influential members of SABRA promoted the immediate establishment of an independent homeland for Coloureds and plans were drawn up for the location of such a homeland in the South-Western Cape.[32] Other SABRA members, however, advocated a more gradual approach, suggesting that a Coloured nation had not yet been built and that the establishment of a Coloured homeland was a long-term rather than an immediate concern.[33] The gradualists also pointed to the fact that Coloureds constituted over half of the Western Cape popu-

29. *The Cape Times,* 13 Dec. 1980, citing Verwoerd in 1959.
30. *Ibid.*
31. South Africa, "Policy Statement issued by the Deputy Minister of Interior", 17 May 1961, p. 5.
32. E. Theron, interview, pp. 4-5.
33. *Ibid.*

lation and could not practically be relocated outside the region. The practical problems associated with attempts to establish a Coloured homeland, together with the pressing strategic concerns which had been highlighted by the campaign of defiance to the regime, led Verwoerd to favour the gradualist approach.[34] He announced that the establishment of a Coloured homeland "was not practical politics".[35] Instead he recommended the development of Coloured self-government "within a White state".[36]

The programme adopted by the Verwoerd government was strongly criticised by many National Party members. In the main, attitudes to Verwoerd's strategy polarised along the north-south divide, with many members of the Cape National Party recommending that Coloureds be exempted from the apartheid political programme. But the extent of regional polarity should not be overemphasised. A minority of Transvaal nationalists were also opposed to Verwoerd's scheme. Included in their number were 15 Afrikaner academics who in 1955 signed a declaration condemning the removal of Coloureds from the voters' roll "on both moral and constitutional grounds".[37] One of the signatories, Prof Kleynhans, later explained that the academics had been opposed to the fact that party leadership had "brainwashed" its supporters into thinking of Coloureds as a threat to White supremacy in South Africa.[38]

In the Cape, Verwoerd's plans were opposed by National Party members of parliament who over time had cultivated a loyal Coloured constituency. Coloured voters, fearing the implications of apartheid, had lent their support to opposition candidates in the 1948 elections. This, we have noted, reinforced the commitment of many Nationalists to the disfranchisement of Coloureds. Some Cape Nationalists, however, held a different view, suggesting that Coloureds would respond to concessions from the government by lending their support to National Party candidates.[39] These advocates of a more incorporative stance pointed towards the Coloured electoral support which Hertzog had enjoyed between 1924 and 1932. In the 1930s and 1940s, it was noted, a number of National Party members of parliament including Bruckner de Villiers

---

34. *Ibid.*
35. *HAD,* 1961, 107, Col. 4191.
36. *Ibid.*
37. W. Vosloo, "The Coloured Policy" in N. Rhoodie (ed.), *South African Dialogue,* p. 380; see also *Star* (Airmail), 22 May 1982.
38. *Ibid.*
39. Central Archives, Evidence to Commission of Inquiry into the Separate Representation of Voters Bill, Record 3813.

(Stellenbosch), J.M. van Zyl (Ladismith) and A. Badenhorst (Riversdale) had depended on the support of Coloured voters.[40]

D.F. Malan had exercised a powerful influence over the development of the National Party. In 1923 Malan had written that

> Segregation obviously is only for the Native. Segregation of the Coloureds is not only impossible but also unnecessary ... The Coloureds can, and with the necessary guidance and sympathetic treatment will, become the pivot of the defence of the European and his civilisation.[41]

Dr Malan was regarded by many Nationalists as the father of Afrikaner nationalism. His attitudes regarding Coloureds, many Cape Nationalists believed, legitimised their incorporative strategy. In 1931, whilst Minister of Interior in Hertzog's cabinet, Malan had attempted to persuade parliament that

> The Natives can be dealt with on the segregation principle, but the position of the Coloured people is different ... The same political rights that we give to the Europeans must in principle also be given to them.[42]

In 1948 Malan himself became Prime Minister. But those expecting him to honour his earlier sentiments regarding Coloureds would have been bitterly disappointed; for before long he had taken the lead in furthering the political and social segregation of Coloureds. Many Cape Nationalists, however, refused to revoke their deep-rooted commitment to an incorporative strategy. Amongst those advocating a more cautious approach were Professor Erica Theron of Stellenbosch University and P.W. Botha, the Nationalist MP for George who was later to become Prime Minister and State President.[43]

The Cape Nationalists who favoured a more incorporative strategy were opposed to the disfranchisement of Coloureds, which, they argued, would serve only to increase opposition to the government and increase the identification of the Coloured élite with the African mass organisations. Other aspects of the Malan programme for Coloureds were warmly endorsed by the Cape Nationalists, who in particular strongly supported the policy of preference for Coloureds in the Western Cape devised by Eiselen and his SABRA collegues. Cape Nationalists were keen to promote Coloured interests and had no quarrel with measures which would prevent African work-seekers from entering employment in the Western Cape.

40. *Ibid.*, Records 3813-3832.
41. *Ibid.*, "United Party Evidence", para. 95.
42. *HAD.* 1931, 16, Col. 986.
43. E. Theron, interview, pp. 3-4.

The Coloured Labour Preference Policy

The SABRA ideologues insisted that the construction of a distinct
Coloured nation could be achieved only through the rearranging of the
material circumstances in which Coloureds found themselves. It was essential, they argued, that Coloureds regard themselves as distinct from
Africans. The undermining of non-European unity became a strategic
priority. A range of measures was adopted which sought to reinforce the
existing distinctions between Coloureds and Africans. A legacy of divide
and rule had already given Coloureds advantages over Africans.
Coloureds were not compelled to carry passes and were not governed by
influx-control legislation. They also had not been directly affected by
measures designed to undermine trade unions and prevent squatting.
From 1948, however, the position of Coloureds deteriorated sharply as
they fell victim to legislation designed to institute residential segregation, disfranchisement and job reservation. At the same time their position was improved relative to Africans: this was achieved through an
unprecedented attack on the African population of the Western Cape.

The Western Cape was regarded by SABRA as the "natural homeland" of the Coloureds and it was in this region that the regime planned
to nurture a Coloured nation.[44] In 1951 it was estimated that 35 per cent
of the Coloured population lived in the Western Cape.[45] Clearly, any
resolution of the thorny question of Coloured identity would have to
take into account the fact that the Western Cape was the home for the
largest concentration of Coloureds. The reluctant recognition of this fact
fuelled the concern of many Nationalists who saw in the Western Cape a
final refuge for White South Africans — a "White homeland".[46] In the
apartheid models the destiny of the Whites was not interwined with that
of the Africans; but the division between the Coloureds and the Whites
was less clear-cut, and led to calls for the elevation of the Coloureds. As
J. Albertyn, a prominent Cape Nationalist, explained,

> We and the Coloureds are here together and we have to live together. That's
> why we have to get the low class of Coloured uplifted, so that he becomes a
> better neighbour.[47]

The disfranchisement of the Coloureds and the enforcement of Group
Areas Legislation had not paved the way for an amicable relationship.

---

44. W. Eiselen, "The Coloured People and the Natives", *Journal of Racial Affairs,* VI, 3,
    1955.
45. South Africa, *Union Statistics for Fifty Years* (Pretoria, Govt. Printer, 1960), A-4.
46. E. Theron, interview, p. 4.
47. J. Albertyn, interview, Cape Town, 22 Jan. 1982, transcript p. 6.

The disaffection of the Coloureds threatened to disrupt the apartheid plans as growing numbers of Coloureds joined the resistance to the regime. In an effort to reduce the damage done but at the same time defend their apartheid scheme SABRA strategists suggested incorporating Coloureds through a Coloured labour preference policy. In 1953 Dr Malan, the prime minister, and Dr Verwoerd, the Minister of Native Affairs, outlined the terms of the bargain when they told a delegation of Coloured notables that

> If you agree to be removed from the common voters' roll, then we would be prepared to talk to our people to provide the means for your development.[48]

The intention of the Department of Native Affairs was to phase Africans out of the Western Cape and replace African with Coloured labour. The department in one stroke intended to achieve two objectives: enforce apartheid through the denial of African residence and employment rights in the Western Cape, and incorporate Coloureds by giving them labour preference. The fortunes of Coloureds were thus inversely related to the predicament of Africans.

The employment preference policy of the National Party was implemented first amongst the government's own employees. Within a year of coming to power 1 696 Africans had been replaced by 1 290 Whites and 406 Coloureds.[49] Building on the existing legislation, the Party immediately set about extending the controls over the employment, residence and movement of Africans. Government Notice 1032 of May 1949 prevented African work-seekers from remaining in the Cape Peninsula for more than 14 days a year.[50] In 1952 the Native Law Amendment Act further streamlined the controls over the residence of Africans in the prescribed (urban) areas. At the same time, the movement of Africans out of the reserves was curtailed. By 1953 this and other legislation had provided the means to implement a strict control over all Africans in the Western Cape. Women in the Western Cape first bore the full onslaught of the apartheid attack. By December 1954 20 000 women had been registered and their employment and residence made dependent on the production of an official permit.[51] The Institute of Race Relations noted in 1954 that "influx control is operated even more strictly in the Western

---

48. Cited in D. Woods (ed.), *Conference at Bulugha: South Africa's first all-race assembly* (East London *Daily Dispatch,* 1951), p. 5.
49. M. Horrell (comp.), *Survey of Race Relations, 1950-1951* (Johannesburg SAIRR, 1951), p. 50.
50. G. Lawrence, interview, Cape Town, 1 Dec. 1981, transcript, p. 5.
51. M. Horrell (comp.), *Survey of Race Relations, 1956-1957* (Johannesburg, SAIRR, 1957), p. 71.

Cape than elsewhere in the Union."[52] The attack on Africans in the Western Cape signalled the initiation of the Coloured Labour Preference Policy.

W.W. Eiselen, Verwoerd's Secretary of Native Affairs and first lieutenant, explained in 1955 that

> Briefly and concisely put, our Native policy regarding the Western Province amis at the ultimate elimination of Natives from this region.[53]

The policy was designed to implement SABRA's plan for a Coloured nation. Eiselen elaborated by saying that the labour preference policy was involved with the

> weal and the woe of the Coloured people and the question of whether they are to be offered the opportunity of progressive development ... The influx and residence for long periods of Natives in the Western Province may well lead to the moral decline and economic impoverishment of the Coloured community ... Even the use of Native migrant workers, which is perfectly permissible in ordinary European areas, can only be permitted in this part of the country, with its permanent Coloured population, as a temporary expedient.[54]

By 1956 the scheme had left a trail of destruction and despair, and 5 000 women had been "endorsed out" of the Western Cape.[55] From this time, the regime turned its attention to the rest of the African population. By 1962 over 30 000 Africans had been endorsed out of the region.[56] Permission to remain rested on the continued employment of the remaining Africans in jobs which Coloureds were unwilling or unable to occupy. The unprecedented attacks on Africans in the Western Cape led, as was hoped, to the assertion of Coloured identity by people desperate to escape the full force of the Coloured Preference Policy.[57] "Passing for Coloured" in the 1950s became as important to working-class people as "passing for White" had been to petty-bourgeois people in the past. Draconian legislation attempted to raise impenetrable barriers to passing for White or passing for Coloured. Nevertheless, passing for Coloured in the 1950s took place on a wide scale.

The Coloured Labour Preference Policy was intimately linked, then,

---

52. M. Horrell (comp.), *Survey of Race Relations, 1953-1954* (Johannesburg, SAIRR, 1954), p. 41.
53. W. Eiselen, *op. cit.*, p. 32
54. *Ibid.*
55. M. Horrell, *Survey 1956-1957*, p. 71.
56. *HAD,* 1962, 108, Col. 1542.
57. R.E. van der Ross, interview, Cape Town, 13 Dec. 1981, transcript, p. 9; L. Abraham, interview, Paarl, 19 Nov. 1981, transcript, p. 5; E. Theron, interview, p. 6; N. Alexander, interview, Cape Town, 25 Nov. 1981, transcript, p.4

with attempts to reconstitute a distinct Coloured "nation" in South Africa. The implementation of the policy was associated with the ascendancy of the Transvaal National Party and the SABRA ideologists under the leadership of Verwoerd. These people aimed to construct a separate political structure for the Coloureds.[58] Arguing that "we definitely do not accept that there will be intermingling of the political structure for the Coloured and for the white man"[59], Verwoerd and his allies demanded the disfranchisement of the Coloureds on the grounds that "they are a race which has completely different racial characteristics."[60] Political equality, the SABRA ideologists argued, was the antithesis of their nation-building plans. For, as a prominent Transvaal nationalist declared,

> If we have political equality, why cannot we also have social equality? ... This is the root of the dangerous attitude of the Coloured people today ... The Coloured people are, after all, a subordinate non-European race.[61]

In the view of SABRA and the Transvaal National Party, the restructuring process and the Coloured Preference Policy would instil in the Coloured people a national identity. Or as Paul Sauer insisted, the aim was "to develop a national consciousness amongst the Coloured people."[62]

Other prominent members of the Cape National Party, however, were opposed to notions of a separate Coloured nation. They saw in the policy of preference an opportunity to enhance the position of Coloureds and to narrow the division between what Piet Marais, the National Party MP for Malmesbury, termed "brown and White Afrikaners".[63] Already, by 1960, the issue of Coloured political identity was proving to be the Achilles heel of Afrikaner unity. In the 1950s, as was to be the case for the next three decades, much of the tension over the issue of Coloured political identity related to Coloured parliamentary representation.

During the 1950s Cape Nationalists were unsuccessful in their defence of the Coloured franchise. However, the campaign of defiance which peaked in 1960 heightened the strategic concerns of the National Party and led to a reconsideration of the Coloured franchise. Fearing the alienation of Coloureds, Cape Nationalists campaigned for the direct representation of Coloureds in parliament. In the main, their campaign

---

58. *HAD*, 1961, 107, Cols. 4192-3, H.F. Verwoerd; *HAD*, 1981, 10, Col. 3737, C.P. Mulder.
59. *The Cape Times*, 13 Dec. 1980, citing Verwoerd in 1959.
60. *HAD*, 1957, 68, Col. 5588, J.E. Potgieter.
61. *HAD*, 1951, 68, Cols. 5587-93, J.E. Potgieter.
62. *HAD*, 1951, 75, Col. 5426.
63. P. Marais, interview, Malmesbury, 21 Jan. 1982, transcript, p. 3.

was conducted through the Cape National Party's mouthpiece, *Die Burger* newspaper. In July 1960, according to "Dawie", the paper's political commentator,

> The drive to a forward movement in Nationalist policy for the Coloureds is becoming stronger and stronger. The most dramatic idea of course is that the principle of the representation of Coloureds in parliament must be recognised, or, put in other words, that Coloureds must be permitted to elect white or brown members ... My impression is that the National Party is already more than half-way in agreement with the principle, and can be completely won for it by strong leadership. The time is approaching for a decision.[64]

Throughout the latter half of 1960, constant prompting by editorials and reports in *Die Burger* fuelled "an overwhelming debate" within the ruling party over the question of Coloured representation.[65] Finally, the cabinet gave approval to a "new vision" for the Coloured people.[66] But Verwoerd, to the bitter disappointment of many Nationalists, firmly rejected direct parliamentary representation for Coloureds.[67] Instead he proposed "Coloured self-government within a White state."[68] His concern was to place Coloureds in a position of preference to Africans whilst at the same time preventing them from rising to the level of Whites. For, as he later explained,

> If the minority group becomes the tail that wags the dog ... surely it is much better to give such a minority limited powers and opportunities ... ensuring at the same time by means of an entrenched section in the constitution that the white man retains absolute supremacy.[69]

The "new vision" frustrated the ambitions of many Cape Nationalists and prompted an unprecedented public debate in *Die Burger*. The paper reported that

> There has never been such a stream of letters on a subject as that which is now overwhelming us in connection with the National Party's Coloured Policy.[70]

The paper in its editorial columns suggested that the Transvaal Party exercised a stranglehold over National Party policy and commented bitterly that it appeared that "nothing which can bring the Coloureds and

64. *Die Burger*, 23 July 1960.
65. *Ibid.; Die Burger*, 19 Sept. 1960. Die Burger, 17 Nov. 1960; *Die Burger*, 26 Nov. 1960; *Die Burger*, 3 Dec. 1960;
66. *Die Burger*, 17 Nov. 1960.
67. *HAD*, 1961, 107, Col. 4191; E. Theron, interview, p. 7.
68. *HAD*, 1961, 107, Col. 4191.
69. *South African Digest*, XII (17), 1965, p. 5.
70. *Die Burger*, 10 Dec. 1960.

Afrikaners closer together must be allowed to succeed!"[71] The paper's
political columnist accepted that although

> the people who are well-disposed to the idea of direct representation for
> Coloureds are in a minority in the Afrikaner ranks, they are a large minority.
> They are also not insignificant.[72]

In its editorials, the paper argued that the Cape National Party should
determine Coloured policy as the Coloureds were "more convincingly a
Cape responsibility" than a Transvaal responsibility.[73] Prominent Cape
Nationalists, the paper had on another occasion reported, believed that
as "the Coloureds have not got their own homeland they must be represented with the Whites in parliament."[74]

Strategic Concerns

By 1960 the campaign of defiance waged against the regime brought a
renewed vigour to the attempts by the cabinet to foster a client
Coloured group. The Minister of Finance, Dr Dönges, drew attention to
the urgency of the situation, declaring that

> The disturbances have taught us another lesson to which the Government has
> also directed attention previously. The lesson is that in those areas where the
> Coloured community forms the natural source of labour, it is wrong to im-
> port Bantu in large numbers, and eventually to create two unprosperous com-
> munities.[75]

The call by the Minister of Finance for stricter controls over Africans
was endorsed by the Minister of Interior and by all the Boland MPs
who, according to *Die Burger*, felt that

> Work must be done on a dramatic scale to implement the policy of removing
> Africans systematically from the Boland.[76]

According to another MP given prominence in *Die Burger*, every
"self-respecting White" should make an "obsession" of getting rid of
Africans from the Western Cape.[77] "The carrying through of the plan in
the Western Cape," the MP declared, "is of the greatest importance,

71. *Ibid.*
72. *Die Burger*, 3 Dec. 1960.
73. *Ibid.*
74. *Die Burger*, 26 Nov. 1960.
75. *HAD.* 1960, 106, Col. 8342, T.E. Dönges.
76. *Die Burger*, 2 Dec. 1961.
77. *Die Burger*, 5 Dec. 1961.

and has been given priority by the government."[78] During this period of crisis, according to the Afrikaans political scientist I.P. de Swardt,

> A part of the White population of the Western Cape were convinced that their safety lay in the ultimate disappearance of Africans from the Western Cape.[79]

According to the National Party representative for Malmesbury, the establishment of a "cleaner whitemansland" in the Western Cape had become a government priority[80]; "We must," he told a public rally, "concentrate everything behind the government's plans for greater action in the disappearance of Bantus from the Western Cape."[81]

The threat of mass resistance which peaked in 1960 strengthened the hand of those who favoured a stricter application of the Coloured labour preference policy. It also served to reinforce the arguments of those Cape Nationalists who sought to promote a closer political alliance with Coloureds. For, with a few notable exceptions, Coloured men and women had not participated in the defiance campaign of the 1950s and the demonstrations which culminated in the declaration of a state of emergency; and according to the Minister of the Interior, "the Coloured community stood calmly on the side of law and order"[82], in marked contrast to the African population of the Western Cape.

The failure of Coloureds to support the campaign of resistance was thus seized upon by those Nationalists supporting a closer alliance with Coloureds. At the same time, the threat posed by the resistance served to underline the necessity of maintaining the division between Coloured and African people. It was noted that a tide of mass resistance to White rule had swept through Africa and now threatened to unite non-Whites in South Africa in a direct onslaught on the regime. As W.C. Malan, the National Party member of parliament for Paarl, told his constituents:

> What does it matter that we in South Africa are getting richer and wealthier if we lose our fatherland ... Take notice what has happened to the rich Whites of the Congo, Tanganyika, Kenya and other African states.[83]

The only solution available to the government in the Western Cape,

78. *Die Burger*, 24 Sept. 1962, F.S. Steyn.
79. I.P. de Swardt, "Administratiewe beheer oor die beweeg na en vertoef van Bantoes in die omskrewe studiegebied Suidwes-kaapland" (Stellenbosch Univ., MA thesis, 1974), p. 30.
80. *Die Burger*, 15 Sept. 1961, P. Marais.
81. *Ibid.*
82. *HAD*, 1960, 10, Col. 5371, J. de Klerk.
83. *Die Burger*, 28 Sept. 1962.

Malan and has colleagues in the Cape National Party suggested, was the systematic removal of Africans from the Western Cape.

From 1960 the administration began to implement even more strictly its Coloured Labour Preference Policy. The position of Africans deteriorated rapidly as they were subject to increased harassment and control. Between January 1959 and March 1962 over 23 000 Africans were deported from the Cape Peninsula.[84] Included in this number were many people classified as "idle and undesirable", a clause widely interpreted to include militant unionists and other "trouble-makers".[85]

Summary

By 1961 Coloured identity had become an ideological battleground of great intensity within the National Party. Under the leadership of Malan and Verwoerd the Party remained firmly committed to the development of a distinct Coloured identity. In the long run, it was believed, the full flowering of such an identity would be expressed in the development of a Coloured nation. The policy of the National Party leadership thus stood in marked contrast to that of previous governments; at no stage had Smuts or Hertzog articulated a strategy for forging a distinct Coloured ethnic grouping.

In the 1950s the National Party was apt to be split along provincial lines — north (Transvaal) and south (Cape) — in its conflict over Coloured identity. All sections of the Party, however, supported the policy of Coloured Labour Preference, which aimed to improve the relative position of Coloured people in the Western Cape at the expense of Africans. The policy represented a particularly strict enforcement of the country-wide plan to limit the employment and residence of Africans in the White (prescribed) areas.

National Party efforts to promote racial identities were associated with a massive programme of legislation. Within three years of coming to power, the Party had invaded virtually every aspect of Coloured people's lives in order to limit their contact with people defined as African, Asian or White. This process of segregation served to fuel the antagonism of the Coloured people towards the state, particularly when this extended to the abolition of Coloureds' parliamentary representa-

84. *HAD,* 1962, 108, Col. 1542.
85. C. Tinto, interview, Cape Town, 8 Jan. 1982, transcript, p. 4; A. Mafeje, interview, New York, 11 Sept. 1982, transcript, p. 2.

tion and the forced removals of Coloureds in terms of the Group Areas Act. The commitment of the National Party to a distinct Coloured identity partly reflected the strategic concerns of the Party and its determination to incorporate a section of the non-White population. At the same time the discrimination against Coloureds — which was part and parcel of the attempt to entrench racial divisions — led to the massive alienation of Coloured people from the government.

CHAPTER FIVE

EMPLOYERS AND THE COLOURED PREFERENCE POLICY: 1948 — 1961

Introduction

By 1880 employers in the Western Cape were complaining of a "serious want of labour".[1] Their response was to recruit African workers from as far afield as Mozambique. African workers were prepared to accept lower wages than the fully proletarianised workers resident in the Western Cape and were also considered by many employers to be less militant and harder-working than the Coloured workforce. By 1900 African workers in the Western Cape had replaced "Cape Boys" in many arduous unskilled tasks and a racial hierarchy in employment had been established. As the principal employer in the Cape Town docks, A.R. McKenzie, explained, "Cape Boys" were preferred for more skilled tasks as they were "well trained and experienced".[2] However, for unskilled and heavy manual tasks "Natives from up-country" were "compounded".[3]

From 1900 to 1948 the pattern of recruitment became further entrenched and employers became convinced that only African workers were suitable for employment as heavy manual labourers. But employers never advocated that Africans should be free to seek work in the Western Cape. On the contrary, from 1901 to 1937 they criticised the failure of the central authorities to control the influx of African labour into the region. Their call for influx controls was muted in times of unskilled labour shortage while in times of labour surplus, as was the case from 1921 to 1934, they were particularly robust in their condemnation of unimpeded African influx. Again from 1937 to 1943, the rapid development of manufacturing industry and the demands of the War economy were associated with a less vigorous defence of state regulation over African influx. By 1945, however, employers had renewed their commitment to a stricter enforcement of the controls.

---

1. Cited in Greenberg, *"Race and State"*, pp.151-2. (See Chapter One.)
2. Cited in Bickford-Smith, "Black labour", p.87.
3. Cited in Saunders, "Ndabeni", p.138.

In 1950, over 23 500 African men were employed in Western Cape industry, the African industrial workforce having doubled in the previous decade.[4] In the Western Cape, African men accounted for over a quarter of the industrial labour force and in agriculture and construction outnumbered other workers.[5] Since the turn of the century, African women had been excluded from Cape industry and in 1950 only 150 African women were registered in industrial employment in the Western Cape; African women were employed in domestic service and in agriculture. Coloured and White women accounted for 27 per cent of the region's industrial labour force; 8 per cent of these women were Coloured whilst 5 per cent were White. White men constituted 21 per cent and Coloured men 28 per cent of the industrial labour force.

In 1949, according to a survey of Cape Peninsula employers conducted by Sheila van der Horst, 90 per cent of Africans were employed in unskilled tasks, compared with 30 per cent of Coloured employees and 1 per cent of White workers.[6] 48 per cent of Coloured workers were classified as semi-skilled, whilst 8 per cent of Africans and 6 per cent of Whites were classed in this category. 93 per cent of White employers were skilled. By contrast, only 15 per cent of Coloured workers and a mere 2 per cent of Africans occupied skilled jobs.

By 1948 a racially hierarchical division of labour was thus firmly established. In terms of this hierarchy, African workers were restricted to unskilled occupations, Coloureds to unskilled and semi-skilled jobs, and White employees exercised a near monopoly over skilled occupations. The National Party, which came to power in 1948, was committed to the extension of this already well-established pattern of employment. The Coloured Preference Policy, it will be recalled, was aimed at placing Coloured men at an advantage to Africans through the strict enforcement of African influx controls and the "ultimate elimination of Natives" from the Western Cape.[7]

4. South Africa, *Industrial Census No. 34,* UG 30/1954, p.75.
5. *Ibid.*
6. This paragraph is based on S. van der Horst, "A note on Native Labour turnover and the structure of the labour force in the Cape Peninsula", *SAJE,* Vol. 25, No. 4, Dec. 1957, Tables 5 to 7.
7. W. Eiselen, "The Coloured People and the Natives", p.15.

Employers and the Coloured Preference Policy

From the turn of the century, employers in the Western Cape had attached a caveat to their commitment to influx controls; they had demanded that any system brought into existence should not restrict their freedom to hire and fire African workers. They insisted that influx controls should at no time threaten the existence of a "labour pool" of unemployed African workers in the urban areas.[8] Without such a "pool", their ability to secure a stable workforce at low wages and to dismiss workers during times of slack business activity or industrial unrest would have been severely restricted.

Cape employers had originally demanded the introduction of influx controls and had acted in collaboration with the central government in the implementation of the controls. From 1937 to 1945, however, the relationship between employers and the Department of Native Affairs had been strained. During the first five years of National Party rule a better working relationship was once again established. In 1954 the Western Cape Urban Areas Commissioner assured Cape employers that their demands would continue to be met.[9] Verwoerd, the Minister of Native Affairs, promised that "he would not induce sudden changes or adopt an unreasonable attitude to the needs of industry", and that "an adequate pool of Native labour would always be retained".[10] Before long, however, Cape employers had come to distrust the Minister of Native Affairs.

In May 1954, in an address to the Federated Chamber of Industries (FCI), he declared that the Western Cape was to be regarded as a preference area for Coloureds.[11] The settlement of Africans in the Western Cape was to be discouraged. Employers at first were left in the dark as to the deeper significance of Verwoerd's statement. They were shocked, therefore, when in 1955 W.W. Eiselen, the permanent secretary of Native Affairs, revealed the details of his Department's plans for the Western Cape. Eiselen announced that the Department was committed to the "ultimate elimination of Natives from the Western Cape".[12]

---

8.   See *HAD*, 1939, 33, Col. 2456, and Chapters One and Three.
9.   Cape Chamber of Industries (henceforth CCI), "Presidential Address", *The Manufacturer*, Feb. 1955, p.31.
10. Cape Chamber of Industries, *Yearbook, 1956* (Cape Town, CCI, 1957), p. 40.
11. CCI, *Yearbook, 1954* (Cape Town, CCI, 1955), p.40.
12. W. Eiselen, *op.cit.*

According to him:

> Through this policy the Department of Native Affairs is endeavouring to put
> the flow of Native families into reverse, so that no large Native population
> will settle side by side with the Coloured community. If additional Native
> manpower is absolutely indispensable, it must come in the form of migrant
> labourers . . .[13]

Eiselen's scheme was immediately condemned by the President of the
Cape Chamber of Industries (CCI) as

> Completely unrealistic and impossible to implement . . . This objective must
> cause grave disruption . . . The essentiality of Natives in certain industries in
> the Cape is indisputable on factual grounds.[14]

"That there should be reasonable influx control has never been dispu-
ted," insisted the CCI, but it questioned the particularly strict application of these controls in the Western Cape.[15] The main concern of the
Cape Chamber was that because

> certain industries in the Western Cape had need of settled urbanised labour
> the policy of ultimately removing Natives from the Western Cape . . . must
> cause grave disruption.[16]

For a short time, the worst fears of Cape employers proved un-
founded; the FCI in 1955 reported that "the labour pattern throughout
the Union is uniform", and Cape employers were able to recruit adequate numbers of unskilled African workers.[17] In fact Cape employers
found some solace in evidence which suggested that the measures used
to enforce influx control in the Western Cape were not unique to that
region.[18] In all urban areas, Verwoerd later explained, the Department
of Native Affairs' attitude was that

> When the Native is employed in the White area (even if he has been there
> for one or two generations) then he is here in the service of the White man
> whose territory it is.[19]

The hopes that Western Cape employers had that they would not be
particularly disadvantaged by the influx controls were shortlived; by the

13. *Ibid.*, p.11.
14. CCI, *Manufacturer*, Feb. 1955, p.31.
15. *Ibid.*
16. CCI, *Yearbook, 1954*, p.40.
17. CCI, *Yearbook, 1956*, p.40.
18. See Federated Chamber of Industries, Memorandum on Influx Controls, 28 June 1956,
    paras. D(1)-D(2).
19. *HAD*, 1957, 9, Col. 4382.

end of 1955 the Western Cape had begun to endure a disproportionate burden of influx control measures. It was in that region, Verwoerd announced in 1955, that "due to a whole series of circumstances, the policy of apartheid in regard to the Bantu can be applied with the greatest ease."[20] It was in the Western Cape that the Department of Native Affairs intended to establish the patterns of control which would eventually be extended throughout South Africa.[21] Already by the end of 1954, the South African Institute of Race Relations had reported that influx control was operated more strictly in the Western Cape than elsewhere in South Africa.[22] Before long the controls had constrained employers in their recruitment of migrant labourers. The clampdown coincided with the summer harvest. In 1956 the Cape Chamber of Industries reported that although

> A general shortage of Native labour was not apparent . . . a seasonal shortage of Native labour, particularly in the last quarter of each year, was occurring. It was feared that as the proportion of migratory labour to non-migratory labour became greater . . . this shortage would increase in severity.[23]

By 1957 the particularly harsh enforcement of influx controls in the Western Cape had led the CCI to complain that "as a result of the tightening of Native influx control, there is no longer an adequate local reserve of Native labour."[24] The CCI was particularly concerned about the uneven enforcement of the regulations, noting that

> If a situation were permitted whereby the inflow of Native labour into the Western Cape were curtailed, whilst it continued to flow in other areas, industry at the Cape would be at an increasing disadvantage.[25]

This, the CCI president had previously warned, would result from the fact that undue restriction of the supply of African labour would inevitably lead to "unprecedented competition for the insufficient Coloured labour".[26] Such competition "would raise cost levels inordinately and seriously weaken the position of both agriculture and industry in the Western Cape."[27]

By 1959 the Department of Native Affairs insisted on the substitution of Coloured for African labour, and the CCI announced that the "pool

20. *HAD,* 1955, 1, Col. 201.
21. H. Verwoerd, "Interview", *S.A. Outlook,* 86 (1019), 1955, p.39.
22. M. Horrell (comp.), *A Survey of Race Relations in South Africa, 1953/1954,* p.41.
23. CCI, *Yearbook, 1956,* p.40.
24. CCI, *Yearbook, 1957* (Cape Town, CCI, 1958), p.41.
25. CCI, *Yearbook, 1958/59* (Cape Town, CCI, 1959), p.54.
26. CCI, *Manufacturer,* Feb. 1955, p.33.
27. *Ibid.*

of Native labour" in the Western Cape had been eliminated.[28] Employers wishing to recruit Africans for unskilled tasks were unable to do so. They were advised by the labour bureau to employ Coloureds instead. The CCI, however, insisted that "Coloureds were not interested in or suitable for performing unskilled work and emphasised the need for a local Native labour pool."[29]

The pleas of Cape industry were ignored and by January 1960 the CCI reported that "the utilisation of Coloured labour for unskilled work was being insisted upon by the authorities."[30] The exhaustion of the "labour pool" and the restrictions on further recruitment of Africans, a political commentator, E. Munger, observed, led to

> an anguished outcry from employers . . . Manufacturers stormed into Cape Town to say that they would have to shut down unless they got replacements for the normal attrition of African labour.[31]

The President of the CCI focused on the "inability" of Coloureds to undertake much of the work done by Africans.[32] He insisted that the issue was a "practical not theoretical one".[33] Cape industry's pleas for a relaxation of the controls were supported by the Cape Chamber of Commerce (CCC), which resolved that

> It was imperative that industry, commerce and agriculture should not be deprived of Bantu labour while alternative labour was unavailable in adequate quantity . . .[34]

By 1961, Munger reported, the replacement policy had adversely affected Afrikaner farmers and other National Party supporters:

> [They] protested that only Africans were efficient on the dairy farms, that the Coloured were too lazy and inefficient for the skilled tasks, and that they must have a steady supply of labour . . . The manager of the local fertiliser works in Bellville got local National Party support for his complaint that: 'We have repeatedly tried to make use of Coloured labour to supplant Native labour . . . This type of labour is unwilling to do the strictly manual work involved . . . We must have African labour'.[35]

28. CCI, *Yearbook, 1959/60* (Cape Town, CCI, 1960), p.23.
29. *Ibid.*
30. *Ibid.*, p.24.
31. E. Munger, *African Field Reports, 1960* (Pretoria, Struik, 1961), pp. 564-565. (*New Age*, 12 March 1959, described Munger's work as "reeking of McCarthyism".)
32. CCI, "Presidential address of Mr D. Banade to the 57th A.G.M. of the CCI", memo, Cape Town, 28 Nov. 1961, p.2.
33. *Ibid.*, p.3.
34. Cited in CCI, *Yearbook, 1962/1963* (Cape Town, CCI, 1962), p.29.
35. E. Munger, *op.cit.*
36. CCI, *Report of the Executive Council, 1962* (Cape Town, CCI, 1962), p.4.

At the same time, the Western Cape Agricultural Union added its weight to the call for moderation, noting that

> The state should be asked to make it possible for these [African] workers to be made available where their services could be shown to be essential.[36]

The particularly strict enforcement of influx controls in the Western Cape was by 1961 being bitterly opposed by employers, many of whom were government supporters. Western Cape Afrikaner farmers, we suggested in the previous chapter, had been among the most ardent advocates of a Coloured labour preference policy. How, then, was this political commitment reconciled with their opposition to attempts to implement the replacement policy?

Politics and Economics

Throughout the 1950s antagonisms increased between the Transvaal National Party, which was led by petty-bourgeois Afrikaners, and the Cape National Party, which was seen to be under the control of Afrikaner "geldmag" (financial power).[37] The Cape party rested on the financial foundations of the Sanlam and Rembrandt empires. By the 1960s, O'Meara has argued, these organisations in alliance with the Cape National Party and its organ *Die Burger* were "virtually an official opposition within the National Party".[38]

O'Meara noted that Sanlam was as much a part of Cape Afrikaner Nationalism as the Party and its press. W.A. Hofmeyer, the founder and first organising secretary of the Cape National Party[39], was at the same time the chairman of the Sanlam Corporation and the Nasionale Pers, the publishing company responsible for *Die Burger* newspaper. This alliance between big business and Afrikaner politics was strengthened in the period of National Party rule by the close association of the Rembrandt corporation with Cape nationalism.

The Cape National Party, it will be recalled, was equivocal in its support for key aspects of the government's Coloured policy. In 1960 *Die Burger* newspaper called for direct representation of Coloureds and their fuller incorporation into White society.[40] But the newspaper also campaigned for a stronger commitment to the policy of Coloured Labour Preference and, emphasising the strategic considerations, called for the

37. O.Meara, *"Volkskapitalisme"*, p.251.
38. *Ibid.*
39. *Ibid.*, p.101.
40. *Die Burger*, 6 Nov. 1960; *Die Burger*, 3 Dec. 1960.

removal of all Africans from the Western Cape.[41] The newspaper, voic-
ing the dominant view within the Cape National Party, implied that the
short-term economic interests of Cape employers would have to be sacrificed to meet political and strategic priorities.[42] Afrikaner farmers and
manufacturers were indignant, but their complaints were overruled by
more powerful business interests within the Cape party.

The Rembrandt and Sanlam corporations' commitment to a Coloured
Labour Preference Policy in the Cape was unequivocal.[43] Without the
continued support of these two, the policy could not have been adopted
by the Cape National Party. At the same time, the support of these financial empires for the Policy of Preference overcame the opposition of
less powerful Cape Nationalists to the particularly strict enforcement of
influx control in the Western Cape.

In the Western Cape Rembrandt and Sanlam had no great need for
the employment of unskilled African labour.[44] The Sanlam corporation
in the Cape employed mainly clerical and administrative staff and made
use of only an insignificant number of African workers. In the 1950s the
corporation still drew a large part of its premium income from farmers
employing African labour, but its activities were no longer centred on
agriculture or the Western Cape.[45] Similarly, the Rembrandt corporation
had by the 1950s diversified production to the extent that activities requiring unskilled African labour were concentrated in the Transvaal and
in Zimbabwe.[46]

The administrative headquarters of the Rembrandt corporation and
one of its factories were located in the Western Cape town of Paarl.
While the headquarters employed no Africans, in 1957 the Paarl factory
employed mainly Africans; in that year the company resolved to replace
its African employees in Paarl with Coloured and White workers.
According to the Western Cape Personnel Manager of the Corporation:

> A decision was taken not to take on any new Blacks and to recruit only
> Coloureds for the Paarl factory . . . When Blacks left they were replaced by
> Coloureds. The decision to take on only Coloured workers was a political
> one, although Rembrandt is mainly interested in business, not politics.[47]

In fact, the decision to employ Coloureds in place of Africans made

41. *Die Burger,* 15 Sept. 1961.
42. *Die Burger,* 6 Dec. 1961.
43. Mr Jagger, Personnel Manager, Rembrandt: interview, Paarl, 20 Jan. 1982, transcript,
    p.2.
44. Mr Killian, Factory Manager, Rembrandt : interview, Paarl, 20 Jan. 1982, transcript p.3.
45. O'Meara, *"Volkskapitalisme",* pp. 251-253.
46. *Ibid.,* pp.202-204; Mr Killian, interview, p.5.
47. Mr Jagger, interview, p.1.

business as well as political sense for the corporation. The Paarl factory was devoted to the manufacture of cigarettes by semi-skilled operatives. Coloured women were able to perform these tasks with ease and, because of the additional costs resulting from the recruitment and regular re-training of African migrant workers, were no more expensive to employ than African semi-skilled workers. Indeed, although the decision to employ Coloureds was not taken with a view to cutting labour costs, such savings did result from the changeover.[48] By supporting the Coloured Preference Policy the Rembrandt corporation was able to improve its stature within the National Party and at the same time make financial gain. The Rembrandt corporation, together with Sanlam, and in marked contrast to the Afrikaner farmers of the Boland, was not adversely affected by the Coloured Preference Policy. Not surprisingly, Sanlam and Rembrandt wholeheartedly endorsed Eiselen's scheme for the "ultimate elimination" of Africans from the Western Cape.[49]

Summary

In the Western Cape the Coloured Preference Policy had by 1961 disrupted traditional patterns of recruitment. Employers, although committed to "reasonable" influx controls, were virtually unanimous in their condemnation of those aspects of the policy which had led to a shrinking of the "native labour pool" and to shortages of African labour. The policy, however, was endorsed by the two most powerful Cape employers: the Rembrandt and Sanlam corporations. The decisive support of these Afrikaner enterprises for the policy of replacing African with Coloured labour stood in marked contrast to the ambivalence of smaller Afrikaner employers to Eiselen's scheme. Nevertheless, as we suggested in the previous chapter, Afrikaner employers had urged National Party candidates to press in parliament for the introduction of policies of Coloured preference and for the stricter regulation of African influx. In 1960 and 1961 it was the Afrikaner farmers of the Western Cape who initiated a call for the swift removal of Africans from the Western Cape. At this time, strategic concerns regarding "the survival of the White man in South Africa" were given priority by many farmers.[50] Boland farmers were at the forefront of demands for the stricter enforcement of influx

48. *Ibid.*, p.2; O'Meara, *"Volkskapitalisme"*, p.204.
49. Mr Jagger, interview, p.4; Mr A. Sol, Sanlam Senior Manager, interview, Cape Town, 19 Sept. 1981, transcript p.2.
50. *Die Burger*, 27 Nov. 1961.

controls in order to create a "cleaner whitemansland" in the Western Cape.[51] Yet it was these same farmers who complained bitterly that their livelihood was threatened by the controls, for they relied on unskilled African labour.

In the late 1950s Afrikaner farmers thus found themselves in a confusing and often contradictory position. Whilst the Sanlam and Rembrandt corporations were spared many of the dilemmas facing smaller employers, pro-Nationalist farmers as well as urban manufacturers and government departments reliant on unskilled African labour placed themselves in a difficult position as they struggled to reduce their African labour complement.

The majority of Cape manufacturers were loyal supporters of the United Party. The policy of the Party mirrored that of the Cape Chamber of Industry (CCI) and of Commerce (CCC).[52] Throughout the 1950s the United Party remained firmly committed to the retention of influx controls and supported the broad principles of the Coloured preference scheme. In 1961, with mass resistance pressing home the strategic advantages of the Coloured Preference Policy, the United Party reconfirmed its commitment to the policy. At the same time the Party heeded the calls of its members and called for an easing of the restrictions. Major van der Byl, a prominent Cape Town United Party MP, provided a rare clarification of United Party policy in 1961:

> Whoever suggested that we wanted millions of Natives coming into the White areas? . . . We never suggested that Natives should be allowed to flock in but what we did ask is that they should be allowed to remain to do certain work, such as stevedoring at the docks, work which neither the White man nor the Coloured man has been prepared to do.[53]

In 1961 the official parliamentary opposition as well as organised industry, agriculture and commerce supported the retention of influx control and the policy of preferential treatment of Coloured people relative to Africans in the Western Cape. Parliament and organised business, however, was divided over the extent to which the policy should be permitted to disrupt the well-established patterns of recruitment of unskilled African labour. The Cape National Party, with the decisive support of the Rembrandt and Sanlam corporations, was unequivocal in its commitment to stricter influx controls. By contrast, organised indus-

51. *Die Burger*, 15 Sept. 1961; *Die Burger*, 2 Dec. 1961.
52. Mr Colinese, Director of Cape Chamber of Industries, interview, Cape Town, 10 Nov. 1979, transcript p.8.
53. Cited in E. Munger, *"Field Reports"*, p.421.

try, commerce and agriculture, with the United Party's parliamentary support, were vocal in their condemnation of those aspects of the policy which aimed to replace African workers engaged in heavy manual tasks with Coloured workers.

In the Western Cape the relationship between employers and the National Party — between economics and politics — was therefore extremely complex. And any account of the development of the Coloured Preference Policy has to take this into consideration.

6. COLOURED POLITICS AND AFRICAN RESISTANCE: 1948 — 1961

Introduction

The Coloured Preference Policy devised by Eiselen cannot be viewed in isolation from the campaign of resistance waged during the 1950s against the National Party. We have seen how anxieties regarding the campaign of defiance against apartheid, and regarding the tide of African nationalism which was sweeping the continent, evoked increasingly shrill calls for a "skoner witmansland" — a "cleaner whitemansland" — in the Western Cape. But the achievement of this was not immediately feasible. In the short run, it was argued, the threat of an alliance of Coloureds and Africans had to be countered even if in the longer run such an alliance could be undermined by the expulsion of Africans from the region.

The Cape National Party never anticipated the eventual relocation of the Coloured population outside the Western Cape. Coloureds, the Cape Nationalists managed to convince the Cabinet, had no "homeland" outside the Western Cape. The implication was that the destiny of Whites and Coloureds was intertwined and that the prosperity of Whites in the Western Cape would inevitably rest on their ability to co-exist with Coloureds resident in the region.

The tide of African resistance, which in the 1950s had swept through South Africa, caused many National Party members in the Western Cape to reinforce their commitment to a closer alliance with Coloured people. These Cape Nationalists were opposed to the disfranchisement of Coloureds and to other measures which led to the disaffection of Coloured men and women. The Coloured Preference Policy was regarded by Cape Nationalists and by Coloured commentators as a concession given to Coloureds in an attempt to mollify resentment to disfranchisement. At the same time the policy embodied the commitment of the National Party to the "ultimate elimination" of the African proletariat in the Western Cape.

From 1948 to 1961, organisations campaigning against apartheid were vocal in their condemnation of racial divisions. Nevertheless during this period the politics of resistance, as had been the case in the pre-Nationalist era, often led to the exacerbation of such divisions. Differences within the radical opposition in the Western Cape, we shall suggest, facilitated the further development of distinct Coloured and African political identities.

In the period 1948 to 1961 Coloured politics in the Western Cape was dominated by radical organisations. Organisations not part of the radical tradition, such as the Coloured Persons National Union (CPNU), had a neglible impact on the political mobilisation of Coloured people. In examining Coloured politics during this period we shall therefore consider only the radical movements. In the 1950s the two major movements were the South African Coloured Peoples' Organisation (SACPO) and the Non-European Unity Movement (NEUM).

Political Organisations

Relations between the NEUM and Anti-CAD on the one hand, and the ANC and CPSA on the other, had been strained throughout the 1940s. Nevertheless, in the Western Cape the first year of National Party rule saw the organisation of a campaign which sought to forge a united opposition to the National Party.

In 1948 the loose alliance against apartheid legislation faced its first test in opposition to the reservation of first-class carriages on the Cape Peninsula railways for Whites. Previously these carriages had been open to all passengers, although in practice only the Coloured élite had been able to afford the cost of first-class travel.[1] The Coloured élite therefore stood to lose the most from the legislation; Africans and the Coloured working class generally travelled in the second- and third-class carriages. Organised into what came to be called the Train Apartheid Resistance Committee (TARC), an ad-hoc committee was established bringing together representatives of the ANC (WC), the Cape Provincial Indian Assembly (CPIA), the Cape Malay Association, the Communist Party of South Africa (CPSA) and the Non-European Unity Movement (NEUM).[2] Before long the ability of the CPSA and the NEUM to coop-

---

1. R. Donaldson, "The train apartheid issue in the Cape Peninsula" (Univ. of Cape Town, BA (Hons) thesis, 1981), p. 8.
2. *Ibid.*, p. 16; Z. Gamiet, "A declaration to the People of South Africa", in *Discussion*, 1, (4), Dec. 1951.

erate was severely tested; the tactics of resistance promoted by the NEUM delegates on the committee, led by Goolam Gool and Ben Kies, were opposed by the CPSA delegates, Sam Kahn, Fred Carneson, Cissie Gool and Jimmy La Guma.[3] For whilst the CPSA sought to use the issue to promote mass civil disobedience, the NEUM wished to confine resistance to boycotts and petitions. The intransigence of both sides sabotaged further organisation and the campaign collapsed into a bitter feud, with the NEUM condemning the CPSA as adventurist and the CPSA retorting that the NEUM was shying away from action.[4]

With the collapse of the TARC, the animosity which had previously existed between the CPSA and NEUM resurfaced, critically undermining attempts to forge a common front against apartheid. The NEUM, recoiling in anger at the failure of the campaign, vowed not to support ad hoc alliances of opposition to apartheid. From this time on, according to S. Makone, writing in the NEUM-associated *Educational Journal,* the NEUM and its affiliates were

> opposed in principle to ad hoc committees and ad hoc campaigns which highlighted one or other aspect of oppression and failed to struggle against it as part of a whole system.[5]

The effect of this "principled" opposition to ad-hoc campaigns against apartheid was to isolate from the ANC (WC) and CPSA the whole generation of Coloured radicals associated with the NEUM. The CPSA was active in organising Coloured and African people whilst the leadership and membership of the NEUM were predominantly Coloured. The opposition of the NEUM to ad-hoc campaigns therefore served to fragment the organisation of Coloured resistance and to draw a large section of the Coloured community away from the African communities. The distancing of the NEUM and CPSA, we shall suggest, served to increase the distance between Coloured and African people in the Western Cape.

In 1951 the radicals, who prior to its banning had been active in the CPSA, took the lead in organising resistance to the Separate Representation of Voters Bill.[6] In January 1951 the Franchise Action Committee (FRAC) was launched at an enthusiatic meeting of 2 000 people.[7] The NEUM refused to support the campaign and, Bunting wrote, "apart

3. T. Karon, "'Vryheid nie op 'n "skinkboord" nie': The Coloured Peoples' Congress and the National Democratic Struggle in the Western Cape, 1951-1962" (Univ. of Cape Town, BA (Hons) thesis, 1983), p.xxiii.
4. S. Mokone, *Majority Rule: Some Notes* (Cape Town, Teachers League of South Africa (TLSA), 1982), p. 65.
5. *Ibid.,* p. 65, citing a 1952 statement.
6. *Guardian* (Cape Town), 25 Jan. 1951.
7. *Guardian,* 9 Feb. 1951.

from indulging in orgies of violent language had remained quiescent."[8] The failure of the NEUM to involve itself was bitterly condemned by Dr Dadoo[9] and Fred Carneson[10] as a betrayal of the struggle against oppression.

The FRAC committee, led by Sam Kahn and Reggie September, rapidly set about extending its base and organising local committees in factories and residential areas throughout the Western Cape.[11] These committees embraced Coloured and African people and worked closely with the ANC (WC). FRAC, according to Carneson, was "engaged in a struggle to defeat the government on this one issue, the disenfranchisement of the Coloured."[12] To achieve this end the committee accepted the tactics of a "broad front", going so far as to accept support from the "racialist" George Golding, who was forced, in his own words, to "throw in [his] lot with the powerful Franchise Action Committee".[13]

The committee organised a mass rally on 8 March, which the *Cape Times* estimated was attended by over 10 000 people, an even larger number than had attended the 1939 protest against segregation.[14] The mainly Coloured meeting resolved to "solemnly pledge to continue the struggle in defence of the Coloured vote with determination and courage."[15] From this time on, the committee concentrated on organising workers in support of a mass strike to be held on 7 May.[16] The strike call was lambasted by the NEUM leadership and the NEUM went out of its way to undermine it.[17] The Anti-CAD National Committee reported that

> It warned the people through pamphlets and from its platforms of the hollowness of this call ... Thousands of pamphlets in English and Afrikaans were distributed all over the country ... That the people heard the anti-CAD's warning is known from the fact that the political stunt did not turn into a national debacle.[18]

8. B. Bunting, *Moses Kotane: South Africa Revolutionary* (London, Inkuleko Publ., 1978), p. 179. (Bunting was a CPSA activist at the time.)
9. *Guardian*, 15 Feb, 1951 (TIC (Transvaal Indian Congress) Pres.)
10. F. Carneson, "The Franchise Action Committee" in *Discussion*, 1, (3), June 1951. (Carneson was a former CPSA activist.)
11. *Guardian* 11 Jan. 1951.
12. Carneson, op. cit., p. 10.
13. *Ibid.*, p. 11; *Cape Times*, 1 March 1951. (George Golding was the president of the CPNU.)
14. *Cape Times*, 9 March 1951.
15. Cited in T. Karon, *op. cit.*, p. 13.
16. *Guardian*, 29 March 1951.
17. *Guardian*, 5 April 1951; *Guardian*, 17 May 1951.
18. T. Karis and G.M. Carter, *From Protest to Challenge: A Documentary History of African Politics in South Africa, Vol. 2, Hope and Challenge, 1935-1952* (Stanford, Hoover Inst. Press, 1972), Document: EN1, 30/2.

But despite the NEUM and in face of victimisation by employers and intimidation by the security police, the strike did achieve considerable success amongst Coloureds in the Western Cape, with support uneven in Cape Town but widespread in Worcester and Paarl.[19] The strike served to politicise many Coloured workers, the majority of whom already had no vote. In so doing the FRAC provided a challenge to the NEUM and a source of leadership to Coloured workers who had never been orga- nised by the NEUM. Significantly, the FRAC also challenged the NEUM within the schools, the strongholds of NEUM support. Approxi- mately 55 per cent of Coloured school-children observed the FRAC stayaway call.[20]

The success of the Franchise Action Committee raised hopes that the Coloured people had demonstrated their commitment to broad cam- paigns of resistance.[21] In August 1951 Johnny Gomas, a Coloured com- munist, wrote that the FRAC

has brought the Coloured people into action as no other organisation has done in the past, and I am sure that under the banner of the FRAC the Coloured people will be able to play their full part in the mass campaign which is to come.[22]

The FRAC, however, seriously miscalculated; future attempts to involve Coloured men and women in campaigns not directly related to their own lives would be far less successful.

In 1952 the preoccupation of the leadership of FRAC with the "Campaign of Defiance against Unjust Laws" led to the decline of the FRAC and the diversion of political campaigning away from issues af- fecting the Coloured communities[23] to those of immediate concern to Af- ricans and the ANC. For the defiance campaign, which was dominated by the ANC, was concerned virtually exclusively with issues affecting African people.[24]

The ANC, which in the 1930s and 1940s had neglected Coloureds, was unable in the 1950s to gain their widespread support for its cam- paigning on the pass law and influx control issues; from 1952 these formed the ANC's focus of resistance. Not surprisingly, the nationwide "Defiance of Unjust Laws" campaign was weakest in the Western Cape.[25] Approximately 300 people are known to have taken part in the

19. *Guardian*, 3 May 1951; *Guardian*, 10 May 1951; *Cape Times* 8 May 1951.
20. *Cape Times*, 9 May 1951; *Guardian*, 10 May 1951.
21. *Guardian*, 21 June 1951.
22. *Guardian*, 9 August 1951.
23. *Guardian*, 27 March 1952. (J. Gomas became the treasurer of the W. Cape co-ordinating committee of the Defiance Campaign.)
24. *Cape Times*, 7 April 1952.

defiance campaign in the Western Cape, less than 4 per cent of the national total.[26] Coloured support for the campaign was negligible in the Cape Peninsula.[27] This was not so much due to what L. Kuper asserted was the "apathy of Coloureds, who are concentrated there"[28], but to the failure of the campaign to address issues of direct relevance to Coloured people. By contrast the Worcester defiance campaign selected issues related to wage demands and segregation which directly affected both Coloured and African people.[29] Coloureds in Worcester participated fully in the units which defied railway and post office segregation in the town.[30] Worcester, however, remained the exception; elsewhere in the Western Cape the response to the campaign was significant among Africans but negligible among Coloured people.

From 1953 the ANC's neglect of Coloured people was justified by the fact that in that year Coloured people were to be organised by the South African Coloured Peoples' Organisation (SACPO). SACPO was established as a broad front and included FRAC radicals such as J. Gomas and R. September and moderates like E. Deane and R. van der Ross.[31] From 1954 to 1955 SACPO campaigned with some success within the Coloured communities on issues which were of direct concern to these communities. In May 1954 legislation initiating apartheid in the Cape Peninsula bus service provided a focus for SACPO activity.[32] By 1955 the bus boycott had fizzled out and SACPO turned its attention to the organisation of opposition to the Group Areas Act.[33]

In March 1955 SACPO formed the Group Areas Coordinating Committee. The Committee embraced a wide range of organisations but failed to solicit the support of the NEUM, which remained to one side because of its "principled" opposition to ad hoc committees.[34] In the .Group Areas Coordinating Committee, as was the case in the other ad-hoc committees in which SACPO was involved, the SACPO activists

25. R. Kingwill, "The African National Congress in the Western Cape: a preliminary study" (Cape Town Univ., BA (Hons) thesis, 1977), pp. 66-68, and L. Kuper, *Passive Resistance in South Africa* (New Haven, Yale Univ. Press, 1957), p. 123.
26. R. Kingwill, *op. cit.*
27. *Clarion*, 3 July 1952; *Clarion*, 10 July 1952; *Clarion*, 14 Aug. 1952; *Peoples World*, 21 Aug. 1952; *Advance*, 27 Nov. 1952. (After the banning of the *Guardian* these new titles were initiated, each of which in turn was banned.)
28. L. Kuper, *op. cit.*, p. 123.
29. *Clarion*, 3 July 1952; *Clarion*, 24 July 1952.
30. *Clarion*, 31 July 1952.
31. T. Karon, *op. cit.*, pp. 48-54.
32. *Ibid.*, pp. 53-55.
33. *Ibid.*, pp. 55-61.
34. R.E. van der Ross, former Chairman of the Group Areas Coordinating Committee: interview, Cape Town, 13 Dec. 1981, transcript p. 8

took a leading role in the organisation of the resistance.[35] Already, however, by 1955 the attention of these activists was diverted away from local issues and into the organisation of the Congress of the People.[36]
Before long, the Group Areas Coordinating Committee had faded into
oblivion.

In the months leading up to the June 12 Congress of the People,
SACPO canvassed widely for the Congress and the proposed Freedom
Charter, putting aside its prior commitments to issues affecting
Coloureds in the Western Cape.[37] The Congress of the People brought
together in close alliance representatives of organisations committed to
the Freedom Charter. In keeping with the intentions of the Congress, its
affiliates on returning to their home regions established committees for
the organisation of joint campaigns. In the Western Cape, Congress affiliates formed the Cape Western Action Council (CWAC). At a report-
back rally attended by over 1 500 people the CWAC began its campaign
to popularise the Freedom Charter and renewed the commitment of
Congress affiliates to anti-apartheid activities.[38] Before long, this show of
militancy triggered fresh campaigns to resist apartheid. In the Western
Cape, SACPO took the lead in a renewed attempt to organise a boycott
of racially segregated buses.[39] Alex La Guma, the SACPO general-secretary, called on all groups to join in the boycott.[40] The NEUM refused to
support the campaign, arguing that it "must have a guarantee first that
the boycott will be a success, before it considers such a proposal".[41]

Despite NEUM condemnation, the boycott was a limited success,
serving to shift the focus of SACPO back to local issues. For Coloureds,
however, the presence of SACPO again was a passing phenomenon, for
in 1956 SACPO was crippled by the arrest of its leaders: the arrest of
La Guma, September and Peake on a charge of treason forced the post-
ponement of the first SACPO conference and seriously undermined the
effectiveness of the organisation.[42] The arrests heralded the decline of
SACPO, for after the acquittal of the three leaders the energies of
SACPO were dissipated by a divisive internal feud over the decision to
give support to candidates in the 1958 general election.[43] Eventually the
SACPO executive decided to support Piet Beyleveld, a member of the

35. T. Karon, *op. cit.*
36. *Advance*, 14 Jan. 1954; *Advance*, 19 Aug. 1954.
37. *New Age*, 26 May 1955; *New Age*, 9 June 1955; *New Age*, 16 June 1955.
38. T. Karis and G. Carter, *op. cit.*, Document DC 17, 14/15.
39. *New Age*, 15 Dec. 1955.
40. T. Karis and G. Carter, *op. cit.*, Document DS 2, 81/2; *New Age*, 10 May 1956.
41. *The Citizen*, 14 May 1956.
42. T. Karis and G. Carter, *op. cit.*, Document D52, 30/4; *New Age*, 20 Dec. 1956.
43. T. Karon, *op. cit.*, pp. 105-128.

Congress of Democrats (COD). For the duration of the election campaign SACPO was engaged in an attempt to fend off the criticisms of
those supporting a boycott of the elections. SACPO stressed that a boycott would be "negative, shortsighted and ineffective"[44] and that whilst
"parliamentary elections are but one front of the struggle for liberation
and unconditional democratic rights"[45], a boycott of the election would
only serve to perpetuate "Nationalist tyranny"[46]. The electorate remained unconvinced.

Most Coloured people refused even to register on the separate voters'
roll. Whereas in 1953 47 849 Coloured men had been registered, in 1958
only 19 138 had registered on the revised roll, despite the fact that the
separate roll was now open to all Coloured men and women over 18.[47]
Less than 20 per cent of the registered Coloured electorate in 1958
voted, and Beyleveld received only 813 votes compared with 2 138 votes
for the United Party candidate, Abe Bloomberg.[48] The success of the
boycott enhanced the prestige of the NEUM and hastened the decline of
SACPO. By 1959 SACPO had almost faded from view. The NEUM, by
contrast, continued to enjoy considerable support. In 1959 a NEUM-
organised boycott of the government's election for the Union Council of
Coloured Affairs (UCCA) forced the Department of Coloured Affairs
to nominate discredited Coloured notables to the 12 Council seats.[49]

From April 1958 to March 1960, SACPO was virtually dormant. The
tragic events of 21 March 1960 provided a fresh challenge to Coloured
radicals, which revitalised SACPO.[50] In Sharpeville the police, in order
to disperse a demonstration of 20 000 Africans, shot into the crowd, killing 69 people and wounding 180 others.[51] In Cape Town on the same
day, police attempts to disperse 10 000 African demonstrators led to at
least three deaths and the wounding of over 50 people.[52] The CPC (formerly SACPO) strongly supported the nationwide strike called by the
Congress alliance for 28 March in remembrance of the police massacre
at Sharpeville and Langa. Approximately 98 per cent of Cape Town's
African workforce observed the strike call, but the response from

44. *New Age,* 30 May 1957.
45. *New Age,* 2 Jan. 1958.
46. T. Karis and G. Carter, *op. cit.,* Document DS2, 84/11.
47. *HAD,* 1959, 4, Col. 1209.
48. *Cape Times,* 9 April 1958.
49. *Torch,* 25 March 1958; M. Simons, "Organised Coloured Political Movements", p. 228.
50. In December 1959 SACPO, in order to reflect its closer links with its Congress partners,
    changed its name to the Coloured Peoples' Congress (CPC).
51. M. Horrell (comp.), *A Survey of Race Relations 1959-60* (Johannesburg, SAIRR, 1960),
    pp. 56-8.
52. *Ibid.,* pp. 59-60; A. Mafeje, interview, New York, 11 Sept. 1982, transcript p. 6, alleged
    that the number people killed at Langa, Cape Town, was over 20.

Coloureds was uneven.[53] Within the Coloured communities the NEUM and moderate Coloured trade unionists refused to support the strike.[54] Predictably, the NEUM condemned the strike as "adventurist".[55] Other Coloureds, including Edgar Deane of the Furniture Workers' Union, J. Keraan of the Garment Workers' Union and George Golding of the CPNU, issued a leaflet calling on Coloureds to "maintain law and order" and continue to work.[56] But despite these divisive actions, approximately 12 factories employing Coloured labour, 50 per cent of Coloured schools and virtually all Coloured shops were closed for the day.[57]

With the Declaration of the State of Emergency and the detention of thousands of activists, including most of the CPC leaders, the CPC was temporarily mothballed.[58] However, following the banning of the ANC and PAC in April 1960 and the release of CPC activists, the Coloured Congress played an active part in the organisation of the 31 May protest and in the successful election of George Peake to the City Council.[59] The following year the CPC continued to make its mark and in March 1961 a series of rallies called by the CPC to commemorate the Sharpeville massacre and to protest against the decision to establish a Republic drew 15 000 people.[60] Buoyed by the success of these rallies, the CPC took responsibility for mobilising a three-day stay-away timed to coincide with the 31 May declaration of a Republic.[61] The stay-away was a dramatic success in the Western Cape, where it was hailed as a milestone in Coloured politics.[62] According to the Executive Council of the Cape Chamber of Industries (CCI),

> Reports from one hundred industrial concerns for the Peninsula revealed absenteeism by Coloured workers had occured in fifty-two firms. This... ranged from 10 to 90 per cent in individual firms affected. Various types of industries were affected.[63]

Tens of thousands of Coloured men and women stayed away from work.[64] For the first time, Coloureds demonstrated a more solid re-

53. *Cape Times*, 29 March 1960; *Argus*, 29 March 1960.
54. *Argus*, 2 April 1960; *New Age*, 15 September 1960.
55. *Ibid.*
56. *Argus*, 2 April 1960.
57. *Ibid.; Argus*, 29 March 1960.
58. *Cape Times*, 6 May 1960.
59. *New Age*, 29 Dec. 1960.
60. *New Age*, 23 March 1961.
61. *New Age*, 11 May 1961; *New Age*, 18 May 1961.
62. *New Age*, 1 June 1961; *New Age*, 8 June 1961.
63. Cape Chamber of Industries (CCI), *Report of the Executive Council for 1961* (Cape Town, CCI, 1961), p. 29.
64. *Ibid.*

sponse than Africans to a campaign of mass resistance.[65] Within a week, a number of key CPC activists were arrested. The arrests were followed by the banning of executive members Alex La Guma, Reggie September and Barney Desai, and, in August 1961, by the death of the national president Jimmy La Guma.[66] Although the CPC was itself never outlawed, the banning of its meetings and the silencing of its leaders led to its demise early in 1962.

The arrest of the Congress and PAC leadership and many rank-and-file activists, and the effective silencing of the organisations, left the NEUM without a rival on the left. The NEUM leadership had not taken part in the mass resistance of 1960 to 1961, preferring to criticise the ANC and CPC from the sidelines. But the wave of repression did not leave the NEUM unaffected; the leadership of the organisation went into hiding and *The Torch*, the organ of the NEUM, was temporarily silenced. In 1962 the NEUM leaders resurfaced and organised themselves into the African Peoples' Democratic Union of South Africa (APDUSA).[67] APDUSA set about promoting the Ten Point Programme of the Unity Movement formulated in 1943. The ANC, CPC, and PAC bore the brunt of repression although the NEUM was not unscathed. Whilst virtually all the leaders of the Congress organisations were arrested or forced into exile, a smaller proportion of the NEUM leadership was banned, jailed or exiled. The NEUM was therefore better placed to organise radical activity in the Western Cape. From 1961 to 1976 the NEUM was able, as a result, to exercise a decisive influence over the Coloured communities of the Western Cape.

The Impact

It is difficult to assess the extent of support for the CPC and the NEUM amongst Coloured people. Both organisations failed to recruit a mass membership and relied instead on enlisting support over particular issues. The leadership of the CPC was mainly petty-bourgeois, as were most of its active members. Howard Lawrence, a CPC activist, recalled that it was generally accepted at the time that the CPC had

> failed to win a mass following amongst the Coloured working class ... Most of our contact and our organisation were among the Coloured middle class.[68]

65. *New Age*, 8 June 1961.
66. *Argus*, 5 June 1961; *Argus*, 10 July 1961; *New Age*, 3 Aug. 1961.
67. K. Hassim, "Hassim on APDUSA", *Work in Progress*, No. 31, May 1948, p. 14.
68. *Morning Star* (Cape Town), 16 Jan. 1963.

The NEUM was no better placed. Teachers and lawyers dominated the executive and exercised a powerful influence over the movement's principles. The NEUM, activists from the 1950s recall, like the CPC was predominantly a middle-class movement.[69] But whereas many CPC activists gave priority to the organisation of workers under the SACTU banner, the NEUM failed to promote worker organisation. In the 1950s the leadership of the NEUM focused on issues relating to secondary education and to the franchise. These matters preoccupied middle-class Coloured people but were not of immediate concern to working-class people; less than 4 per cent of the Coloured population were eligible to vote whilst only a similiar proportion of the school-going population reached high school.[70] In 1956 the government's attitude to Coloured education, in the words of th Cape Director of Education, was that "Coloured children will go into manual labour, so their education must be tailored accordingly".[71]

The NEUM leaders were mainly employed as teachers. The Teachers League was by far the strongest affiliate of the NEUM, whilst its organ *The Educational Journal* was widely regarded as the journal of the NEUM.[72] The preponderance of teachers in the movement from the outset determined the tactics of the organisation. The majority of Coloured teachers were employed by the Department of Coloured Affairs and thus were particularly vulnerable to government victimisation.[73] It was felt by the executive that strike action would threaten not only their own livelihood but also the survival of the movement. Not surprisingly the NEUM president, Ben Kies, a high-school headmaster, together with the other executive members condemned militant action as an adventurist tactic.[74]

Non-collaboration, which for the Congress alliance was a tactic to be used in certain circumstances, became for the NEUM a guiding principle. The preference of the NEUM for boycotts was revealed in the NEUM news-sheet *The Torch*. In an article "Instructions on the boycott" readers were assured that the boycott was the least risky means to resist

69. N. Alexander, interview, Cape Town, 25 Nov. 1981; transcript p. 7; A. Mafeje, interview, p. 3.
70. Calculated from *HAD* 1959, 4, Col. 1209; W. Thomas, "Socio-economic development of the Coloured Community", in H. van der Merwe and C. Groenewald (eds.), *"Occupational Change"*, p. 63. In 1961, 141 518 Coloured youth attended primary school and 6 346 high school.
71. Cited in *Financial Mail*, 25 April 1980, p. 371.
72. See S. Mokone, *Majority Rule: Some Notes*, p. 61-82, and M. Simons, "Organised Coloured Political Movements", pp. 226-6.
73. Department of Coloured Affairs, "Occupational Opportunities for Coloured People", in H.W. van der Merwe and C. Groenewald (eds.), *"Occupational Change"*, p. 143.
74. *New Age*, 15 Sept 1960; *Torch*, 25 March 1958.

apartheid. For, it argued,

IN THIS WAY YOU ARE ACTING WITHIN YOUR RIGHTS; YOU
ARE NOT BREAKING ANY LAWS. NONE CAN PERSECUTE YOU
FOR THE DONT'S. NONE CAN PERSECUTE YOU FOR WHAT YOU
DON'T DO.[75]

The principle of non-collaboration insulated NEUM supporters from state repression. Simultaneously, the unyielding adherence of the NEUM to the politics of non-collaboration served, as we have suggested, to isolate the predominantly Coloured organisation from wider campaigns embracing Coloured and African people. The politics of non-collaboration became, over time, an excuse for inactivity which despite the remarkable rhetoric of the NEUM leadership did little to advance the cause of non-racialism in South Africa.

By contrast SACPO (later CPC), despite its existence as a separate Coloured organisation, from the outset devoted much of its attention to the organisation of African resistance. The ability of the SACPO leadership to involve the Coloured communities in this wider programme of resistance was never easy. In the main, Coloured involvement in ad-hoc campaigns was restricted to those issues which directly affected Coloured people. Coloured men and women throughout the 1950s remained equivocal in their support for Africans, even though the leadership of the CPC shared no such reservations and after the banning of the ANC took over many of its platforms.[76]

Both the NEUM and the SACPO, we have suggested, failed to mobilise Coloureds and Africans under a single banner. Both organisations were vocal in their opposition to Coloured identity. In practice, however, neither organisation managed to escape the racial boundaries of the increasingly divided society. In the years to come, their failure to do so facilitated the further entrenchment of Coloured identity and the continued racial fragmentation of resistance in the Western Cape.

SACPO, the NEUM pointed out, had been established as a separate Coloured organisation and therefore upheld racial distinctions. In 1952 J. Gomas, a SACPO leader, asserted that "the Coloured people must take their stand along with the other non-white peoples through their national organisations — the African and Indian Congresses."[77] Gomas thus expected Coloureds to support other black people in South Africa while at the same time reproducing the National Party notion of distinct Coloured, African and Indian "nations" in South Africa. SACPO in its

75. *Ibid.* (capitals in original).
76. *New Age,* 17 Aug. 1961; *New Age,* 7 Sept. 1961; *New Age,* 19 Oct. 1961.
77. *Guardian,* 13 March 1952.

support for separate organisations from the beginning reproduced racial divisions and between 1948 and 1961 was the only major organisation to confine its membership to Coloureds. But it never sought in its activities to promote a distinct Coloured political identity. In the Western Cape SACPO activists succeeded in including Coloured and African workers in joint campaigns and through their organisation overcame racial divisions.

The NEUM was committed to the organisation of both Africans and Coloureds. However, except in isolated instances it failed to organise Coloureds and African people in the same locality. In the Western Cape it recruited only a handful of African intellectuals. In areas where the NEUM managed to develop a grass-roots base with African communities it failed to organise Coloured people. In the Western Cape, we show below, the greatest possibilities for forging a unity of African and Coloured workers lay in trade union activity. But the NEUM did not meet the challenge.

Workers' Organisations

During the 1950s SACPO activists, together with radicals associated with the Congress of Democrats (COD) and the ANC in the Western Cape, had devoted their energies not only to political activity. In contrast with the NEUM, which failed to involve itself in worker organisation, some activities of the Congress alliance sought to advance non-racial organisations at the work-place. From March 1955 the unions in which these activists predominated were linked together under the umbrella of the Congress-affiliated South African Congress of Trade Unions (SACTU).

Between 1948 and 1961, in the Western Cape, the activities of such unions were very effective in overcoming racial divisions within communities — unlike the NEUM and SACPO. The most prominent of the SACTU unions in the Western Cape was the Food and Canning Workers' Union (FCWU), which in the period 1941 to 1948 had succeeded in organising widely in the conservative Cape hinterland within the food-processing industry. African workers were organised by the union into the unregistered African Food and Canning Workers' Union (AFCWU). In practice both unions mobilised support under the banner of a united FCWU, and according to Mark Stein's history of the Union the division "was not a serious source of weakness to the union"[78]. The organisation of workers by the FCWU broke down many of the barriers between African and Coloured workers.[79] By the 1950s, Stein discovered, a strong correlation existed between the strength of the local FCWU branch and the solidarity which existed between African and Coloured workers.[80]

The success of the FCWU in breaking down racial divisions within the workforce derived in part from its commitment to extend its activities beyond the factory gates. In many areas of the Western Cape, the 1952 Commission of Inquiry into Industrial Legislation reported, the FCWU had become "the focal point of the whole social life" of the community.[81] In rural areas of the Western Cape, FCWU organisers took the lead in campaigns to secure improvements in housing, sanitation, transport, education and wages.[82] The involvement of the union in all aspects of their members' lives increased the presence of the Union in the rural areas and greatly enhanced the prestige of the Union.

The involvement of SACTU activists in political and community organisations followed directly from the close links of the radicals who dominated SACTU with the CPSA and the ANC, SACPO and COD. Until 1952 the executive of the FCWU was dominated by activists of the CPSA.[83] This close association placed the union in the firing line of state repression. In September 1953 the General-Secretary of the FCWU, Ray Alexander, was removed from office and banned under the Suppression of Communism Act. Within a year, four other members of the FCWU executive (Becky Lan, Frank Marquard, Gus Coe and Sarah Wentzel) were also banned.[84]

The close association of the FCWU executive with prominent members of the Congress Alliance was mirrored in the overlap between the executive of the AFCWU and the ANC(WC). Oscar Mpetha, the general-secretary of the AFCWU, was at the same time President of the ANC(WC). Other AFCWU organisers were also prominent within the ANC(WC), including Elizabeth Mafeking, Archie Sibeko, Elijah Loza, "Zollie" Malindi, Bernard Huna, "Looksmart" Ngudle and Christmas Tinto.[85] These individuals were subject to constant harassment and arrest for the part they played in the organisation of the defiance campaign and subsequent resistance.[86] The campaigns of resistance, we have sug-

78. M. Stein, "The Food and Canning Workers' Union, 1950-1960" Conference on Research in Progress, York Univ., York, 26-28 March 1979, p. 2.
79. L. Abrahams, FCWU General Sec., interview, Paarl, 19 Nov. 1981, transcript p. 2.
80. M. Stein, *op. cit.,* p. 3.
81. Cited in *ibid.*.
82. See, for example, *Morning Star/Workers Unity,* 3 (5), October1955.
83. See K. Luckhardt and B. Wall, *Organise or Starve ... The Story of the South African Congress of Trade Unions* (London, Lawrence and Wishart, 1980), pp. 240, 429-432.
84. C. Tinto, interview, Cape Town, 8 Jan. 1982, transcript p. 6.
85. Tinto, interview, p. 6; Luckhardt and Wall, *op. cit.*; *Morning Star/Workers Unity,* July 1956.
86. *Ibid.*; *Truth,* Sept. 1956; C. Tinto, interview, pp. 6-7.

gested, seldom included Coloured men and women. In their role as factory organisers, however, the Union activists were more successful at overcoming the divisions which had defeated them in the communities.

We have seen in Chapter 3 how, in order to comply with the amended Industrial Conciliation Act, the FCWU had in 1947 divided its membership into two distinct unions, the FCWU and the AFCWU. Despite the division of the Union, the FCWU vigorously combated racism within the trade union movement.[87] During the 1950s the FCWU, according to the official biographers of SACTU, was the "bastion of the progressive trade union movement in South Africa"[88]. In 1954 the Union had led the revolt at the Trades and Labour Council after it became clear that the Council intended to exclude Africans. In place of the Trades Council the FCWU had proposed the establishment of a progressive Congress of Trade Unions (SACTU) because, in the words of a motion adopted by the FCWU and twelve other unions,

> Division is the policy directed by the bosses' and not the workers' interests ...
> We are determined to carry on a struggle against the policy of racial discrimination and work for the achievement of a single trade union movement embracing all sections of the working class.[89]

Apart from the AFCWU and the FCWU, other SACTU affiliates in the Western Cape included the combined Textile Workers' Industrial Union (TWIU), the combined National Unions of Laundry and Dry-cleaning Workers (NULDCW), the SA Tin Workers' Union, SA Canvas and Rope Workers' Trade Union, Bag Workers' Union, Metal Workers' Union and the SA Railways and Harbours Workers' Union.[90] The stronghold of SACTU was within the Cape Peninsula.[91] In the rural areas its affiliates the FCWU and the TWIU were also well and widely organised. The role of the TWIU in Worcester was particularly noteworthy; the union under the leadership of Ben Baartman and Julius Busa organised the workforce of African men and Coloured women into a powerful non-racial alliance which for over a generation defied numerous attempts to break the union. In March 1956 a four-day strike by over 1 200 African and Coloured textile workers led to the arrest of 191 strikers.[92] The arrests failed to undermine the remarkable solidarity of Coloured and African workers. In 1957 a boycott of buses in the

87. Abraham, interview, pp. 1-2; Stein *op. cit.*
88. Luckhardt and Wall, *op. cit.*, p.234.
89. *Morning Star*, Oct. 1954.
90. *Morning Star/Workers Unity*, March 1956; *Truth*, March 1957.
91. Tinto, interview, p.7; Abraham, interview, p. 4; R. Magau, former SACTU organiser, interview, Cape Town, 7 Jan. 1982, transcript p. 2.
92. *Morning Star/Workers Unity*, March 1956; *Truth*, Sept. 1956; Luckhardt and Wall, *op. cit.*, p. 236.

Worcester area was supported by African and Coloured workers and led to a reduction in fares.[93]

The success of the TWIU in Worcester in overcoming the racial — and sexual — division of labour in the Boland was repeated by Elizabeth Mafeking and her fellow FCWU organisers. An indication of their achievement was the extent to which Coloured workers were prepared to join in the protests accompanying the banishment of AFCWU organisers to the rural reserves. In 1959 Elizabeth Mafeking, who was the President of the AFCWU and at the same time the Vice-President of the African National Congress Women's League, was compelled to leave her home in Paarl and to resettle in a barren area of the north-eastern Cape.[94] Anger at her banishment culminated in a demonstration of over 3 000 people.[95] Despite the fact that Mrs Mafeking was notionally responsible for Africans and not Coloureds, Coloured protesters outnumbered Africans, for, in the words of the Institute of Race Relations, Coloureds "shared in the indignation of their African fellow-workers"[96]. The demonstration ended after police opened fire, injuring at least 12 demonstrators.[97]

In the Cape Peninsula there were also a number of remarkable successes in organising Coloureds and overcoming the divisions between Coloured and African workers; Ben Turok and later Archie Sibeko recruited Coloured women into the militant Bag Workers' Union, whilst Christmas Tinto and others managed to weld an alliance of unskilled African and Coloured dockers.[98] All these activists operated against a backdrop of growing repression in which the implementation of the Coloured Preference Policy was used as an excuse to endorse Africans active in SACTU out of the region.[99] Amongst those banished from the region were Ben Baartman, Julius Busa, Annie Silinga, Greewood Nqotyana, D. Motloheloa and Charles Makholisa.[100] But despite repression and victimisation, SACTU unions between 1956 and 1961 went from strength to strength. While in 1956 the (combined) FCWU, for example, had fewer than 3 000 members, in 1962 it claimed a membership of 17 630.[101]

93. *Truth,* March 1957. See also R. Kingwill, "The African National Congress", pp. 66-68.
94. Abraham, interview, pp. 6-7; M. Horrell (comp.), *A Survey of Race Relations, 1958-59* (Johannesburg, SAIRR, 1959), p. 225.
95. M. Horrell (comp.), *Survey 1959-60,* p. 57.
96. *Ibid.*
97. *Ibid.*
98. *Truth,* Sept. 1956; *Torch,* 1 May 1956; *Morning Star,* 26 July 1962; Luckhardt and Wall, *op. cit.,* p. 236.
99. M. Wilson, interview, Oxford, 12 June 1981, transcript p. 4; Tinto, interview, p. 7.
100. *Ibid.*; Kingwill, "The African National Congress", p. 104.
101. Luckhardt and Wall, *op. cit.,* p. 235.

Summary

It was no accident that the surge in working-class militancy in the Western Cape coincided with an unprecedented wave of repression in the region and the introduction of the Coloured Preference Policy. This policy was partly a response to the intensification of resistance in the Western Cape; it aimed to undermine the alliance of Coloured and African people and to foster the development of a distinct Coloured identity.

The effect of the policy was to increase greatly the insecurity of Africans in the Western Cape. From 1956 to 1961 over 20 000 Africans were deported from the Western Cape. Included in their number were trade unionists and "trouble-makers". This large-scale victimisation of Africans did not lead to a withdrawal of African support for SACTU or to a moderation of African workers, who found in their joint organisation the only possible escape from the draconian laws. Migrant workers, who were amongst the hardest hit by the Coloured Preference Policy, played a leading role in 1960 in the anti-pass campaign.[102] These workers also provided most of the support for the Poqo insurrectionary movement which arose out of the PAC.[103]

The Coloured Preference Policy had been seen by Western Cape National Party members as a means to stem the rising militancy of Africans in the region. It failed to do so. Perhaps even more remarkably, it failed to further the divisions between Coloured and Africans workers in the Western Cape. On the contrary, in the period 1956 to 1961 — largely as a result of the organisational commitment of SACTU activists — divisions between Coloured and African workers (as well as between male and female workers) were in many instances narrowed. Coloured workers rallied around the SACTU unions.[104]

Initiated in 1955, the Coloured Preference Policy had by 1961 dramatically altered the balance of forces between Coloured and African workers in the Western Cape. Yet whereas Coloured workers had previously failed to support mass resistance campaigns, this support was given in 1961 when Coloured workers participated in the Congress stay-away. The Executive Council of the Cape Chamber of Industries reported that over 50 per cent of the factories employing Coloureds which were sur-

---

102. See T. Lodge, "The Cape Town Troubles, March-April 1960", *Journal of African Studies*, 4, (2), 1978 and T. Lodge, "The Paarl Insurrection" in C. Saunders and H. Phillips (eds.), *Studies in the History of Cape Town, Vol. 2* (Cape Town, U.C.T., 1980), pp. 186-203.
103. *Ibid.*, pp. 200-203.
104. Abraham, interview, p. 6.

veyed were adversely affected, whilst absenteeism ranged from 10 to 90 per cent.[105] According to the Executive Council of the Chamber,

> A serious view was taken of this occurrence as it was the first time that Cape Coloured workers had associated themselves with a demonstration involving a stay-away from work for non-industrial reasons.[106]

The Coloured Preference Policy, there can be little doubt, failed to prevent an alliance of Coloured and African workers in the Western Cape.

105. CCI, *"Executive Council 1961"*, p. 29.
106. *Ibid.*

PART THREE
1961 – 1976

CHAPTER SEVEN

COLOURED PREFERENCE 1961 — 1976

Introduction: The Economy

The killing of African demonstrators at Sharpeville and Langa on 21 March 1960 led to nationwide strikes and protests. On 28 March the militant leaders were arrested and legislation introduced outlawing the PAC and ANC. This draconian action brought to an end a week-long strike which in Cape Town over 57 000 workers had supported.[1] But despite the intimidation a PAC-led march on Parliament on 30 March was joined by 30 000 Africans.[2] On the same day a State of Emergency was declared. By 16 May, 19 918 people had been arrested.[3]

Before long the Government's anxiety was matched by a crisis of business confidence which had a dramatic impact on the economy. Within a year, gold and foreign exchange reserves were cut by half and South Africa was faced by its most severe balance of payments crisis since 1932.[4] The withdrawal of foreign investment and loss of business confidence severely affected the Johannesburg Stock Exchange. By December 1961 industrial and mining shares had collapsed to 70 per cent of their pre-Sharpeville values.[5] The overall effect was that whereas in the period 1948 to 1957 the economy had grown by over 7 per cent a year and in the period 1957 to 1959 by approximately 5 per cent a year, in 1960 and 1961 GDP growth slipped to barely 2 per cent.[6]

By 1962 the resistance had been crushed. It was not long before the economy regained its former strength. Between 1961 and 1969, real GDP growth exceeded 6,5 per cent a year, and in 1969 to 1970 accelerated to 8 per cent a year. But such high growth could not be sustained,

---

1. Horrell (comp.), "Survey 1959-1960", p.61.
2. Lodge, "The Cape Town Troubles", pp.216-39.
3. Horrell, *op.cit.*, pp.68-74.
4. *Financial Mail*, 25 June 1986: "What happened in 1960".
5. *Ibid.*, D. Hobart Houghton, *The South African Economy* (Cape Town, OUP, 1967), pp.172-9.
6. *Ibid.*, pp.172-9, 253-5; A. Dickman, "Investment — the Implications for Economic Growth and Living Standards", *Optima*, 27, (1), 1977, pp. 42-3, cited in B. Hackland, "The South African Progressive Party 1959-1981: Political Responses to Structural Change and Class Struggle" (Oxford Univ., D Phil thesis, 1984), p.25.

and from 1971 to 1974 the economy grew by a more modest 5 per cent a year. Then in 1974 the world-wide recession hit South Africa; from 1974 to 1976 GDP growth slumped to 3 per cent a year.[7] In 1976, we shall note in Part Four, the Soweto riots precipitated a further crisis of confidence and between 1976 and 1978 economic growth was stalled.

Between 1962 and 1974 South Africa recorded some of the highest rates of GDP growth in the world. This achievement in part reflected the success of the government in overcoming resistance by black workers. From 1959 to 1961 the intensification of black trade union and political organisation led to a narrowing of the differential between black and White wages. After 1961, with the smashing of black resistance, the differential again widened; by the end of the 1960s the average wage paid to African workers had dropped from 18 to 17 per cent of White workers' wages, whilst the relative earnings of Coloureds fell to 24 per cent of White earnings.[8]

During the period 1962 to 1970, manufacturing and construction's share of GDP grew from 24,1 per cent to 28,2 per cent. Mining's contribution, by contrast, slipped from 13,3 per cent to 10,5 per cent whilst agriculture's share fell from 12,2 per cent to 9,1 per cent.[9] This restructuring was associated with marked changes in patterns of ownership and control, and in the division of labour in South Africa. Capital investment in the period 1961 to 1976 led to both an increased division between skilled and unskilled labour and an increased demand for all categories of labour. As a result, between 1963 and 1976 black employment in secondary industry grew by 74 per cent compared with a 22 per cent rise in the number of White workers.[10] However, the increase in black employment in the 1960s did not threaten White workers in skilled jobs: they successfully defended their monopoly over skilled and supervisory occupations, and to the extent that black workers were employed in semi-skilled or skilled jobs it was at all times subject to the proviso that, in the words of the Minister of Labour,

> White workers' employment opportunities must be guaranteed at all times and take place so as not to result in the displacement of Whites or in the mixing of race on the same work level.[11]

7. Hackland, _ibid._, pp.124, 297-298; D. Innes, "Monopoly Capital and Imperialism in Southern Africa: the Role of the Anglo American Group" (Univ. of Sussex, DPhil thesis, 1980), p. 392; L. Gordon _et al._ (comp.), _Survey of Race Relations in South Africa, 1978_ (Johannesburg, SAIRR, 1979), p.138.
8. S. van der Horst, "The Changing Face of the Economy", in E. Hellman and H. Lever (eds.), _Race Relations in South Africa, 1929-1979_ (London, Macmillan, 1980), p.98.
9. D. Innes, _op.cit._, p.392.
10. S. van der Horst, _op.cit._, pp. 98-101.
11. _Cape Times_, 5 June 1970, citing M. Viljoen.

In the 1960s well-organised White workers were able to exercise a powerful leverage in the National Party and to entrench further the racial division between White and black workers. By the mid-1970s the influence of White workers had been eroded. By 1977, 74 per cent of the skilled and semi-skilled workforce in the metal, plastics, machinery and motor-manufacturing industries were African and a further 15 per cent Coloured or Asian.[12] In these key sectors it was no longer the case that White workers monopolised skilled and semi-skilled jobs. In the 1970s the upward mobility of Africans and the re-emergence of African trade unions helped reverse the widening differential between White and African workers. Between 1971 and 1977 the real wages of Africans in manufacturing rose by 7 per cent per year and the wage differential between African and White workers narrowed from 6,8:1 to 4,7:1.[13] Outside manufacturing, however, Africans remained confined to unskilled and to a lesser extent semi-skilled employment. Furthermore, in the period 1961 to 1976, despite rapid economic growth, African unemployment increased from approximately 1,2-million to over 2-million.[14]

The growth in African unemployment in the period 1961 to 1976 was associated with a renewed attempt by the government to enforce influx controls. The operation of the controls was entrusted to the labour bureaux system, which was extended to cover the recruitment and screening of all African work-seekers. The revised Bantu Labour Regulations placed the labour bureaux at the centre of the African employment market.[15] The bureaux were used to prevent African work-seekers not legally resident in the urban areas from entering many urban occupations or from engaging in work which was considered the preserve of Africans legally resident in the urban areas. Furthermore, in terms of the regulations, long-term unemployed Africans or those who were deemed to be "idle or undesirable" could be deported from the urban areas to areas which were defined to be the "homeland" of the unfortunate victims. Africans relocated in the rural dumping-grounds (dubbed "native reserves", "bantustans", "homelands" or "national states" by successive government ministers) were mainly confined to unskilled heavy manual employment, if they were able to get a job at all. Not sur-

12. S. van der Horst *op.cit.*, pp.101, 103.
13. *Ibid.*, p.126.
14. N. Bromberger, "South African Unemployment: A Survey of Research", in C. Simkins and C. Desmond (eds.), *South African Unemployment — a Black Picture* (Pietermaritzburg, Dev. St. Research Group, 1978), p.15.
15. South Africa, *Bantu Labour Regulations*, Govt. Gazette Extraordinary 18/1292, 1965. On the role of the labour bureaux see D. Hindson, "The Role of the labour bureaux in the South African State's Urban Policy", Wits. Univ. Seminar Paper, Johannesburg, 12 May 1980, and S. Duncan, "The Central Institution of South African Labour Exploitation", *South African Labour Bulletin (SALB)*, 3, (9), 1977.

prisingly, a disproportionate number of people placed through the "tribal" labour bureaux were employed in agriculture, mining and construction — sectors requiring an abundant supply of unskilled manual labourers.

The influx controls enforced throughout South Africa were even more vigorously applied in the Western Cape. In that region, in terms of the Coloured Preference Policy, the Coloured workforce was regarded by government as adequate to meet employers' semi-skilled and unskilled labour needs. Since the 1930s Coloured workers had been employed in semi-skilled jobs, and although it would be an oversimplification to suggest that a three-tier employment structure existed in the Western Cape coincident with the hierarchical division between African, Coloured and White workers, government had attempted to implement such a division and it had come to be accepted by many employers. By the 1960s employers' preferences for the employment of Coloureds in semi-skilled occupations left them relatively well-disposed to plans to prevent African employment in semi-skilled occupations. We shall show, however, that employers were insistent that they be given a free hand in the recruitment of African unskilled labour.

For over a century the relative contribution of the Western Cape to manufacturing was inversely related to the growth of manufacturing in other regions of South Africa. By 1961 the Western Cape accounted for only 20,9 per cent of total industrial employment and 22,1 per cent of net output.[16] By 1967 the Western Cape's share had fallen to 12,1 per cent of the industrial labour force and 11,2 per cent of industrial output. Between 1967 and 1976 the Western Cape benefited from a countrywide manufacturing boom. Nevertheless, the relative share of the region continued to fall; in 1976 the region contributed only 9,6 per cent of national industrial output and accounted for 11,3 per cent of employment.

The uninterrupted slide in the region's share in manufacturing was not offset by a growth in agriculture's share. By 1969 agriculture in the Western Cape accounted for barely 11 per cent of the regular farm labour force in South Africa, roughly equivalent to its share of manufacturing employment.[17] Within agriculture, as in manufacturing, the racial division of labour was extremely uneven. Whereas the region accounted for 62,5 per cent of Coloured farm labourers and 14,1 per cent of the White farm employees, only 3,1 per cent of African farm workers were employed in the Western Cape.[18] Within Western Cape agriculture,

16. D. Hobart Houghton, *The South African Economy*, p.138.
17. South African Agricultural Union (SAAU), Memorandum on Farm Labour, SAAU Document 134/70, 1970, Table 7.
18. *Ibid*.

Coloured workers accounted for 69,3 per cent of the workforce, Africans for 16,8 per cent and White workers for the remainder. In the country as a whole, the relative share of African and Coloured workers was reversed; Africans constituted 76,8 per cent of the regular farm labour force, Coloured workers 12,9 per cent and White farm workers 10,1 per cent.[19]

In the manufacturing sector of the Western Cape, Coloured workers in 1960 constituted 50,6 per cent of the workforce (men 29,8 per cent, women 20,8 per cent), White workers 29,7 per cent (men 23,0 per cent, women 6,7 per cent) and African workers 19,3 per cent (men 19,1 per cent, women 0,2 per cent). By 1970 the relative share of Coloured workers had increased to 62,1 per cent (men 32,2 per cent, women 29,8 per cent) whilst the relative share of Whites in the manufacturing sector had fallen to 22,3 per cent (men 17,1 per cent, women 5,2 per cent) and Africans to only 15,3 per cent (14,6 per cent men, women 0,7 per cent). Clearly, during the 1960s changes in manufacturing in the Western Cape helped to account for the increasing relative share of Coloured workers and for the increased employment of Coloured women relative to Coloured men. The gain of Coloureds, the statistics reveal, coincided with relative displacement of White as well as African manufacturing employees.

During the 1960s the increasing share of Coloured men and women employed in the manufacturing sector reflected the considerable upward mobility of the Coloured working class. The proportion of Coloured men classified as unskilled fell from 52,0 per cent in 1960 to 42,6 per cent in 1973, whilst the proportion of Coloured women classified as unskilled was reduced from 62,4 to 45 per cent over the same period. These aggregate trends, however, are misleading; although an increasing number of Coloured people entered semi-skilled and white-collar employment, the employment opportunities for Coloured men and women in the period 1960 to 1976 remained extremely constrained. The movement out of unskilled occupations into skilled and semi-skilled occupations masked a much smaller improvement in the real earnings and employment status of the Coloured workforce. Furthermore, Coloured unemployment and underemployment rose rapidly in the period 1961 to 1976.[20] By 1976, according to the (Theron) Commission of Inquiry into Matters Affecting the Coloured Population, there were "no permanent and continuous employment opportunities" for "at least the bottom 30 per cent" of the Coloured workforce.[21]

19. *Ibid.*, Tables 8 and 10.
20. A. Blau, "Unemployment in the Western Cape: a study of Bishop Lavis" (Cape Town Univ., BA (Hons) thesis, 1981), pp.21-23.
21. South Africa, *"Coloured Commission, 1976"*, para. 5.126.

In 1960, 24,5 per cent of Coloured men and 20,8 per cent of Coloured women were classed as skilled or semi-skilled. By 1970 these strata accounted for 35,2 per cent of Coloured men and 26,1 per cent of Coloured women. In the next decade, however, the proportion of Coloureds in these blue-collar categories barely increased. The slow-down in the growth of blue-collar employment in the 1970s was mirrored in the easing of the growth of white-collar employment in the 1970s. In the 1960s the rapid growth of white-collar employment had seen the movement of Coloureds into clerical, sales and supervisory occupations. During the 1960s the proportion of Coloured men employed in white-collar occupations leapt from 3,2 per cent to 10,1 per cent. By 1980 it had crept up to 11,3 per cent. Mainly because of the increased employment of Coloured women in clerical and sales jobs, the proportion of Coloured women in white-collar occupations had by 1980 reached 16,3 per cent, this share having increased from a floor of 2,7 per cent in 1960 to 8,1 in 1970.

Between 1960 and 1980 the proportion of Coloured men classified as professional remained constant at 2,3 per cent. However, the share of Coloured women classified in this category soared from 3,8 per cent in 1960 to 9,0 per cent in 1980. This increase was due to the rapid growth of the teaching and nursing professions. Between 1960 and 1980, 86,1 per cent of the Coloured people classified as professional were employed by the state.[22] In 1970, for example, 18 318 of the 24 860 Coloureds classified as professionals were employed as teachers by the Department of Coloured Affairs.[23]

Despite the desperate attempt of the government to present an encouraging picture of Coloured occupational mobility, in 1976 the Theron Committee was forced to admit that "Coloureds are traditionally a working class who have been landowners only on a very limited scale."[24] Nevertheless Coloured skilled workers in the 1970s were increasingly engaged in jobs which had previously been the preserve of White workers. The political ramifications were considerable; the upward mobility of Coloured workers in manufacturing led to an increasing tension between the White and Coloured working class which fuelled political antagonism associated with the subsequent split in the National Party. It is to a consideration of the National Party and the Coloured Preference Policy in the period 1961 to 1976 that we now turn.

22. Calculated from Administration of Coloured Affairs, "Occupational Opportunities for the Coloured People", in H. van der Merwe and C. Groenewald (eds.), *Occupational Change among Coloured People*, p.143, Table 3.
23. *Ibid.*
24. South Africa, *"Coloured Commission, 1976"*, para. 4.4.

The National Party

The resistance which culminated in the State of Emergency brought to a climax anxieties within the Cape National Party regarding African residence in the region. Prominent Afrikaner Nationalists, alarmed by the extent of resistance, left little doubt about their ambitions to establish a "cleaner whitemansland" in the region and to secure an alliance with Coloured people.[25] The Cape National Party therefore wholeheartedly endorsed the plan proposed by SABRA for the particularly strict implementation of influx controls in the Western Cape. The subject of Coloured identity, by contrast, deepened the growing rift between the Cape and Transvaal National Parties.

From the beginning, the Cape National Party unequivocally accepted that the future of the Coloured people and the White population was intertwined and that a separate "homeland" for the Coloureds could not be found.[26] But Verwoerd, whose commanding position was not dependent on the support of the Cape Nationalists, asserted that in principle the Coloured people were a separate "nation state".[27] Although he accepted that a separate Coloured "homeland" was not at that stage "practical politics", he insisted on Coloured "self-government within a White state"[28]. His aim, he stated in 1961, was to establish within a decade a separate parliament, executive and administration for Coloured people.[29]

With the assassination of Verwoerd in 1966, what appeared to be a compromise between the increasingly powerful Cape National Party and the Transvaal National Party paved the way for the premiership of B.J. Vorster. The stalemate between the warring factions of the Party forced them to shelve their fundamentally opposed plans for the Coloured people. Within the cabinet the Transvaalers, M.C. Botha, C.P. Mulder and A. Treurnicht, attempted to secure the continuation of Verwoerd's principles. The old-guard condemned those Cape Nationalists who sought a closer alliance with "brown Afrikaners".[30] In 1968, for example, Connie Mulder reiterated Verwoerd's principles, noting that

25. See Chapter Four and also, for example, *Die Burger,* 24 Sept. 1962, citing F.S. Steyn, and *Die Burger,* 28 Sept. 1962, citing W.C. Malan.
26. *Die Burger,* 26 Oct. 1963; P. Marais, interview, p.4.
27. *HAD,* 1961, 107, Cols. 4192-3, H.F. Verwoerd.
28. *Ibid.,* Col. 4191.
29. South Africa, *Policy Statement Issued by the Deputy Minister of Interior, 17 May 1961* (Pretoria, Govt. Printer, 1961), p.5.
30. E. Theron, interview, p.8; S.P. Cilliers, interview, Stellenbosch, Sept. 1981, transcript, p.5.

I reject completely the idea that the Coloureds must be regarded as brown
Afrikaners. There is no such concept . . . The Coloureds are a nation on
their own, and they must be led in that direction.[31]

As a result of Cape Nationalist opposition, Mulder and his allies were
unable to lead the Coloureds in the direction charted by Verwoerd;
prominent Cape Nationalists, and notably Theo Gerdener and P.W.
Botha (then Minister of Coloured Affairs), through their influence in
the state executive and cabinet were able to frustrate the development
of a Coloured "homeland".[32] But the Cape Nationalists failed to prevent
the further separation of White and Coloured political and social life.
This failure may be attributed to the iron grip of the Transvaal National
Party over the key ministries of Bantu Affairs and Commmunity Development, and to conflicts within the Cape National Party over the question of Coloured social and political identity.

Under the direction of the Department of Community Development,
150 000 Coloured people were statutorily relocated in the Western Cape
between 1957 and 1980. The largest urban segregation scheme involved
the destruction of the District Six area of Cape Town. Since the turn of
the century the inner city neighbourhood of District Six had provided a
home to working-class people of all races.[33] As a result the area became
a haven for citizens eager to escape the rigid racial boundaries which
isolated other residential areas in the Western Cape: District Six for
many became a symbol of defiance of apartheid. By the same token it
was a blot on the Department of Community Development's grand plan
for residential segregation. Cape Nationalists accepted that the challenge
to apartheid posed by District Six would have to be overcome, but some
recommended that the area should be retained as a Coloured group
area.[34] This recommendation was overruled by the Department of Community Development, which decided instead to redevelop District Six as
a White business and residential area and to relocate the Coloured residents in townships on the urban fringe.[35]

The destruction of District Six, which began in 1961, was initiated almost immediately after the Cape National Party had re-emphasised its

31. *HAD*, 1968, 10, Col. 3737.
32. *Financial Mail*, 6 Feb. 1981; E. Theron, interview, p.8.
33. See T. Grogan, *Vanishing Cape Town* (Cape Town, Nelson, 1976), and R. Hallett,
     "Violence and Social Life in Cape Town in the 1900s", in C. Saunders and H. Phillips
     (eds.), *History of Cape Town Vol. 2*.
34. P. Marais in *Argus*, 2 March 1962; E. Theron, interview, p.10.
35. *Ibid.;* Don Pinnock, interview, Cape Town, 26 August 1981, transcript p.11. It has been
     alleged that powerful Cape National Party investors had considerable speculative inter-
     ests in the redevelopment of District Six as a business area and in the rezoning of large
     tracts of peri-urban land as Coloured residential areas, and that for this reason they gave
     the Dept. of Community Development tacit support in the destruction of District Six.

commitment to solicit the trust of Coloureds. Not surprisingly, however, the fragmentation of families and long-established communities and the forced removal of Coloured people to isolated and soulless peri-urban ghettoes increased the disaffection of Coloured people. As if intending to compound this disaffection, the National Party whilst implementing the Coloured Preference Policy also proceeded with its plan to remove the remaining Coloured representation in Parliament and to establish a separate but entirely subordinate representative assembly for Coloureds.

By 1961 Verwoerd had vowed to establish a set of separate Coloured political institutions to honour the commitment he had made to his constituents in defending the introduction of the 1956 Seperate Representation of Voters Act. As a temporary measure, the Act had allocated four parliamentary seats for the representation of the Coloured electorate by White candidates.[36] Those Coloureds who voted supported opposition candidates for the most part. Brian Hackland has suggested that this was decisive in the National Party's decision to remove the remaining Coloured representation in parliament.[37]

In 1959 tensions within the United Party, the official opposition, over the question of participating in the segregated system contributed to the decision of disaffected members to form the Progressive Party.[38] The infant Progressive Party, however, "out of sympathy with those who advocated boycott" refused to nominate Coloured representatives.[39] By 1962 the Party had reversed its decision in the hope that coloured support would increase its representation in parliament. With Harry Oppenheimer's financial assistance, organisers were employed to canvas the Coloured vote.[40] By 1964 the Coloured membership of the Party had been increased to the extent that, Hackland suggests, "the government became more worried by the success of the party"[41]. In 1965, 1966 and 1967 the passage of amendments to the Separate Representation of Voters Amendment Act extended the terms of the sitting Coloured representatives, and the support of Coloureds for the Progressive Party was not tested. Then, in 1968, the Prohibition of Political Interference Act was passed which ended the representation of Coloureds in Parliament.

---

36. See Central Archives Pretoria, Evidence to Separate Voters Act, SABRA Evidence, para. 29.
37. B. Hackland, "The Progressive Party", pp. 266-268.
38. J. Strangewayes-Booth, *A Cricket in the Thorn Tree: Helen Suzman and the Progressive Party* (London, Hutchinson, 1976), pp.106-7, discusses the resignations of United Party members in relation to the Party's Coloured policy.
39. B. Hackland, "The Progressive Party", p.252.
40. *Ibid.;* p.260.
41. *Ibid.,* p.260.

In the same year the first election for the Coloured Persons Representative Council (CPRC) was held.

The establishment of the Representative Council and the ending of Coloured representation in parliament cannot, however, solely be attributed to the National Party's fears that Coloured voters would give their support to the Progressives. Such anxieties undoubtedly existed and may have influenced the timing of the new legislation; but the ending of Coloured representation in parliament and the establishment of the CPRC was more the culmination of a Verwoerdian scheme that underpinned the Separate Representation of Voters Act and which by 1964 was articulated in the Coloured Persons Representative Council Act.[42]

By 1969 the removal of the remaining Coloured representation in parliament and the creation of an entirely subservient institution for the representation of Coloureds had exhausted whatever goodwill might have remained in the Coloured communities after the destruction of District Six. Almost immediately the Cape National Party began to warn of a growing radicalisation of Coloured people. In an editorial the organ of the Party, *Die Burger,* criticised the harsh treatment of Coloureds. In spite of the earlier denial by Connie Mulder the paper returned to the theme that Coloureds were "brown Afrikaners" and the political "allies" and "junior partners" of the Whites.[43] It was necessary, the paper stressed, to secure "parallel plural co-existence" between White and Coloured people on a more equal basis.[44]

By April 1971 the Cape National Party, with the full backing of the Cape leader, P.W. Botha, had mobilised a campaign within the National Party to reverse what it regarded as the dangerous alienation of the Coloured.[45] As one element of this reformist drive a statement was signed by 138 Afrikaner academics calling for "full citizenship" for Coloureds.[46] Within the Dutch Reformed Churches dissent was also bubbling, with prominent theologians asserting the existence of the "three streams" within the "South African nation" comprising the Afrikaans, English and Coloured sub-cultures.[47] The Prime Minister, B.J. Vorster, appeared to be unmoved by these activities, choosing instead to reaffirm

42. See, for example, Verwoerd's 1961 address to the Union Council for Coloured Affairs in South Africa, *Policy Statement 17 May 1961*, p.5, and Verwoerd in *HAD,* 1961, 107, Col. 4191. It should be noted that the Coloureds were never given the opportunity to vote for Progressive Party parliamentarians. Their vote did, however, help to elect two Progressive Party candidates to the Cape Provincial Council.
43. *Die Burger,* 2 Dec. 1970.
44. *Ibid.*
45. *Die Burger,* 24 April 1971.
46. S.P. Cilliers *et al.,* "Memorandum", 1 April 1971; see also S.P. Cilliers, *Appeal to Reason* (Stellenbosch, Stellenbosch Univ. Press, 1971).
47. See *Woord en Daad,* May 1974, p.4.

his belief that Coloureds were a "nation in the making" and a "nation in its own right".[48] But early in 1973, in order to contain the growing revolt within National Party ranks and to appease moderate Coloured opinion, Vorster conceded to the appointment of a Commission of Inquiry into Matters Affecting the Coloured Population. Professor Erica Theron, one of the few members of SABRA who as a member of the Cape National Party had managed to straddle the gulf between the Cape and Transvaal National Parties, was nominated to chair the Commission. The appointment of the Commission served to remove the issue of Coloured rights from the National Party's agenda and this was no doubt the government's motivation. It was to be three years before the Commission reported. By that time, we shall show in Chapter Nine, Vorster's hold on the National Party's Coloured policies had been weakened further.

Coloured Preference and Employers

From 1961 the policy of Coloured Preference was applied with renewed vigour in the Western Cape. We have noted that anxious Afrikaner nationalists, confronted by mounting civil disobedience and buffeted by the "winds of change" sweeping through Africa, sought to defend themselves by the even more vigorous and far-reaching enforcement of the policy.[49] Whereas previously the policy had been enforced in the area West of the Eiselen line, the zone of preference in 1962 was redefined to include a much larger area; the new boundary included the 68 magisterial districts south of the Orange River and west of a line running between Humansdorp and Port Elizabeth, but excluding Port Elizabeth itself. In 1962 the Standing Cabinet Committee was established with the task of implementing the preferential employment policy for Coloured labour and reducing the number of Africans in the Western Cape. The execution of these goals was entrusted to a Permanent Interdepartmental Committee embracing seven departments. At the local level the policy was to be pursued by "local committees" representing employers, local authorities and the various government departments involved in the scheme.

By 1960 employers' concerns regarding the availability of African labour and a "native labour pool" had led to increasingly strident attacks on the Coloured Labour Preference Policy.[50] The economic crisis which followed the Sharpeville massacre of that year relieved the temporary labour shortage; at the same time the extent of African resistance added

48. *HAD,* 1971, 11, Col. 5110.
49. See Chapter Four.
50. See Chapter Five.

force to the strategic considerations underpinning the Preference Policy. In 1960 employers had been relieved that Coloureds had given only limited support to the nationwide protests and strikes. By 1962 — not surprisingly, given these strategic concerns and the slack demand for labour occasioned by the economic reversal — employers were lending their wholehearted support to the renewed campaign to enforce the Coloured Preference Policy.

In 1962 the Director of the Cape Employers' Association (CEA), Frank Lighton, accepted the post of secretary of the "Cape Peninsula Committee" established to facilitate the implementation of the Preference Policy. His committee, he told employers, believed that "there are many types of work in which the Bantu are at present employed but which could be adequately filled by Coloured labour."[51] The commitment of the Director of the Cape Employers' Association to "assist in the official policy" was echoed by the President of the Cape Chamber of Industries (CCI), who praised the "close and satisfactory cooperation between the Departments of Bantu Affairs and Labour and ourselves"[52]. The Director of the CCI emphasised that it was "not for want of trying" that they were not using more Coloured employees.[53]

In 1964 the passage of the Bantu Labour Act provided the framework for the implementation of the Bantu Labour Regulations. These embodied an overhaul of the labour bureaux system and established a firm link between employment and accommodation of Africans in the Western Cape.[54] The 1964 Act, the (Riekert) Commission of Inquiry into Manpower later clinically explained, was

> a consolidation of the Acts at the time regulating the recruitment, employment, accommodation, feeding and health conditions of the Black labourers.[55]

By 1964, 687 labour bureaux had been established which over the previous four years had processed the employment of over 4-million Africans.[56] With the passage of the 1964 Act the labour bureaux system was extended still further. In the Western Cape the pivotal role of the bureaux in implementing the Coloured Preference Policy was also enhanced.

51. F. Lighton (secretary), Cape Peninsula Local Committee Re Labour in the Western Cape, "Memorandum to Employer Organisations Regarding the Greater Utilisation of Coloured Labour in the Western Cape", memo, Cape Town, 1962, para. 1.
52. *Ibid.*, CCI, "Presidential Address by Mr D. Banade to the 56th AGM of the CCI", mimeo, Cape Town, 29 Jan. 1962, p.3.
53. *Ibid.*
54. See P.J. van der Merwe, "Die Bantoe Arbeidsmark in Suid Afrika" (Pretoria Univ., PhD thesis, 1971).
55. South Africa, *Report of the Commission of Inquiry into Manpower Matters* (Riekert) RP 32/1979 (Pretoria, Govt. Printer, 1979), para. 3.108.

In 1962, as an adjunct to the Permanent Interdepartmental Committee established to implement the Coloured Preference Policy, a housing subcommittee whose purpose was to facilitate the enforcement of the policy was formed. The committee decided that "no new family housing schemes in black areas should be undertaken", and that

> New black housing should be built for single persons (contract workers) in such a way that these hostels could subsequently be converted to accommodate Coloured families.[57]

In 1966, on the grounds that suitable accommodation was not available, the bureaux refused to consider employers' requests for recruitment of African contract workers. Simultaneously, the Department of Bantu Administration froze all additional construction of the hostels in which African migrant workers were compelled to reside.[58] The impact was immediate; employers who had only just begun to enjoy the fruits of the economic recovery found themselves unable to recruit African contract workers. The compulsory accommodation of contract workers in the registered hostels meant that by 1965 a limit had been set on the migrant workforce in the Western Cape. The regulations not only affected migrant workers, however, because there was also a virtual freeze on the construction of family housing. This led to further pressures on the already chronically overcrowded and inadequate accommodation of African families legally resident in the region.[59].

The Bantu Labour Regulations provided the machinery for more effective control of African labour in the Western Cape. All employers within the enlarged preference area were compelled to employ Coloured labour unless they were officially granted exemption. In practice this meant that all employers within the preference region were compelled to apply for Coloured labour to their local magistrate or Department of Labour. In terms of the regulations, if no unemployed Coloureds were registered and the office concerned was satisfied that the employer's wages and conditions of employment were attractive enough to draw Coloureds, but that no Coloureds could be recruited, the employer was issued a certificate indicating that Coloured labour was not available for

56. W. van Breda, *The Employment Process: a Manual on Black Labour* (Bloemfontein, Orange Free State Univ. 1975) Table 3.6.
57. Cited in S. Bekker and J. Coetzee, "Black Urban Employment and Coloured Labour Preference" (Grahamstown, Rhodes Univ. mimeo, 1980), p.6.
58. D. Selvan, "Housing Conditions for Migrant Workers in Cape Town", *SALDRU Working Paper No. 10* (Cape Town, SALDRU, 1976) p.6; for a background to the freeze see also M. Wilson and A. Mafeje, *Langa* (Cape Town, OUP, 1963), p.6, and L. Lee-Warden, "The Crime of Langa", *Africa South*, (3), 1957.
59. G. Lawrence, Deputy Director of Labour Cape Peninsula, interview, Cape Town, 11 Nov. 1979, transcript p.4.

the specific vacancy (or vacancies). On submission of this certificate to the Labour Bureaux concerned,

> supplementary Bantu labour is allowed on a single contract basis through the labour bureau system provided that Bantu labour is not available locally and that there is suitable housing.[60]

The enforcement of the regulations occurred at a time at which Western Cape employers were enjoying an upturn in the economic cycle, and it led to an immediate outcry from employers. The Cape Chamber of Industries complained bitterly that since the passage of the regulations its members had been frustrated in their attempts to recruit African labour. It noted that

> Authorisation has been refused through shortage of housing . . . The thinning-out process begun has been abrupt and drastic, and involved the refusal to allow replacements . . . The action which is being taken is hasty and disruptive. . . . The Chamber is being flooded with reports of cut-backs in production . . . [61]

The "time is surely coming," the Chamber argued, "when those in economic authority will have to face the question as to whether the Western Cape . . .is going to advance economically or not."[62]

The response of the government was to tighten further the "disruptive" policy, whilst at the same time offering some positive tax and other incentives to employers of Coloured labour in designated "decentralised growth points".[63] From 1966 employers in Kimberley, De Aar, Upington and other Northern Cape towns qualified for these incentives. The incentives, however, failed to appease Western Cape employers. On the contrary, their anxieties were compounded by news of further cutbacks in their labour complements.

On 31 January 1966 it was announced that the African labour force in all Western Cape enterprises was to be frozen and that in the following years the African labour force would be reduced at a rate of 5 per cent per annum.[64] To add to the increasing difficulties of employers a system

60   South Africa, *Bantu Labour Regulations,* Govt. Gazette 18/1292, 1965, Chap. 8 para. 21.
61. CCI, Presidential Address by Mr R. Mossop to the 62nd AGM of the CCI, mimeo, Cape Town, 24 Nov. 1966, p.5.
62. *Ibid.,* pp.5-6.
63. South Africa, *Coloured Commission, 1976,* paras. 5.29 (a-c); South Africa, Dept. of Industries, *White Paper on the Report of the Interdepartmental Committee on the Decentralisation of Industries* (Pretoria, Govt. Printer, 1971), paras.34-35. In 1971 Mossel Bay, George, Knysna and Oudtshoorn and in 1973 Darling and Atlantis were added to the list of "decentralised growth points".
64. Mr Pietersen, Bantu Affairs Commissioner for Western Cape, interview, Goodwood, 1 Dec. 1981, transcript p.2.

was introduced in September 1966 by which all employers in the Western Cape were compelled to apply to the Department of Industries, Trade and Tourism for a quota specifying their permissable African workforce.[65]

In 1967 the preference system in Western Cape magisterial districts was entrenced still further with the passage of the Physical Planning Act. By this Act,

> Persons wishing to establish or extend factories in these magisterial districts may use only Coloured or White labour for such establishment or extension. If Coloured labour is not available application to employ Bantu may be made to the Minister of Planning and Environment.[66]

Clearly, as a Department of Industries White Paper later confirmed, the industrial development of the Western Cape was to be subjected to constraints imposed by the political priority of Coloured labour preference.[67] In the words of the Deputy Minister of Bantu Affairs, Blaar Coetzee, the government was "resolved to carry out this plan whatever the cost."[68]

By February 1967 Cape employers had been severely affected by the constraints placed on their recruitment of African workers. Labour shortages in the dairies, in the fishing industry, in the hotel trade and in the furniture industry were reported whilst builders complained of shortages of brick and clay as a result of the impact of the freeze on quarries and brick manufacturers.[69] For farmers, in addition to the direct impact of the regulations, the shortages were aggravated by a knock-on effect of the urban labour shortage as urban employers, particularly in the construction industry, took to recruiting Coloured labour in the rural hinterland.[70] The result, according to Jack Basson MP, was that

> It was rural areas that suffered most from the lack of Coloured labour, because Coloured people were being canvassed in the platteland to work in the towns.[71]

65. *Ibid.*, pp.2-4. The quota system was only applicable in the Western Cape but in 1975 was extended to the rest of the preference region and to Port Elizabeth and Uitenhage. In 1978 Port Elizabeth and Uitenhage were exempted and a system enforced which permitted the recruitment of African labour, providing the level of Coloured unemployment did not exceed 2 per cent.
66. South Africa, *Physical Planning and Utilisation of Resources Act,* No. 88 of 1967, Section 3(1).
67. South Africa, Dept. of Industries, *White Paper,* para. 33.
68. Cited in *Cape Times,* 17 March 1967.
69. *Cape Times,* 8 Jan. 1967, 30 Jan. 1967, 7 Feb. 1967, 1 Feb. 1969, 14 Feb. 1969, 24 Feb. 1969.
70. *Cape Times,* 23 Jan. 1969; *Cape Times,* 14 Feb. 1969.
71. Cited in *Ibid.*

Farmers refused to compete with the higher wages offered by urban employers and bitterly resented the recruitment of rural workers by the predominantely English-speaking industrialists. In late February, when the seasonal harvest commenced, the competition for labour reached unprecedented intensity. Farmers and food-processors soon added their voices to the growing clamour of opposition to the regulations associated with the Coloured Preference Policy.[72] In March, at a rowdy meeting attended by over 200 Hex River farmers, the Deputy Minister of Bantu Affairs, Blaar Coetzee, was forced to concede to the farmers' demands to be exempted from the freeze.[73] This precedent having been set, Afrikaner farmers in other rural areas, many of whom enjoyed considerable local patronage and a close relationship with the National Party, were able to secure similar exemptions. The exemptions were also extended to the docks to prevent fruit exports from being disrupted as a result of shortages of African contract workers.[74] Government departments, furthermore, had little difficulty in gaining exemptions. For example, the Department of Transport successfully petitioned for an exemption on the grounds that it required 2 000 Africans for work which "the Coloureds are not prepared to do".[75] Afrikaner small-businessmen in the towns were less well placed; the Afrikaanse Handelsinstituut from the mid-1960s complained that its members experienced "a severe labour shortage in the Western Cape".[76]

By 1977 Cape urban employers found themselves increasingly subjected to a rigid bureaucracy which considerably restricted their recruitment of African labour. It will be recalled that employers had in broad terms supported the intentions of the Coloured Preference Policy — their objections focused on the practical difficulties of employing Coloured labour in place of African labour in unskilled jobs. During 1965, the Cape Chamber of Industries noted, "complaints continued about the availability and quality of Coloured labour for unskilled jobs and the irregularity of attendance."[77] From 1966, ironically, the Chamber began to blame the problem on the very success of the Preference Policy:

> Attention of the authorities to Coloured education is directing more and more young Coloured to work of a clerical nature, commercial work or,

72. *Cape Times,* 24 Feb. 1967; A. van Niekerk, President, Deciduous Fruit Growers Association, interview, Worcester, 10 Dec. 1981, transcript p.1.
73. *Argus,* 17 March 1967; *Cape Times,* 17 March 1967.
74. D. Hofmeyer, Economist, Elgin Farmers Co-op., interview, 17 Jan. 1980; *Cape Times,* 25 March 1967; *Argus,* 30 April 1970.
75. Unisa Acc. 60, Report No. 26, South African Railways and Harbour Board, "Oral Evidence to the Theron Commission", 4 Feb. 1975, p.3.
76. *Argus,* 30 April 1970, citing F. Kirsten, president of the Handelsinstituut.
77. CCI, *Yearbook, 1965-66* (Cape Town, CCI, 1966), p.27.

when they do turn to industry, at least semi-skilled work. The manual labour-ing class among Coloureds of the Cape is becoming increasingly hard to find . . . In the case of Coloured upliftment there must be a warning and a plea that the sights are not set too high . . . By the example of their fellows' success, enthusiasm for taking on work of a white-collar or clerical nature, or requesting highly paid semi-skilled work for which they are not fully trained, will engender in many that labour work is beneath their capacities. This, oc-curring synchronously with an active drive of Bantu Affairs to decrease the number of Bantu in the Western Cape, is having a sharp and tragic effect on industry.[78]

The Department of Labour implicitly accepted that Coloured labour was not prepared to perform certain unskilled tasks at the wages which employers were prepared to pay. The Department therefore was pre-pared to issue "Certificates of Non-Availability of Coloured Labour" to employers seeking to recruit Africans for heavy manual, low-status occu-pations such as nightsoil duties and shiftwork such as milk delivery.[79] On the other hand the Department refused to consider applications for the recruitment of African contract labour for jobs which it considered to be less arduous and the sole preserve of Coloureds and Africans legally resident in the Western Cape. Such jobs were held by, among others, vehicle-drivers, cleaners, newspaper sellers, petrol attendants, ice-cream sellers, domestic servants and clerks, packers and time-keepers.[80]

In 1967 it was apparent that the commitment of crucial government departments to Coloured preference no longer extended to the "ultimate elimination" of Africans from the region. In practice these departments had capitulated to a number of the employers' demands, and accepted that Africans could continue to be employed in certain categories of work. Furthermore, according to F. Lighton, the Director of the Cape Employers' Association,

> The impossibility of including every firm in the 5 per cent reduction policy was recognised and the policy was changed in an attempt to secure an overall 5 per cent reduction.[81]

This modification provided the Department of Labour with consider-able flexibility, which it used to exempt a range of employers from the cutbacks on the grounds that Coloured workers were unsuitable for the

78. CCI, Presidential Address by Mr R. Mossop to the 62nd AGM of the CCI, Cape Town, mimeo, 24 Nov. 1966, p.4.
79. J. de Reuk, Regional Labour Commissioner, interview, Cape Town, 7 Nov, 1979, tran-script p.9.
80. Unisa Acc. 60, Dept. of Labour (I.P. van Onselen), "The Western Cape" memo, n.d., Appendix D.
81. Cape Employers' Association, "Symposium on Bantu Administration Boards", mimeo, Stellenbosch Univ., 20 Sept. 1974, p.23.

job at hand. Significantly, it was precisely those employers who had initially campaigned for the introduction of a preference policy that were first able to secure exemption from its more disruptive elements. Afrikaner farmers and government employers had access to the state executive in a manner denied to most other employers. As a consequence, urban employers in the private sector suffered most from the reduction policy: they were forced to decrease their African labour force by more than 5 per cent in order to secure an aggregate 5 per cent reduction amongst all employers.

By the end of 1968 the African labour force in manufacturing had fallen 7 per cent below the previous year's level.[82] In October 1969 a survey conducted by the Cape Chamber of Industries revealed that over 85 per cent of the respondents were experiencing difficulties in obtaining African labour and that over half suffered from chronic shortages.[83] The Labour and Non-European Affairs Committee of the Chamber therefore appealed to the Government to allow the further recruitment of African labour.[84] Simultaneously, the committee stressed that

> It must be fairly emphasised that the Committee is not pressing for the abandonment of Government policy, but for a flexible application of that policy in order to alleviate the acute unskilled labour shortage in the Western Cape.[85]

The Committee insisted that practical problems rather than any objections in principle to the Coloured Preference Policy prevented the further substitution of Coloured for African labour. The most pervasive practical problem, it was agreed by the representatives of organised employers, was the perceived inability of Coloured workers to perform arduous manual tasks.

Stereotypes of Coloured Labour

The ability of Coloured workers to resist the levels of exploitation endured by unskilled African workers tended to be viewed by employers in terms of racial stereotypes. In 1973, in its evidence to the Theron Commission, the Cape Chamber of Industries (CCI) pleaded for the maintenance of a supply of African labour to the Western Cape. The CCI

> accepted the Government's policy that Coloureds should be given preference for employment in the Western Cape as their home territory, but subject to

82. *CCI,* Presidential Address by Mr W. Goldberg to the 64th AGM of the CCI, mimeo, 28 Nov, 1968, p.6.
83. CCI, Report of the CCI Industry and Non-European Affairs Committee Regarding the Investigation of the Shortage in Western Cape Industry, mimeo, 1970, p.5.
84. *Ibid.,* p.27.
85. *Ibid.*

the highly important qualification that *Coloureds should be available and adequate for the work required of them.*[86]

It went on to note that

In practice Coloureds have not made themselves available, nor have they become adaptable for certain classes of work, primarily in the unskilled labour field, such as that of heavy manual labour.[87]

According to its members,

Deficiencies amongst Coloureds which are sufficiently prevalent to cause concern to industry are:
(1) *A high rate of absenteeism* (15%)
(2) *Unpunctuality*
(3) *Greater interest in time off than in working and earning.*[88]

The CCI's comments on Coloured labour were reiterated in the submissions of all the Western Cape employer organisations to the Theron Commissioners. In addition to the factors outlined above, the Afrikaanse Handelsinstituut emphasised that Coloureds showed an "unwillingness to do shiftwork or to work at night" and moreover there was an "unwillingness to do heavy work".[89] Absenteeism and high labour turnovers were seen to be further problems associated with employing Coloureds. According to the Handelsinstituut, Natal factories employing "Zulu" workers experienced a turnover a year of less than 25 per cent compared with the 100 per cent experienced in Cape factories employing Coloured labour. Similarly, whilst the mid-week absenteeism rate in the Natal factories was less than 2 per cent, the Cape rate was 15 per cent.[90]

Without exception the evidence of employers' organisations to the Theron Commission claimed that Coloured unskilled labour was "workshy". The Cape Employers' Association (CEA) in its evidence to the Commission noted that employers compelled to employ unskilled Coloureds suffered from "well-nigh intolerable difficulties"[91]. The CEA found that in certain jobs,

Many Coloureds, on seeing the work involved, do not even commence duty and the *maximum period* a Coloured person in fact remains on the job is *THREE WEEKS.* [92]

86. Unisa Acc. 60, CCI "Evidence to Theron Commission, 17 Aug. 1973", para. 1.1 (emphasis in original).
87. *Ibid.*, para.1.2.
88. *Ibid.*, para.2.3 (emphasis in original).
89. Unisa Acc. 60, Afrikaanse Handelsinstituut Evidence to the Theron Commission, mimeo, n.d., para. 34.
90. *Ibid.*
91. Unisa Acc. 100, Cape Employers' Assoc. Evidence, mimeo, 6 Aug. 1973, para. 8.
92. *Ibid.* (emphasis in original).

The CEA complained bitterly that "existing legislation providing for work-shy persons to be committed to rehabilitation centres by a magistrate is not effective."[93] In the view of the Cape Employers' Association, tougher action on "work-shy" Coloureds provided the only alternative to a continuing commitment of the Association to the employment of African workers in unskilled tasks.

The Midland Chamber of Industries, although less robust in its remedy, also pointed to the fact that in its view lower-class Coloureds were "shiftless, irresponsible, work-shy and given to drink".[94] Such a perception of unskilled Coloured was shared by the Western Cape National Development and Management Foundation (NDMF), which emphasised to the Department of Bantu Affairs that

> Coloured labour should not be regarded as a substitute for Black labour in the Western Cape . . . [Coloureds] have an aversion to heavy manual labour . . . Indolence, abhorrence of hard work and limited ambition inhibit progress of most Coloureds . . . The only solution seems to be the employment of Bantu contract labourers.[95]

Overwhelmed by employers' protests, the Theron Commissioners accepted that Coloured preference policies were ultimately flawed by the strength of employer resistance to unskilled Coloured labour. The "most important reason" for the failure of the replacement policy, according to a parliamentary review of the Commission, was that

> Employers in the private as well as the public sector are inclined to prefer Black labour to lower-class Coloured labour, which carried the risk that they may be work-shy or unmotivated.[96]

Sections of the administration in fact had long since accepted that Coloureds were unsuitable for certain jobs. The powerful Department of Native Affairs was, however, less sympathetic to employers' grievances.

In 1937 the *Report of the Commission of Inquiry into the Coloured*

---

93. *Ibid.,* para.9.
94. Unisa Acc. 100, Midland Chamber of Industries Evidence, 10 Aug. 1973, para. 2.
95. National Development and Management Foundation, Cape Western Region, *Long-Term Development of the Western Cape, Proceedings of a seminar held in Cape Town, 16-17 May 1973,* p.34.
96. *HAD,* 1950,87,Col.7467. It should be emphasised that employers do not only discriminate against certain sections of the Coloured population. Our survey of employers found that important distinctions are made between permanently settled, contract and illegal workers. The Coloured Preference Policy, we argue elsewhere, by deepening the division between these three categories of African workers has reinforced the distinctions made by employers between different groups of Africans. For a full discussion of Western Cape employers' attitudes to Africans see I. Goldin, "Economics and Ideology in the Western Cape", *SALDRU Working Paper No.59* (Cape Town, SALDRU, 1984), pp.17-23, 40-91.

Population had noted that employers felt that "generally unskilled Coloureds are less dependable and less efficient than Africans"[97]. The Commission accepted that there was a

> consensus of opinion among employers of Coloured labour that the Native is on the average superior in physique to the Cape Coloured, and in consequence is able to stand the strain of hard manual labour. For these and other reasons employers often prefer to employ the native as labour, even where they are able to obtain the Coloured at the same wage.[98]

Two years later, in 1939, the Minister of Labour cited these reasons and the lower wages accepted by Africans as a reason for the continued influx of African labour into the Western Cape. "The native," he noted, "is very often of a better physical type and moreover has a lower standard of living."[99] Already by 1939, therefore, the Department of Labour had accepted that Coloureds were unable or unwilling to perform certain categories of unskilled manual work. From 1955 this shared conviction of employers and the Department of Labour placed the Department on a collision course with the Department of Native Affairs; under the guidance of Verwoerd and Eiselen, the Department of Native Affairs embarked on a crusade to secure the "ultimate elimination of natives" from the Western Cape.[100] The Department of Labour, however, found the Department of Native Affairs' plan unworkable; in 1955 J. de Klerk, the Minister of Labour, agreed with employers that Coloureds were "work-shy" and unsuitable for certain jobs.[101] But a serious clash between the two departments did not arise until the mid-1960s.

Until 1966 the control of African influx and employment was the sole preserve of the Department of Native Affairs. In that year the overhaul of the Coloured Labour Preference system required increased cooperation between the Department of Native Affairs and the Department of Labour. In terms of a compromise between the contending Departments, the Department of Labour was given jurisdiction to issue "Certificates of Non-Availability of Coloured Labour".[102] These certificates authorised employers to engage Africans legally resident in the local administration board area. Employers wishing to recruit migrant workers

97. South Africa, *"Coloured Commission, 1937"*, para. 34.
98. *Ibid.*
99. *Senate Debates*, 1939, Col. 590.
100. W.W. Eiselen, "The Coloured People and the Natives", p.15.
101. Cited in *The Torch*, 29 Nov. 1955.
102. Mr Keal, Director of Coloured Labour, Labour Department, interview, Cape Town, 17 November 1981, transcript p.1; Unisa Acc. 100, Report No. 26, Dept. of Labour, Oral Evidence to Theron Commission, 4 Jan. 1975, para. 18.2.

faced additional hurdles; they required the Department of Native Affairs to certify that no local Africans were available for employment and that the terms and conditions of employment offered (which necessarily included registered accommodation) met with the Department's approval. The Department of Native Affairs accordingly maintained control over the influx and employment of migrant workers. But the employment of legally resident local Africans came under the jurisdiction of the Department of Labour, which, we have noted, accepted that Coloured workers were unsuitable for many unskilled tasks and as a matter of course allowed local Africans to enter arduous unskilled employment.[103]

By 1973 the Department of Labour had granted exemptions for the employment of Africans within the Coloured preference area as heavy manual labourers, shift workers, cold-storage workers and night-watchmen.[104] These exemptions translated into official policy stereotypes regarding the unsuitability of Coloureds for heavy manual labour as well as prejudices regarding their dishonesty, unreliability and absenteeism. The Department of Labour justified the exemptions on the grounds that

> Coloureds, in general, are not interested in night work or weekend work . . . Over the years employers have developed an attitude towards Coloureds, especially in the unskilled class of work, that they are alcoholics and poor workers.[105]

The Department of labour was not the only government department to call for the continued recruitment of Africans for unskilled jobs. The Department of Transport was similarly disposed. It explained that

> In certain occupations, especially where there is heavy manual labour, preference is given to Bantu because they are better physically adapted than Coloureds for this type of work . . . The urbanised Coloured is reluctant to perform heavy manual labour and overtime work at weekends.[106]

Summary

By the 1870s employers in the Western Cape had shown a preference for the employment of African men in many unskilled manual occupations. A century later, employers' preferences had been sustained and reinforced by deeply embedded stereotypes regarding the particular merits of African labour. In 1973 these prejudices were echoed by Whittingdale, an economic historian of the Western Cape. In a dissertation

103. *Ibid.,* paras. 18.2 — 4.
104. *Ibid.*
105. *Ibid.,* paras. 18.1 — 7.
106, Unisa Acc. 60, Report No. 26, South African Railways and Harbours, Oral Evidence to Theron Commission, 4 Feb. 1975, p.3.

accepted by the University of Cape Town he concluded that Coloureds were prone to absenteeism, drink and violence. He noted, however, that

> The Bantu labourer on the other hand has few personality problems in his character and is admirably suited to dull repetitive work as well as heavy manual labour.[107]

From the outset employers' concerns for a "pool of labour" dogged attempts by the Department of Native (later Bantu) Affairs to enforce its replacement policy. By the mid 1970s public and private sector employers continued to reply on African workers to perform unskilled manual labour. The Department of Labour tacitly accepted the employers' patterns of preference. At the same time, many employers augmented their legal quotas by employing Africans illegally. The overall effect was the failure of the Coloured Preference Policy to act in support of unskilled Coloured workers. The employment of Africans under conditions which Coloured men and women resisted was reinforced by prevailing prejudices. The net result, the Theron Commissioners concluded in 1976, was that within the Coloured population

> The employment prospects for at least the bottom 30 per cent, in terms of education and social status, are very unfavourable. There will be no permanent or continuous employment prospects for this group . . .[108]

This "bottom 30 per cent", Erica Theron later explained, were "unemployable" under the present policy.[109] By contrast, the employment prospects of the skilled stratum of Coloureds, the Theron Commissioners found, were "extremely optimistic".[110] Skilled and educated Coloureds had not been disadvantaged by the Coloured Preference Policy. The Coloured skilled and artisan strata stood to benefit from protection against African training and apprenticeships and from the growth of the Coloured supervisory and clerical occupations. The opportunities for their advancement were nevertheless restricted; the Department of Labour continued to ensure the superiority of White workers within the labour market.[111] Prior to 1976 the movement of Coloured workers into skilled and supervisory positions was not at the expense of White workers. Furthermore, Coloured supervisors and skilled workers except in isolated instances were not permitted to supervise the activities of White workers. The political and trade union muscle of White workers continued to restrict the upward mobility of Coloured skilled work-

107. J. Whittingdale, "Industry in Cape Town", p.169.
108. South Africa, *"Coloured Commission, 1976,"* para.5.126.
109. E. Theron, interview, p.12.
110. South Africa, *"Coloured Commission, 1976"*, para.5.126.
111. See Min. of Labour, M. Viljoen, cited in *Cape Times*, 5 June 1970.

ers. As a consequence the remuneration of Coloured employees in the manufacturing sector declined relative to their White counterparts from 41 per cent in 1945 to 24 per cent in 1970.[112]

Despite the barriers placed on Coloured advancement by the National Party, the Party went out of its way between 1961 and 1976 to promote a small but politically significant Coloured bourgeoisie. In 1962 the Coloured Development Corporation (CDC) was established with the explicit aim of "encouraging and assisting the growth of an entrepreneurial group among the Coloured people."[113] In order to complement the activities of the corporation, the Department of Coloured Affairs increasingly began to employ Coloured men in administrative positions. By 1970 approximately 86 per cent of the 24 860 people classified as Coloured professionals were employed by the state, and by 1974 over 31 000 government jobs were reserved for Coloureds.[114] In the same year the government committed itself to increasing its complement of Coloured employees by over 9 per cent per annum.[115]

For skilled and educated Coloured workers and the petty bourgeoisie, and for the emerging Coloured bourgeoisie, the Coloured Preference Policy offered protected employment and other advantages. The overwhelming majority of Coloured people, however, were no better off as a result of the policy. According to the 1970 census, over 50 per cent of Coloured men earned less than R500 a year, whilst a similar proportion of Coloured women earned less than R240 a year.[116] The poverty datum line at the time was estimated to be R840 a year.[117]

The Coloured Preference Policy had set out to improve the position of Coloured people. However, between 1961 and 1976, despite the renewed commitment of the state to protected employment, the policy had failed to benefit more than a minority of Coloured men and women. Furthermore, whilst the policy aimed to foster a feeling of unity amongst people designated as Coloured, in practice it had the opposite effect; economic and residential stratification reinforced class divisions within the Coloured community. This polarisation, we shall argue in the next chapter, had a profound impact on the development of Coloured political identity.

112. South Africa, *"Coloured Commission, 1976"*, para.5.107 fn.1.
113. South Africa, *Coloured Development Act*, No. 4 of 1962, Preamble.
114. Administration of Coloured Affairs, "Occupational Opportunities" in H. van der Merwe and C. Groenewald, *Occupational Change*, p.143; South Africa, *"Coloured Commission. 1976"*, para.5.85.
115. *Ibid.*
116. *Ibid.*, para. 5.109 fn. 1.
117. W. Thomas, "Socio-economic Development of the Coloured People", in H. van der Merwe and C. Groenewald, *Occupational Change*, p.48.

CHAPTER EIGHT

THE COLOURED POLITICAL RESPONSE: 1961 — 1976

Introduction

Between 1961 and 1976 the Coloured Preference Policy widened the economic gulf between unskilled and petty-bourgeois Coloured men and women. Whereas the Coloured petty bourgeoisie benefited from protected employment, unskilled Coloureds found that the Preference Policy reinforced employers' preferences for African labour.

With the widening of the gulf between the various Coloured strata, many of the remaining strands which held together a notion of a common Coloured identity were torn. By the early 1970s the growing alienation of educated and skilled Coloureds from the lower strata of Coloureds added urgency to the Coloured petty bourgeoisie's demands to be integrated into White society. In 1973, for example, Richard van der Ross, the vice-chancellor of the University of the Western Cape and the first leader of the Labour Party, remarked that

> There is today no greater feeling of unity among the Coloured people than there was ten years ago. Indeed, and herein lies both the irony and the blight of Verwoerd's hopes, it is precisely because of the economic development and educational and social-cultural advances of the Coloured people that they will not unify, but will drift further apart. The strata will drift further apart, those in the upper cultural-economic strata feeling that they have less and less in common with those in the low subeconomic strata. Colour per se is not a unifying factor.[1]

Those in the upper strata, van der Ross commented, aspired to be assimilated with the White middle class.[2]

Over a century before, the vote had been given to better-off Coloureds on the grounds that it was "better to disarm them by letting them participate in the privileges of the constitution" than to drive them into laagers.[3] From 1853 to 1956 the overwhelming majority of Coloureds had remained disfranchised. Nevertheless, until the passage of the Separate Representation of Voters Act the qualified franchise had served to temper the disaffection of the Coloured élite and to prevent

1. R.E. van der Ross, "Political and Social History", pp. 875-6.
2. *Ibid.*, p. 876; R.E. van der Ross, interview, p. 9.
3. William Porter, cited in Trapido, "White Politics", p. 39 (see Chapter One).

them from throwing their full weight behind the African political leadership.

It was no accident that the introduction of the Coloured Preference Policy occured concurrently with the passage of the Separate Representation of Voters Act; the policy aimed to soften the blow of disfranchisement and to limit an alliance of Coloured and African people. With the passage of the Separate Representation of Voters Act the political prospects of the Coloured élite were placed on an entirely separate trajectory to that of Whites. The Preference Policy, however, aimed to provide skilled and petty-bourgeois Coloureds with limited occupational mobility. For, as the Commissioner of Coloured Affairs in 1955 explained,

> The growth in the number of educated Coloureds makes it imperative that more should be done to provide openings for the better class of Coloured, for there is a growing feeling of frustration among the more progressive section of that people.[4]

The Coloured Preference Policy, we noted, promoted the development of the Coloured petty bourgeoisie and the artisan class. The policy, however, never intended to remove the barriers between the Coloured and White petty-bourgeois and artisan strata. In the economic sphere, skilled and relatively wealthy Coloureds found their position relative to Whites limited by statutory ceilings imposed on Coloured job mobility. To compound their frustration, the Preference Policy was linked to the disfranchisement of the Coloured electorate and the establishment of a separate and subordinate system of Coloured representation. The Preference Policy therefore led to improvements in the position of skilled and petty-bourgeois Coloureds compared with the rest of the Coloured population and with Africans; but it failed to improve the position of the Coloured petty bourgeoisie relative to Whites.

The Radical Challenge

By 1962 the Coloured Peoples' Congress (CPC, formerly SACPO) had been silenced and many of its leaders banned or arrested. The NEUM leadership, by contrast, weathered the state of emergency relatively unscathed. Only a handful of NEUM activists were arrested and harassed, and these for activities outside the organisation. From 1962 the NEUM was thus able to assume a virtually uncontested monopoly over radical Coloured politics.

4.   Unisa Acc. 60, Box 51, "Memorandum from Commissioner of Coloured Affairs", p. 2.

The NEUM was vocal in its condemnation of the Coloured Preference Policy and of attempts to promote a distinct Coloured identity. In the Western Cape, however, the Movement failed to translate this commitment into action or to support attempts by "ad-hoc" committees to mobilise Coloured and African people around particular issues. In fact in the Western Cape the NEUM restricted its attempts to organise Africans to the recruitment of African intellectuals. In the late 1940s the Cape African Teachers' Association (CATA) had affiliated to the NEUM, and during the 1950s the NEUM had attempted to weld an alliance of Coloured and African teachers.[5] But because of the failure of the NEUM to support the CATA campaign against the Bantu Education Act the CATA had, by 1962, disaffiliated from the NEUM.[6] From that time, the NEUM failed to recruit the support of more than a handful of African intellectuals.

In 1962 the NEUM established the African Peoples' Democratic Union of Southern Africa (APDUSA). APDUSA, according to a former executive member, was formed "as a specifically political affiliate of the Unity Movement, with the object of recruiting people directly on a political basis."[7] The programme of APDUSA was the Ten Point Programme of the NEUM formulated in 1943. The first official conference of APDUSA was held in Cape Town in 1962 and from this time on APDUSA became virtually synonomous with the NEUM. Like it, APDUSA was dominated by Coloured teachers.[8] These teachers exercised positions of considerable influence within their communities, but their influence seldom stretched beyond the boundaries of the Coloured residential areas.

From 1962 APDUSA and its affiliates followed the well-tested NEUM tactics of non-collaboration. This strategy was not confined to dealings with the government: NEUM affiliates refused to collaborate with other radical organisations engaged in resistance to the regime, and rather focused their energies on a boycott of segregated Coloured institutions. The boycott campaign was given its fullest expression in the organisation of resistance to the separate voters' roll and to the elections for the Coloured Persons Representative Council (CPRC). The CPRC, according to *The Educational Journal,* was a "mock council" which could only "speak as a ventriloquist's doll", which was a "shabby substitute for citizenship rights".[9]

5. A. Mafeje, interview, p. 6; N. Alexander, interview, p. 8.
6. *Ibid.*, pp. 7-8.
7. K. Hassim, "Hassim on Apdusa", *Work in Progress,* 31 May 1984, p. 14.
8. N. Alexander, interview, p. 9.
9. *The Educational Journal*, April/May, 1968. pp. 2-4.

The NEUM focused its attention on the issue of citizenship rights and on the illegitimacy of separate Coloured political institutions. These issues were of pressing concern to many Coloureds, but the fact that the NEUM made little headway in involving Africans or unskilled Coloureds in its campaigns suggests that its policy was not of direct relevance to these groups. The Movement's influence within the Coloured population may be gauged in part from the support for the election boycott called by the NEUM in 1958.

In that year the Coloured Peoples' Congress (CPC) urged Coloureds to support the candidates of the White Congress of Democrats (COD) in the general election. With considerable success, however, the NEUM urged Coloured men and women not to register on the separate voters' roll. As we saw in Chapter Six, 47 849 Coloured men and were registered on the common roll in 1953[10], but by 1958 only 19 138 had registered on the separate roll, despite the fact that the revised roll was open to all Coloured men and women over the age of 21.[11] By 1963 the collapse of the CPC and the increased disaffection of Coloureds from the government, together with an improvement in the NEUM's relative standing within the Coloured communities, had reduced the number registered to a mere 9 839, less than 5 per cent of those eligible for the separate roll.[12] From 1964 the National Party introduced compulsory registration for Coloureds on the separate voters' roll.

The elections for the Coloured Persons Representative Council (CPRC) were held in September 1969. By that time the number of registered voters had reached 637 587, 75 per cent of those eligible.[13] The illegality of boycotting the electoral register together with the willingness of many Coloureds to give the CPRC a chance to prove its merits succeeded in increasing the registered electorate from less than 5 per cent in 1963 to five times that figure, and 47 per cent of the registered electorate voted in the 1969 CPRC election.[14] The poll was highest in the rural constituencies whilst the boycott was most successful in the areas where NEUM claimed greatest support; in seven Cape urban constituencies the percentage poll was less that 30 per cent.[15] By 1975, however, growing disillusionment with the CPRC had led to an 82 per cent drop in the registered electorate and the registration of only 116 030 Coloureds.[16]

10. *HAD*, 1959, 4, Col. 1209.
11. *Ibid.*
12. B. Hackland, "The Progressive Party", p. 253; F. Molteno, "Coloured Politics", in M. Murray (ed.), *"Black Political Opposition"*, p. 634.
13. Unisa Acc. 100, Evidence of Progressive Party to Theron Commission, p. 4; *The Educational Journal*, July-Aug. 1981, p. 16.
14. Unisa Acc. 237, File C. 1.13.1, "Election statistics 1969-1980", p.2.
15. *Ibid.*

The resistance of the Coloured electorate to the CPRC was further reflected in the low turnout for the 1975 elections; the percentage poll was barely 37, and in a number of Cape Peninsula constituencies less than 10 per cent of the registered electorate voted.[17]

The collapse of support for the CPRC was regarded by the NEUM affiliates as evidence of their decisive influence over the Coloured communities of the Western Cape. The monopoly exercised by the the NEUM over radical Coloured politics meant that the NEUM had been alone in calling for a boycott of the polls. The NEUM therefore derived the maximum credit from the opposition to the CPRC elections and from the disillusionment which set in almost immediately the CPRC began to function.

The Coloured Persons Representative Council was comprised of 40 elected representatives and 20 state nominees. The assembly had been constituted with the promise that it would have statutory responsibility for all matters affecting the Coloured population.[18] But in practice the CPRC was subordinate to the Minister of Coloured Affairs. For in terms of the Coloured Persons Representative Council Act,

> No proposed law shall be introduced in the Council except with the approval of the Minister...[19]
> A law ... shall have the force of law as long and as far only as it is not repugnant to any Act of Parliament.[20]

APDUSA and its affiliates savagely attacked the CPRC as a "dummy institution" and condemned the representative councillors as "collaborators".[21] This vitriolic attack on the participating parties heightened the tension within the Coloured communities and brought into the open differences over the question of Coloured identity. The NEUM lumped togther all participants in the Council as collaborators. But it is useful to distinguish between the Labour Party, which may be termed a "discretionary collaborator" for it stipulated the conditions of its participation, and the Federal Party, which had no such reservations.

16. Unisa Acc. 237, File C.1.13.6.3, "1975 election results", p. 1.
17. *Ibid.*
18. L. Curry, interview, Cape Town, 12 Jan. 1982, transcript p. 4; *HAD*, 11, 1968, Col. 2930.
19. South Africa, *Coloured Persons Representative Council Act*, No. 49 of 1964, Section 21(2).
20. *Ibid.*, Section 25 (4)
21. *The Educational Journal*, April-May 1968, pp. 2-5.

The Labour Party

The Labour Party was established in 1965. According to its programme, the priority for the Party was the return of the Coloured people to common roll representation.[22] Richard van der Ross, a founder of the Party, claimed that the Labour Party aimed to use the CPRC as a temporary institution through which to advance "full citizenship for Coloureds".[23] In aiming for the return of Coloureds to the common roll the Party nevertheless accepted the government's political distinction between Coloureds and Africans. This distinction was deeply rooted in the Party's Constitution, which declared that "It is the intention of the Party in the first instance to consolidate the position of the Coloured people in South Africa."[24]

The intention of the Party was to use the CPRC to advance the claim of Coloureds for common-roll representation. The Party, however, did not oppose the existence of a distinct Coloured group or seek to extend its programme to embrace Africans. The Party was unequivocally a Coloured one, with its membership and organisational objectives defined to coincide with racial categories. The Party justified this exclusiveness in terms of the statutory obstacles which prevented official representation of Africans by Coloureds. The law, however, did not demand that the Party ignore the wider interests of the black population. Furthermore, as we shall see, the Party when it so chose was able to extend its brief to include African people.

From the beginning, the acceptance by the Labour Party of the organisation's racial exclusiveness was contested. From 1965, conflicts within the Labour Party over the issue polarised around those who sought to use the CPRC to advance the position of Coloureds as "junior partners" of the Whites, and those who aimed to use the CPRC as a means to campaign for the return of Coloureds to the common roll.[25] The APO, it will be recalled, confronted a similar dilemma to the CPRC. Like Adurahman, Richard van der Ross was faced with the ambiguities arising out of the contradictory position of the Coloured petty bourgeoisie. The Labour Party leadership confined its activities to matters relating only to Coloureds. From 1972 to 1973, however, the Party

---

22. Unisa Acc. 237, File C.1.1.6, "The principles and objects of the Labour Party", pp. 1-2.
23. R. van der Ross, interview, p. 5.
24. Unisa Acc. 237, File C.1.1.2, "Labour Party Constitution, 1967"; Membership Clause 4(a).
25. R. van der Ross, interview, pp. 5-6; Unisa Acc. 237, File C.1.3.1, "Head-office Correspondence with national secretary", 7 Feb. 1968 and 27 Feb. 1978; Unisa Acc. 237 File C.1.3.2.1, "Correspondence of S. Leon with Regions".

flirted with notions of black unity. From 1927 to 1928 the APO had had a similar romance.

In 1972 the term "Coloured" was omitted from the Labour Party constitution because, the amendment read, it was "the intention of the Party in the first instance to consolidate the position of all oppressed South Africans."[26] In that year the Party decided to reject a distinct Coloured identity in favour of a "black" identity. In the words of the Deputy Leader of the Labour Party, "We accept the word black because we are defining ourselves now."[27] The term "Coloured", the National Chairman of the Party, the Rev. H.J. Hendrickse, explained in 1972, was inappropriate because

> an acceptance of this term "Coloured" implies that we accept what other people determine for us. This term "Coloured" has been decided upon by other people and if you look at the circumstances of the South African situation you must ask why? Any Government, any power group can only remain in power, particularly if they are a minority group, if they continue to keep the total majority divided. And this I see as another attempt by the government to further divide us.[28]

The Party's new leader, Sonny Leon, endorsed Hendrickse's comments, and informed the press that "Coloureds cannot talk politics on racially isolated lines. They have to talk on the basis of their oppression with other Black groups."[29]

In 1972, therefore, the leadership of the Labour Party recast its role in terms of a wider struggle for black liberation. In part, this transformation indicated the influence of the black consciousness ideologies of organisations such as the Black Peoples' Convention (BPC) and the South African Students' Organisation (SASO). The BPC and SASO had a considerable impact in the Coloured communities of the Western Cape. Coloured intellectuals associated with the Labour Party found notions of black consciousness particularly attractive.[30] Through sympathetic teachers and the influence of SASO, the black consciousness movement also had a powerful impact on Coloured youth. By 1972 the Labour Party Youth Organisation, sensitive to criticism from SASO,

---

26. Unisa Acc. 237, File C.1.1.3, "Amended Labour Party Constitution, 1972" Membership Clause 6(a).
27. Unisa Acc. 237, File C.1.4.5, "Address to the 7th Labour Party Conference", p.1.
28. South Africa, *Debates and Proceedings of the Coloured Persons Representative Council,* 1972, 15, Cols. 418-419
29. *Rand Daily Mail,* 17 June 1972; see also Unisa Acc. 237, File J.1.1, "Coloureds drift towards black unity".
30. See, for example, Unisa Acc. 237, File C.10.5.2-3, "Sonny Leon's notes on black consciousness", and P. Hugo, *Quislings or Realists? A documentary study of "Coloured" Politics in South Africa* (Johannesburg, Ravan, 1978).

successfully demanded that its parent body respond positively to the calls for black unity.[3] The radical mood expressed within the Labour Party did not, however, represent an unambiguous victory for non-racial ideologies and the Party old-guard was able to resist a concerted effort to secure the withdrawal of the Party from the CPRC. The then leader of the Labour Party, Sonny Leon, explained that the continued participation of the Party in the CPRC was justified on the grounds that

> The purpose of the Labour Party in serving on the Coloured Representative Council is to expose the ineffectuality of the Council. The Party has no confidence in the policy of separate development and all its institutions.[32]

Leon's explanation failed to satisfy his critics on the right or left. Whilst the left plotted his defeat, the most conservative members of the Party departed to form a splinter Social Democratic Party.

Within the Labour Party the struggle between black consciousness and a distinct Coloured identity continued. By 1974 those who supported a separate Coloured identity were firmly in control and the Party leadership had retreated from its romance with black consciousness. The Party Secretary, Fred Peters, later commented that there was "a tendency to think of ourselves as a 'Coloured' organisation instead of a South African political party".[33] According to Peters, the Party once again became "Coloured politics orientated."[34] This preoccupation with Coloured politics was less explicit that that of the Federal Party.

The Federal Party

In 1964 the formation of the Federal Party marked the continuation under another name of a political party which in one form or another had, since 1919, provided pliant political leaders for successive regimes. In 1919, it will be recalled, the National Party had attempted to undermine the influence of the South African Party by sponsoring the development of the United Afrikaner League (UAL) and its newspaper *The South African Clarion.*[35] By 1925 the UAL, with the guidance and funding of

---

31. Unisa Acc. 237, File C.1.10, "Labour Youth Organisation Proposal to 1971 Conference", and File C.10.2.1, "First Youth Conference Minutes, Kimberley, 26 June 1971".
32. *Rand Daily Mail,* 23 July 1973; see also *The Star,* 25 July 1973.
33. Unisa Acc. 237, File C.1.4.9, Secretary's memorandum to Eleventh Labour Party Conference, p. 2.
34. *Ibid.*
35. M. Simons, "Organised Coloured Politics", in H. van der Merwe and C. Groenewald, *Occupational Change,* p. 212; E. Roux, *Time Longer than Rope,* p. 355.

Hertzog, had given way to the Afrikaner National Bond (ANB). But Hertzog's attempt to establish a pro-segregration party failed and by 1931 the ANB had collapsed. Subsequent client parties were similarly unsuccessful.

From 1936 to 1944 the old guard of the African Peoples' Organisation (APO) attempted, at the cost of their own credibility, to mobilise support for the governing United Party. The collaboration of the APO old guard with the United Party served only to increase the conflicts within the APO. In 1940, the year of Abdurahman's death, the APO leadership was usurped and the new executive threw their weight behind the alliance which sought to oppose the Coloured Affairs Department (CAD) initiated by the Smuts government.[36] The opposition of the reconstituted APO to administrative segregation was not shared by the right wing of the APO. In 1944, led by George Golding and Tom Swartz, this conservative fringe formed the Coloured Persons National Union (CPNU) with Smuts's assistance.[37] The aim of the new Party was to mobilise support for the discredited Coloured Affairs Administration and to provide a source of Coloured notables for nomination to various government committees.[38] The strength of opposition to separate political institutions, however, forced the CPNU to adopt a low profile and from 1948 to 1964 it was virtually dormant. In 1964 the remnants of this organisation gave way to the Federal Party (Federale Kleurling Volksparty).

Tom Swartz, the founding president of the Federal Party and government-appointed Chairman of the Council of Coloured Affairs, made no secret of his support for apartheid. In 1973 Swartz confessed that "the Government's policy of separate development in my opinion up to this stage has still been best."[39] The voters disagreed and he was not returned to office. But "Uncle" Tom, previously an Umtata restaurateur, was nominated by Marais Viljoen, the Minister of Coloured Affairs, to act as Chairman of the CPRC; along with the job came a R6 500 salary and substantial fringe benefits.[40] Not unexpectedly, Swartz lavished praise on his political masters, telling Marais Viljoen that the Minister "added lustre to what Mr Botha has so brilliantly achieved".[41] A few months later, without the consent of the CPRC, Swartz sent a mem-

36. S. Mokone, "1943: Preliminary Unity Conference", in *The Educational Journal*, Sept. 1978, pp. 13-14.
37. F. Molteno, "Coloured Politics", in M. Murray (ed.), *"Black Political Opposition"*, p. 636.
38. *Ibid.*
39. Cited in D. Woods (conv.), *Bulugha Conference*, p. 5.
40. *Cape Times*, 4 Oct. 1980.
41. Unisa Acc. 60, Box 28, "Memorandum to the Minister of Labour and the Minister of Coloured Affairs, 1971", p. 4.

orandum to the Prime Minister noting that "This Council reaffirms its full support for the policy of parallel development".[42]

In private the Federal Party executive confirmed its support for apartheid. In public, the Party was compelled to underplay its links with the National Party. Support for apartheid remained an anathema to even the Federal Party's conservative supporters. Federal Party supporters, as Swartz noted in a fascinating glimpse into the limitations of collaborative politics, continued to demand representation on a common roll:

> As leader of my party I feel that if I were to agree to a proposal that that voice should be taken away then I might as well disband my party. With that as a plank and a platform I just cannot face an election, especially in the Cape. I know the feeling of my people and so I want to repeat that if I want to advocate the abolition of their representation in parliament, I will not stand a chance at the election.[43]

In fact, Swartz had never won an election. Other Federal Party candidates, who were less tainted by collaboration, were able to secure a victory at the polls. But the Party never gained more than 11 of the 40 elected seats in the CPRC.[44] Nevertheless, defeated Federal Party candidates were appointed by the government to fill the 20 nominated seats. Labour Party supporters who had secured for their Party a commanding lead in the elections were frustrated to discover that the Party's majority was reversed by the "packing" of the nominated seats with Federal Party candidates. To add insult to injury, Tom Swartz (who almost lost his deposit in the Kasselvlei constituency) was, as we have seen, appointed by the cabinet to chair the CPRC.[45] The National Party thus secured a pro-apartheid majority in the CPRC but at the cost of the further disillusionment and alienation of the Coloured electorate.

In 1976 W. Bergins assumed the leadership of the Federal Party because of the illness of Swartz. Bergins wasted no time in reasserting the Federal Party's support for a separate Coloured identity. He reconstituted the Federal Party as the Freedom Party. But, as Richard van der Ross noted, little had changed:

> The Freedom Party, which used to be called the Federal Party under Tom Swartz, fully accepted separate development ... They saw separate development as a solution, as an end not a means, as a final stage, not just a transition stage.[46]

42. Unisa Acc. 60, Box 28, "Memorandum to the Prime Minister, Hon. B.J. Vorster, Cape Town, 21 Feb. 1972", para. 6.
43. South Africa, *Report of the Commission of Inquiry into Improper Political Interference and Political Representation of the Various Population Groups*, RP 72/1967, p. 148.
44. Unisa Acc. 60, Box 34, "CPRC Election Results", pp. 1-2.
45. *Ibid.*
46. R. van der Ross, interview, p. 8.

Within months of coming to office, as if to underline this commitment, Bergins unequivocally declared that the Coloureds "have an identity of our own ... Our Party will continue with the expansion of our identity."[47]

Attitudes to African Labour

The Federal (later Freedom) Party was the only Coloured political party openly to support the Coloured Preference Policy and to campaign for a stricter implementation of influx controls. The influx of Africans into the Western Cape, Tom Swartz declared, threatened "the character and appearance" of the Coloured community.[48] His successor, W. Bergins, was similarly in favour of discrimination against Africans. Bergins insisted

> that our interests and heritage must be protected against foreigners who at this stage can take bread out of our months. The denial of occupation rights for Africans in our areas is nothing short of justice.[49]

The support of the Federal Party for the Coloured Preference Policy reflected the desire of the Party to secure for its petty-bourgeois and artisan constituents the fruits of collaboration with the National Party. The constitution of the Party left little doubt that the aim of the Party was

> to protect the employment avenues of the Coloured and prevent them from being crowded out by other racial groups. To protect the Coloured people against infiltration by other races in their business areas, and that business licences and other opportunities in every aspect be their exclusive right.[50]

In order to secure the protection embodied in its constitution the Federal Party depended on the paternalism of the government. Under National Party rule this patronage was forthcoming on a scale previously denied to Coloured collaborators. A protective umbrella was established by means of the Coloured Preference Policy: in employment, Coloured employees were in the first instance given protection in terms of the labour bureau's restrictions placed on the employment of Africans in the Western Cape. These discriminatory measures were complemented by Job Reservations in terms of the Section 77 of the Industrial Conciliation Act.

47. W. Bergins, Address to the 11th Annual Conference of the Federal Party, 3 March 1976, cited in P. Hugo, *"Quislings or Realists?"*, p. 373.
48. Cited in M. Horrell (comp.), *A Survey of Race Relations in South Africa, 1965* (Johannesburg,SAIRR, 1966), p. 167.
49. Cited in *The Voice*, 6 May 1978.
50. Unisa Acc. 60, Box 22, "Federal Party Constitution", paras. 6b(iii) and (7).

In 1956 the Industrial Conciliation Act was amended in order to introduce a system by which specified occupations in specified localities could be reserved for members of one of the official race groups. It was no accident that the passage of this Act occurred simultaneously with the National Party's introduction of their Coloured Preference Policy. For the Act provided the basis for a statutory monopoly by Coloured workers over skilled and semi-skilled employment. In the Western Cape, the Act provided Coloured workers with protected employment in the majority of trades associated with vehicle-manufacturing, the garment industry and the liquor and catering industry. From the beginning Tom Swartz strongly supported this statutory protection and, as his lengthy correspondence with successive Ministers of Labour and Coloured Affairs reveals, he attempted at every opportunity to extend the number of occupations monopolised by Coloured workers.[51]

Section 77 of the Industrial Conciliation Act, the Labour Party argued, was a double-edged weapon. It may have offered protection to Coloured workers in some occupations but it also offered protection to White workers, thus preventing Coloured advancement in a whole range of better-paid and more desirable jobs.[52] The Labour Party was convinced that, given a free choice, employers would prefer to employ and train lower-cost Coloured labour than White workers, and that statutory intervention in the labour market was to the net gain of White and not Coloured workers. The Party was therefore opposed to the reservation of certain jobs for members of any one race. It was committed to a free-market ideology which in the words of the second party leader, M.D. Arendse, meant "freedom of entry into all jobs and the removal of all colour bars".[53] The Labour Party, its national chairman, David Curry, later noted, had "always taken a firmly non-racial stand. We believe that a man must do the job he is fit for; so we do not want any protection."[54] In keeping with this philosophy he believed that "the Coloured Labour Preference Policy must go completely."[55] The Party, however, failed to make Coloured preference a political issue. In the debates of the Coloured Persons Representative Council and in the evidence of the Labour Party to the Theron Commission, the Party omitted to call for a revocation of the policy or to condemn those job reservations which excluded Africans from occupations over which Coloureds were granted a monopoly.

51. See Unisa Acc. 60, Boxes 28 and 30.
52. R. van der Ross, interview, p. 8.
53. Cited in F. Molteno, in M. Murray (ed.), *"Black Political Opposition"*, p. 640.
54. D. Curry, interview, p. 2.
55. *Ibid.*

The failure of the Labour Party to be more outspoken was seized upon by the NEUM-associated organisations as evidence of the Labour Party's tacit support for government policy. But the NEUM itself had never actively opposed the policy. In 1955 its newpaper, *The Torch,* had condemned Eiselen as the "most hated man in South Africa", but its criticism of Eiselen was related to his association with measures designed to extend racial segregation in education and not to his Coloured Preference Policy.[56] *The Torch* nevertheless did publicise the problems experienced by Africans as a result of the particularly strict enforcement of influx controls in the Western Cape.[57] From 1962, with the silencing of *The Torch,* NEUM policy was articulated principally through the organ of the Teachers' League of South Africa, *The Educational Journal.* The Journal, we have noted, focused narrowly on educational matters and paid scant attention to issues relating to African workers.

In 1976 *The Educational Journal* engaged in its first analysis of the Coloured Preference Policy. In an editorial responding to the Theron Commission, it argued that the Commission "in its inherently pogromistic discussions" aimed to extend

> the "protection" of "Coloured" workers against "Bantu" workers, particularly in the Western Cape — in effect support for "influx control" and "endorsement-out" in terms of the notorious Urban Areas Act. The Report is completely anti-African ... Nothing can hide the fact that it is pleading for special, patriarchal treatment for the allegedly natural allies of the dominant group...[58]

This "nauseating fraud", the *Journal* noted, was no more than a "whimpering, tribalistic and cynical piece of special pleading" which was to be rejected by the "oppressed" at all costs.[59]

In its editorial *The Educational Journal* left little doubt concerning its attitude to measures associated with the Coloured Preference Policy. In practice, however, the Teachers' League and other NEUM-associated organisations failed to mobilise in defence of Africans or to break down the barriers which existed between African and Coloured people in the Western Cape. We have seen how, by 1961, the movement had alienated whatever support it previously had had amongst African intellectuals. From the beginning the NEUM failed to organise African workers. Between 1961 and 1976 this omission remained a hallmark of the organisations committed to the NEUM programme of action.

56. *The Torch,* 31 May 1955.
57. See, for example, *The Torch,* 23 Aug. 1955; *The Torch,* 22 Nov. 1955.
58. *The Educational Journal,* July-Aug. 1976, pp. 3-4.
59. *Ibid.*

Trade Unions

In the 1950s trade unionists in the Congress alliance had managed at times to overcome the racial divisions which continued to inform the programmes and activities of the Congress affiliates. Although SACPO and the ANC failed to include Coloureds as well as Africans in their campaign of resistance, many of their organisers were also trade unionists in SACTU. On the shop-floor these activists were able, in many instances, to surmount the obstacles which had defeated them in their political campaigns and to successfully weld a solid alliance of African and Coloured workers. In 1960 and 1961 this overlap of the SACTU and Congress leadership compounded the impact of state repression. The banning of the ANC and the arrest of its leaders served a crushing blow on SACTU. By 1963 SACTU had collapsed under the weight of state harassment and the banning of over 160 of its office-bearers.[60]

The destruction of SACTU in the 1960s was associated with the disappearance of nearly all the African trade unions; by 1969 only 13 unions with a combined membership of 16 040 remained, a dramatic decline from the 60 000 workers enlisted in African unions in 1961.[61] The destruction of working-class organisation was also reflected in a sharp drop in militancy. During the 1950s strikes had involved, on average, more than 6 500 workers a year.[62] In the following decade, on average, fewer than 2 000 workers a year were engaged in industrial action.[63] By 1971, however, African workers had begun to recover from the blows of state harassment and to reassert their position in the economy. In that year a strike by over 13 000 Namibian workers and by over 2 000 stevedores in Durban set the stage for a decade which was to be characterised by the rebirth of African trade unionism.[64] In 1973 over 98 000 workers took part in a wave of strikes centred in Durban, and in each year for the rest of the decade over 14 000 workers participated in strikes.[65]

The revival of working-class militancy throughout the country was accompanied by the development of an independent trade union movement. By 1974 21 such unions had been established, many of them linked to advisory and educational groupings set up to assist the fledg-

---

60. D. Hemson, "Trade Unionism and the struggle for Liberation in South Africa", *Capital and Class*, 6, Autumn, 1978, pp. 17-18.
61. Institute for Industrial Education, *The Durban Strikes 1973* (Johannesburg, IIE, 1974), pp. 5-6.
62. *Ibid.*
63. *Ibid.*
64. *Ibid.*
65. L. Gordon (ed.), *Survey of Race Relations, 1980* (Johannesburg, SAIRR, 1981), p. 187.

ling unions.[66] These unions, in contrast to those under the umbrella of the Trade Union Council of South Africa (TUCSA), were from the beginning committed to the organisation of African and Coloured unskilled workers.

The Western Cape was relatively poorly represented in the nationwide strikes in 1973, with the region accounting for less than 2 per cent of the man-days lost.[67] Nevertheless in the Western Cape, as in other major urban centres, the strikes were related to the incipient trade union movement. The formation in 1973 of the Western Province Advice Bureau heralded a new phase in worker organisation in Cape Town. The Bureau set its sights on the organisation of unskilled workers in a range of industries.[68] It reasoned that unskilled workers were particularly vulnerable because they could so readily be replaced. Therefore, the Bureau's founders argued, there was

> a real need for a more general organisation reflecting the numerical strength of these workers and compensating for the lack of bargaining power based on acquired skills.[69]

By 1976 the Bureau was active in over 50 establishments and was assisting some 5 000-6 000 workers, largely concentrated in the iron, steel, engineering and construction industries.[70] In all these industries the Bureau encouraged the formation of democratically elected "works committees" and the participation of workers in the affairs of their incipient union. By September 1976 the Bureau could withstand the blow of the death in detention of one of its founders, Luke Mazwembe, and the arrest and subsequent banning of five of its chief organisers.

The Bureau had by now made a powerful start in its endeavour to organise unskilled workers in the Western Cape. Its acitivities, however, were confined to African workers in the Cape Peninsula. The focus of the Bureau on the Peninsula was based on a recognition that the organisation of unskilled workers in the rural areas and small towns of the Western Cape was being undertaken by the Food and Canning Workers'

---

66. B. Hackland, "The Progressive Party", p. 307.
67. Calculated from M. Horrell *et al.*(comp.), *Survey of Race Relations, 1974* (Johannesburg, SAIRR, 1974), pp. 320-324, and M. Stein, "The Food and Canning Workers' Union", p. 13.
68. J. Maree, "The General Workers' Union, 1973-1981: From Workers' Advice Bureau to General Workers' Organisation", Paper to ASSA Conference, UWC, 29June 1982, pp. 1-3.
69. D. Horner, "The Western Province Workers' Advice Bureau", *SALB*, 3, (2), 1976, p. 75.
70. Z. Mehlomakulu, GWU Chairperson, interview, Cape Town, 21 Dec. 1981, transcript p. 2.

Union (FWCU) and its sister organisation, the African Food and Canning Workers' Union (AFCWU).[71]

In the 1950s, it will be recalled, the FCWU and the AFWCU (henceforth simply FCWU) succeeded in overcoming many of the workplace divisions existing between African and Coloured workers. But the close association of the FCWU with the ANC and other Congress affiliates increased the vulnerability of the union. By 1962 it had been devastated by the constant harassment of its activists which had culiminated in the arrest of its leaders and the endorsement out of the Western Cape of many of the its African organisers. For a decade the crippled union was forced into virtual hibernation. But by the early 1970s the recruitment of new organisers and the termination of the banning orders of many of the former activists had paved the way for the reassertion of the Union's strength.

Having digested the lessons of the 1950s, it no longer sought to combine the task of union-organising with overt political mobilisation. The contraction of employment in the food-processing industry, together with a desire not to strain the still weak union organisation, led to restraint on the factory floor. In 1973 the Union leadership therefore cautioned against joining the national strike wave; during 1973 only one FCWU factory in the Western Cape went on strike.[72] Significantly, however, this was one of the few strikes in 1973 in which Coloured as well as African unskilled workers took part. Both the FCWU and the Western Province Advice Bureau were committed to organising unskilled workers, but only the FCWU focused its attention on Coloured as well as African workers.

According to the Bureau's activists, the Bureau's preoccupation with African workers was the result of its inability to devote its stretched resources to overcoming the "extra-ordinary" problems of organising Coloured workers.[73] "The major problem," Dave Lewis, a Bureau organiser, explained, was that

> when one organises Coloured workers, one quite justifiably finds them so disillusioned with the whole notion of unions as a result of their experience with the TUCSA unions that one is really starting not from square one but square one minus. Because ... they are basically saying, quite justifiably, that unions are no good, we don't want to belong to another organisation that we have to give money to in order to derive a few lousy benefits.[74]

Lewis and other Bureau activists interviewed referred in particular to

71. *Ibid.,* pp. 2-3.
72. M. Stein, *op. cit.,* p. 13.
73. D. Lewis, GWU Secretary-General, interview, Cape Town, 28 Oct. 1979, transcript p. 3.
74. D. Lewis, interview, in *Saspu National,* 2 (9), Nov-Dec. 1981, p. 17.

the negative impact of the Garment Workers' Union of the Cape on Coloured workers.[75]

In the 1960s and 1970s the Garment Workers' Union continued to enjoy a close relation with employers and the state. This had characterised the Union's existence from the start. Throughout the 1950s its leaders had attempted to restrain their members and until 1961 the union successfully managed to avert strike action within the Western Cape industry.[76] But in 1961, despite appeals from the leadership to ignore the strike call, the garment industry was severely disrupted by a stay-away by the Coloured workforce in commemoration of the Sharpeville massacre. True to its tradition, the Garment Workers' Union executive disassociated itself from the stay-away and, it is alleged, in collusion with management and the security police identified and expelled the strike leaders from the Union.[77]

The collaboration of the Cape Garment Workers' Union with employers and the security police throughout the 1960s and 1970s protected the union from successive challenges to its leadership. In 1975, for example, a committee was formed to oppose the union executive's unconstitutional refusal to accept a resolution rejecting the employers' wage offer. Before long the committee members had been dismissed and their supporters intimidated into silence.[78] For, as a large employer candidly explained,

> Management fire workers who question the trade union, and call in the South African Police very quickly if there is any sign of organisation; once fined, the employee will not get a job anywhere in the industry.[79]

In this way the undemocratic, bureaucratic and conservative nature of the union was entrenched. For both employers and the union executive there was much to be gained from close collaboration. Not surprisingly, in interviews employers termed the Cape GWU a "sweet-heart"[80] union,

75. D. Lewis, interview, pp. 2-3; H. Gabriels, GWU Organiser, interview, Cape Town, 2 Dec. 1981, transcript p.4.
76. See Clothing Industry Industrial Council (Cape), *Annual Report 1980* (Cape Town, Clothing Industrial Council, 1981), p. 5.
77. H. Lawrence, former SACPO activist, interview, Cape Town, 20 Oct. 1979, transcript p. 2.
78. J. Bloch, "The Action Committee versus the Garment Workers' Union", in L. Cooper and D. Kaplan (eds.), *Selected Papers on Aspects of Organisation in the Western Cape* (Cape Town, UCT, 1982), p. 56; J. Maree, " Problems with trade union democracy: case study of the Garment Workers' Union of the Western Province", *SALB, 3,* (2) 1976; Articles by H. Lawrence in *Sunday Times (Extra)* of 5 Oct. 1975, 6 March 1976, 28 March 1976 and 11 April 1976.
79. Mr Sacher, interview, Cape Town, 19 Sept. 1981, transcript p. 4.
80. Mr McCarthy, Secretary of Cape Clothing Industrial Council, interview, Cape Town, 26 Aug. 1981, transcript p. 7.

whilst Joanne Bloch in her study of the industry found that many workers regarded Louis Peterson, the Union secretary-general, as their
"boss".[81]

In 1961 the garment industry in the Western Cape employed approximately 25 000 people, over 95 per cent of whom were Coloured.[82] By
1976 the workforce had more than doubled in size.[83] The rapid expansion of the industry had not, however, led to the recruitment of African
labour: since the 1940s the closed-shop agreement secured by the Garment Workers' Union had prevented Africans from being employed in
garment manufacture in the Western Cape. From 1966 this exclusion
was reinforced by the refusal of the Department of Labour to grant per-
mits for the employment of Africans in the garment industry except in
the capacity of night-watchmen or cleaners. The restriction of recruitment to Coloureds should have led wages to be inflated above the levels
prevailing in other regions of South Africa. But the close relationship
between employers and the Garment Workers' Union, as well as the
intervention of the state on the side of the Cape industry, succeeded in
increasing the profitability of the Western Cape industry relative to the
Transvaal industry.

In 1946 wage costs in the Cape were approximately 26 per cent lower
than in the Transvaal.[84] By the mid-1950s the relative improvement in
the position of the Transvaal workers was also reflected in a shortening
of the working week in the Transvaal to 40 hours. From this time on,
Cape employers benefited from two and a half hours more labour a
week than their competitors in the Transvaal. By the early 1960s net
profits in the Cape were 2 per cent above those in the Transvaal.[85] The
power of the Transvaal Garment Workers' Union had brought considerable benefits to its members. The Transvaal employers, however, found
that the Union eroded their position in relation to the Cape industry. In
1968 the Environmental Planning Act compounded the Transvaal industry's problems. The Act stipulated that for every two additional African
workers employed on the Witwatersrand an additional worker of
another race had to be taken on. This measure increased the relative at-
tractiveness of the Cape and "border" garment industries, and between
1968 and 1977 the Transvaal industry declined by 22 per cent.[86] Fearing

81. J. Bloch. *op. cit.*
82. N. Nol, "Manufacturing in the Western Cape", paper to NDMF Conference, Cape
    Town, May 1980, p.8.
83. *Ibid.*
84. H. Barker, *The Economics of the Wholesale Clothing Industry in South Africa, 1907 to
    1957* (Johannesburg, Pallas, 1962), p. 505.
85. J. Lewis, "Industrialisation and Trade Union Organisation", p. 295; "Briefings" *SALB*,
    7, (8), 1982, p. 11.

a further loss of business, Transvaal employers lobbied for the abolition of the Environmental Planning Act's ratios. Their attempt to have this ratio removed was, according to Professor Sadie, an economic adviser to the government,

> very strongly opposed by the Cape clothing industry, which said to the Government that the Cape clothing industry would be destroyed if this ratio was abolished in the Witwatersrand because wage costs would become lower in the Witwatersrand.[87]

The government accepted the Cape garment industry's argument, considering the survival of the industry to be allied to its commitment to protect Coloured jobs in the Western Cape. From the 1930s the Cape garment industry provided one of the mainstays of the Western Cape economy. The influence of the industry over the region extended beyond its contribution to employment and output; the garment industry and the Garment Workers' Union enforced a racial division of labour and entrenched anti-democratic practices in this sector, and this had an important impact on the development of Coloured identity in the region.

We noted that the Garment Workers' Union exercised a remarkable hold over the workforce which thwarted all attempts to democratise the union and which entrenched the union's bureaucratic and conservative leadership. The workforce was thus subjected to an alliance of management and union. In the years between 1961 and 1976 this alliance was associated with a reduction in real wages and the draining of the workers' wages into union funds.[88] These funds offered meagre benefits to the workforce and, as far as many workers were concerned, were channelled into the coffers of the union executive, whose opulence was not hidden from them: the executive visited factories in their fleet of Mercedes vehicles and in appearance had more in common with the employers than the union rank and file. Cape garment workers thus developed a deep mistrust of trade unionism. The disillusionment was not limited to the garment industry; the South African Railways and Harbours, the Post Office and other government departments in the 1960s set up client unions which appeared to serve little purpose other than maintaining an unrepresentative leadership.[89]

86. Clothing Industry Industrial Council (Transvaal), "Evidence to the Riekert Commission", para. 2.
87. Prof. Sadie, interview, Stellenbosch, 8 Oct. 1981, transcript p. 6.
88. See J. Bloch, *op. cit.*; J. Maree, *op. cit.*; *Sunday Times (Extra)* 5 Oct. 1975; *Sunday Times (Extra)* 6 March 1976.
89. Mr Hendrickse, general-secretary, South African Railways and Harbours Staff Assoc. (Coloured), interview, Cape Town, 30 Nov. 1981, transcript pp. 1-2.

The impact of the public service unions and the Garment Workers' Union was to undermine already faded memories of the SACTU unions and to increase the hostility of Coloured workers to the handful of union organisers attempting to overcome these obstacles. As a result Coloured workers in the Cape Peninsula remained isolated from African workers and unaffected by the upsurge in unionism which in the Western Cape was beginning to embrace African workers.

Summary

The period 1961 to 1976 stands in marked contrast to the first 13 years of National Party rule. Whereas from 1948 to 1961 a concerted effort was made, on the political and trade union front, to overcome many of the divisions between African and Coloured people, in the subsequent period such effort were at best half-hearted.

The silencing of the Coloured Peoples' Congress (CPC, formerly SACPO) and the monopolisation of radical politics by the NEUM ended an important alliance of sections of the African and Coloured petty bourgeoisie. At the same time the development of the Labour Party increased the political temperature within the Coloured communities, as the NEUM became locked into a dispute with the Labour Party over participation in separate political and cultural institutions. This battle served to reinforce the preoccupation of both organisations with skilled Coloureds and the Coloured petty bourgeoisie. Neither the Labour Party nor the NEUM in their activities overcame the introspective barriers which divided Coloured and African people. Furthermore, both organisations failed to focus on the working class.

By 1963 the collapse of SACTU had led to a disintegration of its attempts to overcome shop-floor divisions between Coloured and African workers. With SACTU destroyed, the Garment Workers' Union and other racially exclusive and undemocratic trade unions in Cape Town monopolised the Coloured working class. These "sweet-heart" unions provided an unattractive but powerful union image which served to deepen the conservatism of Coloured workers whilst simultaneously increasing the distance between Coloured and African workers.

By 1974, however, a new impetus had been given to the union movement in the Western Cape, although this independent trade union movement was initially slow to make an impact on the Coloured working class. After 1976 many of the barriers between Coloured and African workers were broken. For, we shall demonstrate in Part Four, 1976 marked a crucial stage in trade union organisation and Coloured political identity in the Western Cape.

PART FOUR
1976 – 1984

CHAPTER NINE

ECONOMIC DEVELOPMENTS AND THE NATIONAL PARTY: 1976 — 1984

Introduction: Economic Developments, 1976 — 1983

The vulnerability of the South African economy to the international recession between 1973 and 1976 brought about a slump in real GDP growth from 5 to 1 per cent.[1] Between 1977 and 1978, suffering from the dislocation caused by soaring fuel and labour costs and weakening investor confidence, the economy contracted by 0,25 per cent.[2] By 1979 the tide had turned; soaring domestic demand and a 43 per cent increase in gold revenues inflated GDP by 3 per cent and in 1980 by a remarkable 6,5 per cent.[3] Then in 1981 the bubble burst; a 45 per cent reduction in the value of gold exports and a slackening of consumer demand pulled GDP down to 1 per cent.[4] Partly as a result of the higher cost of imports and owing to the critical shortage of skills, inflation reached a record 16,5 per cent in 1982.[5] By late 1983 a fiscal squeeze had reduced this to 12 per cent. The tight budget strangled further the already depressed economy and precipitated a recession on a scale not seen since 1931. This collapse continued into 1984, with the rand sinking to its lowest-ever value against the dollar, interest rates soaring to 25 per cent and the gross domestic product stagnating.[6]

The wild swings in GDP growth during the 1970s and early 1980s reflected imbalances within the South African economy and the growing concentration of investment in a handful of international corporations —

1. M. Horrell and D. Horner (comp.), *A Survey of Race Relations in South Africa, 1973* (Johannesburg, SAIRR, 1974), p. 192; M. Horrell *et al.* (comp.), *A Survey of Race Relations in South Africa, 1974* (Johannesburg, SAIRR, 1975), p. 220; M. Horrell and T. Hodgson (comp.), *A Survey of Race Relations in South Africa, 1975* (Johannesburg, SAIRR, 1976), p. 150; M. Horrell *et al.* (comp.), *A Survey of Race Relations in South Africa, 1976* (Johannesburg, SAIRR, 1977), p. 266.
2. L. Gordon *et al.* (comp.), *Survey of Race Relations in South Africa, 1978* (Johannesburg, SAIRR, 1979), p. 138.
3. L. Gordon (ed.), *Survey of Race Relations in South Africa, 1979*, (Johannesburg, SAIRR, 1980), p. 174; L. Gordon (ed.), *Survey of Race Relations in South Africa, 1980* (Johannesburg, SAIRR, 1981), p. 73.
4. P. Randall (ed.), *Survey of Race Relations in South Africa, 1982* (Johannesburg, SAIRR, 1983), p. 49.
5. *Standard Bank Review,* May 1983, p. 4.
6. *Standard Bank Review,* September 1984, pp. 1-3.

a concentration associated with capital investment designed to increase labour productivity and manufacturing output. As a result of this intensified production the position of skilled labour was enhanced whilst that of unskilled workers deteriorated. The substitution of capital for African labour increased the rate of unemployment. In 1975 African unemployment had reached 2-million (20,4 per cent of the workforce), by 1977 2,3-million (22,4 per cent) and by 1980 2,5-million (24 per cent).[7]

The increased capital investment led to changes in the labour process; with the fragmentation of skills which were previously monopolised by artisans and technicians, more semi-skilled workers were employed. Black workers benefited most from this restructuring. The strength of White workers who for over 50 years had built a monopoly over the entry of black workers to many crafts was simultaneously eroded. Already by 1977, 89 per cent of the skilled and semi-skilled workers in the metal, plastics, machinery and motor industries were black.[8] Skilled White workers, however, continued to secure a status differential between themselves and black workers; despite more rapid increases in black wages, the wage differential in 1980 remained at over 4:1.[9]

Semi-skilled and skilled Coloured workers were better placed than Africans to move into white-collar and skilled jobs, and benefited most from the rapid, if uneven, development of the 1970s. Within the Coloured population the most noteworthy change was the growth in white-collar clerical and service employment and the declining relative share of Coloured employment in the lower manual and unskilled occupations. Although a country-wide phenomenon, this was most marked in the Western Cape.

In the changing distribution of occupations the divergence between male and female Coloured employment continued, and the gulf widened between blue-collar and white-collar workers on the one hand and unskilled and unemployed workers on the other. In the 1970s and early 1980s Coloured women increasingly moved out of domestic service and agriculture into semi-skilled manufacturing activities and into sales and clerical tasks. In the semi-skilled grades they were paid lower wages than Coloured men for the same task and as a consequence tended to be preferred by employers. Whereas in 1970 40 per cent of Coloured women had been employed as domestic servants, by 1980 the proportion had fallen to 29 per cent. In the Western Cape their place was taken by

7.   N. Bromberger, "South African Unemployment", in C. Simkins and C. Desmond (eds.), *South African Unemployment*, p. 15; L. Gordon *et al.*, *"Survey 1978"*, p. 170; L. Gordon (ed.), *"Survey, 1980"*, p. 88.
8.   S. van der Horst, "The Changing Economy", in E. Hellman and H. Lever (eds.), *Race Relations 1929-1979*, p. 98.
9.   *Ibid.*, p. 126.

African women employed illegally and by Coloured youths. In 1980 it was estimated that over 8 000 African women were employed illegally as domestic servants in Cape Town.[10] The raised penalty for illegally employing Africans from that year persuaded many employers to take on Coloured youths instead. In 1976 it was revealed that it was common practice for householders to visit rural areas to purchase from parents the services of Coloured children who were often no more than 11 years old.[11] In 1980 an Anti-Slavery Society investigation found that the practice was widespread, and as recently as 1982 the *Argus* newspaper documented instances in which a "girl aged 14 was sold as a maid by a man who gets girls for people".[12] Following an investigation by the Domestic Workers' Association its secretary, Maggie Oewies, revealed that "child labour is rife in certain areas" of the Western Cape.[13]

To compensate for the decline in the employment of Coloured women in domestic service, more found their way into blue- and white-collar occupations; whereas in 1970 26,1 per cent of Coloured women were employed as skilled and semi-skilled workers, by 1980 the percentage had risen to 39,2. In 1970 only 8,1 per cent of Coloured women were engaged in white-collar occupations — by 1980 16,3 per cent of Coloured women were so engaged.

By contrast, in the 1970s Coloured men benefited less from the restructuring of manufacturing; the proportion unemployed increased from 13,6 per cent to 27,0 per cent, largely as a result of the contraction in Coloured male unskilled employment from 20,5 per cent to 14,2 per cent and a decline in the proportion employed in agriculture from 23,2 to 15,8 per cent. The proportion of Coloured men engaged in white-collar and professional occupations during the 1970s remained constant. As a consequence unskilled Coloured men bore the brunt of the restructing of labour whilst semi-skilled and skilled Coloured men were able to maintain, although not improve, their position in the occupational hierarchy. In agriculture, mechanisation together with the dramatic decline of the Cape deciduous fruit industry accounted for the relative as well as absolute contraction of the Coloured unskilled workforce. In manufacturing and construction, unskilled Coloured men were replaced by African men.

Between 1976 and 1984 the employment of unskilled African men in place of unskilled Coloured men and the mechanisation of agriculture

10. G. Lawrence, interview, p. 8.
11. *Sunday Times* (Johannesburg), 30 April 1976.
12. Anti-Slavery Society, *Child Labour in South Africa: A General Review* (London, Anti-Slavery Society, 1983), pp. 59-63; *Argus*, 3 Feb. 1982; *Argus*, 5 Feb. 1982.
13. *Cape Times*, 29 Oct. 1980.

led to even higher levels of Coloured unemployment. In 1982 unemployment in the Western Cape was officially estimated to be 5,9 per cent for women and 3,6 per cent for men.[14] A survey conducted in the Cape Peninsula in the same year revealed that, even adopting the government's narrow definition of unemployment, the level actually exceeded 9,1 per cent.[15] A wider definition, which included long-term unemployed, led to an estimation of 13,9 per cent unemployment and 40,4 per cent underemployment.[16] In 1981 a job advertisement at a factory in Parow East, Cape Town, led to over 1 000 people waiting outside the factory gates to be recruited.[17]

Between 1960 and 1980 the mechanisation of agriculture had a dramatic impact on the Coloured population and compounded Coloured unemployment in the Western Cape. Since 1960, over 100 000 Coloured workers have been made redundant in the Western Cape as a result of mechanisation.[18] Together with their families and dependants, these workers left the rural areas and joined the growing army of urban Coloureds searching for a home and a livelihood. The workers most affected by mechanisation prior to 1980 were those in the "Boland" wheat-farming areas.[19] Fruit, wine and vegetable farming, however, could not be mechanised to the same extent as wheat farming and until 1980 unskilled agricultural workers in these areas were consequently relatively insulated from the impact of mechanisation. But since 1980 the collapse of the deciduous fruit export industry and the increased employment of unskilled African labour has undermined the security of Coloured farm-workers in the deciduous fruit areas.

In 1925 the deciduous fruit industry accounted for over 40 per cent of the value of the Western Cape output. By 1983 it contributed only 20 per cent of the regional product.[20] The decline in the industry's share was in part the result of the collapse of the industry's export market.

---

14. *Cape Times,* 12 Jan. 1982.
15. A. Blau *et al.*, "Unemployment in the Western Cape" (Cape Town Univ., BA (Hons) thesis, 1981), pp. 21-23.
16. A. Blau *et al.*, "Unemployment in Bishop Lavis", *SALDRU Working Paper No. 47* (Cape Town, SALDRU, 1982), pp. 19-22.
17. *Cape Times,* 12 Jan. 1982.
18. Calculated from J. Sadie, *Population of the Western Cape 1975 to 2025* (Stellenbosch, Stellenbosch Univ., 1976), p. 3; Deciduous Fruit Board, "Minutes of the sub-committee on the Western Cape Fruit Industry", 17 March 1981, paras. 3(c), 4(a); Cape Divisional Council, "Rural-Urban Migration in the Western Cape, 1960 to 1970", Planning Report No. 29, Cape Town, Sept. 1973, p.3; B. Levy, "Seasonal Migration in the Western Cape", in F. Wilson *et al.* (eds.), *Farm Labour in South Africa* (Cape Town, David Philip, 1977), p. 60.
19. Cape Divisional Council, *op. cit.*, pp. 2-3.
20. A. du Toit, *The South African Deciduous Fruit Industry, Quo Vadis?* (Stellenbosch, Fruit Research Inst. 1981), p.2.

Export earnings in 1976 accounted for 82 per cent of the value of the Western Cape's deciduous fruit crop.[21] By 1982 the appreciation of the rand and increasing competition from Chile and Greece had led to a 76 per cent reduction in fruit-farmers' revenues and the retrenchment of over 6 000 Coloured workers. Many of these workers were made redundant as a result of the closure of 12 fruit farms, while others were replaced by temporary African contract workers; the industry, suffering from what the Minister of Agriculture accepted was an "economic vice", restructured its employment in a manner designed to reduce the permanent workforce to a core of skilled and supervisory Coloured men.[22] This permanent workforce maintained the farms throughout the year and during the peak harvest season supervised the employment of temporary workers. In the mid-1960s, it will be recalled, farmers had secured from · the government exemptions for their recruitment of African seasonal workers. In the 1980s, with the mass redundancies of full-time Coloured farm-workers this reliance on African temporary workers increased.[23] In the deciduous farming areas of the Western Cape, over 50 per cent of the seasonal requirement of farmers was met by the recruitment of African workers. The labour bureau placed no obstacles in the way of further recruitment of African seasonal workers. Farmers, however, preferred to maintain a balance between African and Coloured temporary workers; whereas Coloured workers were employed on a daily basis and presented no fixed overheads in the event of bad weather or delays in harvesting, Africans were recruited on three-month contracts and incurred numerous fixed costs.[24]

From 1976 a mixture of Coloured and African unskilled workers was increasingly employed in urban employment. In 1981 our survey of employers in the metropolitan area of the Cape Peninsula revealed that Africans accounted for 54 per cent and Coloured workers for 46 per cent of the unskilled workforce.[25] No White workers were employed in unskilled grades; 87 per cent of Africans were employed in unskilled grades, 7 per cent in semi-skilled and 6 per cent in skilled grades. For Coloured workers, 25 per cent were employed in unskilled occupations, 54 per cent in semi-skilled occupations, 18 per cent in skilled and 3 per

21. Deciduous Fruit Board, "Minutes of the sub-committee on the Western Cape Fruit Canning Industry", 10 Dec. 1981, p.2.
22. *Cape Times,* 6 Nov. 1981.
23. A. van Niekerk, Western Cape Deciduous Fruit Board, interview, Elgin, 19 Nov. 1981, transcript p.6.
24. *Ibid.,* M. Mitchell, fruit farmer, interview, Somerset-West, 18 Jan. 1980, transcript p. 4; R. Willig, interview, p. 6.
25. This and the next paragraph are based on I. Goldin, "Economics and Ideology in the W. Cape", *SALDRU Working Paper No. 59* (Cape Town, SALDRU, 1984), pp. 46-51.

cent in managerial occupations. By contrast 45 per cent of the White sample population were employed in managerial and administrative jobs, 33 per cent in skilled occupations and 22 per cent in semi-skilled work. The White sample population accounted for 80 per cent of the managerial posts covered by the survey, 32 per cent of the skilled workers and 10 per cent of the semi-skilled workforce. Of the total sample, 40 per cent of the employees were unskilled, 35 per cent semi-skilled, 17 per cent skilled and 8 per cent included in the managerial and administrative grades; 25 per cent of the sample were African, 60 per cent Coloured and 15 per cent White.

An analysis of the sample population revealed that African unskilled workers were concentrated in the construction industry whilst the Coloured semi-skilled workforce was concentrated in the garment, service and retail sectors. Construction was not only the largest employer of African labour but was also characterised by a particularly biased concentration of Africans in unskilled occupations: 97 per cent of the Africans employed in construction were engaged as unskilled labourers, compared with 33 per cent of the Coloured workforce employed in the construction industry. Furthermore, the construction industry employed no women in unskilled occupations.

The ability of the construction industry to secure an abundant supply of cheap and easily retrenchable African labour in the Western Cape allowed the industry, despite the Coloured Preference Policy, to maintain its recruitment of African unskilled workers. The industry emphasised the problems associated with the severe shortage of skilled labour in the Western Cape.[26]

From 1977 a severe shortage of skilled labour was experienced in all industrial sectors in South Africa. In the Western Cape this problem was exacerbated for employers by the drain of skilled workers from the region to the Witwatersrand. Wages in the Witwatersrand in many skilled trades were twice those offered in the Western Cape. In September 1981, for example, bricklayers and plasterers in Johannesburg earned R5,50 an hour while the rate in Cape Town was R3,10 an hour.[27] In order to secure artisans, Cape employers were consequently compelled to improve their terms and conditions of service to levels approximating those on the Witwatersrand.

Between 1976 and 1983 competition between Western Cape and Witwatersrand employers intensified. Western Cape employers formed the

26. D. Allen, President of National Building Industry Federation, interview, Cape Town, 2 Dec. 1981, transcript p. 5; Mr Keal, Murray and Roberts Labour Officer, interview, Cape Town, 17 Nov. 1981, transcript p. 4.
27. *The Argus* (Property Supplement), 12 Dec. 1981.

"Wesgro" organisation to campaign for an improvement in the relative position of the Western Cape. Led by the Mayor of Cape Town and prominent businessmen, Wesgro organised a number of conferences and lobbied parliament for a better deal for the region.[28] Between 1960 and 1980 the Western Cape contribution to national output fell from 14 to 13 per cent and, Wesgro feared, was destined to slide further.[29] In order to arrest the Western Cape's decline, Wesgro campaigned for a reduction in the region's electricty and rail tariffs, which because of the distance of the region from its main market in the Witwatersrand place the region at a comparative disadvantage. Wesgro also complained that Western Cape employers were unfairly disadvantaged by the Coloured Preference Policy, and appealed for an extension to the Western Cape of the same controls over African labour which governed the employment of African labour in other urban areas of South Africa.[30]

The development of Wesgro reflected the growing belief among Western Cape businessmen that the political and economic priorities of the cabinet in the Western Cape were in conflict. Simultaneously, however, the ability of the organisation to enter into a dialogue with the government indicated the new-found closeness between organised industry and the National Party. The attitudes of employers had a marked impact on the reconsideration of the National Party's policy with regard to Coloureds.

National Party, 1976 — 1983

In 1976 the National Party was forced to fundamentally review its policy towards Coloured people. The most dramatic challenge to Party policy was the extent of Coloured participation in the countrywide resistance and stay-aways triggered in June by the Soweto students' protests. We shall show in the next chapter that in the Western Cape Coloured youth took a lead in the demonstrations and entered into a powerful alliance with African scholars. The militancy of the Coloured youth and the widespread sympathy for their cause within the Coloured communities led to a reappraisal of all aspects of National Party policy with regard to Coloureds.

28. National Development Management Foundation (NDMF), *Western Cape: Stagnation or Growth* (Cape Town, NDMF, 1980), pp. 5-15.
29. B. Kantor, "Central Government Policy and the Economic Future of the Western Cape", mimeo, Cape Town, 1981, Table 2.
30. NDMF, *op. cit.*, pp. 14-15; South Africa, Dept. of Environmental Planning and Energy, *A Spatial Development Strategy for the Western Cape* (Pretoria, Govt. Printer, 1980), p. 6, para. 2.4.

The alienation of the Coloured youth and their identification with Africans provided ammunition to Cape Nationalists who since the 1950s had warned of the serious consequences of increasing the division between Coloureds and Whites. In August 1976 Piet Marais, the National Party MP for Malmesbury, led the attack on what he referred to as the disastrous course being steered by the cabinet.[31] His call was taken up by Erica Theron and by other Afrikaner intellectuals including the influential historian F.A. van Jaarsveld.[32] For Van Jaarveld the restoration of the common roll was the only way forward:

> One political mistake was taking the Coloured people off the common roll in 1956 — for which we are today paying the price. To this we must give urgent attention.[33]

In 1977, following the Cape National Congress, the strength of opposition within the National Party was forcefully demonstrated by the ability of the Cape Nationalists to secure in the cabinet a revision of the Party's Coloured policy. The cabinet was presided over by B.J. Vorster but neither he nor Andries Treurnicht were able to sabotage the Cape Party's intentions. The acceptance of the constitutional plan devised by the Theron Commissioners and refined by the Cape National Party caucus represented a decisive victory for the Cape National Party and its leader P.W. Botha, and asserted the supremacy of the Cape Party even before Vorster's resignation as prime minister.[34]

In 1978 after the corruption scandal (which, it has been alleged, was uncovered by the Military Intelligence over which P.W. Botha as Minister of Defence presided), Vorster and his Minister of Interior, Connie Mulder, were forced to resign.[35] P.W. Botha was elected the new leader of the Party, and the commanding position of the Cape National Party was thus assured. The ascendancy of P.W. Botha marked a turning-point in National Party politics. The impact of the change in leadership was especially marked with regard to Coloured policy and in particular to the Coloured Preference Policy. For many Nationalists the Botha government became preoccupied with the question of Coloured identity, sacrificing National Party unity and Verwoerdian principles in an attempt to incorporate Coloureds in a new constitution.[36] For Botha, how-

31. *Cape Times,* 3 Aug. 1976.
32. E. Theron, interview, p. 5.
33. *Argus,* 5 Feb. 1977.
34. E. Theron, interview, p. 9; J. Albertyn, former Speaker of the House of Assembly, interview, Cape Town, 22 Jan. 1982, transcript p. 4.
35. See D. O' Meara, "'Muldergate', the politics of Afrikaner Nationalism and the Crisis of the Capitalist State in South Africa", Univ. of Dar es Salaam, Seminar paper, 1980.
36. J. Albertyn, interview, pp. 5-6.

ever, Coloured political identity was central to the success of his Total National Strategy Plan.

This Plan was devised in 1976 by the military in close collaboration with P.W. Botha, then Minister of Defence. It established certain basic priorities: it was the military's response to the challenge initiated by the Soweto riots and reflected a growing awareness that resistance to the regime could not be contained by repression alone. In the experience of the military, the tactics of the past had led to a cycle of repression and radicalisation.

In 1978 the Chief of the Defence Force, Magnus Malan, explained that by implementing the "Total National Strategy at government level for coordinated action to counter the multidimensional onslaught" the government had "as its goal the continued existence of the Republic of South Africa."[37] Total Strategy, P.W. Botha emphasised, was "not confined to a particular sphere, but is applicable at all levels and to all functions of the state."[38] The Plan, General Malan insisted, would involve a "united and collective effort which includes diplomacy, politics, economics, industry, local authorities and the military."[39] The aim, he stated, was to win the "hearts and minds of the people".[40]

From the outset it was believed that the incorporation of the whole of the South African population was impossible. The "hearts and minds campaign" therefore aimed to secure the allegiance of middle-class Coloured men and women and the African middle class. In the Western Cape, the Plan aimed to win over the Coloured leaders and prevent the further alliance of Coloured and African people.

The focus of the Plan on securing the allegiance of the middle classes was closely associated with the growing bond between the National Party leadership and monopoly capitalists. By the 1970s Afrikaner businessmen had largely discarded their earlier identification with "reddingsdaad"; in 1977 Andries Wassenaar, the chairman of the Sanlam empire, which had at one time been at the centre of the "reddingsdaad" movement, launched into an unprecedented attack on the National Party's economic policy, which, he argued, undermined free enterprise and provided "a freeway to communism".[41] The Sanlam chairman lobbied intensively within the Cape National Party for the development of a re-

37. Cited in *National Student*, 19 Oct. 1979, p. 10.
38. South Africa, *Defence White Paper* (Pretoria, Govt. Printer, 1977), p. 5.
39. *Sunday Times* (Johannesburg), 13 Feb. 1977.
40. *Ibid.*
41. Cited in D. O'Meara, *Volkskapitalisme*, p. 253. "Reddingsdaad" (literally, an "act of rescue") was the term used to refer to the mobilisation of Afrikaaner financial resources behind Afrikaner nationalism.

formist challenge to the growing radicalisation of black workers and students.[42]

The concerns of the Sanlam corporation were shared by the leaders of other large enterprises in South Africa. The influence of these business-men on the Botha government reflected the close links of the Cape National Party with big business as well as the growing interpenetration of Afrikaner and English corporations. This linking of English and Afri-kaner business interests brought together the economic overlords of South African enterprise. From 1976 these powerful individuals shared an acute awareness of the seriousness of the radical challenge and began to mobilise in defence of capitalism in South Africa.

It was not long before the military involved the private sector in the development of the Total Strategy Plan. The aim of the Plan was to act as "a guarantee for the system of free enterprise" in South Africa.[43] In order to underline this commitment and to draw big business into the Total Strategy, the Prime Minister in October 1979 met 500 top busi-nessmen. He endorsed their plea that greater opportunity should be given to middle-class Africans and Coloureds.[44] Botha's economic ad-viser, Dr S. Brand, set the scene, arguing that these people

> must be allowed to take part fully in the free enterprise system if we want
> them to accept it or defend it and make it their own. They must have a
> vested interest in it.[45]

In 1980 the strategic argument through which Botha sought to ad-vance an alliance with the Coloured middle class was given impetus by the recurrence of rioting in the Western Cape. The fresh disturbances added weight to the 1980 Report of the Commission of Inquiry which had been established to investigate the causes of the Riots of 1976 and 1977. The Commission found that in the Western Cape the "sense of solidarity" between Coloured and African youth was the main cause of the riots[46]:

> The Coloured who used to be closer to the White man than the Black man
> had changed to the extent that he was prepared to regard the Black man as
> his comrade in distress and to continue the struggle for improvement with
> him.[47]

42. E. Theron, interview, pp. 8-9.
43. *Paratus,* July 1979, p. 4.
44. *Cape Times,* 23 Nov. 1979.
45. *Rand Daily Mail,* 5 Nov. 1979.
46. South Africa, *Report of the Commission of Inquiry into the Riots at Soweto and Else-where from the 16th of June 1976 to the 20th February 1977* (Cillie), RP55/1980 (2 Vols.), para. 30.24.21.
47. *Ibid.,* para. 30.24.3.

The Commissioners urged the government to reverse the alienation of the Coloureds and to give Coloureds a reason to side with the Whites. The strengthening alliance of Coloureds and Africans, the Commissioners noted, would have a "catastrophic" impact on White security.[48]

In 1980 Coloured youth engaged in protracted rioting and in a boycott of schools. The intensity of the challenge led to calls for a reform initiative. In an editorial the *Citizen* newspaper, reflecting a stronger current of opinion within the National Party, noted that

> Coloured people have become more radical. Far too many Coloured people have thrown in their lot with the Black militants, instead of regarding Whites as friends and natural allies, as people with whom they can join hands to ensure a peaceful and prosperous future for all. The fact that there is a new militancy among Coloured students, a linking up of Coloured youth and Black school radicals, is warning enough that we risk losing the support not only of the older, but of the younger generation of Coloureds as well... [49]

Pointing out that the older generation of Coloured men and women had rejected separate representation and administrative segregation, the paper concluded that

> The government must act, as a matter of some priority, to bring the Coloured people back into their special relationship they had vis-à-vis the Whites. We stress: the alienation of the Coloureds must not be allowed to continue unchecked.[50]

The *Citizen* editorial and other Nationalist commentaries stressed that the Coloured middle class held the key to a successful incorporation of the Coloured population. Nationalist and White opposition spokesmen without fail assumed that the Coloured working class had no will of its own; the militancy of the working class, it was argued, was the result of the radical leadership of that class by educated and better-off Coloureds. In 1975, for example, Nic Rhoodie, a professor at Pretoria University and an influential National Party ideologue, told the Theron Commissioners that

> Revolutions are never planned by the masses, but by a frustrated élite. If the élite becomes frustrated by the outmoded rules of apartheid, they will rally [*opsweep*] the masses.[51]

It was incumbent on the government, Rhoodie insisted, to reverse the dangerous alienation of the Coloured élite. The Coloured élite were the allies of the Whites, and

48. *Ibid.*, para. 2.5.2.
49. *Citizen*, 22 April, 1980.
50. *Ibid.*
51. Unisa Acc. 100, Report No. 34, 29 April 1975, para. 3.3.

Whites and Coloureds are part of the same national community [*gemeenskap*]. I cannot envisage that Coloureds will allow the enemies of the Europeans to overthrow us.[52]

A similar line of argument was developed by Professor Cloete, a respected National Party political scientist. He emphasised to the Theron Commission that

> The future of black identity amongst the Coloureds depends on the measures through which the aspirations of the population group are befriended by the government. If it is not greatly befriended a withdrawal to black identity can be expected as a means to achieve greater political and social rights.[53]

Cloete and Rhoodie's views were shared by Erica Theron and by other powerful intellectuals within the Cape National Party. Their opinions were debated by the Party caucus and endorsed by P.W. Botha, who accepted the responsibility for the translation of the party's strategic concerns into practice.[54]

Botha accepted that the future of the Whites and the Coloureds was inextricably linked. In 1981 in a direct rebuttal of the Verwoerdian scheme he reiterated his argument that

> I have never made a secret of the fact that I do not view the Coloured people as a homogeneous group, or a nation, or a nation in making.[55]

The task of the government, Botha insisted, was to secure the alliance of the Coloured middle class and White people:

> There are thousands of Coloured people who are Christians and anti-communist. I say the time has come to take these people as far as possible with us for the sake of civilisation and the security of the country[56]

"These people", he told recalcitrant officials in his own constituency who had refused to open an agricultural show to Coloureds, "are fighting on our borders and working in our factories. They are loyal citizens of our country."[57]

In 1978 the objective of establishing a fresh initiative to limit Coloured disaffection was made more urgent and at the same time facilitated by the collapse of the Coloured Persons Representative Council. Its collapse placed Coloured men and women in a constitutional vacuum which the Cape National Party insisted had to be filled. In the previous

52. *Ibid.*
53. Unisa Acc. 100, Memorandum submitted by Prof. Cloete, p. 43, para. 8.
54. E. Theron, interview, pp. 8-9.
55. *HAD,* 1981, 4, Col. 1860.
56. *Star* (Airmail edition), 4 April 1981.
57. *Sunday Telegraph* (London), 27 May 1984, citing Botha in 1978.

year the Cape Party had in fact anticipated the demise of the Council: at the Party's 1977 congress a new constitutional framework for Coloureds had been adopted and forwarded to the cabinet for approval. But although accepting the constitution in principle, the cabinet had in practice shelved its implementation.

Under Botha's leadership the ability of the National Party old guard to sabotage the implementation of the constitutional changes was limited by the reshaping of the state executive and legislature. From 1978 government policy was entrusted to the State Security Council, a shadowy committee on which close allies of Botha, including representatives of the military and big business, occupied key positions. The transfer of power to this committee, which functioned as an inner cabinet, and to other nominated committees undermined parliament and, not incidentally, the influence of National Party opponents of P.W. Botha. The reorganisation of the state bureaucracy, in which the number of departments was reduced from 40 to 22, similarly served to centralise control and narrow the responsibilities of administrators opposed to the new leadership.

A further means to deflect internal criticism of the National Party was to shift the debate concerning the new constitution to a newly established institution of White, Coloured and Indian nominees — the President's Council. Established in 1980, the Council served to legitimate Botha's rule and at the same time to include Coloured and Indian notables in the pomp and privilege of government. According to Dennis Worrall, the Chairman of the Cabinet Constitutional Committee which devised the Council, "One of the major tasks of the President's Council would be to find a solution to the identity crisis of the Coloured people." The President's Council, Botha directed, aimed to find a way in which to incorporate Coloureds politically. He explained that

> All the Government is doing is to say to the Coloured people, "We cannot include you in a common voters' role, because if we do there will be agitation to include urban blacks, and soon we'll have black majority rule." Therefore we have to find other methods.[58]

In the event, the Council adopted a constitutional plan not dissimilar to that which had been endorsed by Botha at the 1977 Cape National Party Congress.

Botha publicly staked his political future on the acceptance of the constitution by all sections of the National Party. In July 1982, at a Special Congress held in Bloemfontein, 3 000 delegates from the four

58. *Star* (Airmail edition), 4 April 1981.

provincial parties assembled for the third time in the history of the
Party. For many delegates Botha's promise of an "appointment with the
future" must have been an anti-climax; in an astute move they were simply asked to reconfirm their commitment to the constitutional plan
adopted by the cabinet under Botha's predecessor, B.J. Vorster.[59] The
ploy served to spike the guns of the disaffected Transvaal Party. With
their opposition muted the constitution was unanimously endorsed by
the Special Congress.

The overwhelming support for the new constitution represented a per-
sonal triumph for Botha and clear evidence of his ability to silence the
opponents of constitutional reform within the National Party. From the
beginning, opposition to reform had been led by Connie Mulder, the
former leader of the Transvaal Party, and his successor Andries Treurnicht. Mulder had been forced to relinquish his position following the
"Muldergate" corruption scandal and no longer presented a threat to
Botha within the National Party; he left the Party to form the National
Conservative Party (NCP). Within the National Party, however, Treurnicht continued to mobilise a powerful opposition to Botha's constitutional proposals. At a caucus meeting on 24 February 1982 he raised
objections to Botha's concept of "power-sharing".[60] Following a vote of
confidence in the Prime Minister in which 22 MPs opposed Botha and
one abstained, the dissidents were asked to resign.

On 20 March, Treurnicht launched the Conservative Party with a policy of strict segregation and opposition to any form of "power-sharing".[61]
"A mixed cabinet," he told a crowd of 6 000 supporters, was "unaccep-
table."[62] After a few months the Party was merged with Connie Mulder's
NCP and with Aksie Eie Toekoms, which had been formed in February
1981 by disaffected National Party members opposed to Botha's unwillingness to implement "separate development".[63]

Opposition to the new constitution and a commitment to a separate
Coloured "independent nation" formed a cornerstone of the NCP manifesto.[64] According to Connie Mulder, the leader of the NCP,

> Under National Conservative Party policy the political future of the Coloured
> people would not be accommodated in any political institution for Whites,
> and negotiations would be held with the Coloured people to find a geo-
> graphic accommodation to their political aspirations.[65]

59. *Rapport,* 1 Aug. 1982.
60. P. van Ryneveld, "Divisions in the National Party", mimeo, Oxford University, May
    1984, p. 1.
61. *Argus,* 20 March 1982.
62. *Ibid.;* see also Van Reyneveld, *op. cit.,* pp. 1-2.
63. *Ibid.,* p. 2.
64. *Cape Times,* 3 Nov. 1982.

The proposed Coloured homeland, Andries Treurnicht explained to a NCP by-election meeting, would be "about the size of Swaziland"[66].

The Prime Minister retorted that the segregation of Coloureds would lead only to their further alienation. NCP policy, he warned, would cause "a head-on collision with every population group in South Africa."[67] The purged National Party by contrast promised to guarantee a future for the Whites through entering into alliance with Coloured men and women. For, as Botha challenged the electorate, "Must I estrange these people or must I take them with me so the country's security can be maintained?"[68] The response of the electorate during the by-elections and the subsequent referendum was to endorse the constitutional proposals.

The attempt by Botha to win the hearts and minds of the Coloureds was also an attempt to win wider support from the White electorate and to solicit the English vote. In this the National Party was successful. In 1983 the constitutional changes were supported by over a third of the English-speaking electorate.[69] In reshaping its policy towards Coloureds and Indians the National Party had fundamentally altered the foundations of the Party's support. The attempt to capture the centre ground of White politics had won the allegiance of many English-speakers but at the expense of losing the support of part of the Afrikaner right wing; for the realignment of the National Party and Botha's commitment to "power-sharing" with Coloureds and Asians was opposed by many of the most conservative members of the Party. The Afrikaner Nationalists most threatened by Botha's "power-sharing" scheme were the White working class. It was this class of Whites who provided the major constituency for the new conservative opposition.

Until 1978 the White working class had formed the bedrock of National Party support. In 1975 the general secretary of the Iron and Steel Industry Workers' Union, a stalwart of the National Party, laid down the terms of this support when he reiterated that "no situation will be tolerated in which Whites work under Coloureds".[70] From 1978 the National Party was no longer prepared to guarantee protection to White workers. With the recession over, acute shortages of skilled manpower

65. *Star*, 7 March 1981.
66. *Cape Times*, 3 Nov. 1982.
67. *Star* (Airmail edition), 22 May 1982.
68. *Ibid*.
69. Van Reyneveld, *op. cit.*, p. 7.
70. Unisa Acc. 100, Evidence of W. Bornmann, Gen. sec. of the S.A. Iron and Steel Industry Workers' Union, 21 Jan. 1975, p. 2.

began to constrain production and inflate wages. The mining and industrial barons, who were keen to promote a black middle class and to relieve the skill bottle-neck, pressed for an easing of colour-bar and training restrictions. Despite the furious protests of the White skilled workers, Botha acceded to big business's demands.

For the White working class, Coloured advancement presented the greatest threat; Coloured men with skills and experience which equalled and exceeded that of many White workers challenged the White monopoly over skilled and supervisory positions. Coloured workers were preferred by employers anxious to exploit the lower wages paid to them. For many large employers, White workers had "priced themselves out of the market".[71] Since the 1920s successive governments had, without fail, solicited the White working-class vote by offering them protection from competition by black workers; but the Botha government was less prepared to uphold the privileges won by White workers. It was committed to the abolition of job reservations and to the narrowing of the wage differential between White and other workers. The interests of big business, it was apparent to White workers, had been given priority by the cabinet. Not surprisingly, many White workers refused to support the government. They preferred instead to lend their support to the conservative opposition which promised a return to Verwoerdian ideals and to the political and economic segregation of Coloured and Asian people.

Summary

Between 1976 and 1984 the National Party underwent a dramatic transformation. This upheaval led to fundamental changes in the Party's policy with regard to Coloureds. In 1976 and 1977 the resistance of African and Coloured youth made more urgent the need of the Party to arrest the growing alienation of Coloureds. The publication of the report of the Theron Commission and the collapse of the Coloured Persons Representative Council added impetus to these concerns, which by 1977 had already led the Cape National Party to develop a plan to include Coloureds in a revised constitution.

From 1976 to 1978 the National Party under B.J. Vorster prevaricated on issues related to Coloured political identity. On assuming power P.W. Botha heralded a new era in National Party policies towards the

---

71. F. McLeod, Director of Cape Chamber of Commerce, interview, Cape Town, 3 Dec. 1981, transcript p. 4.

Coloureds. Insisting that Coloured people were the "allies of the Whites in the struggle for South Africa"[72] and that White South Africans must "adapt or die"[73], Botha set out to incorporate the Coloured political leadership.

Botha's reformism led to the disaffection of a part of the right wing of the National Party. At the centre of the conservative opposition's manifesto was their commitment to "separate development" and their opposition to "power-sharing". For many members of the conservative opposition the planned participation of Coloureds in government was proof of Botha's rejection of Verwoerd's principles of "separate development". This opposition voiced the anxieties of many White workers, who feared that the government's commitment to Coloured workers would be at their expense. Previous governments had promoted the interests of Coloureds relative to Africans, but the interests of White workers had always been paramount. Botha's commitment to Coloured advancement was associated with his close alliance with big business and his commitment to end the monopoly of White workers over many skilled jobs.

In the Western Cape the Coloured Labour Preference Policy aimed to protect Coloured workers from African competition, but by 1976 the policy had soured relations between employers and the government. We have shown in this chapter that the Botha government was committed to a closer alliance with organised employers. Simultaneously Botha aimed to renew the commitment of the government to policies of preference for Coloureds. It will be recalled that, in organised industry, employers had opposed the stricter enforcement of the Coloured Labour Preference Policy. The Cabinet's determination to establish a closer relationship with employers could therefore have been expected to conflict with its aims to entrench policies of preference for Coloureds. But we shall show in the next chapter that this was not necessarily the case.

72. *Star*, 7 Aug. 1979.
73. *Ibid.*

CHAPTER TEN

THE COLOURED PREFERENCE POLICY AND EMPLOYERS: 1976 — 1984

The National Party and the Coloured Preference Policy

The Botha government departed from the Verwoerdian plan for the political segregation of Coloureds, but other elements of Verwoerd's Coloured policy were maintained; in particular until 1984 the Botha government resolutely defended the Coloured Preference Policy.

In 1976 the solidarity of Coloured youth with the countrywide protests had emphasised the strategic importance of the Preference Policy. In that year the majority report of the Theron Commission "recommended that the policy be implemented more strictly".[1] The Coloured commissioners, in line with the evidence of the overwhelming majority of Coloureds interviewed by the Commissioners, had been opposed to the policy, but their objections were overruled by Erica Theron, who persuaded the cabinet of the net benefits of the policy.[2] The strength of African resistance did, however, lead to a number of modifications.

In 1977 government anxiety concerning African unrest in the Western Cape highlighted the extent of African unemployment in the region. According to the 1977-78 *Report of the Department of Planning,* it "caused much concern".[3] The cabinet "in order to counter this crisis situation" therefore decided to authorise the employment of 650 African youths (between the ages of 16 and 20) over and above the authorised quotas.[4]

In 1978 the concessions offered by the Vorster cabinet were not renewed by the new Botha government. Botha instead vowed to tighten the existing loopholes and to enforce influx controls even more strictly in the Western Cape. For Botha, an active pursuit of the Coloured Pref-

---

1. *Star,* 10 April 1980.
2. E. Theron, interview, pp.2-3.
3. South Africa, Dept. of Planning and Environment, *Annual Report 1977-1978* (Pretoria, Govt. Printer, 1978), para. 98.
4. *Ibid.*

erence Policy was integral to attempts to incorporate the Coloureds politically and economically.

From 1955, it will be recalled, support for the Preference Policy straddled federal and other divisions within the National Party. This continued to be the case even after the Party was deeply divided on other issues. Thus in the post-1978 period it was supported by an alliance of conservatives such as Andries Treurnicht, Piet Marais, M.C. Botha and J. Albertyn, and by reformists such as P.W. Botha, P. Koornhof and A. van Breda.[5] (Of the conservatives who supported the policy, only Albertyn had, by 1983, not joined the right-wing opposition to the National Party.) Nor was support for the policy aligned along the provincial divisions within the party. A. Treurnicht, the leader of the Transvaal Party, and P.W. Botha, the leader of the Cape Party, found in the policy one of their few points of agreement.[6]

Until 1980 opposition to the Preference Policy from within the Cape National Party was muted. At its 1979 congress the Party voiced its unanimous support for the policy, and the intellectually powerful Stellenbosch branch of the Party, which included Erica Theron, called for a more active commitment to the preference scheme.[7] Since 1980, however, the policy has been opposed by the Stellenbosch branch of the Party. At the 1981 Cape National Party congress a resolution by the Stellenbosch branch called for the scrapping of the policy. Erica Theron, following what she termed a "reconsideration of the evidence"[8], withdrew her earlier support for the policy and began to campaign for its termination. The weight of Coloured opinion, she insisted, had turned against the policy, which was regarded as an unnecessary, paternalistic and possibly counter-productive gesture on the part of the National Party.[9]

The Stellenbosch resolution was roundly defeated by the Party leader, P.W. Botha, in alliance with delegates from the Cape Peninsula northern suburbs (False Bay, Bellville, Parow, Tygervallei and Durbanville) and delegates from Paarl, Worcester, Dekuilen and Oudtshoorn.[10] The Prime Minister was able to rely on the support of his close allies, the chairman of the National Party's Coloured Affairs Group, Piet Badenhorst (MP for Oudtshoorn), and J. Albertyn (MP for False Bay), the

5. *Financial Mail,* 25 April 1980; *Star,* 10 May 1980; *Argus,* 2 Sept. 1981; S.P. Cilliers, interview, p.5;*Argus,* 26 May, 1980.
6. *Argus,* 2 Sept. 1981; E. Theron, interview, p.3.
7. *Ibid.*
8. *Ibid.,* pp.3-4; *Argus,* 2 Sept. 1981; *Cape Times,* 14 Oct. 1982.
9. E. Theron, interview, p.4.
10. *Ibid.,* P. Marais, interview, p.7; J. Albertyn, interview, pp.4-5.

former speaker of the House of Assembly and national organiser of the National Party.[11] For Albertyn the policy could not be disassociated from the wider question of the "survival of the White man in the Cape".[12] In consequence, he noted,

> Even if we admit today that the policy is not a complete success, it must not be rejected or abolished. It must remain the policy . . . it is time we rolled up our sleeves.[13]

From 1978 the renewed commitment of the Cape National Party to the policy led to an even stricter enforcement of influx controls in the Western Cape. Between 1978 and 1981 4 000 women and 11 000 men were, on average, arrested each year for pass law offences.[14] In 1981 the number of Africans arrested in the Cape Peninsula for contravening the influx control regulations exceeded 13 694, more than 10 per cent of the total *de facto* African population of the Peninsula.[15] During the year over R283 500 was collected in fines, with the average R70 fine imposed on the arrested Africans representing approximately two to three weeks' wages for unskilled workers.[16] A total of about 250 000 days of imprisonment resulted from pass law arrests in the Cape Peninsula in 1981.[17]

In October 1982, following the Cape National Congress, controls on influx into the Western Cape were intensified still further. Within three weeks over 3 000 Africans had been arrested and over R60 000 collected in fines.[18] The Commissioners Court in Langa was sentencing over 100 cases a day, of which, according to the Athlone Advice Office, "practically none were defended . . . it is almost impossible for people to request legal defence."[19]

While the number of arrests in other major urban centres declined between 1978 and 1983, influx control arrests increased proportionately in the Western Cape.[20] Between 1978 and 1983 the Cape Peninsula — de-

---

11. *Ibid.*
12. *Ibid.*
13. *Ibid.*
14. L. Gordon (ed.), *"Survey 1979"*, p. 389; L. Gordon (ed.), *"Survey 1980"*, p.301; *HAD*, 1981, 3 Col. 116; *HAD* 1981, 4, Col. 201; *HAD*, 1981, 5, Cols. 229-249. A breakdown of recruitment in the different districts of the Transkei reveals that the W. Cape is the major source of employment in certain districts and these areas are particularly affected by W. Cape labour policy.
15. M. West, "Influx control in the Cape Peninsula", in D. Horner (ed.), "Labour Preference, Influx Control and Squatters: Cape Town Entering the 1980s", *SALDRU Working Paper No. 50* (Cape Town, SALDRU, 1983), p.27.
16. *HAD*, 1982, 4, Col. 165, and M. West, *op.cit.*.
17. *HAD*, 1982, 4, Col. 165.
18. *Cape Times*, 13 Nov, 1982.
19. Athlone Advice Office, "Report for October 1982", mimeo, Cape Town, 1982, p.1.
20. M. West. op.cit., p.21.

spite the fact that African men outnumbered women by three to one —
was the only area in South Africa where more women than men were
arrested for pass law offences.[21] Between 1980 and 1984 the Peninsula
accounted for 30 per cent of all women arrested in the urban areas for
pass law offences.[22] There can be little doubt that since 1978 the Department of Co-operation and Development, on the insistence of the Botha
cabinet, embarked on what the *Cape Times* described as a "war" on Africans in the Western Cape.[23] In 1984 influx controls continued to be enforced more strictly in the Western Cape than in any other region in
South Africa. And yet in that year the Cape National Party abruptly
dropped the policy of Coloured preference which only the year before it
had loyally defended. This "concession" to the policy's opponents was
facilitated by legislative changes which had rendered the particular measures associated with the preference policy largely superfluous.

Legislative Changes and the Coloured Preference Policy

In 1979 the Minister of Co-operation and Development, Piet Koornhof, announced that the Government had accepted the recommenda-
tions of the Riekert Commission and that "influx control measures
should largely rely on the availability of housing and employment".[24] But
the Riekert Commission had specifically refused to recommend the extension of the new system to the Western Cape, noting that the application of the Coloured Preference Policy was a political matter and
therefore outside the Commissioners' brief.[25] All aspects of the revised
influx control legislation were nevertheless already applied to the Western Cape.

The changes meant that in the rest of the country influx control was
made as tight as it had been for almost 20 years in the Western Cape.
Whereas in the rest of the country amendments to the Black Labour
Act in 1980 and 1981 resulted in a considerable modification to influx
controls, in the Western Cape the changes were mainly cosmetic. In the
Western Cape the close association between accommodation and employment had, since 1966, been central to influx control. From 1981 this
association was spelt out in the Black Labour Act, which was applied in

21. *Ibid.*
22. *Ibid.*
23. *Cape Times,* 28 Oct. 1982.
24. P. Koornhof, "Address to the International Housing Conference of the South African
     Institute of Housing Management", mimeo, Cape Town, Oct. 1979, p.9.
25. Pieterson, interview, p.2.

all urban areas. The passage of the new legislation generalised regulations which were already in force in the Western Cape; the extension of these controls to the rest of the country therefore made redundant the existence of a separate body of legislation for the Western Cape.

The Western Cape remained exceptional in three respects, however. In terms of the Black Labour Act African workers employed in all urban areas of South Africa were permitted to transfer between administration board areas if it could be shown that they were to work for the same employer and that approved accommodation was available. In April 1982 an amendment to the Act made the transfer of African workers to the Western Cape dependent on the non-availability of Coloured workers or locally resident African workers.[26] This amendment, according to the Athlone Advice Office, meant that "transfer into the Western Cape is therefore now practically impossible".[27] Secondly, an amendment to the Black Labour Act in May 1982 tightened further influx control in the Western Cape by effectively withdrawing the right of employers in the area to employ an African domestic servant.[28] Finally, apart from these two amendments to the Black Labour Act, influx control in the Western Cape was bolstered by the use of the Admission of Persons to the Republic Regulation Act to deport Africans from the region. In September 1976, prior to the passage of the Black Labour Act, the implications of the Admission of Persons Act were brought home to Africans in the Western Cape when 3 666 people deemed to be Transkei citizens illegally in the area were summarily deported to the Transkei. The Act allowed for the deportation without trial of all suspected "foreigners".

From December 1981, when the Ciskei gained "independence", virtually every African in the Western Cape became technically a foreigner. The Western Cape was the only region in South Africa where deportation was used to bolster influx controls.[29] The cabinet realised that existing legislation, and in particular the Black Labour Act and Admission of Persons to the Republic Regulation Act, made a separate system of influx control in the Western Cape superfluous.

In 1980 the National Manpower Commission in its first report argued that the Coloured Preference Policy was no longer necessary in the light of the revised Labour Act.[30] The new system, the report stated, sought

---

26. South Africa, *Government Gazette No. 8169*, 23 April 1982.
27. Athone Advice Office, "Report of Activities for May 1982", mimeo, Cape Town, May 1982, p.1.
28. South Africa, *Government Gazette No. 8209*, 21 May 1982.
29. *HAD*, 1981, 7, Cols. 390-395; *Argus*, 4 Sep. 1981.
30. National Manpower Commission, *Annual Report 1979-1980* (Pretoria, Govt. Printer, 1980), p.4.

to establish a nationwide pattern of labour control and recruitment. The Department of Manpower stressed that the modified system aimed to distance itself from racial terminology.

The *National Manpower Commission Report* was, indeed, couched in terms of rationality and not of race. For Botha and his technocratic advisers this language provided a means by which to convince foreign governments, investors and big business that apartheid was "dead". The Coloured Preference Policy, according to the Chairman of the Manpower Commission, Hennie Reynders, was an embarrassing anomaly; only in the Western Cape were racial distinctions still explicitly entrenched.[31] The scrapping of the policy, Reynders assured sceptical Nationalists, would not lead to an influx of Africans as statutory measures existed to prevent such an influx. Reynders explained that

> The essential question is whether this policy can be reconciled with certain policy statements by the Government, and whether the system of control over the geographical mobility of manpower, as recommended by Riekert, does not in any case make a separate policy in regard to the Western Cape superfluous.[32]

Reynders' colleague, Dr P. van der Merwe, the Director-General of the Department of Manpower, added his weight to Reynders' call, noting that the Coloured Preference Policy was "unnecessary" and that the removal of the policy "would contribute to a better attitude to the Department and the State in general".[33] The Coloured Preference Policy, he noted, allowed Africans with permanent residence rights to remain in the Western Cape even though they were not always permitted to enter employment.[34] It was, he argued, "difficult to justify a system which allows a person to live in an area but which effectively prevents him from looking for work."[35]

The call for the ending of the Coloured Preference Policy indicated the close relationship which had developed between, on the one hand, the National Manpower Commission and the Department of Manpower (of which it was a part), and, on the other hand, big business in South Africa. P.W. Botha's commitment to promoting a closer relationship between the state and private enterprise stood in marked contrast to the continued refusal of the cabinet to abandon the Coloured Preference Policy. For, as we shall show, the policy was regarded by organised

31. Cape Town Chamber of Commerce, Minutes of Inter-group Affairs Meeting, mimeo, Cape Town, 12 Aug. 1981, para. 8.
32. *Cape Times*, 24 April 1980.
33. *Cape Times*, 25 Oct, 1982; *Cape Times*, 25 April 1980.
34. *Cape Times*, 23 Oct. 1982.
35. *Ibid.*

business in the Western Cape as an unfair impediment to the development of the region, and as an unnecessary and embarrassing hangover from the days in which private enterprise had been at loggerheads with the National Party.

Employers and the Coloured Preference Policy, 1976 — 1983

In the period 1976 to 1983 organised industry and commerce in the Western Cape continued to call for modificiations to the Coloured Preference Policy. But whereas in the 1960s employers' grievances focused on shortages of unskilled African labour, their anxieties in the period 1976 to 1983 were centred on the skilled labour force. This reorientation reflected both the easing of the restrictions on the recruitment of unskilled labour and the reduced reliance of industry and agriculture on unskilled labour.

After 1976 the impact of greater capital investment and the economic recession led to a dramatic increase in the number of unemployed Africans legally permitted to remain in the Western Cape. From 1976 to 1983 African registered unemployment remained above 5 000 in the Cape Peninsula — 9 per cent of the *de jure* workforce — whereas previously it had averaged less than 2 000.[36] The increase in African unemployment posed a "serious predicament" for the Langa labour bureau which it attempted to resolve by reducing the obstacles faced by employers wishing to recruit Africans legally resident in the Peninsula.[37]

After 1976, however, employers had more than satisfied their demand for unskilled African labour; so, for example, of the 3 000 African work-seekers registered at the Langa labour bureau in November 1979 fewer than 20 were offered employment in that month.[38]

The Director of Labour for the Western Cape Administration Board used the high levels of African unemployment amongst the legally resident population as a justification for the tighter enforcement of influx controls on migrant workers and illegal workers.[39] The Administration Board nevertheless continued to permit the recruitment of African migrant workers for certain unskilled jobs. Permanently resident Africans,

36. G. Lawrence, interview, p.7.
37. Mr de Reuk, interview, p.4.
38. G. Lawrence, *op.cit.*
39. Mr Pieterson, interview, p.6.

the administration board accepted, were not suitable for the most arduous and unpleasant unskilled work, such as that associated with night-soil removal, cold-storage work and the construction industry.[40]

In 1980 our survey of 400 African workers in Langa and Nyanga revealed that 76,2 per cent of the workers employed in the construction industry were migrant workers and that the industry accounted for 70,4 per cent of all migrant employment.[41] Employers in the construction industry reported no major obstacles in their recruitment of migrant workers.[42] They noted that although the industry had experienced a chronic shortage of African labour in the 1960s and 1970s, by 1978 the problem had been alleviated. D. Allen, the President of the National Building Industry Federation, explained that

> Although it takes a week or two to get the necessary certificate there's been no serious problem in employing Africans. The only inhibiting factor is the accommodation, and the government has now accepted that you find your own accommodation for them . . . The authorities recognise that the Coloured is reluctant to take on employment in the building industry as a labourer . . . the building industry is not a popular form of employment.[43]

Allen went on to note, however, that the construction industry was faced by a "very serious" shortage of skilled labour.[44]

We have seen how, from 1977, Western Cape employers' anxieties were focused on skilled rather than unskilled labour. By 1981 these employers were campaigning to revise the Coloured Preference Policy in order to permit the training of Africans legally permitted to reside in the Western Cape. In 1981 the Director of the Cape Chamber of Commerce explained that

> the normal requirements of labour for industry have been met. Our problem is the small supply of skilled labour. Wages and salaries are being artifically inflated.[45]

The blame, he explained to a Chamber sub-committee, lay with

> the Coloured preferential labour policy, which adds considerably to the cost structure of local companies and is a critical factor to the growth performance of the Western Cape.[46]

40. *Ibid.*
41. See I. Goldin, "Economics and Ideology", p.70.
42. *Ibid.*, pp.46-50.
43. Mr Allen, interview, p.5.
44. *Ibid.*
45. F. McLeod, interview, p.3.
46. Cape Chamber of Commerce, "Minutes of the Inter-group Affairs Committee, Nov. 1980", mimeo, Cape Town, Nov. 1980, para. 5.

It was argued that in the Western Cape the Preference Policy had restricted the training and job mobility of African workers and given Coloured workers a monopoly over skilled jobs. Since 1977, an economic upturn had meant that the supply of skilled Coloured labour had not matched the growth of manufacturing industry and construction. Skilled workers from 1977 were thus able to command higher wages and to be more discerning in their choice of employers. Employers in the Western Cape, however, were unwilling to compete with the higher rates paid in the Transvaal, and skilled Coloured men migrated to higher-paid jobs in the Witwatersrand. Thus it was that Cape employers urged the government to permit Africans already permanently resident in the Western Cape to be trained for and employed in skilled jobs. The structure of influx control itself was not challenged — employers called for a modification of control rather than an abandonment of the system.

Echoing the strategic concerns of the governent, they expressed their demands in the language of the Total Strategy Plan. The argument of the Cape Chamber of Industries to the (Riekert) Commission of Inquiry into Manpower was that

> It is the Chamber's conviction that unless the "Western Cape Policy" is changed and Blacks who qualify to live in the region are permitted to compete for jobs on an equal basis with Coloureds, dissatisfaction and frustration amongst Blacks who qualify to reside in the area, which has already reached disturbing proportions, will certainly erupt with serious implications for the stability of the region.[47]

The Chamber of Industries in its evidence to the (Wiehahn) Commission of Inquiry into Industrial Legislation reiterated that it was not requesting that

> the inflow of Bantu should in any way be increased; it merely seeks for a review of policy in relation to those who are permanently in the Western Cape and entitled to remain here. Their education and general process of urbanisation is reaching a level which is already causing them to be intensely frustrated by the limitations imposed by their employment. Dissatisfaction on this score is already reaching disturbing proportions and is bound to erupt if this relatively small segment of the Western Cape population is not provided with more satisfactory job opportunities.[48]

The Cape Employers' Association presented similar arguments in its evidence to the Riekert Commissioners. It argued that permanently resi-

---

47. Cape Chamber of Commerce, "Evidence to the Riekert Commission", mimeo, Cape Town, 1977, p.4.
48. Cape Town Chamber of Industries, "Evidence to the Wiehahn Commission", mimeo, Cape Town, 28 Nov. 1977, para. 7.1.

dent Africans should be exempt from influx controls and that "this
would limit the main impact of the influx controls to limiting the number of migrant workers".[49] The Employers' Association noted that

> Many Africans who have the right to permanent residence in the Cape Penin-
> sula are earning sufficient money to afford better houses either on a rental or
> purchase basis . . . The easiest way to permit them to do so is to open a new
> area in the Peninsula where "urban" Africans who can afford to rent or build
> better homes can do so. Besides giving urban Africans a bigger "stake" in the
> peaceful development of the area it would give them the opportunity of mix-
> ing with neighbours of similar social and financial setting.[50]

The plan, the Employers' Association pointed out, would also provide
a much-needed public relations boost for local employers:

> Employers can, for example, readily rebut criticism by overseas visitors in re-
> spect of Coloured housing by showing them what is happening to places like
> Mitchells Plain and Atlantis. We could certainly not do likewise in respect of
> Langa, Nyanga and Guguletu.[51]

The placing of "permanently resident Africans on the same footing as
local people", the Director of the Cape Chamber of Commerce added,
would alleviate the labour shortage and overcome the "frustration and
disappointment which is likely to lead to a lot of social disorder".[52]

The arguments of the Cape Chambers of Commerce and Industry and
the Cape Employers' Association in the post-Soweto years were supported by the Sanlam and Rembrandt Corporations. Through the Urban
Foundation these enterprises, together with other large business concerns, pressed for a better deal for skilled and relatively well-off Africans permanently resident in the African areas. In 1979 the Minister of
Co-operation and Development, P. Koornhof, in lending his support to
the Urban Foundation retracted the government's previous objections to
African leasehold in the urban areas. He noted:

> I believe that the introduction of the 99-year leasehold system will contribute
> greatly towards greater social differentiation in housing on the lines of social
> and economic differentiation . . . be an important factor in the creation of a
> middle class in the Black residential areas and be both a stabilising influence
> and an encouragement to further development.[53]

But despite these powerful arguments in favour of the scheme, the
cabinet continued to block all attempts to extend 99-year leaseholds to

49. Cape Employers' Association, "Evidence to the Riekert Commission", mimeo, Cape
     Town, 17 Oct. 1977, para. 3.1.
50. *Ibid.*, para. 3.2.
51. *Ibid.*, para. 3.3.
52. F. McLeod, interview, p.4.
53. P. Koornhof, Address to S.A. Inst. of Housing Management, pp. 13-14.

the Western Cape.[54] A small-scale, 30-year leasehold scheme for Africans was initiated by the Urban Foundation. This "Uluntu" project was oversubscribed within days of being launched and indicated to local employers' organisations and the cabinet that a relatively well-off stratum of Africans existed in Cape Town who wished to purchase leaseholds.[55] But the "Uluntu" development was restricted to 100 houses and failed to satisfy employers' demands for the extension of African leasehold to the Western Cape. By 1984 the cabinet intransigence had severely strained the relationship between employers and the government. Chris Newton, the President of the Cape Chamber of Industries, warned of the "intolerable potential for dissension and disruption" which would result from the government's refusal to meet the legitimate demands of the African population permanently resident in the region.[56] The private sector, the *Financial Mail* commented, was being prevented from "keeping with the spirit of the Good Hope and Carlton conferences" in which the development of an African middle class had been given priority.[57]

The 1984 Cape National Party Congress

In September 1984 the Cape National Party held its annual congress. The grievances of employers at no stage dominated the debates. Nevertheless, their concerns regarding the African population of the Peninsula were reflected in the Congress's determination to come to terms with African squatting and illegal influx into the Western Cape. In this region, prominent Cape Nationalists pointed out, African squatters provided a direct challenge to the influx control system.

It will be recalled that within months of the introduction of the Coloured Labour Preference Policy the link between employment and accomodation was used to control African influx into the Western Cape. By controlling African accommodation the Department of Native Affairs hoped to control the influx of African people into the Western Cape. The destruction of squatter settlements in which African people resided illegally was for this reason given priority. The largest settlement, Windermere, housed over 15 000 Africans.[58] The reasons for the existence of Windermere were outlined by the editors of the journal

54. Mr Appleton, Urban Foundation, Western Cape Director, interview, Cape Town, 23 Jan. 1981, transcript, p.3.
55. Appleton, interview, p.3.
56. *Argus*, 16 Aug. 1984.
57. *Financial Mail*, 28 Sept. 1984, p.35.
58. *Torch*, 11 Oct, 1955; *Africa South*, Vol. 2, No. 3, 1958, p.1.

Africa South; their comments remain apposite to a discussion of squatting and are worth quoting at length:

> Windermere is an escape-route from the interminable starvation of the Reserves, a passage-way to the factories of the Western Cape. And Windermere is a reconciliation . . . Only to Windermere, and a fistful of squatter camps like it, can the wives and children come, in flight from the famine and desolation of the rural Reserves, to live with their husbands and fathers and help keep each other alive a little longer. For they are "illegal immigrants", smuggling themselves into Cape Town past the barriers of police and Native Affairs Department officials, and the right to live and work in the city lasts only as long as they can escape administrative scrutiny in the confusion of their shacks.[59]

By 1959 Windermere had been destroyed, but the reasons underlying its development soon gave rise to other squatter settlements. Each in turn was demolished, but just as rapidly new settlements developed.

In 1975 the largest and best-known of these communities, located at a busy "Crossroads" near Cape Town, was formed.[60] By 1977, following the demolition of the neighbouring Modderdam, Werkgenot and Unibell squatter camps, Crossroads accommodated over 25 000 people.[61] The Chief Bantu Affairs Commissioner for the Western Cape, F.H. Botha, announced that Crossroads would "have to be destroyed like all the other squatter camps".[62] However, the tenacity of the inhabitants in the face of brutal and persistent attempts to demolish the settlement forced the cabinet in 1979 to concede its first major defeat in its attempts to prevent the further settlement of African families in the Western Cape.[63] Bowing to the resistance of the squatters and in order to end the international media's focus on the demolitions, the Minister of Co-operation and Development, P. Koornhof, accepted that many of the Crossroads residents would be allowed to remain in the Cape Peninsula.[64] Crossroads continued to grow rapidly, however, and as the Government launched repeated attacks on the residents their success in defending their homes became a symbol of defiance.

The defiance became a serious embarrassment to the Government. The MP for False Bay, A. Jordan, in whose constituency Crossroads fell, called for its destruction, arguing, in a strange intrusion of Darwin-

---

59. *Ibid.*
60. See J. Maree and J. Cornell, "Sample survey of Squatters in Crossroads,", *SALDRU Working Party Paper No. 17* (Cape Town, SALDRU, 1978), P.4., and L. Platsky and J. Colle, "Crossroad: from confrontation to co-option", *Reality,* Vol. 13, No. 4, 1981.
61. *Ibid.*, p.13.
62. *Die Burger,* 9 Sept. 1977.
63. *Argus,* 18 Aug. 1979.
64. *Cape Times,* 3 March 1981.

ian ecology into social engineering, that "Coloureds should be protected in their natural habitat"[65], whilst Alex van Breda, the MP for Tygervallei, pointed out that it was "no good having influx controls if they were not applied"[66]. By October 1983, in the words of the Deputy Minister of Co-operation and Development, George Morrison, Crossroads had become

> a symbol of provocation and of blackmail of the Government — we want to destroy that symbol at all costs. We want to destroy that unlawful philosophy . . . [67]

At the September 1984 Congress of the Cape National Party the issue of Crossroads was placed at the top of the agenda. The focus of international attention on Crossroads, according to *Die Burger's* political commentator, caused most concern.[68] The Congress, he noted, felt that

> the history of the squatter camp Crossroads has become a major headache for South Africa . . . Internationally it has become a symbol of an uncaring, inhuman regime which in the winter rains demolished people's shelters. The world's leaders' protests regarding Crossroads are not something which can be wished away. They reinforced prejudices amongst South Africa's major trading partners that in South Africa nothing has changed.[69]

In a display of what *Die Burger* described as "a new realism which will save South Africa", Cape Nationalists decided to bow to international pressures and to house the Crossroads residents in the Khayelitsha township which was to be constructed on the fringe of Cape Town.[70] The township, it was announced, would overcome the acute housing shortage for Africans. By involving the private sector in the township's development the Cabinet hoped at the same time to stimulate the development of an African middle class in the region.

In August 1984 Chris Newton, President of the Cape Chamber of Industries, warned that "the provision of 99-year leaseholds is obviously a prerequisite for private-sector participation in the development of Khayelitsha."[71] P.W. Botha explained to his fellow Nationalists that the government was committed to the promotion of African leasehold.[72] The extension of this leasehold to the Western Cape, *Die Burger* reported, "would lead to a more stable, contented African population in the

65. *Cape Times*, 23 Oct. 1982.
66. *Ibid.*
67. *Star*, 3 Oct. 1983.
68. *Die Burger*, 26 Sept. 1984 ("Dawie").
69. *Ibid.*
70. *Ibid. Die Burger*, 27 Sept. 1984.
71. *Argus*, 16 Aug. 1984.
72. *Die Burger* 27 Sept. 1984.

region" whilst at the same time overcoming the government's financial constraints on African housing development.[73] P.W. Botha strongly supported the reform, noting that

> The intention of the decision is to draw the private sector into measures designed to increase the supply of accommodation for blacks because the state cannot carry the burden."[74]

The Prime Minister and his Cabinet colleagues made it clear that apart from the introduction of the 99-year leasehold and the construction of a new African township at Khayelitsha there would be no change in the policy of influx control. The new dispensation, Botha stated,

> did not imply the approval of uncontrolled influx into the Western Cape. The established interests of the other inhabitants of the Western Cape must not be placed in jeopardy and the government will continue to give attention to influx control.[75]

The Tygervallei constituency, which, it will be recalled, proposed the motion calling for the lifting of controls on permanently resident Africans, was also the first to insist that this relaxation of the policy should not lead to an easing of controls on other Africans. The constituency called for the "repatriation of Africans illegally in the Western Cape to the Nation-states" and insisted that the Cabinet enforce even more strictly the controls on illegal Africans.[76] At the end of the day the Deputy Minister of Interior, Louis Nel, agreed that "Africans not qualified to remain in the Western Cape and those who have no employment or approved accommodation . . . would be repatriated to the Transkei or Ciskei."[77] The scrapping of the Coloured Labour Preference Policy, he reiterated, would not lead to an easing of the restrictions on Africans who were not by law permanently resident in the region[78]: if anything, the opposite was the case. So, for example, the changes were welcomed by G. Colyn, the chairman of the Afrikaanse Sakekamer, on the grounds that "the measures would lead to greater control over African influx and squatting."[79]

Subsequent events were to prove that this was indeed the case. Far from leading to an easing of the position of Africans, the scrapping of

73. *Die Burger,* 26 Sept. 1984.
74. *Ibid.*
75. *Ibid.*
76. *Die Burger,* 27 Sept. 1984.
77. *Ibid.*
78. *Ibid.*
79. *Ibid.*

the policy meant that their position deteriorated rapidly over the next two years. Following intense police activity, which culminated in the arming of the most conservative section of the Crossroads population, a large part of Crossroads housing the community which offered the strongest resistance to the state was destroyed, and over 33 000 people were left homeless.[80] Meanwhile Khayelitsha township, far from offering the opportunity for the development of an African middle class, has proved to be a prison-like compound complete with security fences and arc lights.

Summary

The establishment of the Khayelitsha township and the acceptance of 99-year leaseholds signified the end of the Coloured Labour Preference Policy; a separate set of regulations no longer governed influx control in the Western Cape. From October 1984 influx control in the Western Cape relied on measures applicable in all other urban areas. But since in 1981 the system enforced in the Western Cape was adopted throughout the country, the scrapping of the Labour Preference Policy brought no relief to Africans not (legally) permanently resident in the region.

For Africans permanently resident in the Western Cape, legally, the scrapping of the Coloured Labour Preference Policy provided greater security; for almost three decades their right to remain in the Western Cape had hung in the balance. During this period no attempt was made to provide housing or social services for the permanently resident African population. Furthermore, as a result of the administrative uncertainty, the Western Cape was excluded from the 99-year leaseholds and other measures designed to promote an African middle class. Employers were particularly concerned that this failure would increase the risk of social disruption in the region and also prevent them from training Africans for occupations characterised by labour shortages. P.W. Botha was not unsympathetic to these concerns and argued at the 1984 Cape National Party Congress that the introduction of 99-year leaseholds would appease employers and promote stability in the region.[81] His sentiments were echoed by the Chief Commissioner of Co-operation and Development in the Western Cape, Timo Bezuidenhout. The 99-year leasehold, he insisted, would "lead to greater stability in the communities which I see as a matter of utmost urgency, particularly in these troubled times."[82]

80. *Financial Times,* 10 June 1986; *Financial Times,* 11 June 1986.
81. *Ibid.; Die Burger,* 26 Sept. 1984.
82. *Die Burger,* 27 Sept. 1984.

Between 1978 and 1983 P.W. Botha had refused to ease the commitment of the National Party to the Coloured Labour Preference Policy. He insisted that on the economic level the policy provided a foundation for the incorporation of Coloured people and the maintenance of a division between Coloured and African workers. This renewed commitment to the policy brought about an unprecedented attack on Africans in the Western Cape and in the destruction of the Modderdam, Unibell and Werkgenot squatter settlements.

Employers generally found the National Party under P.W. Botha more accommodating of their interests than had previous Nationalist governments. This closer relationship reflected the growing influence of big business in the National Party and the development of the Total National Strategy Plan. Before long the increasing intimacy of government and business led to the appointment of leading businessmen to key government committees, and to the establishment, with the Cabinet's blessing, of the Urban Foundation. This close relationship was marred in the Western Cape by the intransigence of the Cabinet on the issue of the Coloured Preference Policy.

Employers argued that the training and employment of Africans permanently resident in the Western Cape was a strategic as well as an economic priority. But despite the broad commitment of the Botha government to the promotion of an African middle class, this was at first regarded by the Cabinet as contrary to the objectives of the Coloured Preference Policy. Influential civil servants together with businessmen closely associated with the National Party were convinced, however, that scrapping the policy would not necessarily lead to an easing of influx controls.

By 1983 the Coloured Preference Policy in virtually every respect was embodied in legislation enforced throughout South Africa. The ending of the policy, prominent Nationalists argued, would not lead to an increased influx of Africans into the Western Cape. But it would deflect some of the resistance of African and Coloured people to the government. We shall demonstrate in the next chapter that this opposition accounted for many of the political changes implemented by the Botha government. The scrapping of the Eiselen scheme for the "ultimate elimination" of Africans from the Western Cape resulted (aside from the opposition of employers, resistance of squatters and other factors outlined above) from the failure of the Preference Policy to promote Coloured political identity in the Western Cape.

CHAPTER ELEVEN

COLOURED POLITICAL PREFERENCE AND COLOURED RESISTANCE: 1976 — 1984

Introduction

The 16 June 1976 protests of Soweto students marked a turning-point in South African politics. The first line of defence of the state was repression — within a week over 176 people had been killed and 1 000 detained without trial.[1] But despite the brutality of the police and the death of almost 600 protesters, the campaign of defiance went from strength to strength.[2] In the Western Cape over 107 people (54 Africans and 53 Coloureds) were killed by the police.[3] The new-found solidarity between Coloured and African youth caused grave concern within the National Party. It was, after all, the prevention of such an alliance that lay behind Coloured preference policies.

The main cause of resistance in the Western Cape, the (Cillie) Commission of Inquiry into the Riots concluded, "was undoubtedly the sense of solidarity with Soweto and its people".[4] The Commission found that a large part of the Coloured community rejected "not only the word 'Coloured' but also the notion of a separate Coloured identity" and that they had "joined up with the Black community so as to remove [their] grievances and obtain their rights through concerted action."[5] The attitudes of Coloureds, the Commission argued, "had changed to the extent that they were prepared to regard the Black man as their comrade in distress and to continue the struggle for improvement with them."[6]

1. J. Kane-Berman, *South Africa: the Method in the Madness* (London, Pluto Press, 1979), p.1. For an account of resistance see also B. Herson, *Year of Fire, Year of Ash* (London, Zed Press, 1979).
2. B. Hackland, "Progressive Party", p.306; South Africa, *Commission on Riots*, RP55/1980, part D, Tables 1 and 3.
3. *Ibid.*, para. 2.5.2.
4. *Ibid.*, para. 30.24.21.
5. *Ibid.*, para. 30.24.4.
6. *Ibid.*, para. 30.24.3.

The report of the Cillie Commission confirmed the worst fears of those members of the National Party committed to a closer alliance of Coloureds and Whites.[7] But powerful sections of the National Party were already engaged in a fundamental review of governmemt policy. From 1965, it will be recalled, the leader of the Cape Party and the Minister of Defence, P.W. Botha, had emphasised the importance of the incorporation of Coloureds. In 1977 he was closely associated with the development of a revised constitution in which Coloureds would be brought back into parliament — a recognition of the need to reverse the alienation of Coloured leaders. Until 1980 nothing was done about the new constitution, however.

In 1980 the Government was faced by what the *Observer* newspaper described as "the country's most serious unrest since 1976"[8]. The resurgence of black militancy convinced National Party leaders that brute force alone had failed to overcome the solidarity and radicalism of the younger generation of black youths.[9] In 1976 the riots had been led by Soweto Africans. In 1980 the countrywide upheaval of resistance had its epicentre in the Coloured communities of the Western Cape. The significance of the lead taken by the Coloureds was not lost on the National Party; Coloured preference policies had failed in their primary purpose of preventing the disaffection of the Coloured. Equally important, they had failed to prevent an alliance of Coloured and African people — in the Western Cape, more than anywhere else, resistance was characterised by a solid bond between Coloured and African protesters.[10]

In 1980 the Western Cape challenge was led by a committee of Coloured and African youths. By April 1980 the co-ordinating committee, constituted of representatives from 81 black schools, had secured a near-total boycott of Coloured and African schools in the Western Cape.[11] The joint campaign by over 100 000 black students in the Western Cape highlighted the growing solidarity of Coloured and African people.[12] Through their co-ordinating "Committee of 81" the students

7. E. Theron, interview, p.9; P. Marais, interview, p.6.
8. *Observer*, 1 June 1980.
9. *Ibid.*
10. In addition to the school boycotts and other activities discussed below, the 1980 Commemoration of the 16 June 1976 uprising and the 1980 Electricity Payments Campaign (EPC) succeeded in overcoming some of the divisions between African and Coloured people in the Western Cape. For a discussion of the 16 June Commemoration see the *Cape Herald*, 28 June 1980, the *Financial Mail*, 20 June 1980, and *Grassroots*, Nov. 1980. A summary of the EPC campaign is given in *Grassroots*, May 1981, and *BBSK News*, Sept. 1980.
11. *Cape Times*, 15 April 1980; *Cape Times*, 25 April 1980; *Cape Herald*, 10 April 1980.
12. *Ibid.*; *Cape Times*, 9 April 1980; *Cape Herald*, 29 Nov, 1980.

vigorously opposed what they regarded as the "divide and rule" tactics of the government.[13] In an attempt to defuse the conflict the Director of Coloured Education had offered to concede some of the students' demands; but his jurisdiction was limited to Coloured education and his offer was thus rejected by the students, who refused to consider a settlement which distinguished betwen Coloured and African education. In a manifesto published by the "Committee of 81" it was explained that

> the boycott has deliberately been made a Coloured issue by the ruling-class newpapers and television. To attempt to solve the problem of Coloured education is not enough. In spite of the deliberate tribalism fed into our brains we realise that our inequalities spring from the same root causes and that we are not Bantus, Coloureds or Indians, we are human beings.[14]

The attempt by the students to overcome the divisions between African and Coloured youth was matched by their determination to overcome the generation gap which in 1976 had strained the black communities. The involvement of teachers and parents in the students' cause added weight to the boycott campaign whilst simultaneously politicising the older generation in the African and Coloured communities of the Western Cape. In the process, as the community newspaper *Grassroots* observed, many of the barriers between Coloured and African communities were transcended:

> Western Cape communities from Schotsche Kloof to Stellenbosch, and Guguletu to Ocean View, have shown unprecedented solidarity in support of the students boycotting classes against racial education.[15]

The power of the students and the growing bond between African and Coloured people compounded the anxieties of the National Party, which had previously attempted to dismiss the protests as work of hot-headed youths and outside agitators. The extent of Coloured disaffection could no longer be denied. As if to confirm this failure on the part of the government, the Cabinet was forced in 1980 to accept the final collapse of the Coloured Persons Representative Council. This left Coloureds in a constitutional vacuum and increased the pressure on the Cabinet to implement its shelved constitutional reforms. The demise of the council was due in large part to the withdrawal of the Labour Party from the CPRC.

13. Committee of 81, "Manifesto", mimeo, Cape Town, 14 May 1980, p.2.
14. *Ibid.*
15. *Grassroots,* April 1980, p.1.

The Labour Party and Constitutional Change

Since its formation in 1965 the Labour Party had dominated the arena of institutionalised Coloured politics. In the early 1970s the Party had toyed with black consciousness but by 1976 had again become "Coloured politics orientated".[16] The Party accepted, however, that the growth of black radicalism had reshaped black politics. While radicalism undermined the support of the reformist Labour Party, the disillusionment of many Coloureds with reformism simultaneously served to provide Labour Party leaders with a new tactical argument. For, as the Party leader, the Rev H.J. Hendrickse, emphasised to the Government,

> Our credibility as leaders opting for peaceful change through negotiation is diminishing. This is particularly true of the youth who are impatient . . . We warn Mr P.W. Botha that we are tired of playing games. Nothing but direct representation in parliament for all South Africans is going to satisfy the majority of South Africans and particularly the Labour Party.[17]

In 1980, following the collapse of the CPRC, the development of a new constitution was entrusted to a newly constituted body, the "President's Council". The Council comprised 20 Whites, 10 Coloureds and five Indian nominees, thereby guaranteeing a White majority and excluding Africans.[18] The failure of the Council to include Africans, the Labour Party leadership explained, left it with no choice but to boycott the Council.[19] Those Party members who accepted nomination were expelled from the party; they included the former leader Sonny Leon, who in 1972 had declared that "Coloureds cannot talk politics on racially isolated lines"[20]. For, in the words of the Party's National Chairman David Curry,

> polarisation is the most dangerous process going on in South Africa . . . By serving on the President's Council, without blacks, we will merely be aiding the process of polarisation . . . Unless the Council includes blacks we will have nothing to do with it.[21]

By 1981 circumstances dictated a change of heart in the Labour Party leadership; the already weak hold of the Party on Coloured opinion had slipped. The Party was rooted in the commitment of its leader to com-

---

16. Unisa Acc. 237, File C.1.4.9. Party Secretary to 11th Annual Conference.
17. *Cape Times,* 29 Dec. 1981.
18. *Rapport,* 1 Aug. 1982.
19. *Argus,* 4 Aug. 1981; *Star* (Airmail edition), 15 May 1982.
20. *Rand Daily Mail,* 17 June 1972.
21. *Cape Times,* 1 Oct. 1980.

peting within the arena of institutional politics, and its decision not to participate in the President's Council had left it without an institutional platform. As a result the Party suffered a loss of public exposure for over a year, and according to the columnist Patrick Laurence had "declined with its virtual disappearance from the public eye"[22]. By the year's end the Party leaders had resolved to retract their earlier objections to a constitutional dispensation excluding Africans.[23]

The taking to the streets of Coloured protest, the collapse of the CPRC and the solidarity of Coloured and African people fuelled the anxieties of the cabinet and extended the bargaining position of the Labour Party. Sensing that strategic concerns had come to the fore in the alliance of P.W. Botha, the military and big business, the Labour Party used the language of the Total Strategy Plan to press home its call for greater reform.

During 1981 and 1982 negotiations between the Labour Party and the cabinet focused on the proposed constitutional reforms.[24] David Curry, the Party Chairman, exploited the strategic concerns of the cabinet to the full. He told the cabinet that

> Communism and a future of continuous struggle on the border stare South Africa in the face. Whites therefore have to look for friends and political solutions. The Coloureds have to be drawn into some kind of arrangement so they can help the Whites against the communist onslaught. But the Coloureds are not so amenable and willing to jump on the bandwagon. We know the Whites need us. The politics of becoming hard to get is developing strongly in thinking among Coloureds.[25]

The revised Labour Party constitution in 1981 committed the Party to "opposing communism vigorously" whilst the Party leader, Alan Hendrikse, confirmed that "we are prepared to do what we can to save this country".[26] For this reason the arguments of the Labour Party, the government propaganda sheet *SA Digest* suggested, were accepted by the National Party leadership, which resolved to negotiate for the participation of the Labour Party in the new constitution, even at the price of National Party unity. In July 1982, at a special congress of the National Party, P.W. Botha secured the passage of a revised constitutional package. The subsequent disaffection of the conservative rump of the Party, according to *SA Digest*, "had a dramatic impact on subsequent negotia-

---

22. *Guardian* (London), 3 Jan. 1983.
23. *Star*, 6 Jan. 1982; *Argus*, 30 Dec. 1981.
24. See, for example, *Sunday Times* (Johannesburg), 14 June 1981; *Argus*, 5 May 1982; *Cape Times*, 16 Feb. 1982.
25. *Cape Times*, 26 Nov. 1981.
26. *SA Digest*, 17 Aug. 1984, p.7.

tions between Government and the Labour Party".[27] Within six months, following "intensive wooing" by the Minister of Constitutional Affairs, Chris Heunis, the Labour Party at its annual conference agreed to participate in the tricameral parliament.[28] It will be recalled that the new parliament excluded Africans and guaranteed the continued domination by the White electorate whilst at the same time entrenching the power of P.W. Botha and the National Party.

The Rev Allan Hendrickse justified his Party's about-face on the grounds that the Party aimed to "widen the scope and deepen the content of the reform initiative."[29] "We will give the constitution five years to work," he promised. "If we find it does not work we will withdraw and admit we tried negotiation but it failed."[30] Hendrickse noted that Coloureds had a "calling to find a solution for this country between white and black".[31] Despite criticism the Party was committed to participating in the National Party's new scheme for Coloureds.[32]

Hendrickse insisted that the Coloureds' "position of affinity to both sides" meant that they held "a key position with regard to meaningful change within the present circumstances in South Africa".[33] David Curry was less imaginative in his justification, noting simply that the Party "had been formed to operate within the system".[34] The Transvaal leader of the Party, Jac Rabie, was even less subtle in his support for participation, noting simply that "for the first time you and I are going to be part of the decision-making body that will divide the financial cake."[35]

The decision of the Labour Party to participate in the tricameral parliament led to the resignation of Party members opposed to the new constitution. Prominent amongst these were the deputy leader and Natal chairman of the Party, Norman Middleton, the Natal leader of the Party, Virgil Bonhomme, and four members of the Transvaal executive of the Party, including the leader of the Party in the Transvaal, Sam Soloman, and the vice-chairman, Mohammed Dangor.[36] In the Western Cape, opposition to the Labour Party's collaboration was led by the

27. *Ibid.*
28. *Financial Mail,* 26 Nov. 1982, p.1029; *Cape Times,* 18 Oct. 1982.
29. *Cape Times,* 31 May 1982.
30. *Argus,* 24 Aug. 1984.
31. *Financial Mail,* 11 Feb. 1983, p.50.
32. *Star* (Airmail edition), 19 Feb. 1983.
33. *Financial Mail,* 7 Jan. 1983, p.56.
34. D. Curry, interview, Cape Town, 12 Jan. 1982, transcript p.4.
35. *Star* (Airmail edition), 19 Feb. 1983.
36. *Star,* 27 Dec. 1982; *Cape Times,* 3 Jan. 1983; *Rand Daily Mail,* 6 Jan. 1983; *Rand Daily Mail,* 8 Jan. 1983; *Argus,* 10 Jan. 1983; *Cape Herald,* 15 Jan 1983; *Natal Mercury,* 31 Jan. 1983.

Cape Peninsula branch of the Party. M. Isaacs, the branch secretary, and A. Christians, the branch chairman, together with other executive members and branch activists resigned and joined the alliance committed to opposing the tricameral system.[37] The disaffection of the Cape Peninsula Labour Party leadership and of the Worcester branch leadership was a serious blow to the Labour Party in the Western Cape.

Since 1976 the Western Cape region of the Party had provided a radical challenge to the party's executive. The regional chairman, Hennie Ferus, who was also the leader of the Worcester branch, provided a focus of radicalism within the Party.[38] When he died in April 1981 his funeral, although attended by over 5 000 sympathisers, was boycotted by the Labour Party leaders.[39] They alleged that Ferus had promoted the interests of the African National Congress under the cover of the Labour Party.[40] On the grounds of these and other unsubstantiated allegations, the Worcester branch chairman, David Petersen, and his executive were suspended from the Party and the Worcester branch of the Party dissolved.[41] The suspended members, together with those who had resigned from the Party in Worcester, threw their weight behind the burgeoning community associations.[42]

The Radical Challenge

Between 1980 and 1984 the rapid growth of community organisations had a dramatic impact on the development of Coloured and African political identity in the Western Cape. The revitalisation of such organisations in the Western Cape may be traced to the surge of radicalism initiated by the scholars' boycott in January 1980. The students' grievances focused on the issue of most immediate concern to them — the inferiority of their education. Before long, their frustration spilled over into other areas. By April 1980 there was virtually a total boycott of Coloured educational establishments, and new organisations were being formed to resolve the social ills besetting the Coloured communities. The boycott was joined by African youths and indicated a rejection of the distinction between African and Coloured people. The fledgling

37. *Argus*, 4 Jan. 1983.
38. *Argus*, 27 April 1981.
39. *Cape Herald*, 2 May 1981.
40. *Argus*, 28 Dec. 1981; *Cape Herald*, 20 Nov. 1982.
41. *Ibid.*
42. *Ibid.*

community organisations were similarly committed to non-racial struggle.

The first major community organisation to be initiated in the Western Cape was the Cape Areas Housing Action Committee (CAHAC). Established in April 1980, CAHAC resolved to develop "non-racial democratic movement" based on the principles enshrined in the Freedom Charter.[43] CAHAC's immediate aim was to coordinate organisation, information and resistance over issues relating to community services and the shortage, inadequacy and costs of housing.[44] Its ambitions, however, were far greater. For as its chairman, Wilfred Rhodes, noted at the organisation's first general meeting,

> We must see the increasing rents, bus-fares and electricity charges as being only the smoke. Our work must be geared to extinguish the fire that causes the smoke. Our goal must be to eliminate from this society all the causes of our hardship.[45]

During 1981 and 1982 CAHAC concentrated on grassroots campaigns based on door-to-door visits and street meetings in order to deal with such issues as rents, rates, transport costs, maintenance, street lighting, health services and other matters of immediate concern to the neighbourhood.[46] These campaigns at times culminated in mass protests and demonstrations in which people from various localities were drawn together, and in which Coloured and African residents sometimes campaigned alongside each other.[47].

In each locality in which it had organised ad-hoc campaigns, CAHAC promoted the development of civic associations. By January 1982, 42 such organisations were affiliated under the CAHAC umbrella including associations established in the African townships of Mbekweni (Paarl), Nyanga, Guguletu and Langa.[48] The CAHAC affiliates were broadly committed to the Freedom Charter.[49] CAHAC was thus associated with a dramatic regeneration of ANC-type support within the Coloured communities, on a scale which shadowed that generated by the SACPO organisation in the 1950s. The extent of support for the Freedom Charter, which was closely associated with the ANC, alarmed not only the state; organisations sympathetic to the ideals of the rival NEUM as well

43. CAHAC, Statement read at meetings held in Hanover Park, 10 Jan. 1982.
44. See: *Grassroots*, May 1981; *Grassroots*, July 1981; *Social Review*, Feb./Mar. 1982.
45. *Saspu National*, Aug. 1982.
46. See, for example, *Grassroots*, Dec. 1981; *Grassroots*, March 1982; *Cape Herald*, 19 April 1980; *Cape Times*, 27 Nov. 1982.
47. See: *Grassroots*, June 1982; *Grassroots*, Dec. 1982.
48. *Financial Mail*, 29 Jan. 1982, p.419; *Social Review* Feb./Mar. 1982, p.20.
49. *Grassroots*, Dec. 1981; CAHAC Organiser, interview, Cape Town, 14 Jan. 1984, transcript, p.2.

as the Labour Party regarded the rise of CAHAC as a direct challenge to their primary constituency — the Coloured communities of the Western Cape.

In 1961 the silencing of the Congress Alliance had left NEUM-type organisations with a virtually uncontested monopoly of radical politics. The rise of black consciousness organisations and the development of independent trade unions had by 1973 greatly reduced the sway of the NEUM in Natal and the Transvaal. In the Western Cape, however, the NEUM affiliates — the Teachers League of South Africa (TLSA), the South African Council of Sport (SACOS), the Federation of Cape Civic Associations (FCCA) and the Cape Town Municipal Workers' Association (CTMWA) — continued to exercise a powerful influence within the Coloured communities. True to the form of the NEUM, these organisations refused to participate in ad-hoc committees or to enter into alliances with organisations embracing White activists.[50]

Until October 1981 competition between the NEUM-type affiliates and organisations sympathetic to the Freedom Charter centred on the activities of, on the one hand, the FCCA, and, on the other, CAHAC.[51] Within a year, however, CAHAC had eclipsed the FCCA, and areas which the FCCA had previously regarded as its strongholds had formed residents' associations affiliated to CAHAC.[52] In October 1981 the relationship between CAHAC and NEUM affiliates was strained further by the withdrawal of the FCCA and SACOS representatives from the campaign to oppose the elections for the South African Indian Council (SAIC).[53] The NEUM was particularly dissatisfied by the involvement of the National Union of South African Students (NUSAS) and other White organisations in the campaign, and in the domination of organisations sympathetic to the ANC.[54] At meetings of the anti-SAIC campaign, according to one report, the "green, gold and black flag, the colours of the banned ANC, were raised".[55] By 1981 support for the ANC easily outnumbered that for the NEUM, not least in the Coloured areas. As if to confirm that the balance had shifted firmly in the ANC's favour, a poll conducted by the *Argus* newspaper in the Coloured areas of the Cape Peninsula in 1981 revealed that over 50 per cent of the

50. See: FCCA *et al.*, "Boycott Dummy Institute", mimeo, Cape Town, Nov. 1981; J. Inglis, "White Hegemony", *The Educational Journal,* July – Aug. 1981, pp.11-14.
51. CAHAC Organiser, interview, p.2.
52. *Ibid.*
53. Anti-SAIC Committee, "Call", mimeo, Cape Town, Oct. 1981; FCCA *et al.,* "Boycott Dummy Institutions".
54. *Ibid.*; *Saspu National,* Nov.-Dec. 1981, p.14.
55. *Ibid.*, p.15.

respondents supported the ANC while less than 6 per cent were in favour of the NEUM.[56] In the following years, the tide turned even further in favour of the ANC.

The decision of the Labour Party on 3 January 1983 to contest the elections for the tricameral parliament led to a storm of protest from black leaders. At the forefront of opposition to the Party's decision was Dr Allan Boesak, the Cape Peninsula-based president of the World Alliance of Reformed Churches. Boesak condemned the Labour Party's decision and predicted the formation of a united front of opposition against participation in the new parliament.[57] Within three weeks, at the congress of the Transvaal Indian Congress (TIC) (which in the 1950s had been an affiliate of the Congress Alliance), Boesak and the TIC leadership established a steering committee to initiate such a front and to "consolidate the alliance against the proposals"[58].

The steering committee resolved to form a "United Democratic Front" (UDF) based on the principles of the Freedom Charter.[59] By May 1983 the Front had embraced civic associations, trade unions, students' organisations and churches, and had elected an executive led by the Durban attorney and former ANC leader Archie Gumede.[60] In the Western Cape a UDF regional branch was formed by CAHAC and 21 other organisations.[61] The veteran trade unionist and former leader of the ANC(WC), Oscar Mpetha, was elected president and the imprisoned ANC leader Nelson Mandela nominated as patron of the organisation.[62] At the suggestion of the Western Cape branch of the UDF, a rally to mark the national launch of the organisation was planned for August 1983.[63]

The launch of the UDF on 20 August was attended by approximately 12 000 people, including delegates from over 400 affiliated organisations with a combined membership of between 1 000 000 and 1 500 000.[64] Affiliates included such diverse organisations as the Black Sash, NUSAS, the Muslim Judicial Council, the United Womens' Organisation, the

56. Cited by D. Curry, interview, p.7.
57. *Rand Daily Mail,* 7 Jan. 1983.
58. *Cape Herald,* 29 Jan. 1983.
59. *Ibid.*
60. *Rand Daily Mail,* 23 May 1983; *Sowetan,* 25 May 1983.
61. *Cape Times,* 23 May 1983.
62. *Cape Times,* 26 July 1983.
63 *Cape Times,* 17 Aug. 1983.
64. Estimates of the attendance range from 7 000 (*Argus,* 22 Aug. 1983) to 15 000 (*Cape Herald,* 27 Aug. 1983 and *Cape Times,* 22 Aug. 1983). The majority of reports, however, estimated an attendance of approximately 12 000. See, for example, the *Sowetan,* 22 Aug. 1983; *Argus,* 20 Aug. 1983; *Cape Times.* 23 Aug. 1983. The combined membership figure was cited in the *Argus,* 19 Aug. 1983.

Reform Presbyterian Church, CAHAC, the Transvaal Indian Congress and the South African Allied Workers' Union (SAAWU).[65] The election of the former ANC leaders Archie Gumede, Oscar Mpetha and Albertina Sisula as presidents of the UDF, and the appointment of the imprisoned ANC leaders Nelson Mandela and Dennis Goldberg as patrons of the organisation, left little doubt as to its political leanings.[66]

In the 1950s the ANC had been opposed by the NEUM and from 1959 by the Pan African Congress (PAC). In June 1983, six months after the decision to launch the UDF, the tensions between the ANC and the NEUM and PAC resurfaced in the emergence of a rival to the UDF; on 11 June 1983 an alliance of black consciousness organisations under the umbrella of the "National Forum" was formed.[67] The participants in the Forum rejected the Freedom Charter and adopted instead the Azanian Peoples' Manifesto.[68] The Forum and its Manifesto represented a compromise between black consciousness groupings led by Saths Cooper of the Azanian Peoples' Organisation (AZAPO) and organisations sympathetic to the principles of the NEUM led by Neville Alexander, who had previously been associated with the NEUM.[69] Saths Cooper, who was elected president of the Forum, denounced the Freedom Charter as an "ethnic document" and argued that the National Forum was dedicated to "stamping out all traces of ethnicity".[70] He refused, however, to collaborate with Whites who as "oppressors" were "not needed in the struggle"[71].

The formation of the National Forum might have been expected to have a great impact in the Coloured communities of the Western Cape — a former stronghold of the NEUM. But a year after its formation the Forum had failed to organise meetings or protests in the Western Cape, and the organisation had not yet entered the public domain. The failure of the Forum to make its presence felt in the Western Cape was in part due to the extent of the support for the UDF in the region and the unwillingness of the forum to challenge the UDF on its home territory. The NEUM, which for over three decades had rested on the solid support of the Coloured communities of the Western Cape, found in 1983 that its position had been usurped by the UDF.

65. *Star,* 19 Aug. 1983; *Cape Times,* 20 Aug. 1983; *Sunday Tribune,* 21 Aug. 1983.
66. *Ibid.*
67. *Star,* 25 June 1983; *Rand Daily Mail,* 13 June 1983.
68. *Post,* 22 June, 1983.
69. *Rand Daily Mail,* 8 June 1983; *City Press,* 6 March 1983; *City Press,* 20 March 1983.
70. *Star,* 25 June 1983.
71. *Cape Times,* 21 March 1983.

The impetus for the formation of the UDF had been the desire of individuals committed to the Freedom Charter to oppose the elections for the tricameral parliament. In endorsing the new constitution and accommodating the demand of the Labour Party the National Party had hoped to incorporate Coloureds and to undermine the growing solidarity of Coloured and African people. Ironically this attempt to reconstitute social relations precipitated an even greater challenge to National Party rule. Nowhere was this challenge greater than in the Western Cape. Here the UDF concentrated on opposing the Labour Party's participation in the new constitutional dispensation.

The 1984 Elections

The August 1983 UDF rally initiated the Front's campaign against the Labour Party's decision to contest the elections for the Coloured "House of Representatives". The Rev Allan Boesak, who together with the ANC leader Nelson Mandela was a patron of the UDF, savagely attacked the new constitution which "unashamedly accepts ethnicity" and which attempted to "keep alive tribalism".[72] The Labour Party, he declared, "had been co-opted as junior partners in apartheid".[73]

Opposition to the elections in the Western Cape was coordinated by the CAHAC chairman and regional Secretary of the UDF, Trevor Manuel. From the beginning CAHAC had "strongly condemned and rejected" the Labour Party decision to participate in the constitution, arguing that the party did "not represent the views of the majority but only a tiny fraction of the so-called Coloured community".[74] Trevor Manuel told a Cape Peninsula audience of 6 000 people that the Labour Party was the "junior partner" in an arrangement which by attempting to draw "'Coloureds' and 'Indians' into the White laager threatened the sense of common South Africanness and strengthened the apartheid machinery".[75] His call for a boycott of the polls was supported by a wide range of UDF affiliates including the Muslim Judicial Council, which ruled

---

72. *UDF News*, Vol. 1, No. 2, Oct. 1983; *Cape Times*, 10 Aug. 1983.
73. *Star* (Airmail edition), 29 Jan. 1983.
74. *Grassroots*, March 1983.
75. *Argus*, 15 Aug. 1984.

that it was "haraam" (a religious prohibition) to participate in the elections.[76]

The success of the anti-election campaign in the Western Cape frustrated the Labour Party's attempt to call election meetings. The Party had tried to launch its election campaign in its traditional stronghold of Stellenbosch[77]; the meeting ended in what the *Sunday Times* described as a "near riot" which forced the Party to end advance publicity to all its future meetings in the Western Cape[78]. Two further meetings in the Western Cape were held in which entrance was restricted to Party members. The meetings, in the supposedly conservative Bredasdorp and Vredenburg districts, ended in fiasco with the Party leaders leaving before they were given a chance to speak.[79] Fearing further humiliation, the leaders abandoned meetings in the Western Cape and shifted their attention to the Transvaal.[80] But meetings held in the Coloured townships of Coronationville and Eldorado Park were no more successful than those in the Western Cape and ended in violence and the arrest and teargassing by the police of Labour Party opponents.[81]

The harassment of the Labour Party's opponents culminated in the arrest, on the eve of the elections for the Coloured House of Representatives, of over 40 UDF activists, including virtually the entire executive.[82] The attempt by the police to silence the Labour Party's opponents added weight to allegations that the Party was collaborating with apartheid.[83] These criticisms were reinforced by the decision of the Party to form a "military wing" to deal with the disruption of meetings.[84] The wing was endorsed by the Minister of Law and Order, Louis Le Grange, on the grounds that "if the Labour Party is terrorised by unruly elements, it is entitled to form an internal body to protect itself."[85] Allan Boesak commented that the licensing of political thuggery was a further indication of the Labour Party's and National Party's political bankruptcy.[86]

The antipathy of Coloureds towards the new constitution was evident in the extent to which Coloureds refused even to register on the 1984

76. *Cape Times*, 17 Aug. 1984: *Cape Times*, 18 Aug. 1984.
77. *Cape Times*, 2 Feb. 1983.
78. *Sunday Times* (Johannesburg), 6 Feb. 1983.
79. *Cape Times*, 7 Feb. 1983; *Argus*, 11 March 1983.
80. *Cape Times*, 10 Feb. 1983; *Argus*, 12 Feb. 1983.
81. *Rand Daily Mail*, 18 Feb. 1983; *Cape Times*, 14 Feb. 1983.
82. *Cape Times*, 23 Aug. 1984; *Cape Times*, 18 Aug. 1984.
83. *Argus*, 23 Aug. 1984.
84. *Cape Times*, 14 Feb. 1983.
85. *Cape Times*, 15 Feb. 1983.
86. *Cape Herald*, 21 Feb. 1983.

electoral roll. Between 1969 and 1984 the number of Coloureds eligible
to vote increased by 84,2 per cent from 843 973 to 1 554 307.[87] The number of voters registered over the same period increased by only 38,3 per
cent from 637 587 to 881 984.[88] The percentage of eligible voters registered in 1984 was 56,7 per cent, well below the 75,5 per cent registered
in 1969.[89] In the Cape Peninsula the number registered was well below
the national average, and although the Peninsula accounted for a third
(506 442) of the number of people eligible to vote, only a quarter
(225 000) of all those who registered for the 1984 elections resided in
the Western Cape.[90]

The opposition of Coloured people to the elections was forcefully
demonstrated by the low turnout on polling day. In 1984, despite the
growth in the electorate, the number of votes cast countrywide (272 854)
was actually lower than in the 1969 CPRC election (310 504).[91]The low-
est percentage polls were recorded in the Cape Peninsula, where the average poll was 11,1 per cent, with Table Mountain constituency
recording a 4,1 per cent poll, Manenberg 4,7 per cent, Liesbeek 5,2 per
cent and Hanover Park 5,5 per cent.[92] But there were higher turnouts in
the rural constituencies in the Eastern and Northern Cape, and the
overall poll in the Cape was 29,5 per cent, which was roughly the
national average.[93] The low poll compounded the embarrassment of the
government at the low registration and produced some absurd results,
such as that in the Table Mountain constituency, where the Labour
Party candidate, M. Arendse, gained 118 votes to become a Member of
Parliament entitled to a salary of R40 000 a year, a luxury home,
chauffeur-driven car and numerous other perks.[94]

The Labour Party swept the board in the elections for the Coloured
House of Representatives. The Party's leader, Allan Hendrickse, was
elected leader of the Coloured House and appointed to the cabinet as
Minister without portfolio. But, as Allan Boesak pointed out, it was
"beyond any dispute that the vast majority of people rejected the new
constitution or any participation in it."[95] Boesak attributed the success of

---

87. Calculated from Unisa Acc. 100, Evidence of the Progressive Party, p.7; *Argus,* 24 Aug.
    1984.
88. *Ibid*; Unisa Acc. 100, Evidence of the Progressive Party, p.7.
89. *Ibid.; Cape Times,* 24 Aug. 1984.
90. *Cape Times,* 22 Aug. 1984; *Argus,* 16 Aug. 1984.
91. Unisa Acc. 100 *op.cit.,; Cape Times,* 24 Aug. 1984.
92. *Argus,* 24 Aug. 1984.
93. *Ibid.*
94. *Ibid.; Observer,* 26 Aug. 1984.
95. *Argus,* 23 Aug. 1984.

the election boycott to the efforts of the UDF[96]: door-to-door visits, local meetings and mass rallies called by the UDF in the weeks preceding the election had led Coloureds to accept the hollowness of the new constitution. However, the UDF could not claim sole responsibility for the low turnout in the Peninsula. Newspaper reports revealed that National Forum affiliates, and notably the Federation of Cape Civic Associations and AZAPO, also mobilised opposition to the elections.[97] But National Forum affiliates confined their campaign to public meetings in Coloured areas; by contrast the UDF campaign operated on both a public and a grassroots level, and it was not restricted to Coloured residential areas.[98]

On the day of the elections over 624 000 Coloured pupils boycotted classes, and attendance was limited to 20 per cent.[99] The independent trade unions also supported the election boycott. The FOSATU federation of trade unions called on Coloureds not to vote while its affiliate, the rapidly growing Sweet, Food and Allied Workers' Union (SFAWU), called on its members to show "their united opposition to apartheid".[100] The Food and Canning Workers' Union (FCWU) went a step further, exposing the link between the Union's commitment to non-racialism on the factory floor and its opposition to the tricameral elections, and noting that

> We cannot fight for the unity of all workers and allow a constitutional dispensation which discriminates against people of different races and excludes the majority.[101]

Although supporting the UDF campaign, the FCWU nevertheless refused to affiliate to the UDF.[102] The political profile of the UDF and the close association of the Front with community organisations, it argued, were not entirely compatible with the Union's objectives.[103] Building on the lessons of the past the Union aimed to concentrate on the development of a powerful workers' organisation, and not to sacrifice this goal to what certain Union organisers regarded as the short-run political requirements of organisations such as the UDF.[104]

96. *Ibid.*
97. See the major Cape papers covering the campaign — the *Cape Herald,* the *Argus* and the *Cape Times* — for the period June-Aug. 1984.
98. See, for example, *Argus,* 2 Aug. 1984.
99. *Cape Times,* 23 Aug. 1984; *Cape Times,* 24 Aug. 1984.
100. *Argus,* 22 Aug. 1984; *Cape Times,* 22 Aug. 1984; see also, "Workers Don't Vote", *SALB,* 9(8), July 1984, pp.121-122.
101. *Grassroots,* March 1983.
102. See the debate on Unions and the UDF in *SALB,* Vol. 9, No. 3, Nov. 1983, pp.47-87; "Debating Political Alliances" in *Work in Progress,* No. 34, Oct.. 1984; "General Workers and the UDF" in *Work in Progress,* No. 29, Oct. 1983; *Cape Times,* 20 Oct. 1983.
103. *Ibid.*
104. *Ibid.*

Trade Unions

Between 1976 and 1983 the remarkable development of community organisations in the Western Cape was matched by the rapid development
of the independent trade union movement. The growth in trade unionism in the Western Cape was part of a countrywide regeneration of
workers' organisations. In 1973, it will be recalled, a series of strikes
centred in Durban had given impetus to the development of independent trade unions. By 1982 over 107 unions existed which were committed to organising black workers.[105] These unions were estimated to
have a combined membership of between 400 000 and 500 000 workers.[106] The Western Cape accounted for approximately 10 per cent of the
total. In that region independent trade unions committed to organising
black workers had more than doubled their membership between 1976
and 1982, and by 1982 it stood at some 42 000 workers.[107] Two unions
accounted for over two-thirds of this membership: the Food and Canning Workers' Union (FCWU) (including the AFCWU) and the General
Workers' Union (GWU).[108] Of the two, the growth of the GWU was
particularly rapid.

In 1976 the fledgling General Workers' Union, operating as the Western Province Workers' Advice Bureau, had approximately 5 000 African
members.[109] By 1977 the Bureau had employed full-time organisers, become involved in wage and other negotiations and changed its name to
the Western Province General Workers' Union. From that time it continued to grow rapidly, and by December 1982 it included over 20 000
Western Cape workers.[110] The union was committed to organising in all
sectors employing Africans except those covered by the Food and Canning Workers' Union.[111] Membership was thus scattered over a wide
range of industries employing unskilled Africans. The bulk of the members, however, were employed in construction, the abattoirs, docks, engineering, steel, electricity supply (ESCOM) and hospitals.[112]

105. P. Randall (ed.), *"Survey 1982"*, pp. 147-57.
106. *Ibid.*
107. *Ibid.*; D. Lewis, interview, p.2; J. Theron, interview, p.1.
108. *Ibid.* The independent unions in the Western Cape committed to organising black work-
     ers were the General Workers' Union (membership in the Western Cape approx.
     18 000), the Food and Canning Workers' Union and the African Food and Canning
     Workers' Union (12 000), the Cape Municipal Workers' Association (11 000), the Me-
     dia Workers' Association (650) and the Commercial, Catering and Allied Workers'
     Union (600).
109. See D. Horner, "The Advice Bureau", *SALB*, 3(2),1976 p.75.
110. H. Gabriels, interview, p.2.
111. D. Lewis, interview, p.3.

In 1981 the extension of the union's activities to the docks of Durban and Port Elizabeth led the union to omit "Western Province" from its title.[113] In the same year the union decided to organise unskilled Coloured workers. By mid-1982 over 2 000 Coloured workers had joined the union's ranks.[114] The majority of these workers, Howard Gabriels, a GWU organiser, noted, were employed by the provincial authorities in hospitals and by the Divisional Council as unskilled labourers.[115] By organising these unskilled workers alongside unskilled African workers, the union was breaking new ground in the development of working-class consciousness in the Western Cape. The decision by the union to organise Coloured workers emerged out of its experience of the failure of Coloured workers to support its members during the 1980 meat strike.

The meat strike, the union noted, marked a "watershed" in its short history.[116] For over three months 800 workers stayed away from work in order to press for union recognition.[117] The solidarity of permanently resident and contract Africans constituted "a landmark in workers' struggle in South Africa"[118]. The union called for a boycott of red meat and, according to its spokesmen, "the close alliance between the union and the rest of the community was a particularly outstanding characteristic of the meat strike."[119] This support, it noted, was "matched only in intensity by the extreme measures resorted to by the state in its efforts to smash the strike."[120] Eventually, following the dismissal of the strikers, the banishment of 43 contract workers to the Transkei and the arrest of five activists, the strike crumbled.[121]

The union laid the blame for the collapse of the strike at the door of the Coloured workers who had failed to support the strike. The "failure of the majority of the Coloured workers to join the strike," it reflected, had prevented it from bringing the industry to a standstill.[122] The divi-

112. *Ibid.*
113. *Ibid.*
114. H. Gabriels, interview, p.3.
115. *Ibid.*
116. WPGWU, "The Cape Meat Strike", *SALB*, 6(5),1980, p.77.
117. *Ibid.*; Z. Mehlomakulu, GWU Secretary, interview, Cape Town, 21 Dec. 1981, transcript p.6.
118. WPGWU, *op.cit.*
119. *Ibid.*, pp.49-50.
120. *Ibid.*
121. D. Lewis, interview, p.4.
122. WPGWU, *op.cit.*, p.4.

sion between Coloured and African workers, the union commented, was
an

> ideological victory for the state and the bosses . . . The creation of divi-
> sions between the African and Coloured workers is one of the pillars of
> oppression in Cape Town working-class society, and not even the magnifi-
> cent, selfless support extended by the Coloured community to the workers
> and their union could disguise the fact that the workers and their union
> had not been able to break down these absolutely critical divisions.[123]

The union decided that before embarking on another such strike it
would be necessary to overcome the divisions between the African and
Coloured workers.[124]

The GWU's decision to involve the community in a boycott of red
meat followed the successful "Fattis and Monis" boycott organised the
previous year by the Food and Canning Workers' Union (FCWU).[125] In
August 1978 the FCWU had begun to organise at a Bellville South factory producing "Fattis and Monis" products for the United Macaroni
Group. In April 1979 the demand by the workers for a minimum wage
of R40 a week was met with the dismissal by management of the 10
Coloured union activists.[126] The response of the entire workforce — African and Coloured — was to initiate a strike which was to last seven
months.[127]

The most noteworthy features of the strike were the solidarity shown
between Coloured and African strikers and the success of the boycott of
Fattis and Monis products. Attempts by management and the Department of Labour to divide the Coloureds and African workers, and the
intimidation of the workers by the security police and hired thugs, failed
to undermine the unity of the strikers.[128] The support of the 40 African
contract workers was particularly remarkable; their dismissal led to the
cancellation of their permission to remain in the Western Cape and their
expulsion from the region for the duration of the strike.[129]

The eventual capitulation of the company to the strikers' demands
was due in large measure to the unified response of the workforce to the
strike and to the success of the consumer boycott of Fattis and Monis
products.[130] This countrywide boycott was supported by a wide range of

123. *Ibid.*
124. D. Lewis, interview, pp.4-5; H. Gabriels, interview. p.4.
125. See L. McGregor, "The Fattis and Monis Dispute", *SALB*, 5(6 & 7), 1980, pp.122-131.
126. *Argus*, 27 April 1979.
127. L. McGregor, *op.cit.*, p.131.
128. *Ibid.*, pp.124-131; *Muslim News*, 18 May 1979.
129. J. Theron, interview, p.6.
130. *Ibid.*; V. Engel, interview, p.4.

organisations including Inkatha, the Labour Party and the Western Cape Traders' Association, an organisation representing over 2 000 black traders.[131] By November 1979 the boycott had halved the company's profits and forced management to the bargaining table.[132] Conceding defeat, the company director, F. Moni, warned fellow businessmen not to repeat his mistakes:

> There is no doubt that these boycotts can be effective. We made the mistake of ignoring organised labour. I would advise other firms to negotiate directly with unions as soon as possible.[133]

The agreement signed by the company referred to the registered FCWU and the unregistered African Food and Canning Workers' Union (AFCWU) jointly as "the Union", thereby underlining the fact that the two unions, despite the law, acted as one.[134] The failure of statutory racial boundaries to lead to divisions between the FCWU and the AFCWU showed the union's success in forging a non-racial organisation whilst technically operating within the government's divisive trade union structure, which excluded Africans from joining registered trade unions.

During the Fattis and Monis strike, as one of the strike organisers later commented, "a close relationship was built up" between Coloured and African workers; "differences and prejudices were broken down".[135] "Nowadays", she noted,

> the Coloured workers will travel to the homes of African workers, which they never did before. The township is not a foreign country to the Coloured workers of Fattis and Monis now.[136]

The victory of the Fattis and Monis workers had depended on the ability of the FCWU to overcome the divisions between Coloured and African workers. The General Workers' Union, by contrast, had failed to organise Coloured workers, and the union felt that this failure had contributed to the collapse of the meat strike. It was this experience, together with that of the FCWU, that convinced the General Workers' Union of the need to organise Coloured workers.

However, the GWU restricted its attention to those industries in which Coloureds had previously been unorganised. The decision,

131. L. McGregor, *op.cit.,* p.131.
132. V. Engel, interview, p.4.
133. L. McGregor, *op.cit.,* p.131.
134. *Ibid.*
135. V. Engel, interview, pp.4-5.
136. *Ibid.,* p.5.

according to Dave Lewis, the union's General Secretary, resulted partly from the fact that

> the existence of registered trade unions for Coloured workers has been in the past and remains an enormous difficulty . . . not because the vast majority of the registered unions have any support from Coloured workers, but because certain very key ones are closed shop unions . . . It remains very, very difficult to break that incredible close alliance between the unions and the bosses.[137]

The most obvious example of such an alliance, Lewis noted, was the Garment Workers' Union of the Cape Province.[138]

We have suggested that prior to 1976 the close association of the Cape Garment Workers' Union with the industry's employers entrenched the conservatism of the union and undermined successive challenges to the union. In 1975 an attempt by an "Action Committee" to break the union's hold over the industry led to the dismissal of the activists and the arrest of the Committee's leaders. By 1979 no further challenge to the union executive had been mounted and the Chairman of the Industrial Council for the Cape Clothing, Alan Rosenberg, was able to compliment the union on its "enviable record for stable and excellent industrial relations".[139] A year later Alan Rosenberg had a very different view of the union's ability to prevent unrest.

In 1980 simmering discontent within the workforce erupted when the union failed to press home the workers' demand for an increase in the minimum wage from R15 to R25 a week.[140] The union had pleaded with its members that "it would be ungrateful and singularly ill-timed to hit at our employers."[141] But the workers had reached the limits of their patience and a strike at Rex Truform, the dominant manufacturing company, quickly spread to other enterprises. "The days of cheap labour," a large employer commented, "were over."[142]

The chairman of the Industrial Council was forced to admit that the failure of the union to contain the workers' demands "marred the fine record" of the union.[143] According to Alan Rosenberg,

> A disquieting, ugly new feature which manifested itself in the relationship between employer and employee was "confrontation" at the time of the work stoppages . . . In the history of the Clothing Industry in the Cape demands

137. *Saspu National,* Vol.2, No. 9, Nov.-Dec.1981, p.17; D. Lewis, interview, p.7.
138. *Ibid.*
139. Cape Clothing Industrial Council, *Annual Report, 1980,* p.5.
140. J. Bloch, "The Action Committee", in L. Cooper and D. Kaplan (eds.), *Organisation in the Western Cape,* p.56.
141. *The Clothesline,* Vol. 2, No. 22, 13 June 1980, p.2.
142. *Argus,* 12 Aug. 1980.
143. Cape Clothing Industry, *op.cit.,* p.5.

on employers were always made in an orderly and controlled manner through their trade union representatives. . . . The work stoppages of May, 1980, produced a new phenomenon — the confrontation by a faceless mass of workers with no leaders . . . There is no future for the Clothing Industry in the Cape if illegal work stoppages occur again.[144]

The 1980 strike forced management to take note of the workers' demands and was only resolved after management conceded to demands for a R25-a-week minimum wage. No sooner had the strike been resolved than the industry was once again disrupted by the support of the workforce for the two-day stoppage in commemoration of those who died in the June 1976 uprising. Whereas in previous years Coloured workers had given only limited support to this type of industrial action, in 1980, according to the *Cape Herald,* "commerce and industry were brought to a standstill in the Cape Peninsula."[145] The *Financial Mail* presented a more detailed breakdown of support for the strike. It estimated that approximately 65 per cent of the Peninsula black labour force had remained away from work on June 16 and 17, and that in the clothing industry support for the strike was even greater.[146]

By 1982 the growing militancy of the garment workers led to the formation of a rival union in the industry, the Clothing Workers' Union (CLOWU), which aimed to challenge the hold of the Cape Garment Workers' Union.[147] A combined attack by employers, the security police and the Cape Garment Workers' Union attempted to destroy the fledgling union. But by mid-1984 CLOWU was continuing to make inroads in the industry; CLOWU activists dismissed following a strike were reinstated, and two employers were forced to go against the Industrial Council and recognise the CLOWU leadership as the representative of its employees.[148] However, optimism that CLOWU could repeat its success more widely was premature; after a year and a half in existence its combined membership amounted to less than 1 per cent of the industry's workforce.[149] Furthermore, CLOWU's continuing survival owed much to the financial and organisational support given to the Union by the UDF (Western Cape). The attack by the state on the UDF therefore seriously undermined CLOWU.

144. *Ibid.,* pp.6-7.
145. *Cape Herald,* 21 June 1980.
146. *Financial Mail,* 20 June 1980; see also Cape Town Chamber of Commerce, "Minutes of the Inter-group Affairs Committee", mimeo, 11 June 1980, p.1, Item 3.
147. M. Michell, interview, p.6.
148. *Unity* (Newspaper of the Clothing Workers' Union), July 1984, p.2.
149. Calculated from *Ibid.,* and Cape Clothing Industry, *op.cit.,* p.2.

Summary

Since 1980 the growing militancy of clothing workers was reflected in the birth of CLOWU and the inability of the Cape Garment Workers' Union to prevent industrial conflict in the industry. The radicalisation of the workforce occurred simultaneously with the growing militancy of Coloured youth. In 1976 and again in 1980, Coloured and African youth found in their protests about education a point of convergence from which they could go on to widen the struggle. But in issues unrelated to education, community and student activists committed to non-racial organisation were frustrated by racial divisions. By organising on a local level in communities separated by Group Areas boundaries, the CA-HAC campaign failed in many instances to transcend the racial division between Coloured and African communities.

In the Western Cape, CAHAC provided the organisational base of the UDF. The failure of CAHAC to build a solid base in the African townships therefore tended to reinforce the bias of the UDF towards issues affecting only Coloureds; the impetus for the UDF's formation was provided by the election of Coloureds and Indians to the tricameral parliament. It was therefore not surprising that in the Western Cape the UDF initially focused on mobilising Coloured people in opposition to the elections. With the election over, the challenge to the UDF was to sustain this organisational base in the Coloured areas and to extend its organisation in the African townships. Except on isolated occasions the multiracialism of the executive failed to be translated into grassroots campaigns bringing together Coloured and African rank-and-file members of the Front's affiliates. Furthermore, in the industry in which the UDF first attempted to sponsor the development of a trade union — the garment industry — the workforce was entirely Coloured.[150]

The extent to which structural divisions within the workforce may be overcome depends on the particular history of trade unionism in the locality concerned. The experience of the GWU and the FCWU confirmed that organisation was required to overcome divisions between African and Coloured workers. If unions organise both Coloured and African workers, then, in the experience of Jan Theron, the general-secretary of FCWU,

> the extent of Coloured/African divisions depends to a large extent on the history of the factory concerned. If there has been a long history of strong trade

---

150. The UDF(WC) was also closely associated with the development of the Retail and Allied Workers' Union (RAWU). By August 1984 the union had gained recognition in the major Cape dairies, which employ only African workers. See D. Budlender, "RAWU victory", *SALB* 10(1), Sept. 1984, pp.21-23.

union organisation, then the divisions are minimal; however, in factories where organisation has not been strong there is sometimes antagonism of various forms. The factories with a long experience of trade unionism are definitely less racially divided.[151]

Racism, a FCWU organiser, Virginia Engels, noted, "can be overcome over a number of years but it is a slow process".[152]

In the final chapter we shall evaluate the extent to which organisations have either helped to develop racial prejudice or else helped to break racial divisions down. We shall do so in the context of the attempt by successive governments to implement policies of preference for people defined as Coloured.

151. J. Theron, interview, p.8.
152. V. Engel, interview, p.6.

CONCLUSION

CHAPTER TWELVE

CO-OPTION AND CONTRADICTION

Coloured Preference Policies

The announcement at the September 1984 conference of the Cape National Party that the Coloured Labour Preference Policy was to be scrapped signified the collapse of the most recent of a series of measures instituted by successive governments to promote the employment and residence of Coloureds at the expense of Africans. The retraction of the policy should not, however, be seen to indicate a turnaround in the National Party's attitude to Coloureds. On the contrary, the ending of the policy occurred simultaneously with a renewed attempt by the Party to incorporate Coloured people politically. Furthermore, the extent to which the ending of the Labour Policy will result in changes in controls over African residence and employment has been overstated by liberal commentators. Amendments to the Black Labour Act rendered superfluous many of the regulations associated with the Labour Preference Policy; and the ending of the policy, apart from allowing Africans permanently resident in the region to acquire 99-year leaseholds, is unlikely to lead to changes in the system of controls over Africans in the Western Cape. Controls over housing, employment (and unemployment) and citizenship may together be used to the same effect as influx controls, but they have the advantage of greater flexibility. For this reason the much-heralded abolition of the "pass laws" is of little immediate consequence for Africans in the Western Cape, even if the Abolition of Influx Control Act, which became operative from 1 July 1986, indicates shifts in the framework within which the Government is seeking to control residence and employment.

The Mixed Marriages Act and Section 16 of the Immorality Act were integral to the attempt by the National Party to develop a distinct Coloured political identity. Both items of legislation were important in restricting Coloured upward mobility and assimilation into the White population, and in raising the barriers between Africans, Coloureds and Whites. In 1985 the scrapping of this legislation provided a much-needed boost to P.W. Botha's increasingly hollow reformist image. The change was not simply a public relations exercise; it did mark an important break in Afrikaner nationalist ideology and this led to the further alienation of the most conservative Afrikaners from the National Party. In

practice, however, the abolition of the laws has been of little real significance. It may now be technically possible for people of different race
classifications to marry, but residential areas, government schools, much
public transport and other facilities are still segregated.

The abolition of the Mixed Marriages Act and Section 16 of the Immorality Act has in no way bridged the gulf between the worlds which
Coloured, African and White people in South Africa inhabit. Certainly,
there is no evidence to suggest that it will weaken the commitment of
the National Party to a separate Coloured and White identity.

Meanwhile, the Party's determination to pursue policies of preference
for Coloureds has, far from slackening, hardened in recent years. More
than any of his pedecessors, P.W. Botha is committed to policies designed to achieve this. In the Western Cape the ascendancy of Botha
was associated with a more vigorous commitment to the control of African influx. Since 1978 the position of Africans who had not been able to
obtain permission to reside in the region deteriorated sharply. With the
focus of the controls shifting to housing, attacks on Cape Town's African squatter settlements have come a commonplace occurrence.

From the beginning, policies of Coloured Labour Preference in the
Western Cape coincided with the increasing regulation of African employment and influx. At the turn of the century Coloured people were
exempted from the pass laws and from the health and housing ordinances which in the Western Cape had been used to regiment African
people into segregated townships. As the position of Africans rapidly
deteriorated, the relative position of Coloured men and women improved and the assertion of Coloured identity became a means to escape
pass and other laws. Coloured political identity did not, however, necessarily signify a deep-rooted commitment to it; wherever possible
Coloured people who were able to pass for White were keen to assert a
White identity. For despite the fact that the position of Coloureds relative to Africans had improved, their absolute position and their position relative to White men and women had worsened considerably.

By the 1940s Coloured men had been ousted from virtually every occupation which they had come to regard as their own. The rapid deterioration in the economic position of Coloureds relative to Whites
(despite the relative improvement in their position relative to Africans)
was matched by a dramatic decline in their political position. Selborne
and Hertzog, it will be recalled, were committed to policies of political
incorporation of Coloureds, but their strategic goals did not lead to an
improvement in the position of Coloureds relative to Whites. On the
contrary, the influence of the Coloured electorate was halved in 1930 by
the enfranchisement of White women without any concomitant conces-

sion for Coloured women. Still, the assertion of a Coloured identity did at any rate, despite its shortcomings, provide many Coloured petty-bourgeois men access to political representation denied to Africans, who were virtually excluded from the vote.

Coloured Political Identity

Although a consciousness of racial differences existed prior to the 1890s, the term Coloured until the turn of the twentieth century denoted all non-European people. Events associated with the South African War, the restructuring of labour, the development of social-Darwinism and other factors led to a fundamental shift in racial terminology: by 1905 the different meaning attached to the word Coloured was seen in official documents as well as in the development of political organisations dedicated to the promotion of the position of Coloureds separate from Africans. From the beginning, however, Coloured political identity was a source of intense social conflict.

We have shown that the battle over the existence of a Coloured political identity from the turn of the century to the present day has dominated Coloured politics of the Western Cape. Successive governments have attempted to promote such an identity and to engineer socially an alliance of Coloured and White people. None of these attempts have lived up to their promises. Nevertheless, they have provided the basis for the segregation of virtually all aspects of Coloureds' lives.

It would be surprising if the institutional obligations imposed on people defined as Coloured has not left these people with at the very least a remote notion of Coloured identity. Every person defined as Coloured is compelled to reside in a Coloured Group Area and to carry an identity document which includes a reference to racial status. These and over 100 other statutory measures in South Africa isolate people along racial lines, creating social barriers which correspond with the official racial divisions. By limiting social intercourse at all levels of society these measures have facilitated the development and perpetuation of racial stereotypes and racial prejudice. But while powerful forces exist which encourage the creation of racial identities, so others challenge such an identification.

The significance of racial identities lay in their ability to help rally individuals around a common cause. However, the extent to which Coloured identity was able to bind Coloureds could never be determined *a priori,* for the identity of each person, each group, was a product of a different set of historical circumstances. Racial identities are the unresolved outcome of a conflict which is constantly being reshaped. Individuals ascribed a range of meanings to the term Coloured and defined themselves in different ways according to the context. And of course racial identities at all times co-existed with other forms of identity.

Political Rule, the State and Coloured Identity

Successive governments attempted to adjust social relations in their favour by securing an alliance with sections of the disaffected population. Such policies rested on the preferential treatment of certain groups of people on the basis of symbolic differences between the preferred group and the rest of the subordinate population. Often this preferential treatment was not linked to any absolute improvement in the position of the group given preference; all that was required was that the position of this group did not deteriorate as rapidly as that of the less privileged population.

At the turn of the eighteenth century the alliance of Khoi and Xhosa posed for the colonial military its most serious internal threat. A growing rule of law which distinguished between Bantu-speaking people and Khoisan diffused the challenge but the threat of an alliance continued to alarm successive administrations. In 1853, with the granting of self-government to the Cape, a limited number of non-European males was granted the franchise. By the 1880s, however, Bantu-speaking men were increasingly excluded from the electorate. At about this time a distinct Coloured political identity began to emerge. It was promoted by White political parties who argued that by disassociating themselves from Bantu-speaking people, the rest of the non-European population would be spared the political and economic humiliation suffered by them.

At the turn of the century the introduction of draconian health and housing ordinances led more people, eager to escape the prison-like compounds being erected on the periphery of Cape Town, to seek an identity distinct from that of the Africans. African people were by this time enduring the brunt of the mounting racial prejudice which was reflected in racial stereotyping and in the authorities' ethnic diagnosis of health problems.

It is no accident that the evolution of a distinct Coloured identity took place during a period in which the colonial office was increasingly committed to a strategy of "divide and rule". This policy, informed by late-

Victorian notions of social-Darwinism, was translated in the South African context into a rigid racial hierarchy. The redefinition, in the official census, of the term Coloured to denote a group intermediate between "Whites" and " Bantu" was testimony to this dramatic change in colonial thinking.

The divide-and-rule strategy promoted in the 1850s by the Cape Attorney-General, William Porter, and between 1905 and 1910 by Selborne, the High Commissioner in South Africa, was taken up in 1924 by Prime Minister Hertzog. However, by the time Hertzog finally relinquished power in 1939 the economic and political position of the Coloureds had slipped even further — though as we have suggested, the more rapid deterioration in the position of Africans meant that the position of Coloureds relative to Africans may well have improved. Between 1939 and 1948 the Smuts government entrenched further the division between Coloured and African people. At the same time the gulf between Coloureds and Whites was widened as legislation designed to segregate Coloured and White residential areas, to extend racial divisions at the work-place and to develop a separate Coloured administration was introduced.

By the time the National Party came to power in 1948, policies of preference for Coloureds were deeply rooted in a tradition stretching back for well over a century. The difference between the National Party and previous administrations was that the Nationalists were committed to the establishment of separate "nations" coinciding with racial divisions and that these "nations" were to be segregated geographcally.

Verwoerd accepted that the establishment of a separate Coloured "homeland" was not at the time "practical politics". But he later insisted that

> If we could have settled the Coloureds in a part of the country quite on their own, in their own areas like the Bantu, we certainly would have.[1]

The total segregation of Coloureds, he and his colleagues argued, was a prerequisite for the development of both White and Coloured identity. White identity was seen to be threatened by the vagueness of the distinctions between poor-Whites and Coloureds and by the existence of racially mixed residential areas.

The development of Coloured identity, many National Party ideologues believed, required not only the complete isolation of Coloured people but the establishment of a separate political structure for them. Not surprisingly, the final removal of Coloureds from the common vot-

1.   *HAD.*, 1961, 107, 4193.

ers' roll increased their alienation. However, as a result of the Coloured
Labour Preference Policy the position of Africans in the Western Cape
deteriorated even more rapidly; the assertion of Coloured identity was a
means to escape the pass laws and to remain in the Western Cape. By
offering protection to Coloureds at the expense of Africans, the Preference Policy sought to promote a distinct Coloured identity and to fragment the alliance of Coloured and African people. Significantly, the
policy was vigorously enforced at a time of mounting civil disobedience,
and Cape Nationalists came to see the policy as a strategic priority.

As a result of the stalemate between the contending sections of the
National Party, Verwoerd's death brought little change in the Party's
policy towards Coloureds; the existing schemes for the political and social segregation of Coloureds continued to be enforced and the commitment of the government to the Coloured Labour Preference Policy
maintained. Then in 1978 P.W. Botha wrested power from B.J. Vorster.
Botha represented two forces in the ascendancy in the National Party
and in government: the military and the Cape National Party.

Both of these were firmly committed to forging a closer alliance with
Coloureds. Their commitment was reinforced by the growing alienation
of Coloureds evident from the extent of Coloured participation in the
1976 and 1980 riots and from the collapse of the Coloured Persons Representative Council. Coloured resistance placed the Cabinet on the defensive and they were compelled to fundamentally review their Coloured
policy. The new constitutional arrangement excluded Africans and guaranteed the continued domination of Whites, but Coloureds and Indians
were offered representation in a racially segregated, tricameral parliamentary system. This arrangement was opposed by the overwhelming
majority of Coloureds. At the same time it was condemned by many
right-wing National Party members as contrary to Verwoerdian apartheid.

Whereas the National Party, largely because of its increasing preoccupation with strategic concerns, was committed to a closer alliance with
Coloureds, the new conservative opposition condemned what it described as "power-sharing" and called for a return to Verwoerdian principles. In the 1950s the SABRA think-tank had been influential in the
development of Verwoerd's policies towards the Coloureds; now in the
1980s this institution remained loyal to the same ideology and, having
purged its reformist members, continued to develop plans for the establishment of a separate Coloured "homeland".[2]

---

2.   See, for example, A.J. Antonites, "Selfbespreking en die pad vorentoe", *Journal of
     Racial Affairs*, 34 (4), Oct. 1983, pp.108-115.

Employers

History shows us that government policy is constantly frustrated by tensions within the ruling party and the government machinery. For example, in the 1930s the refusal of the Department of Justice to implement the Department of Native Affairs' regulations sabotaged its attempts to control the residence and employment of Africans in the Western Cape. By the 1950s the Department of Justice had been compelled to arrest pass-law offenders. But the Department of Labour circumvented these controls and agreed with employers that only Africans were suitable for many jobs. By the late 1960s employers of certain categories of unskilled African labour were automatically exempted from the Coloured Labour Preference Policy.

Considerable tensions existed within the employer class and between that class and the various, often antagonistic, branches of government. These render unsatisfactory any interpretations of "capital and the state" which rest on a simple one-to-one correspondence between a particular group of employers and government policy.

The fact that many people who loyally support the government's political programme may as employers be opposed to some of its policy implications has been demonstrated with reference to the Coloured Labour Preference Policy. In the Western Cape many National Party members who were vocal in their support for the Preference Policy were equally determined to gain exemption from those aspects of it which adversely restricted their recruitment of unskilled African labour.

Already by the 1880s employers had found in unskilled African labour a means to overcome resistance by local workers to low wages and arduous conditions of employment. By 1900 a clear division of labour had emerged in the Western Cape, and employers had come to insist on the employment of Africans in unskilled manual occupations; from the beginning, however, the employers sought to "compound" Africans and to restrict the influx of Africans into the Western Cape.

Employers' demands for the stricter regulation of African influx in the early 1920s were translated into central government policy. With the encouragement of employers and sections of the Coloured population, the government introduced strict controls on the residence of Africans in the Western Cape. The extent to which employers were actually prepared to endose these controls was influenced by the stop-go economic cycle; employment opportunities for Coloured workers were at all times limited by the determination of employers to secure an adequate supply of cheaper and more exploitable African labour.

In 1955 the introduction of the Coloured Labour Preference Policy
was greeted with dismay by many Western Cape employers, who saw
the policy as placing them at an unfair disadvantage to employers in
other regions. However, certain large corporations which were powerful
within the Cape National Party supported the policy, which they regarded as integral to the National Party's nation-building plans and as
the basis for an urgently needed alliance of Coloureds and Whites. The
support of these powerful businessmen and the opposition of other employers, including many who were considered to be loyal National Party
supporters, highlighted some of the contradictions within the capitalist
class.

The Cape Chambers of Industry and Commerce as well as the Cape
Employers' Association, the Western Cape Afrikaanse Handelsinstituut
and the Western Cape branch of the South African Agricultural Union
condemned those aspects of the Coloured Labour Preference Policy
which restricted their employment of unskilled Africans. Nevertheless,
all these pressure groups were broadly in favour of the policy and were
utterly opposed to the unregulated influx of Africans into the Western
Cape.

By the early 1980s a growing consensus had emerged between various
employers' groups and between these groups and the National Party
leadership. In order to overcome their acute shortage of skilled labour,
and to give effect to their strategic concerns regarding the development
of a black middle class, the employers lobbied for the extension of African leasehold to the Western Cape and for the scrapping of what had by
1981 become the superfluous provisions of the Coloured Labour Preference Policy.

Coloured Political Organisation

Until the 1890s Coloured people were anxious not to establish a political
identity of their own. In the next decade the situation changed dramatically and by 1904 a separate Coloured organisation — the APO — had
begun to campaign for the protection of Coloured people at the expense
of the rest of the non-European population.

From the beginning the APO was engaged in a rear-guard defence of
the rapidly deteriorating position of Coloured people. By defending
their position in isolation from Africans it became a willing partner to
policies of preference for Coloureds. These policies improved the posi-

tion of Coloureds relative to Africans. Nevertheless, the rapid deterioration in the political and economic position of Coloureds led to the alienation of a growing number of Coloured men and women. By the 1930s the APO's domination of Coloured politics had been challenged by political organisations which, although firmly based in the Coloured communities, were antagonistic to policies which sought to advance the position of Coloureds in isolation from Africans. But the ability of these organisations to overcome the political divisions between Africans and Coloureds was limited by the ANC's pre-occupation with African identity and its exclusion of Coloureds. Radical Coloureds found themselves thrown back on to their own communities. The association of these Coloureds with other radicals opposed to the ANC led to the formation of the NEUM.

The NEUM in the Western Cape confined itself mainly to the Coloured communities and failed to transcend the barriers between Coloured and African people. Its major source of competition within the Coloured communities came from Coloured communists who, although excluded from the ANC, from 1950 co-ordinated joint campaigns with that organisation. The formation of SACPO and its membership of the Congress Alliance gave institutional form to the close collaboration of Coloured and other radicals opposed to the NEUM — a collaboration that brought about joint campaigns of African and Coloured people. But attempts to mobilise Coloureds around issues which did not affect them directly (such as pass laws) met with little success, and in the political arena SACPO failed to break down the divisions between Coloured and African people.

With the silencing of SACPO and the NEUM, Coloured politics centred on participation in the Coloured Persons Representative Council. The only Coloured political party with a semblance of legitimacy to compete in this arena was the Labour Party. Like the APO, the Party was from the beginning ambivalent about its support for a distinct Coloured identity; this reflected tensions within the Party as well as the desire of Party leaders to exploit to the full the strategic concerns of the National Party.

The strategic concerns came to a head in 1976 and again in 1980 when the failure of the government's attempt to co-opt Coloureds — and in particular the younger generation of Coloureds — became painfully obvious to the cabinet. Simultaneously, the withdrawal of the Labour Party from the CPRC forced the government to abandon the Council and to implement a constitutional scheme which at the very least would secure the participation of the Labour Party. The introduction of the new constitution was a measure of the success of resistance to previous attempts to develop separate Coloured political institutions. But the latest attempt to incorporate the Coloureds politically was doomed, like earlier attempts, to failure; the elections for the Coloured House of Representatives were boycotted by the overwhelming majority of those eligible to vote. Even more significantly, the introduction of the tricameral system, by excluding Africans and by entrenching the domination of the National Party, occasioned the formation of a fresh challenge to the government in the form of the United Democratic Front (UDF). In the Western Cape the UDF provided a focus for Coloured radicalism which for the first time placed the Coloured communities at the forefront of struggles associated with the ANC-oriented Freedom Charter. This proved the UDF's ability to overcome many of the divisions which have hampered the development of such organisation in the Coloured communities, and the development of the growing radicalism of these communities. Despite state repression, the UDF is attempting to overcome the divisions between the African and Coloured communitites of the Western Cape, break down racial prejudice and so lay the foundations for a non-racial society.

Trade Unions

By organising across racial boundaries trade unions have the potential to do away with racial divisions at the work-place. At the same time they may also have the opposite impact: in the Western Cape the development of racially exclusive craft unions at the turn of the century provided a powerful impetus to the development of Coloured political identity. Their formation was a defensive response to de-skilling and other pressures placed on the workforce.

By the turn of the century, trade unionism was itself a focus of conflict over racial identities. In opposition to the racial protectionism of the craft unions, members of the International Socialist League and other organisations in the docks and elsewhere sought to organise non-racially. From the beginning these radical organisations posed a challenge to the racially segregated unions.

The exclusion of Coloureds from the ICU, and the wave of repression which followed the brief but remarkably successful campaign by the ANC to organise African and Coloured workers, had by 1930 left Coloured workers in the hands of less radical union officials. These unionists were committed to racially exclusive organisation and, in the case of the Cape Garment Workers' Union, gave priority to the interests of the employers rather than the workers. But if the 1930s marked a low point in trade unionism in the Western Cape, the 1940s pointed the way to a non-racial trade union movement. At the forefront of this movement was the Food and Canning Workers' Union (FCWU). From 1941 the Union instilled a new radicalism into Coloured workers which through their joint organisation with African workers chipped away at racial divisions in the workforce.

In the 1950s the close links between radicals associated with the FCWU and the Congress Alliance increased the vulnerability of the Union to state repression. The Union nevertheless went from strength to strength and, together with other members of the SACTU alliance, managed to overcome many of the divisions between Coloured and African workers — a feat which the political side of the Congress Alliance was unable to achieve. However, the declaration of a State of Emergency and the associated wave of repression brought to an abrupt end these activities, and by 1962 the non-racial trade union movement was a shadow of its former self.

For a decade, trade unions which perpetuated racial divisions were given a near-monopoly over the workforce of the Western Cape. Since 1974, however, their position has again been challenged by unions committed to breaking down the barriers between Coloured and African workers. These unions have had a marked impact on the working class of the Western Cape and, despite the weight of repression, the divisive tactics of employers and the deeply rooted racial prejudices within the working class, have in certain circumstances been remarkably successful in forging non-racial organisation.

The extent to which racial divisions exist within the workplace can never be determined *a priori*. The development of racial prejudices and their dissolution depends critically on the nature of workers' organisation and the specific historical experience of the workforce. Racial divisions between Coloured and African workers, in the words of the Cape Chamber of Industries, "vary to such an extent from factory to factory that it is not possible to make a valid general comment about them".[3] The role of trade unions is decisive, and trade unions dedicated to forging non-racial organisation can, over time, achieve their objective.

Conclusion

It has been shown that Coloured preference policies have been intimately associated with the making of Coloured political identity. By im-

---

3.   Unisa Acc. 100, Evidence of the Cape Chamber of Industries, p.8.

proving the position of Coloureds relative to Africans these policies have increased the advantages of an assertion of Coloured identity. Simultaneously, however, the position of Coloured people has deteriorated sharply. Their exclusion from White society and the segregation of all aspects of their lives have increased their alienation. For many Coloureds, increasingly disillusioned by the failure of White and Coloured politicians to advance their position, the only way forward is through their joint organisation with African men and women.

This radicalisation of Coloureds since 1976 has propelled Coloureds to the forefront of struggles being waged against the regime, and compelled the government to develop new strategies in their attempt to engineer an alliance of Coloureds and Whites. The determination of the state to shore up its defences and to undermine non-racial organisation has been resisted by the UDF and the increasingly powerful independent trade-union movement. These organisations are committed to the promotion of a democratic and non-racial society; in striving for this goal they are engaged in a long and bitter struggle against racial identity. On this struggle rests the hope and challenge of all those who are interested in progressive change in South Africa.

BIBLIOGRAPHY

(1) PRIMARY SOURCES

Athlone Advice Office — *Monthly Report of Activities,* January 1977 to December 1982

Annual Reports

Barker, H.A.E. — *The Economics of the Wholesale Clothing Industry in South Africa 1907 to 1957* (Johannesburg, Pallas Publications, 1962)

Batson, E. (Ed.) — *The Social Survey of Cape Town* Report No.SS4, The Distribution of Poverty Among Coloured Households in Cape Town (UCT, 1941)

Black Sash — "Memorandum on the Pass Laws and Influx Control" (*Sash* Vol.16, No.8, February 1974)

Bureau of Market Research — *Urban Coloureds in Cape Town* (Cape Town, Bureau of Market Research, Report No.9, 1955.

Bureau for Economic Research — *Interim Report on the Economic Potential of the Western Cape* (Stellenbosch, University of Stellenbosch, 1979)

Greater Saldanha and the Development of the Western Cape (Cape Town, Syfrets-UAL Group, 1973)

Further Report on the Economic Potential of the Western Cape (Stellenbosch, University of Stellenbosch, 1980)

Cape Chamber of Industries — *Annual Reports:* 1932-1946 (Cape Town, CCI, 1933-1946)

Yearbooks: 1946-1982 (Cape Town, CCI, 1947-1983)

Report of the Executive Council, 1962 (Cape Town, CCI, 1962)

Cape of Good Hope, Colony of — *Census, 1865* G20/66 (Cape Town, Government Printer, 1866)

Census, 1875 G18/76 (Cape Town, Government Printer, 1876)

	Census, 1891, G6/92 (Cape Town, Government Printer, 1892)
	Report of the Commission on the Labour Question, 3 Volumes. G39/93 G3/94 (Cape Town, Government Printer, 1894)
	Census, 1904 G19/1905 (Cape Town, Government Printer, 1905)
Cape Provincial Administration	*Report of the Committee of Inquiry into the Establishment of Separate Local Authorities for Coloured Group Areas* (Cape Town, CPA, 1961)
Cape Town City Council	*Towards Cheaper Housing* (Cape Town, CTCC, 1950)
	Native Affairs Department Annual Report, 1946 (Cape Town, CTCC, 1947)
Clothing Industry Industrial Council (Cape)	*Annual Report, 1980* (Cape Town, Clothing IC, 1981)
Coloured and European Conference	*Report of the Proceedings* (Cape Town, 26-28 June, 1933)
Committee of '81	*Manifesto* (Cape Town, SRC Press, 14 May 1980)
Community Action Committee	*We do not buy Fattis and Monis Products* (Cape Town, pamphlet, n.d.)
Cooper, C.	*Strikes: January to June 1982* (Johannesburg, SAIRR, 1982)
Cosas	*Each one teach one* (Pamphlet, 1982)
Eiselen, W.W.M.	"The Meaning of Apartheid", *Race Relations*, Vol.XV, No.3, 1948
	"The Coloured People and the Natives", *Journal of Racial Affairs* Vol.6, No.3, April 1955
Feldman-Laschin, G.R.	*Income and expenditure patterns in South Africa: Coloured Households Cape Peninsula* (Pretoria, Univ. of South Africa, Pretoria, 1965)
	Income and expenditure patterns in South Africa: Urban Bantu Cape Town (Pretoria, University of South Africa, 1968)
Hancock, W.K., and van der Poel, J.	*Selections from the Smuts Papers, 4 Vols.* (Cambridge, CUP, 1966)

Heard, K.A.	*General Elections in South Africa, 1943-1970* London, 1974)
Hofmeyer, D.	*Report of an Economic Survey of the Elgin/ Vryeboom Area* (Elgin, Elgin Co-operative Fruitgrowers Ltd, 1975)
Kadalie, C.	*My Life and the ICU* (London, Cass, 1970)
Long Range Planning Society	*Aspects of the Long-Term Future of the Western Cape; Conference Papers* (Cape Town, LRPS, 1981)
National Productivity Institute	*Productivity of the Women's and Girls' Clothing Industry in South Africa* (Pretoria, National Productivity Institute, 1971)
Nicholls, G. Heaton	*South Africa in My Time* (London, 1961)
Potgieter, J.	*Household Subsistence Levels of the Major Urban Centres of the Republic* (Port Elizabeth, Bureau of Market Research, 1977)
Schoeman, B.	*My lewe in die politiek* (Johannesburg, Nasionale Pers, 1978)
South Africa, Republic of	*Report of the Economics and Wages Commission 1925,* UG14/1926
	Evidence to the Select Committee on Native Bills, SC10/1927
	Report of the Commission of Inquiry into Coloured Persons Rights, SC10/1927
	Joint House of Assembly and Senate Select Committee on Representation, 1927/1929
	Department of Census and Statistics, Industrial Censuses, 1928-1952
	Report and Proceedings of the Joint Committee on the Representation of Natives and Coloured Persons in Parliament and Provincial Councils, Joint Committee No.1 1935
	Report of the Commission of Inquiry regarding the Coloured Population of the Union, UG54/1937
	Report of the Commission on Mixed Marriages in South Africa, UG30/1939
	Conditions existing in the Cape Flats and similarly affected areas in the Cape division, UG18/1943

South Africa, Republic of

Report of the Inter-departmental Committee on matters affecting Coloured Persons on Coloured Mission Stations, Reserves and Settlements, UG33/1947

Coloured Advisory Council, *Annual Reports* (1st 1943/1944 to 4th 1949)

The Economic and Social Conditions of the Racial Groups in South Africa, Report No.13 of the Social and Economic Planning Council UG53/1948

Report of the Native Laws Commission of Enquiry, UG28/1948

Population Registration Act, Act No.30 of 1950

Industrial Legislation Commission of Inquiry Report, UG62/1951

Report of the Commission of Inquiry into the Subject Matter of the Separate Representation of Voters Act Validation and Amendment Bill, 1953, Part 1, UG20/1954

Summary of the Report of the Commission for the Socio-economic Development of the Bantu Areas, UG61/1955

Report of the Industrial Tribunal to the Minister of Labour on Reservation of Work in the Clothing Industry of South Africa (Pretoria, Government Printer, 1957)

Department of Coloured Affairs *More Opportunity for the Coloured People* (Policy statement by the deputy Minister of the Interior, Mr P.W. Botha, 17 May 1961)

Department of Census and Statistics *Union Statistics for Fifty Years* (Pretoria, Government Printer, 1960)

Report of the Commission of Inquiry into Events of the 20th to 22nd November 1962 at Paarl and the causes which gave rise thereto, RP51/1963

Report of the Commission of Inquiry into the system of local government which applied to the city of Cape Town, G682, 1964

Bantoe behuising in Wes-Kaaplandse Stedelike Gebiede, in Verslag van die Subkomitee van die Interdepartementele komitee insake Vervanging van Bantoe-arbeid in Wes-Kaapland GP S7525409 1965/66100 (Pretoria, Government Printer, 1965)

Report of the Commission of Inquiry into Improper Political Interference and the Political Representation of the Various Population Groups, RP72/1967

Verslag van die Interdepartementele Komitee insake Beheermaatreëls, Department of Bantu Administration and Development 1967

Physical Planning and Utilisation of Resources Act, No. 88 of 1967

Report of the Select Committee on the Immorality Amendment Bill, 2 parts, SC7/68 and 3/69

Community Development Amendment Bill 1972 Report of the Select Committee, SC9/1972

Press Statement by Mr B. Lindeque, Secretary for Labour, concerning work reservation in the Building Industry, 1973

Department of Planning, *Decentralisation Growth Points 1975*

Report of the Commission of Inquiry into Matters Affecting the Coloured Population Group, RP38/1976

Department of Census and Statistics, *Census of Manufacturing 1976. Principle Statistics on a Regional Basis,* Report No.10.21.33

Housing Matters: Report of the Commission of Inquiry, RP74/1977

South Africa, Republic
of

Department of Planning and Environment
Decentralisation — Growth Points 1977, 1977

Press Statement by the Minister of Bantu Administration and Development and the Minister of Community Development in connection with Illegal Squatting in the Cape Peninsula, 1977

Department of Planning and Environment Annual Reports

Department of Interior and Social Services Statistical Labour Reports

Second Bantu Laws Amendment Act, 1978, Act No.102, 1978. Government Gazette 1978 No.6095

Report of the Commission of Inquiry on Legislation affecting the Utilisation of Manpower, RP32/1979

Report of the Commission of Inquiry into Labour Legislation, RP47/1979

White Paper on the Report of the Commission of Inquiry into Legislation affecting the Utilisation of Manpower, WPT 1979

Laws on Plural Relations and Development Second Amendment Act, 1979, No.98 of 1979, Government Gazette Vol.169 1979

Report of the Commission of Inquiry into the Riots at Soweto and elsewhere from the 16th June 1976 to 20th February 1980, RP55/1980

Department of Environmental Planning and Energy *A Spatial Development Strategy for the Western Cape* (Pretoria, Government Printer, 1980)

Industrial Council Agreement, Clothing Industry, Government Gazette Vol.191, 1981

Industrial Council Agreement: Printing and Newspaper Industry, Government Gazette Vol.191, 1981

House of Assembly, *Hansard Votes and Proceedings*, 1948-1983

House of Assembly, *Hansard Debates* (HAD), 1948-1983

Department of Coloured Relations and Affairs, *Annual Reports*

Department of Census and Statistics, Census of Wholesale and Distribution 1971

Department of Census and Statistics, *Census of Population*, 1939, 1946, 1960 and 1970

Department of Census and Statistics, *Gross Geographic Product of factor incomes by Magisterial Distribution*

Department of Census and Statistics, *Census of Manufacturing*, 1963-1964, 1965-1966, 1968, 1970 and 1972

Department of Census and Statistics, *Labour Statistics: Annual Reports*, 1968-1975

Annual Reports of the Department of Environment 1978-1983

Annual Reports of the Department of Planning 1968-1977

Bantu Affairs Administration Accounts, *Auditor General: Report on the Accounts of the Bantu Administration Boards 1973-1975*, RP108/1976

Coloured Affairs Department Annual Reports 1957-1979

Trade Union Council of South Africa (TUCSA)   *Official Trade Union Directory 1981-1982* (Johannesburg, TUCSA, 1982)

United Party   *The Cape Coloured Vote: A common role or political apartheid* (Cape Town, Juta, 1954)

Unity Movement of South Africa   *The Revolutionary Road Ahead* (Lusaka, NEUM, 1969)

(2) SECONDARY SOURCES

Abercome, N. and Turner B. — "The Dominant Ideology thesis", *British Journal of Sociology*, Vol. 29 No.4, December 1978

Abraham, K. — *From Race to Class: Links and Parallels in African and Black American Protest Expression* (London, Grassroots, 1982)

Adam, H. (ed.) — *South Africa: Sociological Perspectives* (London, Oxford University Press, 1971)

Adam, H. — *Modernising Racial Domination* (Los Angeles, Univ. of California, 1971)

Adam, H. and Giliomee, H. — *Ethnic Power Mobilized. Can South Africa Change?* (New Haven, Yale University Press, 1979)

Adler, T. (ed.) — *Perspectives on South Africa: A Collection of Working Papers* (Johannesburg, African Studies Institute, Univ. of Witwatersrand, 1977)

Allen, S. — "The Institutionalisation of Racism", *Race,* Vol. XV, No. 1.

Alexander, R., and Simons, H. — *Job Reservation in the Trade Unions* (Cape Town, Enterprise, 1959)

Althusser, L. — Ideology and Ideological State Apparatuses, in L. Althusser, *Lenin and Philosophy and other Essays* (London, NLB, 1971)

Anderson, P. — *Considerations on Western Marxism* (London, Verso, 1979)

Arguments within English Marxism (London, Verso, 1980)

Anti-Slavery Society — *Child Labour in South Africa: A General Review,* Anti-slavery Society, Child Labour Series, Report No. 7. (London, Anti-Slavery Society, 1983)

Antonites, A.J. — "Selfbeskikking en die pad vorentoe", *Journal of Racial Affairs,* 34, (2), Oct. 1983,

Apter, D. (ed.) — *Ideology and Discontent* (New York, Free Press, 1964)

Ashenfeller, O., and Rees, A. (eds.) — *Discrimination in Labour Markets* (Princeton, Princeton Univ. Press, 1973)

Asheron, A. — "Race and Politics in South Africa", *New Left Review* Vol. 53, 1969

Ashford, D.E.	*Ideology and Participation* (London, Sage, 1972)
Attlee, M.	"The Coloured People of South Africa", *African Affairs* Vol. 46, No. 184, July 1947
Baldwin, A.	*Uprooting a Nation: a Study of 3 million Evictions in South Africa* (London, Africa publ. trust, 1974)
Ballinger, V.M.L.	*From Union to Apartheid: a Trek to Isolation* (Folkestone, Bailey Bros., 1969)
Ballinger, W.G.	*Race and Economics in South Africa* (London, Day, 1934)
Banton, M.	*The Idea of Race* (London, Tavistock, 1977) *Racial and Ethnic Competition* (Cambridge, CUP, 1983)
Barnard, P.N.	"Die Kleurling-vraagstuk...kan Suid-Afrika 'n Tuiste vir die Nageslag bly?" *Onderwysersblad vir Christelike en Nasionale Onderwys en Opvoeding 51 (563), 1974*
Barrat, J. (ed.)	*Accelerated development in South Africa* (London, Macmillan, 1974)
Barrington-Moore, Jr.	*Social Origins of Dictatorship and Democracy* (Harmondsworth, Penguin, 1966)
Baskin, J.	"Farm Workers and the National Manpower Commission" *South African Labour Bulletin* 8 (2), 1982 "Dockworkers and the General Workers' Union" *SALB* 8 (5), 1982 "Factory workers in the Countryside: The Food and Canning Workers' Union in Ceres and Grabouw", *SALB* 8 (4), 1983
Batson, E.	"A Contribution to the Study of Coloured Poverty", *Race Relations* Vol.9, 1942 *The Poverty Line in Cape Town: Social Security and the Coloured People* (Cape Town, Social Survey Conference, 1942) *Social Security and the Coloured People* (SAIRR, Johannesburg, 1946)
Bell, R.T.	"Migrant Labour: Theory and Policy", *South African Journal of Economics Vol. 40, 1972*

Industrial Decentralisation in South Africa (London, Oxford University Press, 1973)

"Some Aspects of Industrial Decentralisation in South Africa", *SAJE* Vol. 43 pp.401-431, 1975

"Capital Intensity and Employment in South African Industry", *SAJE* Vol. 46, No.1, pp.48-61, 1978

Ben-Tovim, J.G., and Ben-Tovim, G.   "Marxism and the Concept of Racism", *Economy and Society* Vol.7, No.2, May 1978

Benyon, J.A. (ed.)   *Constitutional Change in South Africa* (Pietermaritzburg, Univ. of Pietermaritzburg, 1978)

Beteille, A. (ed.)   *Social Inequality* (Harmondsworth, Penguin, 1969)

Bickford-Smith, V.   "Black Labour of the Docks at the Beginning of the Twentieth Century", in C. Saunders and H. Phillips (eds.), *Studies in the history of Cape Town, Vol.2* (Cape Town, Univ. of Cape Town, 1980)

"Dangerous Cape Town: Middle-class Attitudes to Poverty in Cape Town in the late Nineteenth Century" in C. Saunders *et. al.* (eds.), *Studies in the History of Cape Town, Vol. 4* (Cape Town, UCT, 1981)

Biesheuvel, S.   "Black Industrial Labour in South Africa", *SAJE* Vol. 42, 1974, pp.292-311.

Binghamton Collective   "Race and Class in Twentieth Century Capitalist Development", *The Insurgent Sociologist* Vol.10. No.2, Feb. 1980

Blau, A., T.J., *et. al.*   "Unemployment in Bishop Lavis", *SALDRU Working Paper No. 47* (Cape Town, South African Labour and Development Research Unit (SALDRU), 1982)

Bloch, Joanne   "The Action Committee versus the Garment Workers' Union", in L. Cooper and D. Kaplan (eds.), *Selected Papers on aspects of organisation in the Western Cape* (Cape Town, UCT, 1982)

Bloch, N., and Weichel, K.	*A Profile of African Employment in the Cape Peninsula* (Cape Town, Urban Problems Research Unit (UPRU), Univ. of Cape Town, 1977)
Bloch, R., and Wilkinson, P.	"Urban Control and Popular Struggle: A Survey of State Urban Policy 1920-1970", *Africa Perspective* No.20, April 1982, pp.2-40.
Boaden, B.G.	"The Urban Housing Problem in an Apartheid Economy", *Africa Affairs* Vol. 77, 1978, pp.499-510,
Boesak, A.	"Die Theron-Kommissie: Die Witskrif — 'n Grafskrif?", *Deurbraak* Vol.6, No. 4, June 1977
	"Die Wat by Ons Is, Is Meer as die Wat by Hulle Is", *Deurbraak* Vol. 3, No. 2, July 1980
Boeseken, A.J.	*Slaves and Free Blacks at the Cape 1658-1700* (Cape Town, Tafelberg, 1977)
Bonacich, E.	"Class Approaches to Ethnicity and Race," *The Insurgent Sociologist* 10 (2), 1980
Botha, C.J.	*Die Kleurlinge* (Pretoria, Departement van Onderwys en Wetenskap, 1964)
Botha, D.	"Die Verhouding van die Afrikaner Teenoor die Kleurling," *Deurbraak* Vol. 6, No. 3, April 1977
Bozzoli, B. (ed.)	*Labour Townships and Protest: Studies in the Social History of the Witwatersrand* (Johannesburg, Ravan, 1979)
	The Political Nature of a Ruling Class: Capital and Ideology in South Africa, 1890-1933 (London, Routledge and Kegan Paul, 1981)
Brindley, M.	*Western Coloured Townships: Problems of an Urban Slum* (Johannesburg, Ravan, 1976)
Bromberger, N.	"South African Unemployment: A Survey of Research", in C. Simkins and C. Desmond (eds.), *South African Unemployment — a Black Picture* (Pietermaritzburg, Dev. Studies Research Grp., 1978)
Brookes, Edgar, H.	"The South African Race Problem in the Light of General Hertzog's Proposed Legislation", *The International Review of Missions*, Vol. 16, 1927

The Colour Problems of South Africa (London, Kegan Paul, 1933)

Browett, J.G., and Fair, T.J.D. — "South Africa 1870-1970; a View of the Spatial System", *South Africa Geog. Journal* Vol. 56, pp.111-120

Bruwer, J.J. — "Arbeid en Meganisasie in die Suid-Afrikaanse Landboubedryf," *Tydskrif vir Rasse-Aangeleenthede* No. 3, July 1974

Buchan, J., — *Prester John* (London, Thomas Nelson Sons, 1910)

Bundy, C.J. — *The Rise and Fall of the South African Peasantry* (London, Macmillan, 1979)

"Vagabond Hollanders and Runaway Englishmen: White Poverty in the Cape before poor Whiteism", pp.11-23, in Institute of Commonwealth Studies, *Collected Seminar Papers on the Societies of Southern Africa in the 19th and 20th Centuries,* Vol. 13 (London, Univ. of London, 1984)

Bunting, B. — "Liquor and the Colour Bar", *Africa South* Vol. 2, No. 4, July-Sept. 1958

Moses Kotane: South African Revolutionary (London, Inkuleko Publ., 1978)

Burawoy, M. — "Race, Class and Colonialism", *Social and Economic Studies* Vol. 23, 1974, pp. 521-550.

Manufacturing Consent (Chicago, Univ. of Chicago Press, 1979)

"Migrant Labour in South Africa and the United States", in Nichols T. (ed.), *Capital and Labour — A Marxist Primer* (Glasgow, Fontana, 1980)

Butler, J. — "The Significance of Recent Changes within the White Ruling Caste", in L. Thompson and J. Butler, *Change in Contemporary South Africa* (Berkeley, Univ. of California Press, 1975)

Callinicos, A. — *Southern Africa after Zimbabwe* (London, Pluto, 1981)

Cape Coloured Franchise (Anon.) — "Mr Havenga's Agreement with Dr Malan", *Round Table* No. 111, June 1938

Cape Flats Committee for Interim Accommodation — *Crossroads: Some Facts and Figures* (Cape Town, CFCIA, n.d.)

Carneson, F. — "The Franchise Action Committee", *Discussion* 1, (3), June 1951

Carchedi, G. — "On the Economic Identification of the New Middle Class", *Economy and Society* 4 (1) 1978

Carstens, W.P., — *The Social Structure of a Cape Coloured Reserve: A study of Racial Integration and Segregation in South Africa* (New York, OUP, 1966)

Carter, G.M., and O'Meare, P. (eds.) — *Southern Africa in Crisis* (Bloomington, Indiana Univ. Press, 1977)

Centre for Contemporary Cultural Studies (eds.) — *On Ideology* (London, Hutchinson, 1977)

Christian Council of South Africa — Interview with Minister of Native Affairs, Dr Verwoerd, *S.A. Outlook* 86 (1019) 1 March 1955

Cilliers, S.P. — *The Coloured People of South Africa: a Factual survey* (Cape Town, 1963)

Wes Kaapland — 'n Sosio-ekonomiese Studie (Stellenbosch, Kosmo, 1964)

Appeal to Reason (Stellenbosch, Stellenbosch Univ. 1971)

"The Social, Political and Economic Implications of Industrial Progress with particular reference to the position of the Coloured Population", *Social Dynamics* Vol. 1. No. 1., June 1975

Cilliers, S.P., and Bekker, S.B. — *Die Arbeidsituasie van die Swartman in die Wes-Kaapland met besondere aandag aan die toestand in die Kaapse Skiereiland* (Stellenbosch, Univ. of Stellenbosch, 1980)

Civilised Labour Policy (anon) — "The Civilised Labour Policy versus the Displacement of non-European Labour", *Race Relations* Vol. 2, 1935 pp.55-61.

Clarke, D., and
  Simkins, C.,
Structural Unemployment in South Africa (Univ. of Natal, Pietermaritzburg, 1978)

Clifford-Vaughan,
  F.McA.
International Pressures and Political Change in South Africa (Cape Town, OUP, 1978)

Close, R.
New Life (Cape Town, FCWU, 1950)

Coetzee, J.H.
Volk Sonder Land: Versamelde Opstelle oor die Kleurlinge in Suid-Afrika (Potchefstroom, Pro Rege-press, 1971)

Cohen, G.A.
Karl Marx's Theory of History: A Defence (Oxford, OUP, 1979)

Cohen, R., Gutkind, D.,
  and Brazier, P. (eds.)
Peasants and Proletarians, the Struggle of Third World Workers (London, Hutchinson Co., 1979)

Colby, D., *et. al.*
"Determinants of Black Wages: a Case Study", SAJE Vol 45, 1977, pp.243-256.

Comm. Comm.
Nyanga Bush: The Story of the Squatters (Cape Town, Nusas, 1981)

Conradie B.
"Die Blanke en die Kaapse Kleurling", *Journal of Racial Affairs* 3 (3), 1952

Cook, A.
Akin to Slavery: Prison Labour in South Africa (London, International Defence and Aid Fund, 1973)

Cooper, L., and
  Kaplan, D. (eds.)
Selected Research Papers on Aspects of Organisation in the Western Cape (Cape Town, UCT, 1982)
Reform and Response: Selected Research Papers on Aspects of Contemporary South Africa (Cape Town, UCT, 1983)

Cope, R.K.
Comrade Bill: The Life and Times of W.H. Andrews, Workers' Leader (Cape Town, Stewart, n.d.)

Corrigan, P.
"Feudal Relics or Capitalist Monuments? Notes on the Sociology of Unfree Labour", *Sociology* Vol. 11, No. 3, 1977

Cory, G.E.
The Rise of South Africa, Vol.1. (London, Longman, 1910)

Cowley, J., *et. al.* (eds.)
Community or Class Struggle? (London, Stage 1, 1977)

Cox, O. Cromwell
Caste, Class and Race: a Study in Racial Dynamics (New York, MRP, 1970)

Curthorpe, A., and Spearrit, P. (eds.)	*Who are our Enemies? Racism and the Working Class Australia* (Sydney, Hale and Iremonger, 1975)
Danziger, K.	"Ideology and Utopia in South Africa: a Methodological Contribution to the Sociology of Knowledge", *British Journal of Sociology* 14, 1963, pp.59-76
Davenport, T.R.H.	*The Afrikaner Bond: The History of a South African Party, 1880-1911* (Cape Town, OUP, 1966)
	"The Consolation of a New Society: The Cape Colony", in M. Wilson and L. Thompson (eds.), *The Oxford History of South Africa Vol. 1.* (London, OUP, 1969)
	"African Townsmen" in *African Affairs,* Vol.68, April 1969
Davids, A	"Politics and the Muslims of Cape Town: A Historial Survey", in C. Saunders *et. al.* (eds.), *Studies in the History of Cape Town, Vol.4* (Cape Town, UCT, 1981)
Davies, R.	"The Class Character of South Africa's Industrial Council Legislation", *SALB* 2(6), 1976
	Capital, State and White Labour in South Africa 1900-1960 (Brighton, Harvester, 1979)
Davies, R., and Kaplan, D.	"Capitalist Development and the Evolution of Racial Policy in South Africa", in *Tarikh* Vol. 6, 1979, pp.46-62
de Kadt, E., and Williams, G. (eds.)	*Sociology and Development* (London, Tavistock, 1974)
de Kiewiet, C.W.	*A History of South Africa* (London, OUP, 1957)
de Klerk, N.C.	"Bantoe-Arbeid en Beleid in Wes-Kaap", *Tydskrif vir Rasseaangeleenthede* Vol. 14, No. 2, 1962
	"Die Kleurling: Kroniek van Twee Landsbewoners", *Deurbraak* Vol. 5, August 1976
Desmore, A.	"The Cape Coloured People Today", *Journal of the Royal African Society* Vol. 36, 1937, pp.347-56.

Dewar, D., and
Watson, V.
"Comment on 'A Spatial Development Strategy for the Western Cape'", *Working Paper No. 15* (Cape Town, Upru, 1980)

Diamond, C.R.
White paper on the Riekert Committee Report — An Appraisal, *SAJE* Vol. 40, 1972, pp.44-60.

Dickie-Clark, H.F.D.
The Marginal Situation (London, Routledge & Kegan Paul, 1966)

"The Coloured Minority of Durban", in N.P. Gist and A.G. Dwarkin (eds.), *The Blending of Races: Marginality and Identity in World Perspective,* pp. 25-38 (New York, John Wiley and Sons, 1972)

Doman, E.J.
"The In-Betweeners: a look at the Coloured People of South Africa", in *Optima* 25 (3), 1975

Doxey, G.V.
The Industrial Colour Bar in South Africa (Cape Town, OUP, 1961)

"Enforced racial stratification in the South African Labour Market", in H. Adam (ed.), *South Africa: Sociological Perspectives* (London, OUP, 1971)

Drucker, H.M.
The Political Uses of Ideology (London, Macmillan, 1974)

Dubow, S.
"African Labour of Cape Town Docks, 1900-1904: Processes of Transition", in C. Saunders *et. al.* (eds.), *Studies in the History of Cape Town, Vol.4* (Cape Town, UCT, 1981)

Duncan, P.
South Africa's Rule of Violence (London, Methuen, 1964)

Duncan, S.
"The Central Institutions of South African Labour Exploitation", *SALB* 3 (9), Nov. 1977

"Idle and Undesireable", *Sash* 20 (3), Nov. 1978

"The Effects of the Riekert Report on the African Population", *SALB* 5 (4), Nov. 1979

du Plessis, I.D.
The Cape Malays (Johannesburg, New Africa Pamphlet Series, 1948)

	"Die Kleurling in die Raamwerk van ons Ras-severhoudings", *Journal of Racial Affairs* 8 (3), April 1957
du Toit, B.	*Ukubamba Amadolo: Workers' Struggles in the South African Textile Industry* (London, Onyx, 1978)
du Toit, B.M.	"Stress, Crisis and Behaviour — a South African case", *Journal of Modern Studies* Vol. 17, 1979, pp.117-140.
Edelstein, M.L.	*What do Coloureds Think?* (Johannesburg, Labour and Community Consultants, 1974)
Edwards, R., Reich, M., and Gordon, D.M.	*Labour Market Segmentation* (Toronto, Heath Co., 1979)
Edwards, R.	*Contested Terrain* (London, Heinemann, 1979)
Ellis, G., *et. al.*	"Aspects of the squatter problem in the Western Cape", *South African Outlook* Vol. 107, No.1269, pp.35-39
Elphick, R.H.	*Kraal and Castle, Khoikhoi and the Founding of White South Africa* (New Haven, Yale Univ., 1979)
Elphick, R., and Giliomee, H. (eds.)	*The shaping of South African Society 1652-1820* (London, Longman, 1979)
Enloe, C.	*Ethnic Conflict and Political Development* (Boston, Little, Brown and Co., 1973)
	Ethnic Soldiers: State Security in a Divided Society (Harmondsworth, Penguin, 1980)
Etherington, E.N.	"Labour Supply and the Genesis of the South African Confederation in the 1870s", *Journal of African History* Vol. 20, 1979, pp.235-253.
Evans, G.	"The Leyland Strike", in L. Cooper and D. Kaplan (eds.), *Selected Research Papers in Aspects of Organisation in the Western Cape* (Cape Town, UCT, 1982)
Fair, T.J.D.	"Polarisation, Dispersion and Decentralisation in the South African Space Economy", *South African Geog. Journal,* Vol.58, 1976, pp.40-56.
Fantham, H.B., and Partner, A.	"Notes on Some Cases of Racial Admixture in South Africa", *South African Journal of Science* Vol.24, Dec. 1927

February, V.A.   *Mind your Colour: The "Coloured" Stereo-*
                          type in South African Literature (London, Ke-
                          gan Paul International, 1981)

Feit, E.,   *Urban revolt in South Africa 1960-1964: a*
                          Case Study (Evanston, Northwestern Univ.
                          Press, 1971)

Findlay, G.   *Miscegenation* (Pretoria, Pretoria News,
                          1936)

Fine, B., and   *Rereading Capital* (London, Macmillan,
   Harris, L.   1979)

Finnegan, B.   "Unlearning Apartheid: A White Teacher
                          and Black Students Come of Age in a Class-
                          room in Cape Town", *Mother Jones,* Decem-
                          ber 1982, pp.16-45

Fisher, F.   "Class consciousness among Colonised
                          Workers in South Africa", in L. Schlemmer
                          and E. Webster (eds.), *Change, Reform and*
                          Economic Growth in South Africa (Johannes-
                          burg, Ravan, 1978)

Food and Canning   "A Search for a Workable Solution", *SALB* 7
   Workers' Union   (8), July 1982

Forster, J.   "The Workers' Struggle — where does FO-
                          SATU stand?" *SALB* 7 (8), July 1982

Fox, A.   *Beyond Contract: Work, Power and Trust Re-*
                          lations (London, Faber, 1974)

Franklin, N.N.   "Industrial Expansion and Native Policy in
                          South Africa", *Journal of African Studies*
                          Vol. 1, 1942, pp.201-206.

Frankel, P.   "The Politics of Passes: Control and Change
                          in South Africa", *The Journal of Modern Af-*
                          rican Studies, Vol. 17, No. 2, June 1979, pp.
                          199-218.

Fredrickson, G.M.   *White Supremacy: a Comparative Study in*
                          American and South African History (Ox-
                          ford, OUP, 1981)

Freund, W.   "Race Relations in Southern Africa at the
                                    turn of the Nineteenth Century: The Cape
                                    Colony in the Batavian Era, 1803-1806",
                                    The Institute of Commonwealth Studies,
                                    *Societies of Southern Africa Collected Semi-
                                    nar Papers, Vol. 1* (London, ICS, 1970)

Friedman, A.L.   *Industry and Labour: Class Struggle and
                                    Monopoly Capitalism* (London, Macmillan,
                                    1977)

Fugard, A.,   *The Blood Knot* (Cape Town, Simondium,
                                    1964)

Galton, F.,   *Inquiries into the human faculty and its Devel-
                                    opment* (London, Macmillan, 1883)

General Workers'   "Reply to Fine, de Clergq, Innes", *SALB* 7
   Union   (3), Nov. 1981

                                    "Retrenchment and Organised Workers,"
                                    SALB 8 (2) November 1982

Genovese, E.D.   *In Red and Black: Marxian Explorations in
                                    Southern and Afro-American History* (New
                                    York, Vintage, 1971)

Gerdener, T.   "Grondslae vir Vernuwing", *Deurbraak* Vol.
                                    3, No.3, April 1974

Gerson, J.   "Projections of the expected shortage of
                                    Coloured Housing", *SALDRU Working
                                    Paper No. 21* (Cape Town, SALDRU, 1979)

Gibson, R.   *African Liberation Movements: Contempo-
                                    rary Struggles Against White Minority Rule*
                                    (London, OUP, 1972)

Goldin, I.   "The Poverty of Coloured Labour Prefer-
                                    ence: Economics and Ideology in the Western
                                    Cape", *SALDRU Working Paper No. 59*
                                    (Cape Town, SALDRU, 1984)

Gorz, A. (ed.)   *The Division of Labour: the Labour Process
                                    and Class Struggle in Modern Capitalism*
                                    (New York, Harvester Press, 1976)

Graaff, J.   "Interviews with African Workers", *SALB* 3
                                    (2), September 1976

Graaff, J., and   "Residential and Migrant African Workers in
  Maree, J.   Cape Town", *SALDRU Working Paper No.
                         12* (Cape Town, SALDRU, 1977)

Graaff, J., and   *Employment Survey of Black Workers Living
  Weichel, K.   in Crossroads* (Cape Town, SAIRR, 1978)

Greenberg, S.   *Race and State in Capitalist Development:
                         Comparative Perspectives* (New Yaven, Yale
                         Univ., 1980)

Greenberg, S., and   "Labour Bureaucracies and the African Re-
  Giliomee, H.   serves", *SALB* 8 (4), Feb. 1983

Griessel, A.   "CATAPAW and the Anti-Pass Campaign in
                         Cape Town in the late Fifties", in L. Cooper
                         and D. Kaplan (eds.), *Selected Research
                         Papers on aspects of Organisation in the West-
                         ern Cape* (Cape Town UCT, 1982)

Grogan, T.   *Vanishing Cape Town* (Cape Town, Don Nel-
                         son, 1976)

Guelke, A.   "Apartheid and the Labour Market", in C.
                         Hill and P. Warwick (eds.), *Southern African
                         Research in Progress: Papers given at a Con-
                         ference of the Centre for Southern African
                         Studies, Univ. of York. Dec. 1974* (York,
                         Univ. of York, 1975)

Gutkind, P., and   *African Social Studies: a Radical Reader*
  Waterman, P. (eds.)   (London, Heinemann, 1977)

Hackland, B.   "The Economic and Political Context of the
                         Growth of the Progressive Federal Party in
                         South Africa 1959-1978", *Journal of Southern
                         African Studies* (JSAS), Vol. 7, No. 1, Oc-
                         tober 1980

Hall, S.   "The Political and the Economic in Marx's
                         Theory of Classes", in A. Hunt (ed.), *Class
                         and Class Structure* (London, Lawrence and
                         Wishart, 1977)

                         "Race, Articulation and Societies Structured
                         in Dominance", in UNESCO, *Sociological
                         Theories: Race and Colonialism* (Paris, UN-
                         ESCO, 1980)

                         "Teaching Race", *MultiRacial Education*,
                         Vol. 9, No. 1, Autumn 1980

"Moving Right", *Socialist Review* No. 55, Jan.-Feb. 1981

Hall-Gardiner, K.   "City Government: A Critical study of the Machinery and Principles of Local Self-government with Special Reference to Cape Town", *S.A. Architectural Record,* Vol. 29, Nos. 1 and 2, 1944

Hallet, L.G.   *Problem of Union's Coloured Races,* (Durban, Theosophical Book Depot Pamphlet, 1924)

Hallett, R.   "The Hooligan Riots", in C. Saunders (ed.), *Studies in the History of Cape Town Vol. 1* (Cape Town, UCT, 1979)

"Policemen, Pimps and Prostitutes — Public Morality and Police Corruption", in C. Saunders (ed.), *Studies in the History of Cape Town Vol. 1.* (Cape Town, UCT, 1979)

"Violence and Social Life in Cape Town in the 1900s", in C. Saunders and H. Phillips (eds.), *Studies in the History of Cape Town, Vol. 2* (Cape Town, UCT, 1980)

Hampton, J.D.   "The Role of the Coloured and the Bantu in the Economic Pattern of the Cape", *SAJE* Vol. 30, No. 4, December 1962

Hancock, W.K. (ed.) and van der Poel, J.   *Selections from the Smuts Papers* 4 Vols. (Cambridge, CUP, 1966)

Harries, P.   "Mozbiekers: The Immigration of an African Community to the Western Cape 1876-1882", in C. Saunders (ed.), *Studies in the History of Cape Town Vol. 1* (Cape Town, UCT, 1979)

Harrison, W.   *Memoirs of a Socialist in South Africa 1903-1947,* (Cape Town, Harrison, 1948)

Harsch, E.   *South Africa: White Rule, Black Revolt* (New York, Monad, 1980)

Hart, G., and Fair, T.   *The National Physical Development Plan (NPDP): A Summary and Review* (San Francisco, 1975)

Harvey, D.   "Labour, Capital and Class Struggle around the Built Environment in Advanced Capitalist Societies", *Politics and Society* 6 (3), 1976

Hellman, E., and Lever, H. (eds.) — *Race Relations in South Africa, 1929-1979* (London, Macmillan, 1980)

Hendrie, D., and Horner, D. — "The People and Workers of the Cape Peninsula: a Sketch", *SALB* 3 (2), Sept. 1976

Hermer, C. — *The Diary of Maria Tholo* (Johannesburg, Ravan, 1980)

Hindson, D. — "The New Black Labour Regulations: Limited Reform, Intensified Control", *SALB* 6 (1), July 1980

Hirsch, A., and Nicol, M. — "Trade Unions and the State: a Response", *SALB* 7 (3), Nov. 1981

Hoare, Q., and Smith, G. (eds.) — *A. Gramsci: Selections from Prison Notebooks* (London, Lawrence and Wishart, 1971)

Hobsbawm, E.J. — *Primitive Rebels* (Manchester, Manchester Univ. Press, 1959)

"Labour History and Ideology", *Journal of Social History* Vol. 7, No.4. 1974, pp.220-24.

Hofmeyer, W. — "Rural Popular Organisation Problems: Struggles in the Western Cape, 1929-1930", *Africa Perspectives*, No. 22, 1983

Horner, D., and Maree, J. — "The Duens Bakery Dispute", *SALB* 2 (9 and 10), May-June 1976

"The Western Province Workers' Advice Bureau" *SALB* 3 (2) Sept. 1976.

Horrell, M. *et. al.* (comp) — *A Survey of Race Relations in South Africa, 1950-1981* (Johannesburg, SAIRR, 1951-1981)

Houghton, D. Hobart, and Dagut, S. — *Source Material on the South African Economy, 1860-1970* (3 Vols.) (Cape Town, OUP, 1972)

Houghton, D. Hobart — *The South African Economy* (Cape Town, OUP, 1973)

Hubbard, M. — *African Poverty in Cape Town, 1960-1970* (Johannesburg, SAIRR, 1972)

Education for Underemployment (Johannesburg, SAIRR, 1975)

A Survey of opportunities for Blacks in Langa (Cape Town, SAIRR, 1976)

Hudson, W., *et. al.*	*Anatomy of South Africa: a Scientific Study of Present Day Attitudes* (Cape Town, 1966)
Hugo, P.	"Die Kleurling", *Deurbraak* Vol. 1, No. 3, May 1972
	Quislings or Realists? A Documentary Study of "coloured" Politics in South Africa (Johannesburg, Ravan Press, 1978)
Hume, I.	"Notes on South African Wage Movements", *SAJE,* Vol. 38, 1970, pp. 240-256.
Hunt, A. (ed.)	*Class and Class Structure* (London, Lawrence and Wishart, 1978)
Hutt, W.H.	"Economic Aspects of the Report of the Cape Coloured Commission", *SAJE* Vol. 6, No. 2, June 1938
	"Wage Fixation and the Coloured People", *Race Relations* 9, 1, 1942
	The Economics of the Colour Bar (London, Inst. of Economic Affairs, 1964)
Inglis, J.	"A brief history of the Franchise in South Africa", *The Educational Journal,* July-Aug. 1981
Innes, D.	*Forced Removals of Coloureds in South Africa* (London, Africa Publications Trust, 1975)
Innes, D., and O'Meara, D.	"Class Formation and Ideology: the Transkei Region", in *Review of African Political Economy* No. 7, Sept.-Dec. 1976
Institute for Industrial Education	*The Durban Strikes* (Johannesburg, Inst. for Ind. Ed., 1974)
Jacobson, E.	*The Cape Coloured: a Bibliography* (Cape Town, UCT, 1945)
Jeeves, A.H.	"South Africa and the Politics of Accommodation", *International Journal* Vol. 30, 1975, pp.504-517.
Jeffrys, M.	"Where do the Coloureds come from?" *Drum,* Nos. 102-106, 1959
Jessop, B.	*The Capitalist State* (Oxford, Martin Robertson, 1982)
Joubert, D.	*Met Iemand van 'n Ander Kleur* (Cape Town, Tafelberg, 1974)

Joubert, E.

The Story of Poppie Nongena (London, Hodder and Stoughton, 1980)

Johnstone, F.

Class, Race and Gold: A Study of Class Relations and Discrimination in South Africa (London, Routledge & Kegan Paul, 1976)

Kamfer, P.

"Colouredism: the Last Grovellings", *Educational Journal*, Jan.-Feb. 1977

Kaplan, D.E.

"The South African State: the Origins of a Racially Exclusive Democracy", *The Insurgent Sociologist* 10 (2), 1980

Karis, T., and Carter, G.M. (eds.)

From Protest to Challenge: a Documentary History of African Politics in South Africa, 1882-1964 (3 Vols.) (Stanford, Hoover Institution Press, 1973)

Kellerman, A.P.R.

"Kontak van Kleurlinge met Bantoes in die Kaapse Skiereiland met Besondere Verwysing na die Werksituasie", *Suid-Afrikaanse Raad vir Geesteswetenskaplike Navorsing, Verslag No. 5-8* (Pretoria, SARG, 1971)

Kidd, B.

Social Evolution (London, Macmillan, 1894)

Kies, B. (ed.)

"Theronausea", *The Educational Journal* Vol. XLVII No. 8, June 1976

"The Theron Report: A Postscript", *The Educational Journal* July-Aug. 1981

Kinloch, G.C.

The Sociological Study of South Africa: an Introduction (London, Macmillan, 1972)

Knight, J.B., and McGrath, M.D.

"An Analysis of Racial Wage Discrimination in South Africa", *Oxford Bulletin of Economics and Statistics* Vol. 34, No. 4, Nov. 1977

Kotzenberg, H.R.

"The Policy and Program for the Decentralisation of Industry in South Africa", *Finance and Trade Review,* December 1973

Kraak, G.

"Financing African Worker Accommodation in Cape Town", *SALDRU Working Paper No. 35* (Cape Town, SALDRU, 1981)

Kuper, L.

Passive resistance in South Africa (New Haven, Yale University Press, 1957)

An African Bourgeoisie: Race, Class and Politics in South Africa (New Haven, Yale University Press, 1965)

Kuper, L., and Smith, M.G. (eds.) — *Pluralism in Africa* (Berkeley, University of California, 1969)

Kuper, L. — *Race, Class and Power: Ideology and Revolutionary Change in Plural Societies* (London, Duckworth, 1974)

Labour Research Committee — *The Local State: Cape Town: A Case study* (LRC, Cape Town, 1982)

Lacey, M. — *Working for Boroko: The origins of a coercive labour system in South Africa* (Johannesburg, Ravan, 1981)

Laclau, E. — *Politics and Ideology in Marxist Theory* (London, New Left Books, 1977)

La Guma, A. — *A Walk in the Night* (London, Heinemann, 1967)

In the Fog of the Season's End (London, Heinemann, 1972)

Lambley, P. — *The Psychology of Apartheid* (London, Secker and Warburg, 1980)

Larrain, J. — *The Concept of Ideology* (London, Hutchinson, 1979)

Lee-Warden, L.B. — The Crime of Langa *Africa South* 1 (3) April-/June 1957

Leftwich, A. (ed.) — *South Africa: Economic Growth and Political Change* (London, Allison and Busby, 1974)

Legassick, M. — "The Concept of Pluralism: a Critique", in Gutkind, P.C., and Waterman, P., *African Social Studies: a Radical Reader* (London, Heinemann, 1977)

"Legislation, Ideology and Economy in post-1948 South Africa," *Journal of South African Studies* Vol. 1, 1974

"The Northern Frontier to 1820: The emergence of the Griqua People", Elphick, R., and Giliomee, H. (eds.), *The Shaping of South African Society 1652-1820* (London, Longman, 1979)

Leggett, J. — *Class, Race and Labour: Working-class Consciousness in Detroit* (New York, OUP, 1968)

Legum, C. — "The Southern African Crisis", *Africa Contemporary Record* Vol. 10, 1978, pp. A3-A31.

Leistner, G.M.E.   "Economic and Social Aspects of Physical Control over Rural and Urban Population Movements", *Journal of Racial Affairs* **Vol. 19, No. 3, 1968, pp.3-10.**

Le May, G.   *British Supremacy in South Africa 1899-1907* (London, OUP, 1965)

Leslie, R.   "Coloured Labour and Trade Unionism in Cape Town", *Journal of the Economic Society of South Africa* Vol. 3, No. 6, 1930.

Lever, J.   "Capital and labour in South Africa: The passage of the Industrial Conciliation Act, 1924", *SALB* 3 (10) December 1977

Levy, B.   "Seasonal Migration in the Western Cape", in F. Wilson, A. Kooy and D. Hendrie (eds.), *Farm Labour in South Africa* (Cape Town, David Philip, 1977)

Lewis, D.   "Trade unions and class stratification: a preliminary analysis of the role of working-class organisations in the Western Cape", in Van der Merwe, H.W. (ed.), *Occupational and Social Change among Coloured People in South Africa* (Cape Town, Juta, 1976)

Lewis, D.   "Registered trade unions and Western Cape workers", *SALB* 3 (2), September 1976

Lipschitz, M., and   "Living Conditions in a squatter camp", *Race Greshoff, N.M.   Relations Journal* Vol. 21, No. 41, 1954

Lodge, T.   "The Cape Town Troubles, March-April 1960", *Journal of Southern African Studies* Vol. 4, No. 2, April 1978
                          "The Paarl Insurrection", in Saunders, C., and Phillips, H. (eds.). *Studies in the History of Cape Town* Vol. 2 (Cape Town, UCT, 1980)

Long Range Planning   *Some Aspects of the Long Term Future of the Society of Southern   Western Cape: Proceedings of a Conference Africa   (Cape Town, LRPSS, 1981)

Lonsdale, J., and   "Coping with the Contradictions: the Devel- Berman, B.   opment of the Colonial state in Kenya 1895-1914", *Journal of African History* Vol. 20, No. 4, 1979

Lotter, J.M.   *The Social-Economic position of the Coloured in the Western Cape* (Pretoria, Govt. Printer, n.d.)

Loudon, J.B.   *White farmers and black labour tenants* (Cambridge, CUP, 1970)

Loveridge, R., and Mok, A.L.   *Theories of labour market segmentation* (The Hague, Martinus Nijhoff, 1979)

Luckhardt, K., and Wall, B.   *Organise ... or starve. The history of the South African Congress of trade unions* (London, Lawrence and Wishart, 1980)

Macmillan, W.M.   *The Cape Colour Question: an historical survey* (London, Faber, 1927)
Bantu, Boer and Britain (Cape Town, UCT, 1929)

McCracken, J.L.   *The Cape Parliament, 1854-1910* (Oxford, OUP, 1967)

Macrone, I.D.   *Race attitudes in South Africa* (London, 1937)

McGregor, L.   "The Fattis and Monis Dispute", *SALB* 5 (6 and 7) March 1980, pp. 122-131.

Mafeje, A.   "The Ideology of Tribalism", *Journal of Modern African Studies* 9, 2, 1971
"Religion, class and ideology in South Africa", in M. West and M. Whisson (eds.), *Religion and Social Change in South Africa*, pp. 164-184

Magubane, B.   *The Political Economy of Race and Class in South Africa* (London, Monthly Review Press, 1979)

Malan, D.F.   *Die Groot Vlug* (Cape Town, Longman, 1967)

Mantzaris, E.A.   "Another victory for trade unionism: the 1918 Cape Town Musicians' Strike", in C. Saunders *et al.* (eds.), *Studies in the History of Cape Town Vol. 3* (Cape Town, UCT 1980)

Manuel, G., and Hatfield, D.   *District Six* (Cape Town, Longmans, 1967)

Marias, G., and van der Kooy, R.   *South Africa's Urban Blacks: Problems and Challenges* (Pretoria, Rousseau, 1978)

Marais, J.S.   *The Cape Coloured People 1652-1937* (Johannesburg, Wits. Univ. 1957) (first publ. 1939)

Mare, G.   *African Population Relocation in South Africa* (Johannesburg, SAIRR, 1980)

Maree, J.   "Problems with trade union democracy: case study of the Garment Workers' Union of the Western Province", *SALB* 3 (2) September 1976

Maree, J., and Cornell, J.   "Sample survey of squatters in Crossroads, 1977", *SALDRU Working Paper No. 17* (Cape Town, SALDRU, 1978)

Marks, S., and   *Economy and Society in Pre-Industrial South*
  Atmore, A. (eds.)   *Africa* (London, Longman, 1980)

Marks, S.   "Khoisan Resistance to the Dutch in the Seventeenth and Eighteenth Centuries", *Journal of African History,* Vol. 13, No. 1, 1972, pp. 55-80

Marks, S., and Gray, R.   "Southern Africa and Madagascar", pp. 384-468, in Gray, R. (ed.), *The Cambridge History of Africa Vol. 4, from c. 1600 to c. 1790* (Cambridge, CUP, 1975)

Marquard, L.   *The Peoples and Politics of South Africa,* Revised 3rd edition (Oxford, OUP, 1962)

Marx, K.   *Capital* (Vols. I — III) (London, Lawrence and Wishart, 1974)

                              The German Ideology (London, Lawrence and Wishart, 1970)

Matheson, A.   *The Coloured People of the Cape* (London, 1948)

Meer, F.   *Race and suicide in South Africa* (London, Routledge & Kegan Paul, 1976)

Mettler, J.   "Die Kleurling: Steeds meer verwydering", *Deurbraak* Vol. 5, No. 5, August 1976

Mhlongo, S.   "An Analysis of the Classes in South Africa", *Race and Class* Vol. 16, 1975, pp. 259-294.

Millin, S.G.   *God's Stepchildren* (London, Constable, 1924)

                              The Dark River (London, Collins, 1919)

                              The South African (London, Constable, 1926)

Mkele, N.   "The Emerging African Middle Class", *Optima* Vol. 10, 1960, pp. 217-226.

Mokone, S.   *Majority Rule: Some Notes* (Cape Town, Teachers League, 1982)

Molteno, F.   "Colour-caste and Ruling Class Strategy in the South African Class Struggle: the Case of 'The Coloured People' and Collaborationist Politics", pp. 623-650, in M. Murray (ed.), *Black Political Opposition* (Cambridge, Schenkman, 1982)

Moodie, J.W.   *Ten years in South Africa* (2 Vols.) (London, 1835)

Morse, J.J., and Peele, S.   "'Coloured Power' or 'Coloured Bourgeoisie?' Political Attitudes among South African Coloureds", *Public Opinion Quarterly* Vol. 38, No. 3, 1974

Mouffe, C.   *Gramsci and Marxist Theory* (London, Routledge & Kegan Paul, 1979)

Muller, A.L.   *Minority Interests: The political economy of the Coloured and Indian Communities in South Africa* (Johannesburg, SAIRR, 1968)

Muller, C.F.J.   *Five hundred years: a history of South Africa* (Cape Town, Academia, 1969)

Muller, H.   *Aanwesigheid van kleurlingvroue in diens by twee klerefabrieke in die Kaapse Skiereiland* (Stellenbosch, Stellenbosch Univ., n.d.)

     The role of the Coloured people in the economic pattern of the Republic of South Africa (Pretoria, SABRA, 1965)

Muller, S.   "Juvenile delinquency and the colour bar", *Africa South* Vol. 3, No.3, 1959, pp. 35-41.

Munger, E.   *African Field Reports 1960* (Cape Town, Struik, 1961)

Nairn, T.   "The Modern Janus", *New Left Review* 94, 1975

National Development Manpower Foundation   *Long Term Development of the Western Cape,* Résumé of Seminar held at Cape Town on 16 and 17 May 1973 (Cape Town, NDMF, 1973)

     Stagnation or Growth, Proceedings of a Conference held in Cape Town, May 1980 (Cape Town, NDMF, 1980)

Nattrass, J.   "Migrant Labour and South African Economic Development", *SAJE* Vol. 44, 1976, pp. 65-81.

"The narrowing of wage differentials in South Africa", *SAJE* Vol. 45, No. 4, December 1977

Capital intensity in South African manufacturing (Durban, Natal University, 1977)

The South African Economy: Its Growth and Change (Cape Town, OUP, 1981)

Newton-King, S.   *The Rebellion of the Khoi in Graaff-Reinet 1979-1803* (Cape Town, UCT, 1980)

"The labour market of the Cape Colony 1807-1828", in Marks, S., and Atmore, A. (eds.), *Economy and Society in Pre-Industrial South Africa* (London, Longman, 1980)

Nichol, M.   "Riches from Rags: Bosses and Unions in the Cape Clothing Industry 1926-1937", *Journal of Southern African Studies* April 1983, 9 (2), pp. 239-257

Nicolaus, M.   "Proletariat and Middle Class in Marx: Hegelian Choreography and the Capitalist Dialectic", *Studies on the Left* Vol. 7, 1967

Nikolinakos, M.   "Notes on an economic theory of racism", *Race* Vol. XIV, 4, 1975

No Sizwe   *One Azania, One Nation: The National Question in South Africa,* (London, Zed Press, 1979)

NUSAS   *The Union is strength: The resurgence of black trade unionism in the 1970s* (Cape Town, NUSAS, 1980)

Olivier, N.J.   "Die Naturel in die wes-Kaapland" *Journal of Racial Affairs* 4 (2), January 1953

O'Meara, D.   *Volkskapitalisme: Class, Capital and Ideology in the development of Afrikaner Nationalism, 1934-1948* (Cambridge, C U P, 1983)

Pansegrouw, H.M.   The influx of natives, *Journal of Racial Affairs* Vol. 2, No. 4, 1951, pp. 35-39

Patterson, S.   *Colour and Culture in South Africa: A study of the status of the Cape Coloured People within the social structure of the Union of South Africa* (London, Routledge & Kegan Paul, 1953)

	"Some speculations on the status and role of the Free People of Colour in the Western Cape", in Patterson, S., and Fortes, M. (eds.), *Studies in African Social Anthropology* (London, Academic Press, 1975)
Pearson, K.	*The Chances of Death and Other Studies in Evolution* (London, Scott, 1897)
Perrings, C.	"A moment in the 'proletarianisation' of the new middle class: race, value and the division of labour in the Copperbelt, 1946-1966", *Journal of South African Studies* Vol. 6, No. 2, April 1980
Phillips, C.	*The Coloured Problem in South Africa* (Johannesburg, n.d.)
Phillips, H.	"Black October: Cape Town and the Spanish Influenza Epidemic of 1918", in C. Saunders (ed.), *Studies in the History of Cape Town Vol. 1* (Cape Town, UCT, 1979)
Phizacklea, A., and Miles R.	*Labour and Racism* (London, Routledge & Kegan Paul, 1980)
Picard, H.	*The Grand Parade: the birth of Greater Cape Town* (Cape Town, Struik, 1969)
Pickvance, C.G. (ed.)	*Introduction to urban sociology: critical essays* (London, Tavistock, 1976)
Pinnock, D.	"From Argie boys to skollie gangsters: the lumpen-proletariat challenge of the street-corner armies of District Six, 1900-1957", in C. Saunders *et. al.* (eds.), *Studies in the History of Cape Town Vol. 3* (Cape Town, UCT, 1980)
	Elsies River, Institute of Criminology (Cape Town, 1980)
	Group Areas, Criminology Source Book No. 1 (Cape Town, Inst. of Criminology, UCT, 1982)
Platsky, L., and Collie, J.	"Crossroads: from confrontation to co-option", *Reality* 13, (4), July 1981
Plaut, M., and Ward, D.	*Black trade unions in South Africa* (London, Spokesman, 1982)
Poulantzas, N.	*Political Power and Social Class* (London, NLR, 1975)

	Classes in Contemporary Capitalism (London, Verso, 1978)
Prior, C., and Prior, A.	Some aspects of unemployment in the Western Cape, *SALB* 4 (4), July 1978
Projects Committee	*Fattis and Monis strike* (Cape Town, pamphlet, n.d.)
Rabie, J.	Wit-bruin blokvorming teen swart is gevaarlike spel, *Deurbraak* Vol. 6, No. 5, August 1977
Randall, P. (ed.)	*Survey of Race Relations in South Africa, 1982* (Johannesburg, SAIRR, 1983)
Ratcliffe, A.E.	"Industrial Development policy: changes during the 1970s", *SAJE* Vol. 47, No. 4, December 1979
Rautenbach, P.S.	The Development of Regional Planning in South Africa, in Lombard, J.A. (ed.), *Economic Policy in South Africa* (Cape Town, HAUM, n.d.)
Rex, J.	The Plural Society: The South African case, in *Race* Vol. 12, No. 4, 1971
	Race Relations in sociological theory (London, Weidenfeld and Nicholson, 1970)
Rex, S., and Moore, R.	*Race, community and conflict* (London, OUP, 1967)
Rex, P.	"The Lineage Mode of Production", *Critique of Anthropology* No. 3, Spring 1975
Rhoodie, N.J. (ed.)	*South African Dialogue: Contrasts in South African thinking on Basic Race Issues* (Johannesburg, McGraw Hill, 1972)
	The Coloured Policy of South Africa, in *African Affairs* Vol. 72, No. 286, 1973
	Sosiale Stratifikasie en kleurlingskap (Johannesburg, McGraw Hill, 1977)
Rich, P.	"Ideology in a Plural Society: the cause of South African segregation", *Social Dynamics* 1 (2), Dec. 1975
Rive, R.	*Emergency* (London, Faber and Faber, 1970)
Romanovsky, P.	Louw's Bush: A socio-economic analysis, *Divisional Council of the Cape Town Planning Data Bank Report No. 17* (Cape Town, CDC, 1973)

	Rural-urban migration in the Western Cape, 1960 to 1970, *Divisional Council of the Cape Engineers Department Planning Report No. 29* (Cape Town, CDC, 1973)
Roux, E.P.	*S.P. Bunting: A Political biography* (Cape Town, The African Bookman, 1944)
	Time Longer Than Rope: A history of the Black Man's Struggle for Freedom in South Africa (London, Univ. of Wisconsin, 1978)
Ruberry, J.	Structured Labour Markets, *Cambridge Journal of Economics,* March 1978
Russel, M.	*Afrikaners of the Kalahari* (Cambridge, CUP, 1979)
SABRA	"Gesigspunte in Verband met die Kleurling en sy plek in die samelewing", *Journal of Racial Affairs* 5 (3), 1954
	Jaarboek van die Suid-Afrikaanse Buro vir Rasse-Aangeleenthede Nr 9, 1973 (Pretoria, SABRA, 1973)
SAIRR	*African Housing in the Peninsula* (Cape Town, SAIRR, 1954)
Sachs, E.S.	*Rebel's Daughters* (Alva, MacGibbon, 1957)
	The Anatomy of Apartheid (London, Collets, 1965)
Sadie, J.L.	"Demografiese aspekte van die Kleurlingbevolking", *Journal of Racial Affairs,* Vol. 5, No. 4, 1954,
	Population of the Western Cape 1975 to 2025 (Stellenbosch Univ., Bureau for Economic Research, August 1976)
Sandbrook, R., and Cohen, R. (ed.)	*The Development of an African Working Class: Studies in Class Formation and Action* (London, Longman, 1975)
Saul, J.	"The Dialectic of Class and Tribe", in Saul, J., *The State and Revolution in Eastern Africa* (London, Heinemann, 1979)
Saunders, C. (ed.)	*Studies in the History of Cape Town Vol. 1* (Cape Town, Univ. of Cape Town, 1979)
Saunders, C., and Phillips, H. (eds.)	*Studies in the History of Cape Town, Vols. 2 and 3* (Cape Town, UCT, 1980)

Saunders, C.,
Phillips, H., and
van Heyningen, E.
(eds.)

Studies in the history of Cape Town, Vol. 4 (Cape Town, UCT, 1981)

Saunders, C.

"From Ndabeni to Langa", pp. 167-204, in C. Saunders (ed.), *Studies in the history of Cape Town Vol. 1* (Cape Town, UCT, 1979)

"The creation of Ndabeni: Urban segregation and African Resistance in Cape Town", pp. 132-166, in Saunders, C. (ed.), *Studies in the history of Cape Town Vol. 1* (Cape Town, UCT, 1979)

"Africans in Cape Town in the Nineteenth Century: an outline", in Saunders, C., and Phillips, H. (eds.), *Studies in the History of Cape Town, Vol. 2* (Cape Town, UCT, 1980)

Schapera, I.

Migrant Labour and Tribal Life (Cape Town, OUP, 1947)

Scheepers, G.

"The political consciousness of African urban workers: a review of recent publications", *African Perspectives* 1978, 2, pp. 83-98

Schlemmer, L., and
Webster, E. (eds.)

Change, Reform and Growth in South Africa (Johannesburg, Ravan, 1978)

Schonstein, P.

Influx Control: Greater Cape Town (Cape Town, Institute of Criminology, 1982)

Schoeman, B.M.

Van Malan tot Verwoerd (Pretoria, Human and Rousseau, 1973)

Segal, R.M.

"Even we", *Africa South* Vol. 2, No. 3, April-June 1958

Selope-Thema, R.V.

"In defence of the Cape Native Franchise", *South African Outlook* (September 1928)

Selvan, D.

"Housing conditions for migrant workers in Cape Town, 1976", *SALDRU Working Paper No. 10* (Cape Town, SALDRU, 1976)

Semmel, B.

Imperialism and Social Reform: English Social-Imperial thought, 1895-1914 (London, Allen and Unwin, 1960)

Shanin, T.

"The peasants are coming: migrants who labour, peasants who travel and Marxists who write", *Race and Class*, Vol. XIX, No. 3, Winter 1978

Shorten, J.   *Cape Town* (Cape Town, John Shorten Ltd, 1963)

Simkins, C.   "Socio-economic characteristics of 16 squatter settlements in Cape Town area in 1975", *SALDRU Working Paper No. 21* (Cape Town, SALDRU, 1978)

Simkins, C., and   *South African Unemployment — a Black Pic-*
Desmond, C. (eds.)   *ture* (Pietermaritzburg, Dev. St. Research Grp, 1978)

Simkins, C.E.W., and   *Social Dynamics* 5 (2), December 1979
Hindson, D.

Simkins, C.E.W.   "The distribution of the African population of South Africa by age, sex and region-type 1960, 1970 and 1980", *SALDRU Working Paper No. 42* (Cape Town, SALDRU, 1981)

Simons, H.J.   "The Coloured Worker and Trade Unionism", *Race Relations* 9, 1, 1942

Simons, H.J., and   *Class and colour in South Africa: 1850-1950*
Simons, R.E.   (Penguin, Harmondsworth, 1969)

Simons, M.   "Organised Coloured Political Movements", in H.W. van der Merwe and C.J. Groenewald (eds.), *Occupational and Social change among Coloured People in South Africa* (Cape Town, Juta, 1976)

Sivananadan, A.   *A different Hunger: writings on black resistance* (London, Pluto, 1982)

Sklar, R.   "Political Science and National Integration — A radical approach", *Journal of Modern African Studies* 5, 1, 1967

Small, A.   *Kanna Hy Ko Hystoe* (Cape Town, Tafelberg, 1965)

                             The Coloured people: a 1970 appraisal: one view (Johannesburg, SAIRR, 1970)

                             "Ons Jongmense het trots geleer", *Deurbraak* Vol. 6, No. 1, November 1976

Snitcher, F.   "The Eiselen scheme," *Africa South* Vol. 1, No. 3, April-June 1957

Stadler, J.J.   "The Gross Domestic Product of South Africa, 1911-1959", *SAJE* Vol. 31, 1963, pp. 194-201

Stedman-Jones, G.   *Outcast London: a study in the relationship between classes in Victorian society* (Oxford, OUP, 1971)

Stevens, E.J.   *White and black: an inquiry into South Africa's greatest problem* (London, 1914)

Steyn, J.H.   *The free enterprise system as the vehicle for the fulfilment of black aspirations* (Alice, 1978)

Stone, C.   "Industrialisation and female labour force participation of Coloured women in the Cape Peninsula", *Centre for Intergroup Studies Collected Seminar Papers No. 62* (Cape Town, UCT, 1975)

Stone, G.L.   "Identity among Lower-Class Cape Coloureds", in M.G. Whisson and H.W. van der Merwe (eds.), *Coloured Citizenship in South Africa* (Cape Town, Inst. of Interracial Studies, 1972), pp. 20-47

Strangeways-Booth, J.   *A Cricket in the Thorn Tree: Helen Suzman and the Progressive Party* (London, Hutchinson, 1976)

Strauss, J.   "Kleurling identiteit", *Journal of Racial Affairs,* Vol. 30, No. 3, July 1979

Surplus Peoples Project   *Report of Findings* (Five Volumes) (Cape Town, Surplus Peoples Project, 1983)

Susser, I.   *Norman Street: Poverty and politics in an urban neighbourhood* (New York, OUP, 1982)

Suzman, A.   *Race Classification and Definition in the Legislation of the Union of South Africa 1910-1960* (Johannesburg, SAIRR, 1960)

Swanson, M.W.   "Urban origins of separate development", *Race* Vol. 10, No. 1, July 1968

"The sanitary syndrome: 'Bubonic plague and urban Native policy in the Cape", *Journal of African History* 18 (3), 1977

Tabata, I.B.   *The awakening of the people* (Nottingham, Spokesman, 1974)

Tate, C.M.   *Shadow and substance in South Africa: A study of land and franchise policies affecting Africans 1910-1960* (Pietermaritzburg, Univ. of Natal Press, 1962)

Theal, G.M.	*History and Ethnography of Africa South of the Zambesi Before 1795,* Vol. 2 (London, Sonnenschein, 1909)
Therborn, G.	*The ideology of power and the power of ideology* (London, Verso, 1980)
Theron, E., and Swart, M.C.	*Die Kleurlingbevolking van Suid-Afrika* (Stellenbosch, Univ. of Stellensboch, 1964)
Thomas, W.H. (ed.)	*Labour Perspectives on South Africa* (Cape Town, David Philip, 1974)
	"Socio-economic development of the Coloured Community", in H.W. van der Merwe and C.J. Groenewald (eds.), *Occupational and Social Change Among Coloured people in South Africa* (Cape Town, Juta, 1976)
Thompson, E.P.	"'Revolution Again' or Shut your Eyes and Run" *New Left Review* Nov.-Dec. 1960, No. 6.
	On the Poverty of Theory and other Essays (London, Merlin, 1980)
Thompson, L.M.	*The Cape Coloured Franchise* (SAIRR, Johannesburg, 1949)
	"The Non-European Franchise in the Union of South Africa", *Parliamentary Affairs* Vol. 4, 1950
	The Unification of South Africa, 1902-1910 (Oxford, OUP, 1960)
Trapido, S.	"The origins and development of the African Peoples' Organisation", Institute of Commonwealth Studies, *Collected Seminar Papers on the Societies of Southern Africa,* Vol. 1 (London, University of London, 1970)
	"South Africa in a Comparative Study of Industrialisation", *Journal of Development Studies* April 1971
	"'The friends of the natives': merchants, peasants and the political and ideological structure of liberalism in the Cape, 1854-1910", in Marks, S., and Atmore, A. (eds), *Economy and Society in Pre-Industrial South Africa,* (London, Longman, 1980)

Unterhalter, B.

"Changing attitudes to passing for white in an urban Coloured community", *Social Dynamics* Vol. 1, No. 1, 1975, pp. 61-62.

Uytenbogaardt, R.S.

"The making and meaning of urbanism: a case study in Cape Town", *Optima* Vol. 28, 1979, pp. 46-64.

van Breda, W.W.

The employment process: A manual on black Labour (Bloemfontein, Orange Free State Univ., 1975)

van den Berghe, P.L.

"Miscegenation in South Africa", *Cahiers d'Etudes Africaines* No. 4, 1960

South Africa: A Study in Conflict (Berkeley, Univ of California, 1967)

Race and Racism — a comparative perspective, (New York, Wiley, 1967)

"Race and Racism in South Africa", in A. Beteille (ed.), *Social Inequality* (Harmondsworth, Penguin, 1969)

Race and Ethnicity: Essays in Comparative Sociology (New York, Basic Books, 1970)

van der Horst, S.T.

"Notes on the Occupation Distribution of the Coloured People", *Race Relations* 21 (1) 1954

Native labour in South Africa (Oxford, OUP, 1942) (reissued Frank Cass, 1971)

"Labour policy in South Africa, 1948-76", in Truu, M.C., *Public Policy and the South African Economy* (Cape Town, OUP, 1976)

"Statutory and Administrative Measures and Policy Directly Affecting the Employment of Coloured Persons", in H.W. van der Merwe and C.J. Groenewald (eds.), *Occupational and Social Change among Coloured People in South Africa* (Cape Town, Juta, 1976)

The Theron Commission Report — a Summary (Johannesburg, SAIRR, 1976)

"The Changing Face of the Economy" in E. Hellman and H. Lever (eds.), *Race Relations in South Africa, 1929-1979* (London, Macmillan, 1980) van der Merwe, H.W., and Groenewald, C.J. — *Occupational and Social Change Among Coloured People in South Africa,* (Cape Town, Juta, 1976)

van der Merwe, S.P. — "The economic influence of the Bantu labour bureau system on the Bantu labour market", *SAJE* Vol 37, March 1969, pp.42-54.

van der Ross, R.E. — "Afrikaners soos gesien deur Kleurlinge; Die Kleurling-gister en vandag", *Deurbraak* April 1974, Vol. 3, No. 3.

The Founding of the African Peoples' Organisation in Cape Town in 1903 and the role of Dr. Abdurahman (Pasadena, Munger Africana Library, 1975)

Myths and attitudes: an inside look at the Coloured People (Cape Town, Tafelberg, 1979)

van Eeden, I.J. — "Die Bantoe in die Metropolitaanse Gebied", *Journal of Racial Affairs,* Vol. 26, 1975, pp.61-73.

van Heyningen, E. — "Refugees and relief in Cape Town, 1899-1902", in C. Saunders *et al.* (eds.), *Studies in the History of Cape Town Vol. 3* (Cape Town, UCT, 1980)

"Cape Town and the plague of 1901", in C. Saunders, *et al.* (eds.), *Studies in the History of Cape Town, Vol. 4* (Cape, UCT, 1981)

van Selm, R. — *This History of the South African Mutual Life Assurance Society 1845-1945* (Cape Town, 1945)

van Westerhuizen, D. — "Die Kleurling van Suid-Afrika: 'n Bibliografie", *National Bureau of Education and Social Research Information, Series No. 13* (Pretoria, NBE, 1967)

van Zyl, G.N. — "Ruimtelike patrone van ekonomiese aktiwiteite in die Westelike Kaapprovinsie", in Long Range Planning Society, *Aspects of the Long Term Future of the Western Cape* (Cape Town, LRPS, 1981)

Venter, A.J. — *Coloured: A profile of Two Million South Africans* (Cape Town, Human and Rousseau, 1974)

Verwoerd, H.F.

"Interview with Minister of Native Affairs in 1956 on subject of Africans in the Western Cape", *South African Outlook* Vol. 86, No. 1019, March 1956, pp. 40-43

Viljoen, S.P.

"Future of the free enterprise Economy in South Africa", *South African International* Vol. 8, pp. 39-50

Vosloo, W.B.

"The Coloured Policy of the National Party", in N.J. Rhoodie (ed.), *South African Dialogue* (Johannesburg, McGraw Hill, 1972)

Wade, M.

Peter Abrahams (London, Evans Brothers, 1972)

"Myth, Truth and the South African Reality in the Fiction of Sarah Gertrude Millin", *Institute of Commonwealth Studies Collected Seminar Papers on the Societies of Southern Africa in the 19th and 20th Centuries Vol. III* (London, ICS, 1972)

Wages Commission

Riekert: Don't worry everything's okay (Cape Town, UCT, Wage Commission, 1980)

Wagner, I.J.M.

Poverty and dependency in Cape Town (Cape Town, Maskew Miller, 1937)

The structure and size of households in Goodwood and Elsies River, *Journal for Social Research,* December 1951

Walker, C.

Women and Resistance in South Africa (London, Onyx Press, 1982)

Walker, E.

A history of Southern Africa (London, Longman, 1968)

Walker, I.L., and Weinbren, B.

2000 casualties, a history of the trade unions and the labour movement in the Union of South Africa (Johannesburg, 1961)

Wassenaar, A.D.

Assault on Private Enterprise Cape Town, Tafelberg, 1977)

Waterman, P.

"Workers, unions and protest at the periphery of capitalism", *Development and Change* Vol. 10, No. 2, April 1979

	"The state and the control of labour: the case of Lagos Cargo Handling Industry", in Collins, P. (ed.), *Administration for Development in Nigeria* (Lagos, African Education Press, 1980)
Watson, G.	*Passing for White* (London, Tavistock, 1970)
Webster, E., and Kuzwayo, J.	A Research Note on Consciousness and the Problem of Organisation, in F. Fischer *et al.*, *Change, Reform and Growth in South Africa* (Durban, 1975)
Weichel, K., Smith, L., and Putterill, M.	*Nyanga and Crossroads — Some aspects of Social and Economic Activity* (Cape Town, Project Report, 1978)
West, M., and Whisson, M. (eds.)	*Religion and Social Change in South Africa* (Cape Town, David Philip, 1975)
West, M.	"From Pass Courts to Deportation: Changing Patterns of Influx Control in Cape Town", *African Affairs* Vol. 81, No. 325, October 1982
Western, J.,	*Outcast Cape Town* (London, George Allen and Unwin, 1981)
Western Province General Workers' Union	"Comments on the question of registration", *SALB* Vol. 5, No. 4, November 1979
	"Registration and organisation: the case of the stevedores", *SALB* 5 (6 and 7) March 1980, pp. 57-75
	"Dispute in the meat industry", *SALB* 6 (1) July 1980
	"The Cape Meat Strike: struggle for a Democratically Elected Workers' Committee", *SALB* 6 (5) Dec. 1980
Whalley, M.F., and Perkins, A.E.	*Of European Descent* (Johannesburg, Juta, 1909)
Whisson, M.G., and van der Merwe, H.W.	*Coloured Citizenship in South Africa* (Cape Town, Inst. of Interracial studies, 1972)
Whisson, M.G.	*The Fairest Cape? An Account of the Coloured People in the District of Simonstown* (Johannesburg, SAIRR, 1972)
Whisson, M.G., and Kahn, S.	*Coloured Housing in Cape Town* (Cape Town, Board of Social Responsibility of the Diocese of Cape Town, 1969)

Whisson, M., and Weil, W.	*Domestic servants: a microcosm of the race problem* (Johannesburg, SAIRR, 1971)
Whisson, M.G.	*The Coloured People* (Cape Town, Abe Bailey Inst., 1971)
Wickins, P.L.	*The Industrial and Commercial Workers' Union of South Africa,* (Cape Town, OUP, 1978)
Williams, R.	*Problems in Materialism and Culture* (London, Verso, 1980)
Williamson, G.E.	Labour and Industry, *Race Rels. Journal* Vol. 18, 1951, pp. 170-186
Wilson, F.	*Migrant Labour in South Africa,* (Johannesburg, Sprocas, 1972)
Wilson, F. (ed.)	*Farm labour in South Africa* (Cape Town, David Philip, 1977)
Wilson, M., and Mafeje, A.	*Langa* (Cape Town, OUP, 1963)
Wilson, M., and Thompson, L.	*The Oxford History of South Africa,* (Oxford, OUP, 1969)
Wilson, W.J.	*The declining significance of race* (Chicago, Univ. of Chicago, 1978)
Wollheim, O.D. (ed.)	*The Theron Commission Report: an evaluation and early reactions to the report and its recommendations* (Johannesburg, SAIRR, 1977)
Wolmarans, C.P.	"Die arbeidsituasie en werkgesindheid van die Kaapse Skiereiland", *Suid-Afrikaanse raad vir geesteswetenskaplike navorsing, verslag no. MM-58* (Pretoria, 1976)
Wolpe, H.	"Industrialism and Race in South Africa", in S. Zubaida (ed.), *Race and Racialism* (London, Tavistock, 1970)
	"Class, race and occupational structure", Institute of Commonwealth Studies, *Collected Seminar Papers on the Societies of Southern Africa in the 19th and 20th Centuries, Vol. 2* (London, London Univ., 1971)
Worsley, P.	"Proletarians, Sub-proletarians, lumpenproletarians, marginalisation, migrants, urban peasants and urban poor", *Sociology* Vol. 10, January 1976

Woods, D. — *Conference at Bulugha: South Africa's first all-race assembly* (East London, *Daily Dispatch, 1973*)

Wright-Mills, C. — *The Sociological Imagination* (New York, OUP, 1959)

Yudelman, D. — "Industrialisation, Race Relations and Change in South Africa: an ideological and academic debate", *African Affairs* Vol. 74, pp. 82-86, 1975

Ziervogel, C. — *The Coloured People and the Race Problem* (Cape Town, 1936)

Brown South Africa (Cape Town, Maskew Miller, 1937)

Who are the coloured people? (Cape Town, African Bookman, 1944)

Zubaida, S. (ed.) — *Race and Racialism* (London, Tavistock, 1970)

INDEX

workers, 174-5
  and African workers, 174-5
  male and female, 174
  white- and blue-collar jobs, 174-5
  youth, and Africans, 180, 183
Coloured Affairs Council, 56, 73
Coloured Affairs Department, (CAD), 56, 73
  and Anti-CAD, 56 73
Coloured Development Corporation (CDC), 150
Coloured Labour Preference Policy, 88-9, 105-7, 122, 137-44, 151-2, 178
Coloured labour, 144-5
  CEA's view on, 145-6
  characteristics of, 145
  contrast with African, 147
  Departments of Labour's views on, 147
  and Theron Commission, 144-5
Coloured Peoples' Association of South Africa (CPA), 30
Coloured Peoples' Congress (CPC), 115-16, 152
Coloured Peoples' Vigilance Society, 30-1
Coloured Persons' Educational Union (CPEU), 58
Coloured Persons Enfranchisement Bill, 39
Coloured Persons National Union (CPNU), 108, 159
Coloured Persons Representative Council (CPRC), 136, 153-4
  attacked by APDUSA, 155
  collapse, 155, 184, 209-10
  composition, 155
Commission of Inquiry into Matters Affecting the Coloured Population of the Union, 3, 44-5, 67-8, 131-2, 137
Commission of Inquiry into Industrial Legislation (Wiehahn), 120, 199
Commission on Mixed Marriages, 3-4
Communist Party of South Africa (CPSA), 49, 108
  and ANC, 49
  and Anit-CAD, 58-9
  Marxist-Leninist, 59
  and NEUM, 58-9
  Trotskyist, 59
Congress of Democrats, (COD), 113-14
  and trade unions, 120
Congress of the People, 113
Conservative Party, 186-7
Consolidation of Urban Areas Act, 71
  effect on Cape, 71-2
Constitution Amendment Act, 21
CPC, 116-19

"Crossroads" squatter settlement, 202-3

Dadoo, Dr, 110
Deane, E., 112
Desai, Barney, 116
Department of Coloured Affairs, 114
  employment policy, 150
Department of Industry, Trade and Tourism, 141
Department of Native Affairs
  and Cape employers, 97
  and Cape influx control, 68
  and Cape Town Council, 37, 38-9
  control by Transvaal National Party, 83
Depression, Great
  and division of labour, 44
  effect on Coloured population, 44
Die Burger
  and Cape National Party, 101-2
  supports direct Coloured representation, 101
  supports Coloured Labour Preference, 101-2
"divide and rule" strategy, viii, 237
dock strikes, 17-18
dock workers and racial divisions, 63

economic growth, 127-8
  and Black and White earnings, 129
  and relative earnings, 128
  and White jobs, 129
economic recession, 13, 174
Eiselen, W.W.
  and Coloured problem, 78
  condemmed by CCI, 98
  elimination of Africans from Western Cape, 97-8
  policy, xvi, 137
employers, 239-40
  and African labour, 197-8, 200-1
  and Coloured labour, 198-9
  and Coloured Labour Preference Policy 197-201
  and influx control, 199
Erasmus, H.S. 78, 80
Essau, Abraham, 20
ethnic hierarchy and early settlement, 4-5
  stereotyping, 23
  see also race, Coloured identity
eugenics *see* social-Barwinism

Fagan, Henry, 67
Federal Party, 158-61
  and Coloured identity, 160